The Economics of Exploration for Energy Resources

CONTEMPORARY STUDIES IN ECONOMIC AND FINANCIAL ANALYSIS, VOLUME 26

Editors: Professor Edward I. Altman and Ingo Walter, Associate Dean
Graduate School of Business Administration, New York University

CONTEMPORARY STUDIES IN
ECONOMIC AND FINANCIAL ANALYSIS

An International Series of Monographs

Series Editors: **Edward I. Altman and Ingo Walter**
Graduate School of Business Administration, New York University

The Economics of Exploration for Energy Resources

by JAMES B. RAMSEY
Chairman
Department of Economics
New York University

 JAI PRESS INC.

Greenwich, Connecticut   *London, England*

338.272
E19

WF

Library of Congress Cataloging in Publication Data
Main entry under title:

The Economics of exploration for energy resources.

Contemporary studies in economic and financial
analysis ; v. 26)
  Includes bibliographies and index.
  1. Energy development—Cost effectiveness. I. Ramsey,
James Bernard. II. Series.
HD9502.A2E25   338.2'72   82-477
ISBN 0-89232-159-8   AACR2

Copyright © 1981 JAI PRESS INC.
36 Sherwood Place
Greenwich, Connecticut 06830

JAI PRESS INC.
3 Henrietta Street
London WC2E 8LU
England

ISBN NUMBER: 0-89232-159-8

Library of Congress Catalog Card Number: LC82-477

Manufactured in the United States of America

CONTENTS

**THE RELATION BETWEEN EXPLORATION ECONOMICS
AND THE CHARACTERISTICS OF MINERAL DEPOSITS**

PART V. POSTSCRIPT

**WHAT WE HAVE LEARNED: WHAT DO WE
EXPECT NEXT?**

LIST OF CONTRIBUTORS

E. D. Attanasi	United States Geological Survey Department of the Interior
Ben C. Ball	Massachusetts Institute of Technology M.I.T. Energy Laboratory
Laurence A. Bruchner	Los Alamos Scientific Laboratory, New Mexico
John C. Davis	Senior Scientist, Kansas Geological Survey, University of Kansas
Elmer L. Dougherty	University of Southern California
Lawrence J. Drew	United States Geological Survey Department of the Interior
Dennis N. Epple	Graduate School of Industrial Administration, Carnegie-Mellon University
Richard Engelbrecht-Wiggans	University of Illinois Urbana-Champaigne
John J. Gilbert	Department of Economics University of California, Berkeley
Lars Hansen	Graduate School of Industrial Administration, Carnegie-Mellon University
John W. Harbaugh	Department of Applied Earth Science, Stanford University
John Houghton	Massachusetts Institute of Technology M.I.T. Energy Laboratory

Myrle M. Johnson	Los Alamos Scientific Laboratory, New Mexico
Gordon M. Kaufman	Massachusetts Institute of Technology M.I.T. Energy Laboratory
Z. Livne	Massachusetts Institute of Technology M.I.T. Energy Laboratory
John Lohrenz	Chief of the Applied Research and Analysis Section, Conservation Division, United States Geological Survey
D. L. Mosier	United States Geological Survey
Richard Newcomb	Department of Mineral Economics, West Virginia University
Robert S. Pindyck	Department of Economics, Massachusetts Institute of Technology
James B. Ramsey, Chairman	New York University, Department of Economics, C. V. Starr Center for Applied Economics
D. H. Root	United States Geological Survey
W. Runggaldier	Massachusetts Institute of Technology M.I.T. Energy Laboratory
D. A. Singer	United States Geological Survey
James L. Smith	Massachusetts Institute of Technology M.I.T. Energy Laboratory
James L. Sweeney	Energy Modeling Forum, Stanford University
John P. Weyant	Energy Modeling Forum, Stanford University
John W. Whitney	John W. Whitney, Inc.

ACKNOWLEDGMENT

"I am indebted, as are all the contributors to this volume to the Challenge Fund of New York University for providing in part the funds required for the convening of the Conference and the initial editing of the manuscripts which enabled this volume to be completed."

James B. Ramsey, Chairman
Department of Economics
New York University

INTRODUCTION

Economics is a misunderstood discipline. The ubiquitous phrase "the economics of . . ." illustrates and compounds the confusion, because its use derives more often from the noneconomist than from the economist. So that the efforts of those attending the Energy Exploration Conference held at New York University in May of 1979 can be appreciated, let me take a little time to explain what the economist means by "the economics of . . ." and what the noneconomist may mean.

The noneconomist's use of the term is usually a synonym for "the financial accounting of . . . ." In short, the term is usually reserved for an accounting of the estimated monetary outlays and revenues of a project, whereby, if the latter exceed the former, the project is declared to be "economic." That such usage of language causes the economist to shudder is the least of our concerns; much more important is the result that communication between economists and others is debilitated. The first difficulty is that even when an economist engages in such accounting exercises, which are then called cost–benefit analyses, the costs and benefits recorded are usually, and are certainly intended to be, far different from the figures obtained from accounting records. The reason for this is that the economist tries to see through the monetary mirage and record net real costs and benefits, carefully labeling them either private or social. The "ideal" situation is one wherein *real incremental* private costs equal *real incremental* private returns, which in turn equal the corresponding real incremental social costs and returns. Social costs and returns are the costs and returns borne by society as a whole. Much of the economist's time is taken up in trying to discover, determine, and measure social costs and returns and relate them to the private costs and returns. One of the benefits of competitive markets is that this equation of social and private costs and benefits is automatically achieved.

The output of operations research analysis is often called economics, but it is not. Operations research is concerned with deriving operating procedures, generating information, solving optimality problems, or providing rules-of-thumb even, in order to facilitate the successful managing of the firm or enterprise. The subject matter of economics, however, is less concerned with the details through which solutions to the firm's problems are obtained and more concerned with relating the behavioral outcome to the basic "economic" forces impinging on the firm. For example, economics is more concerned with the impact of a technological change in the firm's use of different types of resources, the quality of the product, all relevant prices, the possible effects on industrial structure, and even in evaluating the circumstances that either encourage or impede the very process of technological change and innovation. By and large economics is not concerned with the specific details of how firm A as opposed to firm B sets about utilizing a technological change.

These introductory remarks are more important in this particular volume because of the number of noneconomists contributing to it in areas that do border on economic analysis. The reader, however, will benefit by keeping in mind the distinctions mentioned above, because the mix of contributions covers the gambit from geology, to accounting, to operations research analysis, and to economics itself.

In this connection, a fundamental aspect of the intent of the conference was to bring together a disparate, but potentially interactive, group of scholars and practitioners. The main idea in this regard was to provide a mechanism through which geologic and economic scholars could begin to communicate more effectively with each other, where scholars as a group could interact with practitioners, and where both scholars and practitioners could discuss problems with bureaucrats in a less politically unnerving climate than Washington's.

It is my belief that most of this objective was successful; although the interaction with the bureaucracy was indecisive due to the government's relative lack of participation.

The subject matter of the conference itself provided overwhelming reasons for its promulgation. First, energy exploration, not exhaustion, is the dominant issue of this decade and the next. Secondly, the public in general and the economics profession in particular have ignored this crucial issue. Consequently, the social, private, geologic, and technical forces impinging upon and thereby determining the course and nature of exploration are unknown and are themselves unexplored.

To be sure, there has been and there will continue to be a massive *operations research* type of interest in energy exploration; individual firms have much at stake, even their survival, which ensures close attention to the specifics of exploration—where to drill and how deep is therefore an all-engrossing issue. But the resolution of the economic and political forces that interact with the geologic and technical realities is a neglected topic.

Exhaustion, at least for the foreseeable future, is an irrelevance. The fact that there are a finite number of metric tons of oil in the earth's crust is as true today, but no more so, as it was when the first well was dropped. There is a difference between exploration today and yesteryear. Today our exploration tools are more sophisticated, but that technological gain is needed to compensate for the fact that we have already discovered the most easily accessible oil; it is most unlikely that anyone will trip over an enormous new field in Texas or Louisiana. But it is not unlikely that new search areas, such as the offshore, or that regions previously unsuspected of containing energy-bearing rock at any depth, will produce new oil discoveries and even the occasional mammoth field. The main difference between today and the past is that the marginal finding cost is now much greater than it was formerly. That is a hard, inescapable fact, but it is not exhaustion.

If exhaustion is not the contemporary issue, then what of the use of "exotic fuel sources," such as so-called "synthetic fuels," oil shale, solar, geothermal, and tidal power. The majority of these potentialities are in the initial basic research stage; very little is known at present of their possible economic benefits, other than they are not cost effective, at present, even with substantial, if not massive, subsidies. Whereas basic research efforts quite properly deal with possibilities, innovation and implementation must deal with not just the probable, but the highly probable. The alternatives to oil and gas, especially for motive power, are not visible on the immediate horizon. Consequently, at the very least, more oil and gas are needed to bridge the gap between now and our indefinite future. Once again exploration is the key issue.

However, as the reader is probably aware, the importance of exploration seems to be virtually ignored by the press, bureaucracy, and the general public, the last group for presumably the very good reason of not having been made aware of the situation. In organizing the conference we discovered the lack of enthusiasm by the media for the subject of exploration and even at one point were accused of engaging in a conspiracy of silence about the supposed benefits of solar power. For those of us actively engaged in analyzing exploration problems, it is important to keep in mind this situation of voluntary ignorance on the subject of energy exploration. The importance lies first in recognizing that matters that appear to us to be of the first importance are not so perceived by the public. The second aspect is that ignoring this difference in perception will seriously impede, if not prevent entirely, any successful communication between exploration researchers and the public, not to forget the various departments of the government bureaucracy.

One of the contributing factors to the potential success of the conference was the facility the conference provided for economists to learn more about the role played by geology in the process of discovering oil. Conversely, the conference enabled geologists to discover that oil exploration is not just "geologic predictions," but an outcome of political–economic forces.

While this comment might appear to be a simple truism, its startling vital implications are revealed, once one recognizes the policy effects from confusing the outcome of political–economic forces with geologic and technical ones. If our current level of discoveries were purely the outcome of geologic and technical factors, that is one thing, but if they are the outcome of political–economic forces, that is something else again. To declare a low output discovery rate a geologic phenomena is to recognize the futility of future search; but to see the matter as a political–economic result is to begin contemplating a solution. Oil and gas believed not to exist will not be found, no matter how abundant it may be.

This book is in five parts, each part representing an aspect of the concerns mentioned above. The first part of the book is concerned with a brief indication of some of the strengths and weaknesses of the current "state-of-the-art" energy supply models. As will be seen, all models leave something to be desired, many a lot. By and large economic models (so-called "econometric") are weak on incorporating geological and technical constraints in an effective manner and tend to ignore bureaucratic and political market intervention almost entirely. Economists are beginning to recognize these omissions as serious mistakes that significantly inhibit the usefulness of their models. The noneconomic models, in contrast, are weak in the incorporation of economic and political forces; these models tend to view the supply and discovery process as purely mechanistic, depending essentially and almost exclusively on geological and technical factors. There is a third type of extant supply model, what might best be termed an attempt to simulate the operational activities of individual firms. While these models can be most useful in providing a summary framework for tracking individual firm activities under existing circumstances, they are not so useful at providing qualitative insights into the fundamentals of market behavior. By analogy, such models provide a great amount of information on how the leaves are attached to branches, which in turn are attached to the trunks, but they do not provide much information about the growth process of the forest as a whole.

Part II of this book cites two papers in full plus an abstract. The contents concern the almost totally ignored subject matter of the theoretical economic analysis of exploration. This part of the book then is of prime importance for the economist's contribution to the understanding of the process of exploration and the role of economic forces. As usual, the objective of theoretical analysis is to provide insights into general firm behavior, and the contributions in this book are not lacking in this regard. The implications for policy are of far-reaching significance, provided, and only provided of course, that the theoretical analysis proves to be a useful and viable analytical tool.

Part III is not as extensive as might be wished; it is concerned with enumerating some of the political and economic realities faced by energy explorers of all types.

The fourth part seeks to gain greater perception about the economics of oil and gas exploration, those areas most fully researched to date, by comparing that situation with those pertaining in coal and other minerals.

Part V is a postscript. A brief answer to the question of what we have learned is given together with some speculation about what the research scholar should explore next.

PART I
EMPIRICAL MODELS OF
EXPLORATION, APPRAISAL, AND
SUPPLY FOR OIL AND GAS

PHYSICAL VARIABLES AND THE PETROLEUM DISCOVERY PROCESS

E. D. Attanasi, L. J. Drew, and D. H. Root

I. INTRODUCTION

Accurately forecasting the future supply of petroleum by the use of economic variables has a twofold benefit. First, it would enable one to know the total future petroleum supply, and second, because these economic variables are artificial, the promise exists that the future supply can be controlled for the general good. These two benefits are not independent, for to the extent that future supply cannot be controlled by economic variables, it cannot be forecast by economic variables. For example, if large price increases do not result in supply increases, then knowing the future price does not tell one the future supply because supply is obviously being controlled by something else. If physical limits rather than economic variables are the most important determinants of petroleum production, then these physical limits must be incorporated into any supply model. In general, each barrel of oil taken from a field is physically more difficult to extract than the barrel before. From one barrel to the next, this increase in difficulty is imperceptible,

3

but over a 30-year period, it can reduce production from an oil field from several hundred thousand barrels per day to almost nothing.

In order for a nation, or the world, to maintain a level of crude oil production, new fields must be discovered and brought into production to make up for the declining production in older fields. Models concerned only with short-term forecasts need not consider the physical limits on the rates of discovery, but models concerned with long-term forecasts must do so. Physical limits to crude oil production in a single field are contracting limits. The same equipment and extraction methods applied to the same field will be less productive this year than they were last year. The phenomenon of contracting limits occurs also in exploration. The same methods and equipment that found many 100-million-barrel oil fields in Texas in the 1930s and 1940s will not find many 100-million-barrel oil fields in Texas in the 1980s and 1990s. This growing difficulty in discovering crude oil must be incorporated, perhaps implicitly, in any model that attempts to forecast petroleum supply.

We argue that physical properties of petroleum field occurrence induce a regularity in the discovery process of a region. This dependence of the discovery process on physical characteristics can serve as a basis for constructing rather simple analytical models that can be used to reproduce the discovery history of a given area with a high degree of accuracy. In this paper several economic models of the petroleum industry are examined for their consistency with physical properties of the petroleum discovery process. Several physical discovery process models are reviewed, and one is applied with an engineering cost algorithm to estimate the incremental costs of future discoveries for a major U.S. oil producing region, the Permian Basin.

II. ECONOMIC MODELS OF THE PETROLEUM INDUSTRY

A. *The Fisher Model*

Franklin Fisher, the author of the first widely publicized petroleum industry econometric model (Fisher, 1964), used three equations to predict the annual number of wildcat wells drilled, success ratio (proportion of wildcat wells that resulted in a commercial discovery), and the average size of predicted discoveries. The product of the values produced by these three predicted variables yields the supply of new reserves. According to Fisher, exploration takes place at both the extensive margin (i.e., frontier areas) and the intensive margin (i.e., partially explored areas). Discoveries at the intensive margin are generally small but of low risk, whereas discoveries made on the extensive margin tend to be large but infrequent.

Fisher believed that the initial industry reaction to increases in price was to shift exploration to areas classified at the intensive margin (from frontier areas). The most important physical relationship in Fisher's model predicted the average size of new discoveries during a specific time period and had the following analytical form

$$S_t = \frac{\alpha_0 S_{t-1}^{\alpha_1} F_{t-1}^{\alpha_2}}{N_{t-1}^{\alpha_3} P_t^{\alpha_4}} \tag{1}$$

where S_t is the average size of oil fields discovered in period t, F_{t-1} is the previous period's oil and gas success ratio, N_{t-1} is the average size of natural gas fields discovered in period $t-1$, P_t is the price of oil in period t, and the parameters (α_i's) are positive. In summary, the average size of new discoveries is directly related to the size of fields discovered in the previous period and to the previous period's success ratio and is inversely related to the average size of natural gas fields discovered in the previous period and the current price of oil.

There are many more factors that influence the rate of petroleum discovery than can be included in a model. In order to make a selection one must rank factors according to their importance and the availability of data. The choices of what factors to include can be based upon *a priori* considerations and then tested empirically, or they may be made by a process of trial and error; but a rationale for the choices made should be evident either before a model is tested on real data or after. Fisher gives no rationale for including either the previous year's success rate or the average size gas field discovered in the previous year in his equation for determining the average size oil field discovered this year. We are unable to supply a rationale for the inclusion of either of these, though of course, that is no proof that there isn't one. The success rate seems to be a poor indicator of average field size because it is determined by the large number of small fields whereas the average field size is determined by the total oil discovered, which is primarily the result of a few large discoveries, which hardly effect the success rate at all. The relation between the average size of oil fields found in one year and the average size of gas fields discovered the year before is the reverse of what we would expect, that is, it is inverse rather than direct. This is surprising because the discoveries in the two populations (oil and gas fields) proceed on the average from the larger to the smaller, with exploration shifting between oil and gas according to which offers the more valuable targets. This shifting of exploration between oil and gas means that if one knows the sizes of gas fields being discovered then one would expect that the oil fields being found would be of comparable value so that the relation between sizes of oil and gas fields being discovered would be direct and not inverse. The relation between the sizes of oil fields found this year and gas fields found in the previous year would be weaker than that between oil and gas fields found in the same year, but the relation would still be direct.

The complete model was estimated and the short-run price elasticity was found to be .3, indicating a modest price responsiveness of reserves from new discoveries. The model's estimated price elasticity has been applied to long-run supply problems although the model may not have been constructed to predict petroleum supply. The model's structural equations do not reflect the finiteness of the physical resource base because field sizes are not forced to zero by the form of the model. In order to increase the number of observations, data from various regions were pooled and dummy variables were relied upon to capture regional differences. Price data for a particular region typically showed little variation during the time period considered. It is possible that by pooling the data, variations in price data and consequently the estimated elasticities were more the result of differences in the quality of the oil than in the incremental discovery costs. Fisher's original formulation was later elaborated by Erickson and Spann (1971) by including an equation for predicting the average size of natural gas deposits by using the same functional equation specification.

B.   The MacAvoy and Pindyck Model

Fisher's basic approach was used by MacAvoy and Pindyck (1975) in their petroleum industry econometric model. That is, they forecast the reserves from new discoveries by predicting the number of wildcat wells to be drilled, success ratios for oil and gas exploration, and the average size of oil and natural gas discoveries. Again, the most important physical relation is associated with the prediction of average discovery size (S_t), which took the following form:

$$S_t = S_R \exp[WR(-\alpha_0 + \alpha_1 D_1 + \alpha_2 D_2 \\ + \alpha_3 D_3 + \alpha_4 X - \alpha_5 PG_R + \alpha_6 PO_R)] \tag{2}$$

where $X = (PGO_0 - XO - CO_0)/PGO_0$; S_R is the average discovery size in the previous 3 years; WR is the number of successful oil wells in the reference period immediately preceding the current period; D_1, D_2, and D_3 represent, respectively, dummy variables for South Louisiana, the Permian district, and a single large area covering East Texas, Kansas, and Oklahoma; PO_R is a 3-year average of oil prices; and PG_R is a 3-year average of natural gas prices. The variable X, an index of oil depletion, is specified as a function of PGO_0, an estimate of original oil in place for the production district; XO, end-of-year oil reserves; and CO_0, cumulative production. The model's specification implies that predicted average size of new oil discoveries is directly related to the price of oil (the reverse of the previous model) and inversely related to the price of gas and the advancement of depletion. The model has obvious difficulties when depletion is complete because it does not force discovery sizes to zero. MacAvoy and Pindyck claim that their model captures long-run supply adjustments because estimated coefficients indicate that price is directly related to deposit size.

This direct relationship is not consistent with the U.S. experience. Comparison of the relevant historical data and simulations revealed that the model substantially overestimated the price responsiveness of new reserves. Revisions of the model by Pindyck (1978) produced the following structural equation specification for the average size of oil discoveries for period t (S_t):

$$S_t = \exp(\Theta_0 + \Theta_1 D_1 + \Theta_2 D_2 + \Theta_3 D_3 - \Theta_4 CW_t) \qquad (3)$$

CW_t is the cumulative number of exploratory wells drilled through period t; D_1, D_2, and D_3 are the same dummy variables used in Eq. (2). Average oil discovery size is divorced from economic variables and merely declines as a function of the cumulative number of exploratory wells increases. Alternatively, the equation used to predict the average size of natural gas discoveries in period t (N_t) has the form:

$$N_t = \exp(\beta_0 + \beta_1 D_1 + \beta_2 D_2 + \beta_3 D_3 + \beta_4 PG_R - \beta_5 PO_R - \beta_6 CW_t) \qquad (4)$$

where PG_R and PO_R are reference prices for gas and oil, respectively. Differences in the specifications of the oil and gas equations reflect the viewpoint that for oil the only relevant factor is the degree of exploration an area has been exposed to but for natural gas, economic variables (the price of oil and natural gas) play a part in determining average discovery sizes. In this article it is argued that determinants of the discovery process—sequence of discoveries—are fundamentally physical in nature.

III. PETROLEUM FIELD SIZE DISTRIBUTIONS AND THE REGULARITY IN THE DISCOVERY PROCESS

Figure 1 presents the size distribution of oil and gas fields from the Permian Basin, with natural gas converted to barrels of oil equivalent (BOE) at the rate of 5270 cubic feet of (wet) natural gas per barrel. This field size distribution is typical of other basins or petroleum provinces. Within a particular petroleum province, fields have a wide range in sizes; most of the fields are small and most of the reserves discovered are in a few large fields. Figure 2 is the same as Figure 1 but is drawn to scale without breaks in the y-axis in order to emphasize how much more common small fields are than large in the same petroleum prov-

Figure 1. Histogram of the Size Distribution of Oil and Gas Fields
Discovered in the Permian Basin by December 31, 1974.
(1 BOE = 1 BBL Crude Oil = 5270 cf Natural Gas).
Fieldsize Estimates Were Made in 1977 by the
U.S. Department of Energy, Energy
Information Administration,
Dallas, Texas, Field Office
(Written Commun.)

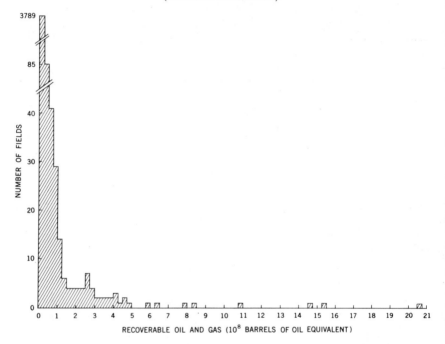

ince; at the scale used in Figure 2, the large deposits are too few to be
graphed. Table 1 gives the proportion of aggregate petroleum contained in various size classes of fields. The largest 38 fields (less than
1 percent of the total) contain more than half of the oil whereas the
3789 fields contained in the smallest size class account for only 16
percent of the oil discovered. The figures and table indicate why success
ratios convey little information about future discoveries. Although most
of the oil is found in a few very large fields, the success ratio is driven
by the numerous small deposits.

A consequence of the wide range in field size is a declining discovery
rate (BOE per exploratory well or foot drilled). Figure 3 presents the
average field sizes for 14 drilling increments of approximately 2000
wells each in the Permian Basin. The reason the unequal sizes of fields
implies a declining discovery rate is that a given large field is easier to

Figure 2. Histogram of the Size Distribution of Oil and Gas Fields Discovered in the Permian Basin by December 31, 1974 Drawn Without a Break in the Y-Axis. Same Data as Graphed in Figure 1.

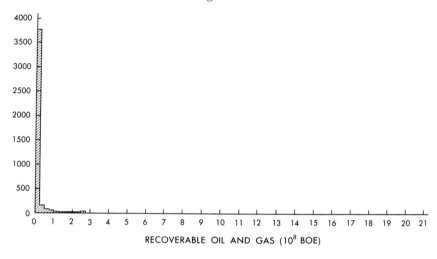

RECOVERABLE OIL AND GAS (10^8 BOE)

discover than a given small field, so that as exploration progresses, the size of fields discovered tends to decrease. Large fields are frequently in large geologic structures that are more easily detected than small structures. If the fields in an area are not typically in structures, large fields are still easier to hit than smaller fields because of their large surface areas. For example, the East Texas Field, which contains about 6 billion barrels of oil, has a surface area of over 200 square miles. Even if drilling were random, the larger fields, by virtue of their surface areas, would on the average be found earlier in the discovery sequence than smaller fields. Any improvement in the skill of the explorationist (over purely random drilling) accelerates the discovery of large fields, thereby accentuating the decline in the discovery rate. Because of the regularity of the sequence of discoveries and the regularity in discovery rates, the discovery process is amenable to being modeled. These principles of petroleum exploration are the basis of discovery process models, several of which are reviewed in the next section.

IV. DISCOVERY PROCESS MODELS

Although structures and data requirements of discovery process models can differ, they all seem to use the central assumption that the larger the field, the more likely it is to be discovered. In the model authored by Barouch and Kaufman (1977), the size distribution of fields is as-

Table 1. Proportion of Aggregate Petroleum in the Permian Basin Contained in Various Size Classes of Fields

Size class[a]	Number of fields in class	Cumulative number of fields	Percentage of petroleum total in class	Cumulative percentage
2050–2075	1	1	5.6	5.6
1500–1525	1	2	4.0	9.6
1450–1475	1	3	3.9	13.5
1075–1100	1	4	2.9	16.4
825–850	1	5	2.3	18.7
775–800	1	6	2.1	20.8
625–650	1	7	1.7	22.5
575–600	1	8	1.6	24.1
475–500	1	9	1.3	25.4
450–475	2	11	2.5	27.9
425–450	1	12	1.2	29.1
400–425	3	15	3.3	32.4
375–400	2	17	2.1	34.5
350–375	2	19	2.0	36.5
325–350	2	21	1.8	38.3
300–325	2	23	1.6	39.9
275–300	4	27	3.1	43.0
250–275	7	34	4.8	47.8
225–250	4	38	2.6	50.4
200–225	4	42	2.3	52.7
175–200	4	46	1.9	54.6
150–175	4	50	1.8	56.4
125–150	6	56	2.2	58.6
100–125	14	70	4.1	62.7
75–100	29	99	6.8	69.5
50–75	41	140	6.7	76.2
25–50	85	225	7.8	84.0
0–25	3789	4014	16.0	100.0

[a] In millions of barrels of oil equivalent (BOE).

sumed to be lognormal and the probability of discovery is proportional to size. Discovery process models developed by Arps and Roberts (1958) and Drew, Schuenemeyer, and Root (1979) make no assumption with respect to the ultimate field size distribution but do assume discovery proportional to field size.

In the Barouch and Kaufman model, the size distribution of remaining fields is estimated from the size and the sequence of past discoveries. Under the assumptions of sampling without replacement from a finite population, the ultimate number of fields in that finite population is estimated. Barouch and Kaufman (1978) used the first 15 discoveries in the Leduc reef play in the western Canadian sedi-

Figure 3. Graph Showing Average Sizes of Fields Discovered in 14
Intervals of Exploratory Drilling Between 1921 and 1974 in the
Permian Basin (1 BOE = 1 BBL Crude Oil = 5270 cf Natural
Gas). About 2,000 Wells Were Drilled in Each Interval. Field
Size Data and Discovery Dates from the U.S. Department
of Energy, Energy Information Administration,
Dallas, Texas, Field Office (Written Commun.);
Exploratory Drilling Data from Petroleum
Information, Inc., Denver, Colo. (1977).

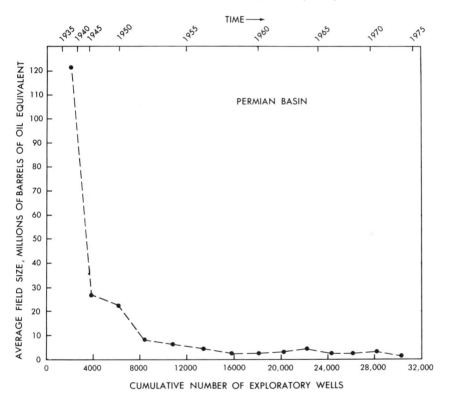

mentary basin to forecast the sizes of the sixteenth through the fifty-
fifth discovery. The model was found to predict the total volume of
petroleum contained in the 28 additional discoveries made to date to
within 7 percent of what was actually discovered.

The model developed by Arps and Roberts (1958) is based upon the
following assumptions: For any size class of fields, the probability of
discovery is directly proportional to the number of fields remaining to
be found and their areas. This model asserts that the proportion of

undiscovered targets in a given size class declines exponentially with cumulative drilling; that is,

$$F_A(W) = F_A(\infty)[1 - \exp(-CAW/B)] \qquad (5)$$

where $F_A(\infty)$ is the ultimate number of fields having an average areal extent equal to A; $F_A(W)$ is the number of discoveries expected to be made by the drilling of W cumulative wells; B is the basin area; and C is the efficiency of exploration. For the case of random drilling, C equals 1; for the case where exploratory drilling is carried out twice as efficiently as random drilling, C is equal to 2.

Before forecasts can be produced, the values of the two parameters (B, basin size, and C, exploration efficiency) must be estimated. Arps and Roberts (1958) first tested their model in the Denver Basin area and relied upon their extensive knowledge of the area to estimate subjectively these two parameters. In retrospect, their parameter estimates were very accurate. Using their parameter values and data from the first 7 years of exploration (1949–1955) to estimate the ultimate number of deposits in each size class, a forecast of the number of fields to be found for an additional 9000 wells (1956–1974) was made for each size class. Figure 4 indicates the relatively high predictive power of the model.

Another discovery process model, the area of influence model, was developed by Drew, Schuenemeyer, and Root (1979). The basic assumption of this model is that the fraction of undiscovered deposits in a given size class is equal to a power of the fraction of the basin area that is unexplored. For a given size class, the model takes the form

$$1 - F = (1 - A/B)^C \qquad (6)$$

where F is the fraction of targets discovered; A is the area exhausted; B is the basin area; and C is the exploration efficiency. For purely random drilling, C is equal to 1 and Eq. (6) implies that the fraction of discovered fields in a size class is equal to the fraction of the basin explored. If, for example, C were equal to 2, the efficiency of exploration would be twice that of random exploration, suggesting that when one third of the basin is explored (that is, A/B is equal to 1/3) then 5/9 of the fields for that size class have already been discovered. The area of influence model was applied to the Denver Basin (Drew, Schuenemeyer, and Root, 1979) and the results are shown in Figure 5. Like the Arps and Roberts model, the area of influence model can be applied to basins with multiple plays or multiple producing horizons by estimating the models for different depth intervals.

Figure 4.   Graph Showing Actual Total Discoveries of Petroleum in
the Denver Basin by 1974 and Discoveries Predicted for 1956–1974
by Using Arps and Roberts' (1958) Discovery Process Model
and the 1949–1955 Actual Data from Petroleum
Information, Inc., Denver, Colo. (1975).

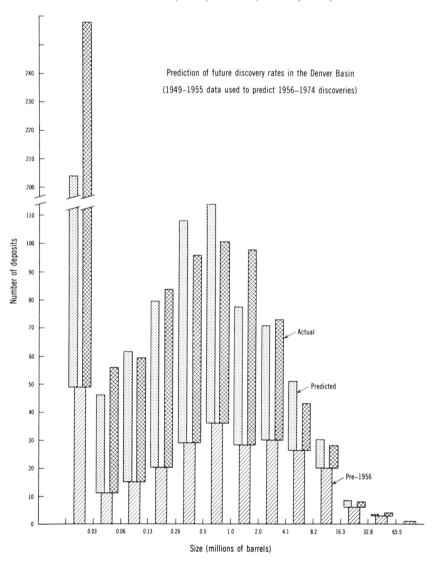

Figure 5. Graph Showing Actual Total Discoveries of Petroleum in
the Denver Basin by 1974 and Discoveries Predicted for
1956–1974 by Using Drew, Schuenemeyer, and
Root's (1979) Discovery Process Model and
Actual Data for 1949–1955.

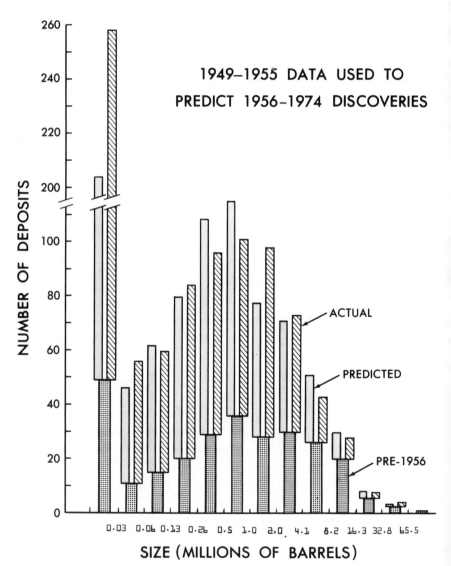

An Application of Discovery Process Models

Incremental costs of future discoveries in the Permian Basin, which is located in western Texas and southeastern New Mexico, were estimated by using a discovery process model (Drew, Root, and Bawiec, 1979) to predict future discoveries in conjunction with an economic costing algorithm (Attanasi, Garland, Wood, Dietzman, and Hicks, 1979) to estimate costs of finding and developing these discoveries. The parameters of the Arps and Roberts model were estimated separately for four 5000-foot depth intervals and were used to predict the size distribution of new oil and gas discoveries in terms of barrels of oil equivalent. A complete explanation of the models is available in Drew, Root, and Bawiec (1979) and Attanasi, Garland, Wood, Dietzman, and Hicks (1979).

Given the size distribution of future discoveries, an engineering discounted cash flow analysis for the representative well of the average field in each size and depth class was carried out (assuming a given output price and required rate of return) to determine ultimate recovery or whether it was indeed economic to develop the well and field at all. Past trends were used to determine the proportion of fields that would be (1) oil fields (including associated gas) and (2) nonassociated gas fields subject to primary recovery. It was further determined for oil fields whether they would be subject only to primary recovery or to both primary and secondary recovery. The detailed engineering cost analysis was also carried out for all classes of fields. A field was determined to be economic if the after-tax net present value of the representative production well was greater than zero. The amount of exploration that would be undertaken was calculated internally by the cost algorithm. It was assumed that the positive surplus of present value obtained through developing the various fields must eventually provide a cash flow adequate to repay the number of exploratory wells drilled in advance of development. Operationally, the discovery process model predicted the frequency and size distribution of fields for successive increments of 1000 exploratory wells. For a given price and discount rate, exploration stopped when the sum of the net present values of deposits discovered by the next 1000 exploratory well increments were no longer sufficient to cover costs of that exploration effort. The cumulative estimated reserves discovered and developed, of course, varied with the price of oil and gas used in the calculations.

Assuming mid-1977 costs and land acquisition costs of $50 per acre, the estimated marginal costs of future (post-1975) discoveries from the Permian Basin are presented in Figure 6. Here, marginal costs are not defined with respect to time. The last 1000 exploratory wells predicted

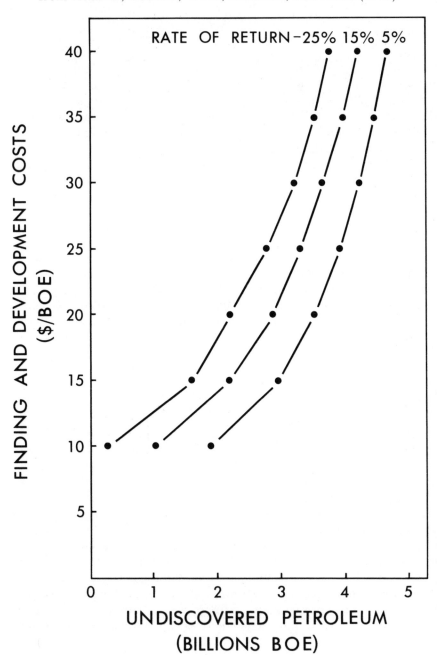

Figure 6. Graph Showing Incremental Costs (in Mid-1977 Dollars) of Finding and Developing Undiscovered Petroleum Reserves in the Permian Basin After 1974 for Three Required Rates of Return (1 BOE = 1 BBL Crude Oil = 5270 cf Natural Gas). Data from Attanasi, Garland, Wood, Dietzman, and Hicks (1979).

to be drilled were those for which the sum of marginal finding and production and development costs are equal to price. Through 1974 in the Permian Basin 37.4 billion BOE were found by 30,340 exploratory wells. The results of the study (see Attanasi, Garland, Wood, Dietzman, and Hicks, 1979) indicate that, at a 15 percent required rate of return and a price of $15 per BOE, an additional 2.2 billion BOE (found by 11,000 additional exploratory wells) will be economic; at the same rate of return and $40 per BOE, finding and developing an additional 4.2 billion BOE (found by 36,000 additional exploratory wells) will be economic. At the 1974 production level (1.4 billion BOE) for the Permian Basin, total economic discoveries even at $40 per BOE will amount to only approximately 3 years production. If oil and gas resources were to be priced at their replacement costs, as some advocate, the required price increases would indeed be very large.

CONCLUSIONS

If one wants to model the discovery process, out of the myriad of factors that could conceivably affect petroleum discoveries, only a few factors can be studied. Evidence presented here suggests that the discovery rate is principally controlled by the size distribution of oil fields present and their order of discovery. The search for oil in the United States was far less successful after World War II than before. This unfortunate change did not arise from government policy nor was it dictated by the laws of the market place. The U.S. discovery rate declined because there were not many big fields left to be found. This lack of big fields was not apparent at the time but has since become obvious. For petroleum exploration where the limiting factor is the finite number of large fields, forecasts should be based upon studies of field size distributions. Prices and costs control economic behavior, but the amount of oil discovered is determined by the size distribution of undiscovered fields.

REFERENCES

Arps, J. J. and Roberts, T. G. (1958). Economics of Drilling for Cretaceous Oil on East Flank of Denver-Julesburg Basin, *American Association of Petroleum Geologists Bulletin* **42**: 2549–2566.

Attanasi, E. D., Garland, T., Wood, J., Dietzman, W., and Hicks, J. (1979). Economics and Resource Appraisal: The Case of the Permian Basin, *Proceedings of 1979 SPE Economics and Evaluation Symposium*, Dallas, Texas, pp. 227–234.

Barouch, E. and Kaufman, G. M. (1977). *Estimation of Undiscovered Oil and Gas in Mathematical Aspects of Production and Distribution of Energy*, Proceedings of Symposia in Applied Mathematics, Vol. XXI, American Mathematic Society, pp. 77–91.

——— (1978). The Interface Between Geostatistical Modelling of Oil and Gas Discovery and Economics, *Journal of the International Association of Mathematical Geology* **10:** 611–627.

Drew, L. J., Root, D. H., and Bawiec, W. J. (1979). Estimating Future Rates of Petroleum Discoveries in the Permian Basin, *Proceedings of the 1979 SPE Economics and Evaluation Symposium,* Dallas, Texas, pp. 101–106.

Drew, L. J., Schuenemeyer, J. H., and Root, D. H. (1979). *Resource Appraisal and Discovery Rate Forecasting in Partially Explored Regions, Part A—Application to the Denver Basin,* U.S. Geological Survey Professional Paper No. 1138.

Erickson, E. W. and Spann, R. M. (1971). Supply Response in a Regulated Industry: The Case of Natural Gas, *Bell Journal of Economics and Management Science* **2:** 94–121.

Fisher, F. M. (1964). *Supply and Costs in the United States Petroleum Industry,* Johns Hopkins University Press, Baltimore, p. 177.

MacAvoy, P. W. and Pindyck, R. S. (1975). *The Economics of the Natural Gas Shortage (1960–1980),* North Holland, Amsterdam, p. 259.

Pindyck, R. S. (1978). Higher Energy Prices and Supply of Natural Gas, *Energy Systems and Policy (2),* 1978, pp. 177–209.

A SIMULATION MODEL FOR OIL EXPLORATION POLICY ON FEDERAL LANDS OF THE U.S. OUTER CONTINENTAL SHELVES

John C. Davis and John W. Harbaugh

ABSTRACT

Effective appraisal of the petroleum resource potential of a frontier OCS region requires that statistical methodology be used. The most effective approach may involve a comparison on a prospect-by-prospect basis of the frontier region with maturely explored regions that are geologically similar. Where seismic data are available in the frontier OCS region, a probability distribution can be assigned to each seismic prospect on the basis of a comparison with prospects in the mature region. Each probability distribution can incorporate both a dry hole probability and a spectrum of oil or gas volumes. The resource potential for the region as a whole can be regarded as the Monte Carlo sum of the distributions attached to the individual prospects. A simulation model can be developed to test the consequences of different federal exploration policies.

I. INTRODUCTION

Many spokesmen have stressed the need for objective estimates of the nation's petroleum resources. Effective planning for the next two decades will require a series of estimates that will be progressively modified

19

as exploration proceeds. These estimates should be as free from bias as possible, and ideally they should be provided by organizations or individuals that are politically neutral. Estimates from industry or government agencies are automatically suspect, as witnessed by the current controversy involving revision and refutation of early optimistic resource estimates by the U.S. Geological Survey (Theobald et al., 1972; McKelvey, 1973, 1974; Miller et al., 1975). These differences may be legitimate, especially considering the enormous uncertainty that surrounds any petroleum resource forecast, but the whole matter is clouded by assertions that the differences may be politically inspired (see, for example, Sporn, 1974; Cook, 1975).

Many aspects of national policy will be influenced by the assessment of the nation's oil and gas resources. Leasing policies in the outer continental shelf (OCS) regions, federal tax regulations with respect to oil and gas, conversion from oil to coal, and the establishment and development of national petroleum reserves will be strongly affected. Yet, in spite of this obvious need for independent appraisals of petroleum resources, there is no group within the Federal government that is making resource forecasts using procedures that are demonstrably unbiased and hence appropriate to the task. Steps should be undertaken to develop objective evaluation procedures and to apply them to the OCS regions, including the Atlantic OCS. The principal qualities that should be incorporated in the resource assessment process are enumerated below.

A. Use of Relevant Data

A resource assessment must make effective use of relevant data if it is to be valid. Within the Atlantic and other relatively virgin OCS areas, such data consist of seismic information and some subsurface information from COST wells and exploratory wells. Each exploratory well has a large bearing on the assessment of the petroleum potential of the region, but the assessment must also involve a detailed analysis of the extensive seismic coverage. The seismic surveys in the Atlantic OCS, for example, have revealed a large number of structures, many of which are regarded as prospects. An effective resource assessment must include a detailed analysis of such individual prospects.

B. Incorporation of Realistic Exploratory Practices

A petroleum resource appraisal should reflect the procedures that actually are used in exploration. Only those oil and gas deposits that are potentially discoverable and producible should be entered into the resource base. In most OCS regions, and certainly the Atlantic OCS, the industry's practice is to locate geologic structures with seismic surveys and to drill those that appear most attractive. Thus, almost all of the petroleum that may be found and produced will occur in traps that consist of structures that have been defined seismically. There also may be petroleum present in traps that are not seismically discernable, but the current resource assessment should be confined to oil and gas associated with perceived structures that are potentially drillable under economic and technological conditions that apply to the OCS within the next two decades. The inclusion of other possible hydrocarbon deposits, whose discovery is highly problematic, in the resource base has been severely criticized as being misleading (Cook, 1975).

The industry's practice is to run widely spaced reconnaissance seismic lines and then to run more closely spaced surveys over major structures that appear prospective. Some of the structures that retain their attractiveness after detailed seismic exploration may be candidates for drilling. Thus, in assessing OCS regions, it is essential to (a) consider the proportion of the region that has been seismically reconnoitered, (b) consider the proportion that has been seismically investigated on a detailed scale, and (c) tabulate the number of structures that form prospects that are drillable under the assumed economic conditions. A useful definition of its resource potential, therefore, is the Monte Carlo sum of the potentials of the drillable prospects, plus additional increments assigned to parts of the region that either have not been seismically surveyed or where the seismic surveys are too widely spaced to detect most of the structures.

C. *Presentation of the Appraisal in Probabilistic Form*

There are many sources of uncertainty in a resource assessment, including uncertainty in seismic surveying and interpretation, the volume of petroleum that may occur in a trap, and of course the presence of petroleum itself. For example, the existence of a structure having apparent low relief on a seismic profile may be highly uncertain. Not only is there uncertainty about its existence, but about its shape, areal extent, and vertical relief as well. These uncertainties must be coupled with the uncertain presence of oil within the structure. Even if the presence of the structure and its size and shape were known with absolute certainty, there would still remain large uncertainty as to the presence of petroleum, and to the volume of oil and gas, if present. All of these sources of uncertainty must be considered simultaneously in the resource estimation process. A weighted probability estimate for each drillable structure is needed and should reflect the possible nature of the structure, as well as the uncertain volume of associated oil and gas. A single probability distribution per structure is capable of representing the dry hole probability, plus the probabilities attached to different oil and gas volumes. The structures that form drillable prospects can then be summed together by Monte Carlo methods to yield a single, composite probability distribution for the region as a whole. A resource assessment in this form satisfies the requirements that we have set. It is based on relevant information, it accords with industrial exploration practices, and it incorporates an appropriate degree of uncertainty. Furthermore, such an estimate can be objectively revised upon receipt of new information using Bayes' rule. We can expect that any resource appraisal of immaturely explored OCS regions will undergo drastic revisions as drilling results are obtained. It is important, therefore, that the revision process be as unbiased as the initial estimation process.

II. RESOURCE APPRAISAL METHODS IN CURRENT USE

Current petroleum resource appraisal techniques applied to relatively virgin areas such as the OCS regions can be grouped into two approaches. The first, utilized by the USGS Resource Analysis Group (in the so-called "RAG" studies; Miller et al., 1975), derives an expert consensus about the existing resources from geologists knowledgeable about the area being evaluated, using a Delphic approach. The experts consider factors such as the approximate volume of sedimentary rocks in the area, number of currently discerned structural prospects, the results of any drilling, current assumptions about regional sedimentological and geochemical conditions, and the production in more mature areas believed to be geologically similar. Usually, the experts are asked to specify points on a cumulative probability distribution of the resource volume. Their subjective appraisals of the "most likely volume" define the median of the distribution. In addition, the experts specify a "lowest likely volume," corresponding to a 95% probability that "at least this minimum quantity exists," and a "greatest likely volume," corresponding to less than 5% probability that "more than this amount may exist." By asking members of the panel to reconsider their estimates in the light of the opinion of the other members, a consensus is forced in a few iterations.

The drawbacks of the Delphi method of resource estimation are readily apparent, and include the possibility of conscious or unconscious bias in the selection of the panel of "experts," statistical nonindependence of the probability estimates as the successive rounds of revision are undertaken, and many psychometric considerations. Sackman (1974) discusses these in great detail and suggests that advantages of the Delphic approach are completely outweighed by its shortcomings. Biases will be expressed as an incorrect assessment of the median probable resource value. Even worse, the Delphic feedback process ensures that the extremes of the distribution will be underestimated, emphasizing an apparently universal human tendency to underestimate the likelihood of rare events. Because the bulk of the petroleum resource of many regions is contained in extremely rare, "giant" fields, the tendency to underestimate probabilities associated with the upper extreme of the resource distribution is especially troublesome. Harris (1976) provides a critique of Delphic procedures applied to resource estimation problems and presents a number of examples, chiefly for uranium resources and metallic ores.

The most widely used alternative to the Delphic approach is a methodology adopted from petroleum reservoir analysis. Originally an engineering procedure to investigate the merits of different development schemes for reservoirs or fields, it has been extended to the appraisal of prospects where no reservoir has yet been discovered. It consists of identifying specific prospects (usually seismic structural anomalies), estimating certain geologic parameters for the prospects, and then calculating potential reservoir volumes. Cost factors concerned with drilling and development can be appended, with economic assumptions about future oil prices and other factors, and the appraisals expressed as expected monetary values based on discounted net cash flow calculations. It should be emphasized, however, that the procedure consists of two distinct operations; the first being a volumetric calculation of the oil in place in the reservoir, and the second a financial analysis of the worth of the oil that can be economically produced, expressed as a succession of cash flow forecasts discounted to the present. These, in turn, are merged together to yield a single expected monetary value or EMV.

Even in a reservoir that has been discovered and in which a number of wells have been drilled, there is uncertainty about the amount and spatial distribution of producible oil. The factors that control reservoir volume vary from place to place within the pool at a rate much greater than the sampling density of the wells, so there is always uncertainty as to the volume of recoverable oil. This uncertainty is accommodated by considering the components of reservoir volume (thickness, areal extent, and porosity) not as point estimates but as probability distributions. The volumetric calculation is then performed by Monte Carlo methods to yield a probability distribution of oil volume. This methodology is widely used in the industry and is described in detail in several texts (Newendorp, 1975; McCray, 1975).

When applied to prospect evaluation, the uncertainties associated with the volumetric calculations increase enormously, because there is *no* direct evidence of the magnitudes or ranges of the critical variables. In addition, there is no certainty of even the existence of oil in the prospect, so the entire calculated volume must be tempered by a "dry hole probability" or "risk factor." In many petroleum provinces, the dry hole probability may be so large (typically 75 to 95 percent) that it dominates the calculations and is the single most influential factor in the financial analysis. Unfortunately, in a virgin province, the dry hole probability is unknown and cannot be estimated in an objective manner except by analog comparisons with other, more mature petroleum provinces.

Although there is no direct evidence of the magnitudes of critical geologic variables in an undrilled prospect, the most important of these can be estimated from seismic information. Sensitivity analyses show that the dominant variables in volumetric calculations are areal extent of the prospect, its height of structural closure, and the proportion of the trap that is filled with oil or gas. Other variables, such as porosity, thickness, gas–oil ratio, and oil–water ratio are less important. Fortunately, two of the most critical variables can be estimated from the configuration of the prospect as perceived seismically. The other variables must be assumed on subjective grounds and hence, suffer from greater uncertainty. If these less certain variables are entered into a Monte Carlo analysis with extremely wide variances, as would be appropriate considering their conjectural nature, they have little effect on the final calculated distribution of volume.

The USGS Conservation Division uses this Monte Carlo procedure to evaluate tracts nominated for leasing in the outer continental shelf areas (Akers, 1976). The Canadian Geological Survey uses a similar program for regional resource estimation by aggregating the appraisals for all prospects in a region (Canadian Dept. Energy, Mines and Resources, 1977). Most major oil companies use Monte Carlo methods for prospect appraisals, and in some instances for basin evaluation. Akers' (1976) Range-of-Values program of the USGS requires as input the probability distributions for 13 geologic variables to be used in the volumetric calculations; this program is regarded as typical of those used by industry. Estimating the probability distributions for these variables is an onerous and time-consuming task, and this effort (on the basis of sensitivity analyses) probably contributes very little to the final appraisal. The difficulty of assigning realistic values to many of these distributions is dramatically illustrated by the current practice of using parameters originally derived for tract evaluations in the Louisiana OCS for evaluation of tracts in the Atlantic OCS.

The Conservation Division evaluates tracts only in those portions of the OCS regions that potentially will be part of a lease sale and that have been nominated by the industry. This policy causes the Conservation Division's evaluations to be highly localized. In the Atlantic OCS, for example, such evaluations aggregate only a fraction of the total area of the Atlantic shelf, and there is no attempt to appraise the petroleum resources of the region as a whole. Regional resource appraisal is not a function of the Conservation Division, and its role in the OCS regions is to calculate the so-called "fair market value" for each tract that has been nominated. The fair market value is defined as the EMV, which the Bureau of Land Management then establishes as the minimum acceptable lease bonus. The fair market value established for a tract is highly confidential. Maximum bids that are less than the figure established are rejected. The Conservation Division's obligation with respect to each tract is essentially ended once the fair market value has been obtained and the tract leased. Furthermore, there is no obligation to revise the estimate of the producible oil in a tract unless the tract should be leased again at a later time. Thus, the current practices of the Conservation Division are not directly applicable to regional resource estimation, these obligations being handled within the USGS by the Resource Analysis Group of the Geologic Division.

III. AN ALTERNATIVE TO CURRENT APPRAISAL TECHNIQUES FOR FRONTIER OCS REGIONS

The objective of a Monte Carlo prospect appraisal is to estimate the volume of oil within a reservoir that may occur in a prospect. Because much of the substantive information used is derived from seismic reflection-time contour maps, it seems feasible to relate these seismic variables directly to the volume estimates, by-passing the Monte Carlo volumetric calculations entirely. In effect, this acknowledges that the other variables that are components of reservoir volume are so poorly known in a prospect that they cannot be used to reduce the uncertainty in the volume estimate. All sources of variation other than those that can be extracted from the seismic structure maps are confounded in a general error term in a simple linear regression model of the form

$$Y_i = \alpha_0 + \beta_1 X_i + \varepsilon_i$$

where Y_i is the estimated volume of petroleum in the ith prospect, α_0 and β_1 are coefficients of the linear relationship, X_i is the size of the *i*th prospect as perceived seismically, and ε_i is an independent random deviate representing the uncertainty in the resource estimation. Dimensional considerations suggest that the relationship may be loglinear, with Y_i best taken as the logarithmic transform of reservoir volume and ε_i assumed to have the form of a lognormal distribution about the regression line. The variance of ε_i supplies estimates of the upper and lower probabilistic limits of reservoir size equivalent to the "maximum probable volume" and "minimum probable volume" that emerge from a Monte Carlo simulation.

If suitable estimates of the parameters α_0 and β_1 can be found and an operational definition formed for "size" of a seismic anomaly, use of this simple model should produce several significant benefits:

1. The model would significantly reduce the analytical effort necessary to evaluate a prospect because only a limited number of input variables would be required.
2. Because data requirements are minimal, *all* prospects perceived on regional seismic maps can be evaluated, rather than only those within tracts that have been nominated.
3. Adjustment of the parameters of the prediction equation could be performed by statistically orthodox procedures as new data become available, rather than by empirical adjustments as is now done.
4. The statistical model is extremely flexible, and can easily be expanded to include other predictive variables if their inclusion seems warranted. By contrast, the Monte Carlo techniques as embodied in the USGS Range-of-Values program are relatively inflexible and cannot be modified without significant programming efforts.

The major criticism of the regression procedure that we propose is that it must rely initially upon relationships found in other regions where both reservoir volumes as well as seismic structural sizes are known, such as in the Louisiana OCS. The statistical methodology thus requires an investment in background analysis of mature regions in order to obtain the parameters. Care can be taken, however, to select those regions that are reasonable analogs on the basis of similar overall geology.

Figure 1 shows the relationship between areas of seismic anomalies and the oil-field volumes associated with these, in the offshore part of the Potiguar Basin of Brazil. Although there are only six fields in this part of the Potiguar Basin, a rough linear relationship exists.

Figure 1. Relation between Area of Seismic Anomaly and Estimated Reservoir Volume of Producing Structures in Potiguar Basin, Offshore Brazil.

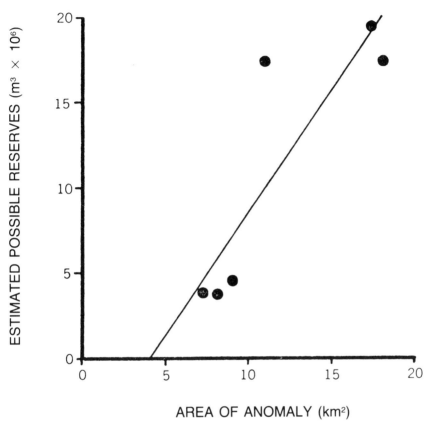

Producible oil $= -5.119 + (1.393)$ Area, with a correlation of $r = +0.66$.

Figure 2 illustrates the form of statistical relationships that can be rapidly extracted from seismic reflection-time maps and other data for offshore Louisiana. The plot illustrates information from only one area, the North Extension of the Salt Marsh Island district, which encompasses 280 thousand acres, divided into 56 tracts of 5 thousand acres each. Within this region, there are 11 prospects or seismic structures apparent in the Upper Miocene, accounting for approximately 28 percent of the total area of the district. Of these, seven structures have been tested and six have yielded production. In addition, four structures apparent in shallower horizons but not in the Miocene have been tested

Figure 2. Regression between a Measure of Reservoir Volume (Dollar Equivalents of Barrels of Oil and Thousands of Cubic Feet of Gas) and Area of Seismic Prospects.

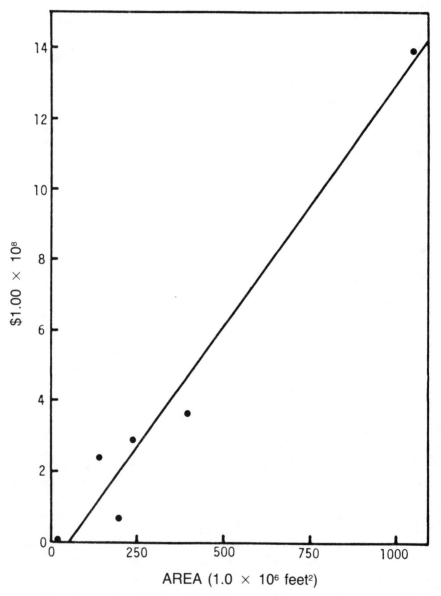

Data from North Extension of Salt Marsh Island district, Louisiana OCS.

and all have proven dry. One Miocene productive structure was removed from the data set because it is a major piercement dome and therefore has a large barren core of salt; the simple measures of anomaly size used could not reflect the true area of structure available to contain oil or gas pools around this feature.

The fitted regression, considering only prospects that have been tested, is

reservoir volume $= -1.1125 + 0.01405$ prospect area

Note that "reservoir volume" is given in monetary units of $\$1.00 \times 10^8$ in order to equate oil and gas content of the reservoirs, and "prospect area" is given in units of 1.0×10^6 square feet of equivalent ellipses having the same lengths and widths as the prospects. The correlation coefficient is $r = 0.98$, indicating an extremely good fit of the function to the observational data. The extremely high correlation reflects in part the small sample size and the overriding influence of the largest reservoir but is nevertheless encouraging and indicates that statistical approaches are feasible.

In addition to the relation established between reservoir volume and prospect size for the North Extension of the Salt Marsh Island division, other data are relevant to the construction of a statistical model of prospects. For example, Figure 3 shows the relation between lengths and widths of anticlinal features in the area and indicates a general consistency in structural style for most sizes of prospects at various seismic horizons. Information on height of prospect closure to production (Figure 4) and to "drainage distance," a measure of the gathering area through which hydrocarbons might have migrated into the trap, is also relevant. The success ratio, or proportion of dry wells drilled on each prospect, was examined and shows no strong correlation with size of prospect. The average success ratio (SR) for all ultimately productive prospects in the area is SR $= 0.47$, with a standard deviation of $s = 0.19$. This success ratio can be used to calculate the probabilities attached to a series of failures when a prospect is first tested (Figure 5). The histogram gives the probability that more than the specified number of wells must be drilled before the initial discovery and is based on the geometric probability distribution. Such distributions are significant because they can be used to provide a probabilistic answer to the question of when a prospect has been adequately tested and can be abandoned as truly dry.

The problem of classifying prospects into homogeneous populations was briefly investigated using the Louisiana OCS data to provide insight as to how this might be done in the Atlantic OCS and elsewhere. Within

Figure 3. Plot of Lengths versus Widths of Anticlinal Features Shown
on Reflection-Time Maps of Three Seismic Horizons in the North
Extension of Salt Marsh Island District, Louisiana OCS.

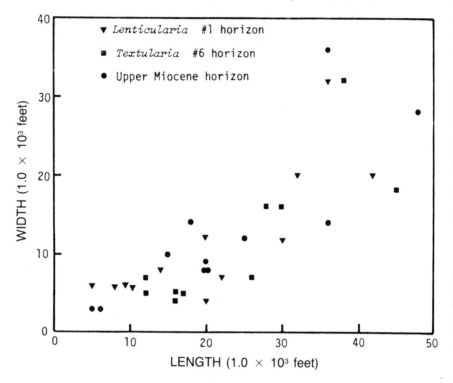

the Louisiana OCS, three broad categories of prospects can be distinguished: (1) salt or shale piercement features of major structural relief
and great complexity; (2) nonpiercement anticlines of major relief, both
with and without faulting; and (3) low amplitude anticlines, usually
unfaulted or with a simple pattern of faulting. On the Louisiana regional
seismic contour map prepared by Perry Geophysical Services, Inc., at
a scale of 1 inch = 20,000 feet, 136 major structures of Type 1 can
be distinguished. The map shows approximately 270 features of Type
2, and about 400 smaller features of Type 3. All may be considered
to be prospects.

Within the North Extension of the Salt Marsh Island division, there
is 1 piercement dome, 2 major faulted anticlines, and 13 minor anticlinal
structures, of which 8 have been tested. Figures 6 to 8 are illustrations
of hypothetical structures typical of the three categories within this area.
It should be noted that all of the structures of Type 1 and Type 2

Figure 4. Plot of Height of Closure of Seismic Prospects versus a
Measure of Reservoir Volume.

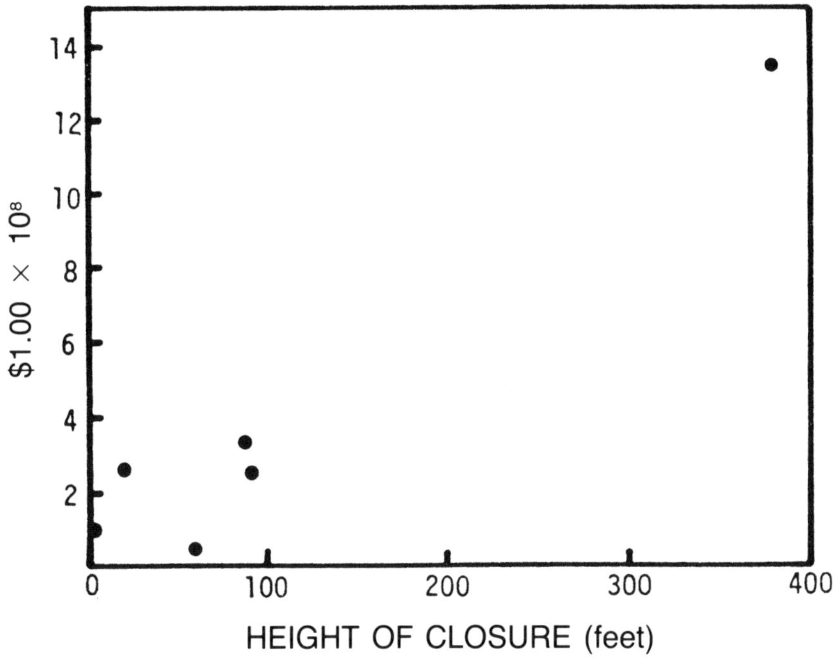

Conventions are the same as in Figure 2.

produce in this area, while only three of eight tested structures of Type
3 have so far yielded production.

Within the Atlantic OCS, most structures seem analogous to Type
3 Louisiana OCS structures, with a few Type 2 structures. Piercement
domes of Type 1 seem to be almost entirely absent except in deeper
water along the continental margin in the northern part of the Atlantic
OCS. Preliminary examination of the reconnaissance data from both
the Louisiana OCS and the Atlantic OCS suggest that a large population
of tested structures can be defined in the Gulf Coast and will be analogous to most structures discerned at present in the Atlantic OCS.
Therefore, it should be possible to estimate the parameters of a statistical
estimation model that could be used successfully for reserve estimation
throughout the Atlantic OCS and possibly in other OCS areas as well.

Figures 6 through 8 are drawn to the same scale. Horizontal dimensions are typically on the order of a few miles and vertical contours are
100 feet apart.

Figure 5. Probability That More Than the Indicated Number of Exploratory Wells Will Have To Be Drilled on a Seismic Prospect before the First Discovery.

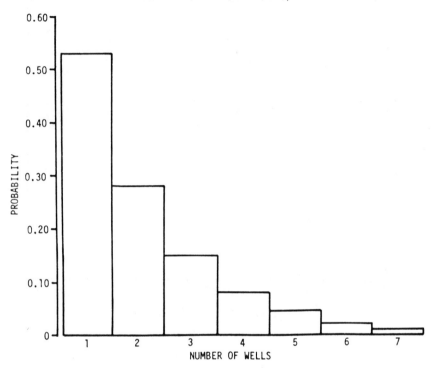

Values derived from the geometric probability distribution using the success ratio of wells on productive structures in the North Extension of Salt Marsh Island district, Louisiana OCS.

IV. SEISMIC STRUCTURE OF THE ATLANTIC OCS

Until a decade ago, the Atlantic OCS (AOCS) ranked as one of the United States' least known geologic provinces. This has changed, however, with the oil exploration activities of the past decade, and the area has lost some of its frontier status. The earlier general interpretation of the AOCS was that of a wedge of sedimentary strata of Jurassic, Cretaceous, and Cenozoic age, characterized by gently undulating, more or less uniform dip toward the Atlantic basin. The extensive seismic surveys of the past 5 years, however, have revealed an AOCS that is much more structurally complex, and indeed, locally, the AOCS rivals parts of the Louisiana OCS in structural complexity. In places, the AOCS is still apparently characterized by a more or less uniformly

Figure 6. Type 1 Seismic Prospect, a Hypothetical Piercement Salt Dome as It Might Appear in the Upper Miocene of the Louisiana OCS.

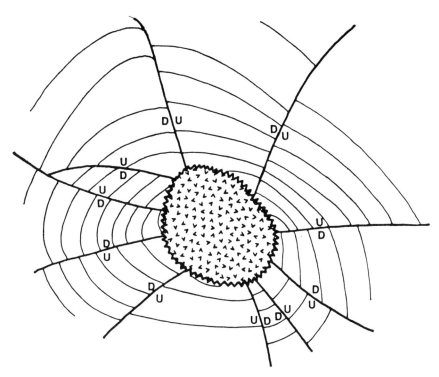

dipping homocline with minor undulations. Elsewhere, however, the area is now known to be faulted and folded, with some very large features. For example, the so-called "Stone Dome," which lies northeast of the Baltimore Canyon area, is a fold of only moderate complexity but of immense areal extent. It is perhaps the most attractive "prospective" structure discerned in the AOCS, stimulating the highest lease bonus yet received within the AOCS ($107 million for one tract), and has been drilled by Mobil, resulting in an extremely disappointing dry hole.

The exploration history to date in the AOCS follows the classic pattern consisting of a progression of seismic surveys of greater density. The initial seismic reconnaissance involved widely spaced parallel traverses. Structures of interest detected in these initial surveys were then "detailed" by networks of progressively closer spaced seismic lines. A few of the structures are large enough to have been outlined by the widely spaced reconnaissance lines ("Stone Dome," for example), but many

Figure 7. Type 2 Seismic Prospect, a Hypothetical Faulted Anticline as
It Might Appear in the Upper Miocene of the Louisiana OCS.

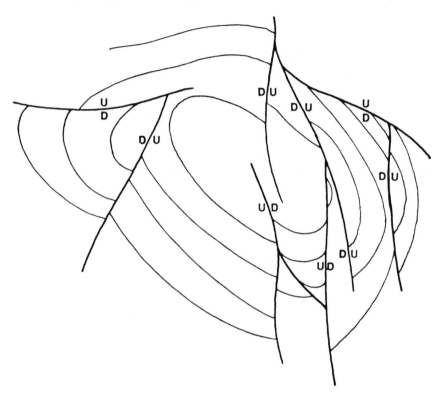

This style of structure is similar to larger structures in the Atlantic OCS.

others could not be defined until additional lines were run. Much of
the area of the AOCS is still in the reconnaissance seismic stage, with
the remainder crossed by seismic nets of varying degrees of density.
The current perception of the AOCS is, therefore, strongly influenced
by these differences in seismic line density.

Among the surprises revealed by the extensive seismic surveys are
locally complex fault and fold systems, which appear to be due to
diapiric intrusions of rock salt or plastic shale that has flowed from a
deeply buried horizon. There are also several northeast–southwest
trending zones of complex faulting and folding that provide attractive
prospects. Some of the structures are elongate anticlines up to 5 or
more miles long with structural closure of as much as 500 feet, or more.
Present structural interpretations are based on seismic reflection times

Figure 8. Type 3 Seismic Prospect, a Hypothetical Gentle Anticline as It Might Appear in the Upper Miocene of the Louisiana OCS.

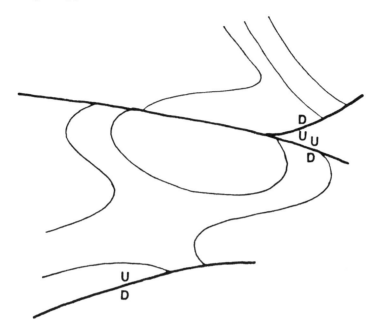

Most structures apparent in the Atlantic OCS seem similar to this style.

and are subject to the errors inherent in seismic surveying and interpretation. Even if these errors are substantial, however, the structures of high vertical relief should "survive" when explored by drilling. On the other hand, some of the low-relief seismic structures may prove to be illusory upon seismic reinterpretation, much less drilling. For example, a number of broad, gentle, elongate anticlines in the Blake Plateau are based on widely spaced reconnaissance seismic lines. These anticlines have vertical relief of less than a hundred feet and may simply represent errors in the seismic interpretive process, including seismic velocity variations and irregularities in topography of sea floor. The number of structures that form potentially exploitable prospects (disregarding economics for the moment) in the AOCS is large, probably aggregating more than 100, and there are undoubtedly others that will be discerned with additional seismic surveys.

A comparison of seismic maps of the Gulf Coast OCS and the AOCS indicates that the two are much more similar structurally than would have been assessed earlier. Indeed, the appraisal of the AOCS by the

Conservation Division and the mode of exploration by industry in the AOCS are very strongly influenced by experience in the Gulf Coast OCS. The structural complexity in parts of AOCS is somewhat less than that seen in the Louisiana and Texas parts of the offshore Gulf Coast, but greater than that of the Mississippi–Alabama–Florida (MAFLA) segment of the Gulf Coast OCS.

V. THE EFFECT OF SEISMIC LINE DENSITY IN RESOURCE APPRAISAL

Effective resource appraisal of an OCS region requires that the density of seismic lines be considered. As we have emphasized, present knowledge of the Atlantic OCS is derived largely from seismic surveys, although information from wells also will become immensely important in the next several years. The present seismic line density in the AOCS is highly variable because much of the area is covered only by a reconnaissance net of lines. However, most of the presently interpreted major structures are crisscrossed by closely spaced seismic lines. This suggests that there are probably many smaller, undetected features that will be found if the seismic line density is increased. Therefore, it is essential that those areas of the AOCS that have not been surveyed at the reconnaissance level also be entered into the appraisal process. To do so, it will be necessary to forecast the number of anomalies or prospects that will be encountered when areas that have been only seismically reconnoitered are subsequently surveyed in detail.

Reconnaissance surveys detect general areas of "interest," which are then detailed with a seismic net having a line spacing that may be eight times as dense as the reconnaissance survey. The general pattern is usually a rectangular grid, with the initial spacings up to 10 by 20 miles or more. Subsequent surveys often involve progressively halving the distances between lines, although it is not uncommon for later lines to deviate from an ideal rectangular grid. For example, sometimes a network of lines inclined at 45° to the original network is employed.

There is an important "feedback" effect in seismic exploration, which stems from general exploration philosophy and which decrees that effort will be concentrated where there are features of interest. Thus, seismic detail tends to have the greatest density where "interesting" anomalies have been found in reconnaissance surveys. However, it is also true that prospects that are potentially drillable are more likely to be detected and outlined with detailed surveys. A consequence is a strong bias in the seismic sampling process, with the majority of prospects located in areas that have been surveyed in detail. Of course, some structures such as Stone Dome are so large that they are readily outlined by reconnaissance surveys, but most seismic features that form prospects are smaller and may require line spacings much closer than the initial spacing in order to be appropriately delineated. Note, however, that there is a general tendency for geophysicists and geologists to devise optimistic structural interpretations regardless of seismic line density, and prospects are often devised that are unsubstantiated by the data.

The apparent structural complexity in a frontier OCS region is a consequence of both the true complexity and the seismic line density. The efficacy of the seismic procedures in measuring differences in elevation of reflecting horizons and errors in the surveying process also influence the results. Regardless of these diverse influences, there is strong correlation between seismic line density and parent structural complexity. A glance at the regional seismic maps will confirm this generalization for the AOCS. Much of the area of the Atlantic shelf that has been surveyed only at the reconnaissance level is interpreted as a gently dipping homocline with minor undulations, whereas most of the areas of seismic detail are interpreted as structurally complex.

It is obvious that seismic line density will have strong influence on estimated regional resource potential based on seismic prospects. If we define the resource potential for the region as a whole as the Monte Carlo sum of the probability distributions attached to individual seismic prospects, it follows that the regional estimate is dependent on the number of prospects. In turn, this number depends partly on the density of seismic lines. Ideally, there are functional relationships that relate changes in exploitable prospects detected to changes in line density. The form of this function can be deduced. Assume that we are dealing with an area that is structurally complex and that the degree of complexity is more or less uniform throughout. If the seismic line spacing is extremely wide it will not be possible to define the three-dimensional outlines of prospects of economic interest, even though a single line may cross an anomaly, because an interpretation in three dimensions requires a succession of crossing lines. As the line density progressively increases, our ability to define prospects in three dimensions will also increase up to a point, beyond which an increase in line density will not yield any more anomalies of economic interest, either because the features discerned are too small to constitute viable prospects or because there are limits to the seismic resolution process itself.

The form of the function is shown in Figure 9, which is a hypothetical graph of changes in number of "exploitable prospects" per unit area versus seismic line density per unit area. The unit area should be reasonably large relative to the dimensions of exploitable structures, per-

Figure 9. Hypothetical Function Relating Number of Exploitable Seismic Prospects per Unit Area (as for Example, in an Area of 1000 Square Miles) versus Seismic Line Density (Number of Miles of Line per Unit Area).

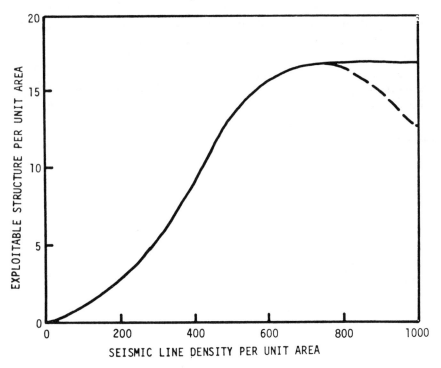

haps on the order of 1000 square miles in a frontier OCS region. The seismic line density may be expressed as the number of miles of seismic line per unit area.

The slope of the curve representing the function is a measure of the relative efficiency of the detection process. Theoretically, the efficiency progressively increases up to the inflection point, beyond which the efficiency progressively decreases, finally reaching a point where an increase in line density does not bring about an increase in number of structures detected. In reality, the function probably peaks and then declines as density increases, because closer line spacing may cause some previously attractive features to "split" into lesser anomalies that are too small to be attractive.

There are many examples of the discovery of oil fields in which the original geological interpretations proved to be seriously in error. The original interpretations were important in that they provided the rationale for drilling. "Hindsight" experiments by Griffiths and Drew (1964; 1966) and by Drew (1966; 1967) indicate that fields in most of the maturely developed oil producing regions of the United States could have been found more efficiently by procedures that did not rely on geological or geophysical exploration at all but instead used grid or even random drilling. We may be confident, however, that any exploratory holes drilled in a frontier OCS region such as the Atlantic shelf will require the traditional geological rationale that demands that an attractive seismic structure be present. The dashed extension of the curve in Figure 9 represents the hypothetical effect of "too much" seismic information, reducing the technical incentive to drill.

There are published tables that relate the probabilities of detecting randomly located elliptical targets with gridded exploration surveys (Singer and Wickman, 1969). A later section of this paper provides equations relating detection probabilities to seismic line spacings, as a function of the dimensions of anomalies as defined by lengths of their major and minor axes. Because the AOCS is relatively nonisotropic with respect to structural style, it is perhaps appropriate to devise several different functions of the form shown in Figure 9, relating the number of exploitable structures per unit area to seismic line density, each function corresponding to a particular structural style.

The function may be developed empirically by analyzing seismic reflection-time maps for particular areas that have been surveyed initially at the reconnaissance level and then subsequently resurveyed with progressively closer line spacing. Unfortunately, maps based on reconnaissance surveys are usually updated when new seismic lines are added, and previous interpretations of prospects may undergo substantial transformations as the line density increases. Of course, extremely large features such as Stone Dome will survive with only relatively small changes, such as minor undulations and small faults, but the gross outline will be only slightly modified.

The actual structural style should have substantial effect on the form of the function. Some areas of the Atlantic OCS are interpreted to be uniformly dipping homoclines with minor undulations. With wide line spacing, relatively few prospects appear, except possible subtle features of moderate or low relief and of marginal interest. If the apparent structural style interpreted at this stage is close to reality, an increase in line density will detect a small number of new prospects. The functional relationship would then take the form shown in Figure 10.

If functions of the form shown in Figures 9 and 10 can be developed for the AOCS, it would be possible to forecast statistically the number of prospects per unit area in those parts of the Atlantic shelf that have

Figure 10. Hypothetical Function Similar to That of Figure 9, Except That It Pertains to an Area of Much Less Structural Complexity.

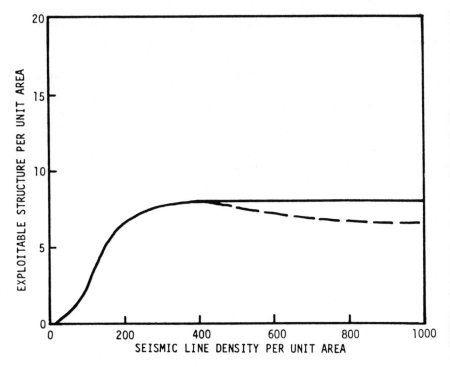

been surveyed at the reconnaissance level. In turn, regression relationships could be used to make resource forecasts for those areas. Obviously, these forecasts will have much greater uncertainty than those for areas of close seismic control. Nevertheless, the prospects that are undiscovered but statistically forecast could be entered into the resource base estimate. Thus, an important aspect of such an estimation procedure is that the uncertainty can be compartmented geographically and considered in the overall resource estimate in a more objective manner than with Delphic methods.

VI. ASSESSING THE WORTH OF SEISMIC EXPLORATION BEYOND THE RECONNAISSANCE STAGE

Two presumptions are necessary in order to evaluate the worth of a "nondirect" exploratory action, such as the shooting of additional seismic lines. The first is that drilling activities will be confined to perceived seismic anomalies. The second is that there is a positive relation between the size of a perceived seismic anomaly and the size of reservoir that may exist within the anomaly. Both of these assumptions seem reasonable both on theoretical grounds and on the basis of experience in more mature offshore areas.

A minimum reservoir volume of interest can be defined on a purely economic basis, as a smaller reservoir will not yield sufficient income to offset the cost of its discovery and development. The size of the seismic anomaly likely to be associated with this minimum reservoir volume can be estimated from the regression between reservoir volumes and anomaly sizes in a geologically similar training area or from expert subjective opinions. This provides the minimum dimensions for prospects to be sought in the seismic phase of exploration.

The initial seismic network usually consists of widely spaced parallel traverses, with a few perpendicular tie-lines whose effect on the probability of discovery can be neglected. The probability that an anomaly of the minimum size can be determined by the geometric relationship (Uspensky, 1937) is

$$Pr = \frac{Q}{D}$$

where $Q = 2[(a^2 + b^2)/2]^{1/2}$ and D = spacing between seismic lines. (The equation given assumes the anomalies are elliptical in form with major and minor semiaxes a and b; the relation can be generalized to

$$Pr = \frac{P}{\pi D}$$

where P is the perimeter of any convex figure; but as a first approximation, an elliptical target shape is adequate.)

The number of prospects of minimal size encountered on the reconnaissance seismic search can be counted. Then, the total number of minimal-sized prospects within the exploration area can be predicted by the relationship

total number of prospects
$$= \frac{\text{number of prospects detected on reconnaissance}}{\text{probability of detection}}$$

This number, minus the number already detected, gives the number of undetected prospects remaining. Similarly, the number of undetected prospects of other sizes can be estimated. This procedure assumes the prospects are randomly distributed with respect to the seismic lines, so the anomalies observed are an unbiased sample from the population of prospects within the search area. It also presumes that the areal size of anomalies can be estimated from the reconnaissance seismic net. In fact, sampling theory suggests that the sizes of individual prospects will be overestimated. If the minimal anomaly of interest is very small with relation to the spacing between seismic lines, the number detected in the reconnaissance phase is likely to be low because of the difficulty of discerning small features on the profiles.

From the reconnaissance seismic net, a distribution of sizes of perceived anomalies can be constructed. From this, an estimated distribution of prospect sizes that exist in the search area can be calculated. The proportion of prospects that will prove productive must be estimated on the basis of relative frequencies of success in a similar area or by expert subjective opinion. (Ideally, this probability of success should be conditional upon the size of the perceived anomalies, but information necessary to establish such statistics has not yet been gathered.)

If a relationship can be established between size of anomaly and size of contained reservoir, these anomaly size distributions can be turned into field size distributions. The relationship logically should be positive monotonic with some upper constraint, but the exact form has not been investigated. It may be determined by regression for well-explored areas such as offshore Louisiana and then extrapolated to the area being evaluated, or the relationship may be subjectively estimated by experts. Possible forms of the relationship include

$$\text{field size} = \beta_0 + \beta_1(\text{anomaly size}) + \beta_2(\text{anomaly size})^2$$

or

$$\text{field size} = \beta_0(\text{anomaly size})^{\beta_1}$$

Once the size distribution of fields in discovered anomalies and the size distribution of fields in predicted anomalies have been estimated, the expected monetary value of each set of fields can be calculated. The difference in EMV for the two distributions, minus the cost of the additional seismic exploration necessary to find the anomalies missed by the reconnaissance survey, is the net worth of the additional seismic effort.

The cost of the additional seismic exploration necessary to locate the anomalies of minimum size of interest may be estimated from geometric considerations. The spacing between seismic lines is given by

$$D = \frac{Q}{Pr}$$

If it is essential that all minimal-sized anomalies be located with certainty, the relation reduces to $D = Q$. That is, the space between traverses cannot exceed the size of the anomalies being sought. Within a bounded area, the number of additional seismic lines necessary to achieve the required spacing between adjacent lines can be found, and the cost assessed on a simple cost-per-mile basis.

A test of this appraisal method was performed on the Potiguar Basin, which is off the northeast coast of Brazil, about 1200 km southeast of the mouth of the Amazon River. The area being appraised by PE-TROBRAS, the Brazilian national oil company, is approximately 50 km by 25 km, an area of 1250 km^2. A reconnaissance seismic survey consisting of six lines spaced approximately 5 km apart covers the basin. The minimum size of anomaly said to be of interest is approximately 2 km in length and about 1 km in width (a typical anomaly is about double this size). About 20 anomalies are detectable along the reconnaissance seismic lines, of which four appear to be near the minimum size of interest. The probability that a 5-km search pattern will detect randomly located targets measuring 2 × 1 km is $Pr = 1.58/5 = 0.31$, where $Q = 2[(1^2 + 0.5^2)/2]^{1/2} = 1.58$. The total number of anomalies of minimal size must be about 13, since $.31 × 13 = 4$. As four of these have already been found by the seismic reconnaissance, nine must remain undiscovered.

The maximum spacing between parallel seismic lines required to discover an anomaly having dimensions 2 × 1 km with 100 percent certainty is about 1.6 km. In the Potiguar Basin, a seismic line spacing of 2 km was chosen, giving a discovery probability of about 80 percent for the smallest anomaly of interest.

The reconnaissance seismic survey of the Potiguar Basin contains about 300 km of seismic lines. A detailed survey with lines spaced 2 km apart would require about 450 km of additional seismic information. If the cost of marine seismic data is estimated at $400/km, a detailed seismic survey for the basin will require an additional investment of $180,000, or $20,000 per expected anomaly.

So far, 4 of the 11 anomalies tested in the Potiguar Basin have proved productive, giving a success ratio of 36 percent. Assuming the success ratio does not change significantly with either time or size of seismic anomaly, we expect three of the anomalies undetected by the reconnaissance search to be productive. The cost of additional seismic data per discovery is thus $60,000.

In most areas, and up to some limiting anomaly size, we expect a complicated (but in general, monotonically positive) relation between size of perceived seismic anomaly and size of contained reservoir. In the Potiguar Basin, the relationship has a linear correlation of +66 percent between estimated possible reserves and area of anomaly. This relationship can be expressed as reserves $(m^3 \times 10^6) = -5.119 + 1.393$ area of anomaly(km^2).

On this basis, an anomaly of the minimum size of interest (which contains approximately 6.28 km^2) may contain a reservoir with possible reserves of 3.6×10^6 m^3 of oil, or approximately 22.5 million barrels. If three additional reservoirs of this magnitude are discovered by detailed seismic surveys, the cost per barrel of the entire detailed seismic survey is less than 0.3¢.

(Within the Potiguar Basin, two additional generations of seismic lines were actually run after the initial reconnaissance phase. These consisted of a set of seismic lines parallel to the initial reconnaissance set, and a second set of tie-lines perpendicular to the first two sets. The result is a more-or-less regular seismic grid having a spacing of about 2 km by 3 km. The probability that an anomaly of the minimum size of interest will be found by this search pattern is

$$Pr = \frac{Q(D_1 + D_2 - Q)}{D_1 D_2} = \frac{1.58(2 + 3 - 1.58)}{6} = 90\%$$

where $D_1 = 2$ km; $D_2 = 3$ km; $Q = 2[(1^2 + 0.5^2)/2]^{1/2} = 1.58$. With this grid, we would expect to find 12 of the 13 anomalies estimated to be present within the exploration area. In fact, 11 anomalies of this size can be discerned on the map, a close accord with predicted results.)

VII. EXPLORATION SIMULATION MODEL FOR LEASING POLICY IN OCS REGIONS

To formulate a rational and acceptable prelease exploration policy for federal lands (particularly the outer continental shelf), it is essential that the economic and social consequences of alternative policies be assessed in an objective manner. Because there are powerful vested interests concerned with the development of federal lands, the methodology and assumptions incorporated in the analysis of alternatives must be free of bias and must be based upon factual, objective sources of data wherever possible.

Because it is obviously impossible to experiment with actual leasing procedures on a large scale and because subjective appraisals of policy are highly susceptible to criticism because of the possibility of extreme bias, modeling the exploration process under different constraints imposed by leasing policy seems the most appropriate mode of investigating the alternatives. The Kalter–Tyner cash flow model (Kalter et al., 1975) provides an analytical modus based upon accepted techniques of economic appraisal. However, it is essential that the inputs to such cash flow models be closely tied to the specific geologic conditions that not only govern the occurrence of oil and gas but that also guide the exploratory process. If geologically dependent sources of input are not used, the only alternative is to derive inputs from broad resource appraisals. Such resource appraisals are subjectively based and notoriously inconsistent, as Kalter and others point out. It is essential, therefore, that independent sources of inputs to the cash-flow model be developed that would take into account the mode of exploration in high-cost, high-risk frontier areas and that would be acceptable on methodological grounds to all concerned parties.

The exploration simulation model suggested here is based on empirical frequency distributions derived from actual petroleum provinces considered analogous to areas that will be leased in the future. It also recognizes the fact that modern exploration does not consist of drawing from a population of field sizes, as used by Kaufman in numerous studies (Kaufman, 1974; Kaufman et al., 1975), but rather in the drawing from a population of *prospects* that have a conditional relation to reservoir sizes. In offshore frontier regions, these prospects are perceived almost exclusively by seismic methods. The nature of the perception of a prospect depends strongly upon the density and quality of the seismic survey, adding an element of uncertainty to the selection process. Geologic conditions in some areas make seismic analysis extremely difficult and cloud the interpretations; nevertheless, in high-cost frontier areas, exploration generally will not proceed in the absence of perceived seismic anomalies. This means that the "serendipitous discovery" that has characterized the development of many onshore petroleum provinces is unlikely to occur in the OCS, at least in the initial stages of exploration.

Within an offshore exploration area, seismic reconnaissance surveys adequate to delineate most of the potential prospects are available to the industry and government in advance of leasing. Therefore, the total number of prospects in the population can be defined reasonably well. The probability that prospects of specified dimensions have been missed by the seismic survey, as well as the number of missed prospects, can be estimated by methods of geometric probability. It will be necessary (1) to define a measure of attractiveness of seismic anomalies and establish the conditional relationship between this measure and the size of associated reservoirs within anomalies. It also will be necessary to (2) define dry hole probabilities, (3) define the conditional probabilities that a reservoir remains undetected after an initial test, and (4) specify the geographic density of anomalies within a test area.

Basically, the proposed exploration model consists of a Monte Carlo simulation procedure that samples from a distribution of the magnitudes of seismic prospects. The conditional relationship between magnitude of seismic anomalies and size of associated reservoirs allows a reservoir volume to be drawn for each prospect. This may be accomplished in various ways, including two-step sampling from one of a series of reservoir size distributions (each of which is equated to a category of prospect magnitude) or by calculating and then randomly perturbing a reservoir volume estimated as a function of anomaly magnitude. The dry hole risk may be incorporated in the distribution of reservoir volumes or appended as a separate operation. Output from the model consists of a sequence of hypothetical prospects, each barren or associated with a reservoir volume. The sequence will be sorted by rank of perceived magnitude of anomaly, as any realistic appraisal will most likely proceed from most attractive to least attractive prospect. Attached to each anomaly that contains a reservoir is some small but significant probability that the reservoir will not be detected by the initial drilling effort, but could be detected by subsequent drilling.

The sequence of prospects could now be sampled according to rules defined by the leasing strategy being tested, and an economic appraisal performed. The procedure would then iterate through successive sequences until a stable distribution of economic outcomes is obtained. Alternative leasing strategy rules could be tested using the same sequences or with other random realizations of the exploration model.

There are, of course, endless refinements that can be incorporated in the exploration model, including the use of multiple criteria of attractiveness of prospects, and the incorporation of geographic considerations. The latter embellishment would allow simulation of "interactive" leasing strategies that increase the apparent probability of success (or "*ex ante* expectation" in Kalter and other's terminology) of lease tracts near prior discoveries.

Constructing a computer program for the Monte Carlo simulation procedure is relatively straightforward, following procedures outlined in, among many other sources, Hammersley and Handscomb (1964). Geologic modeling using Monte Carlo procedures is discussed at length by Harbaugh and Bonham-Carter (1970). The major challenge will be to generate the necessary probability distributions and conditional relationships required by the model. Arbitrary or subjective distributions and relationships can be provided that will permit testing of the model and its interface with the econometric analysis procedure. However, the major effort in constructing the exploration simulation model must be devoted to obtaining realistic estimates of actual distributions and conditional probabilities in areas suitable to serve as analogs to OCS regions. Unless this is done, the modeling effort will remain vulnerable and subject to justifiable criticism.

VIII. MONTE CARLO SIMULATION MODEL OF OCS PROSPECTS

Provided suitable input distributions can be obtained, Monte Carlo simulation programs can readily be written that will generate sequences of prospects having attributes that match those observed in an analogous area or believed to exist in an OCS leasing area. A simple model conditionally simulates a distribution of reservoir volumes for a distribution of prospect (seismic anomaly) sizes. Successive realizations can be created, all of which accord to the parameters specified by the input distributions. Various selection criteria, specified by alternative leasing policies, can be applied to choose from among these realizations, and the financial consequences of their selection computed with an economic evaluation program.

There are numerous alternative ways in which such a program could be structured. For example, rather than generating lognormal distributions of field sizes conditional upon anomaly size, field sizes could be selected randomly from within independent distributions, each relating to a specific category of anomaly magnitude. Choice of procedure may depend upon the relative ease with which the anomaly size and field size distributions can be obtained.

A more complex algorithm introduces geographic constraints to ensure that the simulated reservoirs are distributed in a spatially realistic manner. This may be of value in some types of leasing simulation, for example, if leases are to be preferentially issued for prospects a certain distance from shore or in certain depths of water. Also, it would allow investigation of the effects of changes in the size of lease tract issued or the merits of dispersing or concentrating tracts in one geographic area.

A more elaborate algorithm for a prospect simulator would involve the use of multivariate conditional relations to generate multiple characteristics of prospects and their associated reservoir sizes. Such multivariate characteristics might include measures of seismic anomaly area, heights of closure, or axial ratios; length and heights of the throw of faults; and other features specific to the seismic anomalies themselves. These characteristics are interdependent to some degree. It would also be possible to introduce a perturbing factor related to the quality of seismic information. Poor quality seismic information would have the effect of inflating the variances of the anomaly distributions. Obtaining objective estimates of this factor may prove difficult, however.

The highest level of elaboration would involve combination of geographic considerations with multivariate considerations. This would allow incorporation of independent geologic factors into the calculation of reservoir volumes. Such independent factors might include regional information on sedimentary facies changes, regional organic geochemical considerations, regional heat flow, and depth of burial of the prospective horizons. These independent factors could be expressed as functions of the geographic coordinates (assuming they have a simple spatial structure) or even as digitized maps. After a random prospect location had been generated, the values of the independent geologic factors for that location could be found by evaluating the geographic functions or by querying the stored maps and then the information entered into the multivariate equation used to predict the field size distribution.

Of course, an increasingly sophisticated model requires ever greater numbers of input parameters. Determining which of the many possible geologic factors influence reservoir presence and size is a challenging research problem, let alone objectively determining their parameters. No doubt the final design of a multivariate simulation model should be dictated by the practical constraints of time and by the availability of data from which meaningful estimates of parameters can be derived.

ACKNOWLEDGMENTS

We acknowledge the support of the U.S. Department of Energy's Leasing Programs Office, which provided support for preparation of reports on which this present paper is based. We specifically acknowledge Drs. Robert J. Kalter and Anthony A. Prato of the Leasing Programs Office for their support and encouragement. Ms. Jo Anne De-Graffenreid provided secretarial and editorial assistance.

NOTE

This article was presented at the Conference on the Economics of Exploration for Energy Resources, New York University, May 17–18, 1979.

REFERENCES

Akers, H., Jr. (1976). Monte Carlo range-of-values program description, U.S. Geological Survey Conservation Division internal report.

Canadian Dept. Energy, Mines, and Resources (1977). Oil and natural gas resources of Canada, 1976, Dept. Energy, Mines, and Resources Report EP 77-1, Ottawa, Ontario, Canada.

Cook, E. (1975). Undiscovered or undeveloped crude oil "resources" and national energy strategies, Am. Assoc. Petroleum Geologists Studies in Geology, No. 1, p. 97–106.

Drew, L. J. (1966). Grid drilling exploration and its application to the search for petroleum, Ph.D. dissertation, Pennsylvania State University.

———— (1967). Grid-drilling exploration and its application to the search for petroleum, *Economic Geology*, **62**: 698–710.

Griffiths, J. C. and Drew, L. J. (1964). Simulation of exploration programs for natural resources by models, *Colorado School of Mines Quarterly*, **59**: 187–206.

———— (1966). Grid spacing and success ratios in exploration for natural resources; Sixth Annual Symposium and Short Course on Computers and Operations Research in Mineral Industries, Pennsylvania State University.

Hammersley, J. M. and Handscomb, D. C. (1964). *Monte Carlo Methods*, Methuen, London.

Harbaugh, J. W. and Bonham-Carter, G. (1970). *Computer Simulation in Geology*, Wiley-Interscience, New York.

Harris, D. P. (1976). A survey and critique of quantitative methods for the appraisal of mineral resources, U.S. Energy Research and Development Administration report GJO-6344.

Kalter, R. J., Tyner, W. E., and Hughes, D. W. (1975). Alternative energy leasing strategies and schedules for the Outer Continental Shelf; Dept. Agricultural Economics, Cornell Univ., Ithaca, New York, p. 1–40, 112–139.

Kaufman, G. M. (1974). Statistical methods for predicting the number and size distribution of undiscovered hydrocarbon deposits, *in* K. H. Crandall and J. W. Harbaugh (eds.), *Methods of Estimating the Volume of Undiscovered Oil and Gas Resources*, AAPG Research Symposium, Stanford, California, p. 247–310.

Kaufman, G. M., Balcer, Y., and Kruyt, D. (1975). A probabilistic model of oil and gas discovery, *in* J. D. Haun (ed.), *Methods of Estimating the Volume of Undiscovered Oil and Gas Resources: AAPG Studies in Geology*, **1**: 113–142.

McCray, A. W. (1975). Petroleum Evaluation and Economic Decisions, Prentice-Hall, Englewood Cliffs, New Jersey.

McKelvey, V. E. (1973). Mineral resource estimates and public policy, U.S. Geol. Survey Prof. Paper 820, p. 9–19.

———— (1974). U.S. Geological Survey releases revised U.S. oil and gas estimates, U.S. Dept. Interior News Release, March 26, 1974.

Miller, B., Thomsen, H. L., Dolton, G. L., Conry, A. B., Hendricks, T. A., Lennartz, F. E., Powers, R. B., Sable, E. G., and Varnes, K. L. (1975). Geological estimation of undiscovered recoverable oil and gas resources in the United States, U.S. Geological Survey Circular 725.

Newendorp, P. D. (1975). *Decision analysis for petroleum exploration*, Petroleum Publ. Co., Tulsa, Oklahoma.

Sackman, H. (1974). Delphi assessment—expert opinion, forecasting, and group process, Rand Corp. report R-1283-PR.

Singer, D. A. and Wickman, F. E. (1969). Probability tables for locating elliptical targets with square, rectangular and hexagonal pointnets, Pennsylvania State University Mineral Science Experiment Station Special Publication 1-69.

Sporn, P. (1974). Multiple failures of public and private institutions, *Science* **184**: 284–286.

Theobald, P. K., Schweinfurth, S. P., and Duncan, D. C. (1972). Energy resources of the United States, U.S. Geol. Survey Circular 650.

Uspensky, J. V. (1937). *Introduction to Mathematical Probability*, McGraw-Hill, New York.

A PLAY APPROACH TO HYDROCARBON RESOURCE ASSESSMENT AND EVALUATION

L. P. White

I. INTRODUCTION

This paper presents a methodology developed by the U.S. Department of the Interior to simulate oil and gas exploration activity for petroleum provinces. The analytical construct is an integral part of a larger microeconomic simulation model of petroleum exploration, development, production, transportation, and distribution activities that have been used to evaluate public policy alternatives for the National Petroleum Reserve in Alaska.

The National Petroleum Reserve in Alaska (NPRA) is an area of approximately 37,000 square miles located on the northern coast of Alaska west of Prudhoe Bay. The Naval Petroleum Reserves Production Act of 1976 required the President to conduct a study to determine the best overall procedures to be used in the development, production, transportation, and distribution of any petroleum resources in the Reserve and the economic and environmental consequences of alternative procedures. The Office of Minerals Policy and Research Analysis was directed to develop an economic and policy analysis in support of the legislative requirement and has designed a petroleum process and decision model that probabilistically simulates the major activities involved in oil and gas exploration, development, production, transportation, and distribution. Public policy alternatives are tested by the model to evaluate their economic consequences over an extended time period (e.g., 50 years). The modeling philosophy is process and decision oriented in order to capture the important interdependencies among the various petroleum activities and the sensitivity of economic decision making to various public policies.[1]

The model allows partitioning of the surface area of large basins or provinces into activity areas (delineated surface areas of arbitrary size, shape and number) that serve as the basic geographic frame of reference for analyzing petroleum or other land use activities in the province. The size, shape, number, land use classification, connecting transportation corridors, and availability sequence of activity areas are major public policy options for which alternative policies and procedures may be tested. For example, a province may be divided into two sets of activity areas, one set representing areas closed to petroleum activity and the other set representing areas that could be opened for petroleum activity according to a particular schedule. (Figure 1 presents an example set of activity areas for the National Petroleum Reserve in Alaska.)

Among the activities the integrated model explicitly simulates are two of the major economic decisions that occur repeatedly in the development of a petroleum province. The first decision involves the determination of whether a particular prospect merits testing with an exploratory well; the second, whether the resources contained in a discovered deposit, or combination of deposits, merit development, production, transportation, and distribution to market. This paper addresses the procedures developed to simulate the exploration decision. In the following sections an overview of the play approach is presented, followed by a discussion of alternative approaches. A geology model and an exploration model based on the play approach are then developed.

II. OVERVIEW OF THE PLAY APPROACH

The exploration process is simulated through the integration of two independent submodels: a geology model, which is based upon a probabilistic assessment of the most important geologic parameters in a province, and an exploration model, which simulates the search for oil

Figure 1. Example Activity Areas for the National Petroleum Reserve of Alaska (March 1, 1979).

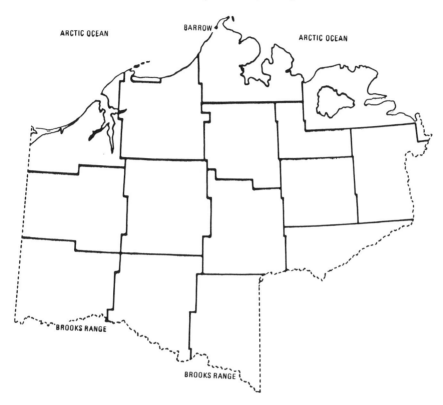

and gas in the province. The geologic model generates a list of prospects (potential drilling targets) and a resource appraisal of the oil and gas in place using subjective probability distributions developed by experts familiar with the geology of the area. The exploration model simulates both the economic evaluation of prospects by an explorer and the drilling decision, generating a sequence of discoveries that form an inventory of pools to be evaluated for development.

These two submodels are integrated in a Monte Carlo simulation of exploratory activity over an extended time period. Each Monte Carlo pass begins with the geologic submodel sampling from probability distributions for the important geologic parameters to simulate a possible state of geologic nature for the province. This state of geologic nature is composed of a particular number of prospects, some of which are simulated as actual deposits of oil and gas, with the remaining ones dry.

After simulating their expected size, these prospects are ranked according to expected volume to form a simulated target list for the discovery process.

The discovery process is then represented, on a year by year basis, as the sequential evaluation of prospects on the target list. The status (i.e., a deposit or dry) of the prospects is unknown to the simulated explorer. If the expected economic value of a particular prospect justifies drilling an exploratory well, the simulated decision is to test it and determine whether it contains hydrocarbons. This procedure continues each year in the Monte Carlo pass or until all prospects have been tested. The learning process in exploration is simulated by using the drilling results each year to update the simulated explorer's perceived state of geologic nature. The output of the exploration model each year is a list of dry wells and discovered deposits of oil and gas. The discovered deposits are added to an inventory of pools to be considered for development. A large number of Monte Carlo passes are made to generate frequency distributions for the important output variables, such as total oil and gas resources in place, discovered reserves, and production.

III. EXISTING APPROACHES TO RESOURCE APPRAISAL AND EXPLORATION MODELING

Existing approaches to resource appraisal and exploration modeling generally fall into one of three categories. A brief description and discussion of their usefulness to situations similar to the National Petroleum Reserve in Alaska (NPRA) follows.

Historically, volumetric analysis has been the primary assessment procedure applied to a large province. First, an area that has received substantial exploration and development and that is geologically analogous to the area of interest is identified. Then, the results of the analog area per unit of sedimentary volume are used as a surrogate for the hydrocarbon potential per unit volume in the area of interest. A good example of the volumetric approach may be found in Jones (1975).

Two shortcomings exist with this approach when used to estimate the economic value of the potential resources of a frontier province such as the NPRA. First, since the degree to which the analog area matches the target area is difficult to assess, it is difficult to quantitatively estimate the geologic uncertainty and, in turn, the economic uncertainty for the area of interest. Second, the level of geologic information is far too limited to be useful for economic analysis. Many of the geologic characteristics critical in determining economic value are lost (e.g., number of deposits, sizes of deposits).

Prospect analysis, a second approach to the assessment of an area, involves the identification and relatively detailed evaluation of all the potential targets for exploratory drilling that exist in an area. This approach is widely used and well developed (see, for example, Wansbrough et al., 1976 or Newendorp, 1975).

Again, there are two shortcomings in applying this latter technique to an area such as the NPRA. First, the levels of effort and data required in a prospect analysis are substantial and generally are not available for the initial economic evaluation of provinces or basins. Second, prospect analysis typically treats each prospect independently and ignores any regional correlation of geologic characteristics across prospects. The probability that a particular prospect is actually a deposit—the dry hole risk factor—is commonly used to independently risk each prospect. In essence, this implies that the presence of oil or gas in one prospect is totally independent of its presence in other deposits, even though the prospects exist in a relatively homogeneous geologic setting. Therefore, whereas prospect analysis is appropriate for certain applications, the amount of information necessary for its application and the fact that it ignores regional geologic correlation make it unattractive for the assessment of large areas such as the NPRA.

A more recent approach to modeling the exploration process uses the early results of exploration to estimate the returns to future drilling. In general, initial discoveries are used to estimate the parameters of a statistical model of the discovery process. Two examples of this approach may be found in papers by Kaufman et al. (1979) and Drew et al. (1979). A shortcoming of this approach, in its present state of development, is that it requires information that is not available until after some actual discoveries have been made in an area.

IV. A GEOLOGIC MODEL BASED ON THE PLAY APPROACH

The geologic assessment procedure developed for application to the National Petroleum Reserve in Alaska focuses on the play—a stratigraphic unit of relative homogeneous geology—as the basic unit of geologic analysis.[2] A fundamental assumption is that the geologic characteristics within the play are significantly correlated but show substantially less correlation across plays. In particular, if all the regional geologic characteristics necessary for the occurrence of trapped hydrocarbons are present in the play area, it is likely that the play will contain deposits of oil or gas. However, if one or more of these regional characteristics is missing or unfavorable, it is likely that all the prospects within the play will turn out to be dry.[3]

The play approach divides the geological characteristics of a potential deposit into three categories: play-specific, prospect-specific, and reservoir-specific attributes. Play-specific attributes consist of geologic characteristics common to the play as a unit and include hydrocarbon source, timing, migration, reservoir rock, and the number of prospects. The occurrence of these attributes is a necessary, but not sufficient, condition for the existence of oil or gas deposits in the play.

Prospect-specific attributes are the geologic characteristics common to the individual prospects within the play and include the existence of a trapping mechanism, minimum effective porosity, and hydrocarbon accumulation. Conditional on the existence of the necessary play characteristics, the simultaneous occurrence of these three prospect attributes results in the presence of oil or gas in a prospect.

Reservoir-specific attributes are the reservoir characteristics of an individual deposit of oil or gas in the play and include the area of closure, reservoir thickness, effective porosity, trap fill, reservoir depth, water saturation, and hydrocarbon type (i.e., oil or dry gas). These reservoir attributes jointly determine the volume of oil or gas present in a deposit.

Probability judgments concerning each of these three sets of characteristics for the play are developed by experts familiar with the geology of the area of interest. The experts first identify the major plays within the basin or province, review all existing data relevant to the evaluation, and then make subjective probability judgments concerning the three sets of attributes for each identified play.[4]

The play-specific attributes are assessed in the following manner. First, a probability distribution is developed for the number of potentially drillable prospects that may exist in the play area. Second, a probability of existence or occurrence is assigned to each regional play characteristic. For example, the probability that a hydrocarbon source exists for the play may be assessed as .75, the probability that timing in the play area has been favorable at .8, the probability that hydrocarbons could have successfully migrated from the source to traps in the play at .9, and the probability that the play contains reservoir grade rock at .84. The product of these four probabilities is termed the marginal play probability—the joint probability that all the regional geologic characteristics necessary for the accumulation of hydrocarbons in the play area are simultaneously favorable. For the above example, the marginal play probability would equal .454.

The second set of probability judgments required for the assessment concerns the likelihood that each of the three prospects attributes is present in a prospect. These probability judgments are made on the condition that all of the play-specific attributes are favorable. The product of the three prospect-specific attribute probabilities is the joint probability that a prospect is a deposit and is called the conditional deposit probability (conditional on favorable play geology).

The third set of probability judgments required involves assessments of the range of values for the reservoir characteristics of an individual deposit within the play. Given that a prospect actually contains oil or gas, each characteristic is assessed as a probability distribution, with the exception of the hydrocarbon mix that is assessed as a point estimate of the likelihood that a deposit is oil rather than dry gas.

These three basic sets of probability judgments are made for each of the identified plays and comprise the basic geologic input data to the geologic model. Figure 2 presents an example data form for recording these judgments for a particular play.

At the beginning of each Monte Carlo pass, the geology model uses the three sets of probabilities for each play to simulate one possible state of geologic nature. The geologic model proceeds in the following manner for each identified play in each pass.

Step 1.   The probability distribution for the number of potentially drillable prospects is sampled to determine the number of prospects that will be simulated as existing in the play during the particular pass.

Step 2.   Each of the reservoir volume distributions is sampled for each of the prospects to simulate the amount of oil or gas present should the prospect be a simulated deposit during the pass.

Step 3.   The marginal play probability is sampled to determine whether or not the play will be simulated as dry or as potentially productive during the pass.

Step 4.   For each prospect in a productive play, the conditional deposit probability is sampled to determine whether it will be simulated during the pass as a deposit or as dry. All prospects in a dry play are simulated as dry.

The particular state of geologic nature determined in each pass in the geology model is not made known to the simulated explorer, who must proceed with an exploration drilling program in order to learn the status of the individual prospects and thus make discoveries.

Figure 2. Sample Data Form for Recording Probability Judgments for a Play.

EVALUATOR: <u>Red White</u>　　　　　　　　PLAY NAME: <u>Alpha Sandstone</u>

DATE EVALUATED: <u>5/13/79</u>

	ATTRIBUTE		PROB. OF FAVORABLE OR PRESENT							COMMENTS
PLAY ATTRIBUTES	HYDROCARBON SOURCE		.75							
	TIMING		.80							
	MIGRATION		.90							
	POTENTIAL RESERVOIR FACIES		.84							
	MARGINAL PLAY PROBABILITY		.454							
PROSPECT ATTRIBUTES	TRAPPING MECHANISM		.90							
	EFFECTIVE POROSITY (≥3%)		.50							
	HYDROCARBON ACCUMULATION		.70							
	CONDITIONAL DEPOSIT PROBABILITY		.315							
HYDROCARBON VOLUME PARAMETERS	RESERVOIR LITHOLOGY	SAND	XX							
		CARBONATE								
	HYDROCARBON MIX	GAS	.75							
		OIL	.25							
	FRACTILES / ATTRIBUTE		PROB. OF EQUAL TO OR GREATER THAN							
			100	95	75	50	25	5	0	
	AREA OF CLOSURE (×10³ ACRES)		2	10	25	50	75	125	150	
	RESERVOIR THICK- NESS/VERTICAL CLOSURE (FT)		5	25	50	100	150	180	200	
	EFFECTIVE POROSITY (%)		3	5	10	15	20	25	27	
	TRAP FILL (%)		5	10	20	30	40	55	75	
	RESERVOIR DEPTH (×10³ FT)		10	11	12	15	18	19	20	
NUMBER OF DRILLABLE PROSPECTS (Play Attribute)			30	32	35	45	55	58	60	
PROVED RESERVES (×10⁶ BBLS; TCF)			0.0							

An important input to the geology model is the percentage of prospects from each play that are likely to fall within each activity area. It may be directly assessed by the geologist or it may be estimated as the percentage of the play covered by the activity area. The geology model uses this estimate to assign each specific prospect generated at the beginning of a Monte Carlo pass to a particular activity area. The result is a projection of the three-dimensional geologic column in which plays are vertically stacked into a two-dimensional realization at the surface, with each activity area assigned the number of prospects estimated to underlie it.

The list of prospects for each activity area is the primary output of the geologic submodel; a second major output, after completion of all Monte Carlo passes, is an appraisal of the oil and gas resources for the area. The resource appraisal is generated by cumulating the simulated deposits for each Monte Carlo pass, over a large number of passes, to develop a probability distribution for oil and gas resources. Figure 3 presents a flow chart of the geology model.

V. AN EXPLORATION MODEL BASED ON THE PLAY APPROACH

The exploration model simulates the search for oil and gas deposits as a dynamic discovery process, integrating the important elements of both the geology and the economics appropriate to the province. The primary function of the exploration model is to take the prospects generated by the geology model at the beginning of each Monte Carlo pass and simulate their evaluation and drilling by an explorer. Exploration is modeled as a decision process under uncertainty in that the simulated explorer does not know prior to drilling if a particular prospect has been simulated as a deposit or as dry by the geology model. That is, perfect information about the simulated state of the geologic world is not available at the exploration decision point. Rather, the evaluation of a prospect and the decision whether or not to test it with an exploratory well are based on an imperfect perception of the geology derived from the original probability distributions. Given that his decision is to test a particular prospect, the cost of an exploratory well is charged and the status of the prospect (a deposit or dry) is revealed to the explorer.

The discovery process continues each year until all prospects perceived to be economic have been tested or until the termination year for the particular Monte Carlo pass has been reached. The outcome, in terms of discoveries and dry prospects, represents the returns to

Figure 3. Flow Chart of the Geology Model Based on the Play
Approach.

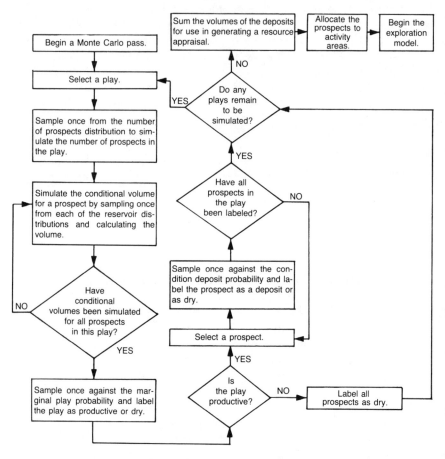

exploratory drilling for one particular realization of geologic and economic conditions. A large number of such passes are made, each time
using the geologic model to generate a possible state of geologic nature
against which the exploration model simulates the discovery process.
Outcomes of interest (e.g., total oil and gas in place, total oil and gas
discovered) from each pass may be accumulated and frequency distributions developed as outputs of the Monte Carlo simulation.

Once a particular geologic state of nature has been generated for
each activity area in the geology model, the year-by-year exploration
process for the particular Monte Carlo pass is simulated in the exploration model. Associated with each activity area is the year that explo-

ration is scheduled to commence. More than one activity area may be scheduled for initial exploration in the same year, whereas some activity areas may never be scheduled for exploration. This flexibility permits testing the economic consequences of alternative configurations for Federal lease sales in a province.

The exploration model follows a four-step procedure simulating the discovery process over time in activity areas open to exploration (Figure 4 presents a more detailed flow chart).

Figure 4. Flow Chart of the Exploration Model Based on the Play Approach.

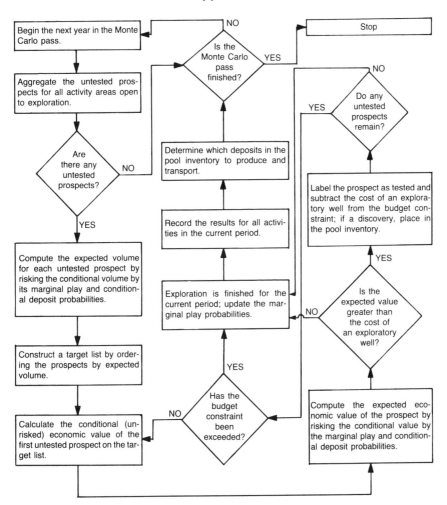

Step 1.   A target list containing all untested prospects in activity areas open to exploration is formed by ranking the prospects according to expected (risked) volume.

Step 2.   Prospects on the target list are economically evaluated, taking into account the perceived geologic risks (the marginal play and conditional deposit probabilities).

Step 3.   The decision on which prospects, if any, to test with an exploratory well is made based on expected value, drilling costs, and an exploration budget constraint.

Step 4.   The explorer's geologic perception is updated, by revising the marginal play probabilities he uses in estimating expected volume and economic value, to reflect previous drilling results.

The four steps are repeated each year that exploration is allowed until either the termination year is reached or all of the prospects perceived to be economic have been tested.

Step 1 in the exploration model is the formation of a target list. All the untested prospects allocated to activity areas open to exploration are aggregated and the expected volume of petroleum for each is computed by risking the conditional volume with the appropriate marginal play and conditional deposit probabilities. The target list is formed by ranking the prospects according to expected volume and represents the order in which the prospects will be evaluated for exploratory drilling in Steps 2 and 3. Table 1 presents an example.

Step 2 involves the economic evaluation of a prospect on the target list. The expected net present value of the prospect, conditional upon its actually being a deposit of oil or gas, is estimated by using a pro-

Table 1.   Example Target List.

Prospect rank	Play	Activity area	Conditional volume	MPP[a]	CDP[b]	Expected volume	Status
1	Alpha	H	2000	.454	.315	286	Dry
2	Beta	A	3000	.650	.120	234	Dry
3	Alpha	B	1500	.454	.315	215	Deposit
4	Alpha	B	1000	.454	.315	143	Dry
5	Alpha	H	700	.454	.315	100	Dry
6	Beta	F	1200	.650	.120	94	Dry
7	Alpha	A	600	.454	.315	86	Deposit
8	Beta	H	900	.650	.120	70	Dry
9	Beta	F	850	.650	.120	66	Dry
10	Alpha	A	400	.454	.315	57	Dry

[a] Marginal Play Probability.

[b] Conditional Deposit Probability.

duction model, a transportation model, and a distribution model. The production model estimates a simplified time profile of production conditional on the prospect's becoming a developed discovery. The transportation and distribution models estimate the cost of moving oil or gas to market, conditional on any existing transportation network serving the area. The transportation model dynamically develops a pipeline network for the area as discoveries are made and placed in production. Field development, transportation, and distribution costs are estimated by the production, transportation, and distribution models to arrive at a time profile of the costs that must be incurred to market the oil or gas that the prospect might contain. The associated revenue stream is generated by matching the potential production profile with a time profile of market prices (an exogenous input to the model) and the present value of net revenue is computed using an appropriate discount rate.

It is necessary to incorporate geologic risk into the economic calculations because up to this point the prospect has been economically evaluated on the condition that it is a deposit. The geologic risk consists of two components: the risk that the regional geology of a play is unfavorable and the risk that, even in cases in which the overall play geology is favorable, the geology specific to the particular prospect is flawed. Therefore, it is necessary to risk the prospect by multiplying its conditional net present value by the marginal play probability and the conditional deposit probability. The result is the expected economic value of the prospect.

Step 3 in the exploration model is the application of a decision rule to determine whether or not a prospect merits testing with an exploratory well. The decision rule is based on expected net present values and a budget constraint. The budget constraint sets an upper bound on the number of exploratory wells that may be drilled in any particular period. The expected economic value of the prospect is compared to the cost of an exploratory well and only if the expected value equals or exceeds the cost of testing the prospect will an exploratory well be simulated as drilled.

During each time period, the process of comparing prospect expected values with exploratory well costs continues down the target list until one of the following three events occurs: (1) exploration in a particular year ceases when the sum of the costs for wildcat wells exceeds the budget constraint; (2) a prospect is reached for which the wildcat well costs exceed its expected net present value; or (3) no additional prospects remain on the target list. At this point the drilling decisions are assumed to be implemented, exploration costs recorded, and the results of the drilling revealed. Any discoveries are placed in a pool inventory to await a development decision in following periods.

Step 4 involves updating the explorer's geologic perception to reflect the results of exploratory activity in the current year. Results from all wells are assumed to become available simultaneously at the end of the period. Prospects that have been tested with an exploratory well during the period are removed from the target list, reducing the number of available prospects for exploration consideration in following periods.

Further, an attempt to capture some of the learning that takes place during the discovery process can be made by taking advantage of the way in which the geologic risk has been factored into two components. The marginal play probability for each play in which only dry prospects have been drilled is revised according to Bayes formula; each time a dry prospect is drilled in a play, the marginal play probability is reduced as specified by the formula. (An example is presented in the Appendix.) The first time a prospect in the play is tested and revealed to be a simulated deposit of oil or gas, the marginal play probability for that play is set equal to 1 to reflect the fact that all of the regional play characteristics must be favorable for an oil or gas deposit to exist. These revisions in the perceived marginal play probability do not affect the simulated state of geologic nature because it has been fixed at the beginning of the Monte Carlo pass; the revisions only influence expectations, the perception of nature, and thus simulate the learning process that will take place over time during exploration.

The revised marginal probabilities influence exploration decisions in future periods through their impact on the expected volumes and net present values computed in Steps 1 and 2. In the case of a play that is yielding an initial series of dry prospects, the marginal probability is continually revised downward. Thus, after a series of dry wells, the expected values of the remaining prospects in the play can become too small to justify further exploration in the play even though some of them may be simulated deposits and commercial if discovered by the explorer. In the case of a play in which a prospect has been tested with an exploratory well and demonstrated to be a simulated deposit, the risking of remaining prospects in the play is based only on the conditional deposit probability because the marginal play probability is equal to 1. Remaining prospects will have, therefore, higher expected values than would be the case if there had been no discoveries in the play.

The oil and gas discoveries generated by the exploration model form an inventory of pools that represent the input to the development decision. These pools are economically evaluated for possible production, transportation, and distribution, and those combinations of pools expected to be commercial are simulated as being produced, transported, and distributed to markets.

VI. CONCLUSION

The procedures developed here have been designed to achieve an analytical melding of geology and economics; the objective has been to develop a resource assessment and economic evaluation methodology for a large area, under conditions of substantial uncertainty, and in a manner conducive to policy analysis.

A play approach to resource assessment and evaluation for large basins or provinces has been selected for several reasons. First, it provides a direct assessment of the geologic characteristics and uncertainty for the area of interest. While analogs are certainly of great use to the geologist in developing his judgments concerning an area, his final judgments are tailored explicitly to the information and perceptions of the target area. Second, the level of geologic detail provided by the play approach is rich enough to support meaningful economic analysis. Furthermore, the results of actual exploration in an area are quite easily incorporated into the play format. Third, while the play approach treats exploration as a process of prospect evaluation and decision, it does not require explicit identification and substantial detail for each prospect. Fourth, the play approach recognizes a regional component to the geology within a play that causes prospects to be geologically correlated. In essence, the play approach divides the traditional dry hole risk factor into two components. The first component is the risk that is common to all prospects in the play because they share a common potential for source material, migration, timing, and reservoir rock. The second component is the risk that an individual prospect may have a geological flaw specific to it and independent of other prospects in the play. Finally, the approach does not require actual discoveries in a play for assessment purpose; judgments may be based on whatever data exist and can explicitly reflect the uncertainty in the data.

Initial efforts to advance the analysis will focus on the simplifications that currently exist in the exploration model. For example, the target list is formed by ranking the prospects according to expected volume and only a few prospects are fully evaluated to determine expected economic value. The number of prospects fully evaluated is a function of the budget constraint. In principle, the target list should be based on economic value but volume is used as a surrogate to save computation time. Alternative approaches that more closely reflect economic value (e.g., production rate) without adding substantially to the computation time are being investigated. The use of a budget constraint to limit the number of exploratory wells each period is a second simplification that can be improved—perhaps with a more explicit model of the investment process.

APPENDIX

Bayesian Revision of the Marginal Play Probability: An Example

Marginal Play Probability = P(favorable play) = 0.454
Conditional Deposit Probability = P(discovery|favorable play) = 0.315
P(dry well|favorable play) = 1.0 – P(discovery|favorable play) = 1.0 – 0.315 = 0.685
P(dry well|unfavorable play) = 1.0
P(unfavorable play) = 1.0 – P(favorable play) = 1.0 – 0.454 = 0.546
P (favorable play|one dry well)

$$= \frac{[P(\text{dry well|favorable play})][P(\text{favorable play})]}{[P(\text{dry well|favorable play})][P(\text{favorable play})] + [P(\text{dry hole|unfavorable play})][P(\text{unfavorable play})]}$$

$$P(\text{favorable play|one dry well}) = \frac{(.685)(.454)}{(.685)(.454) + (1.0)(.546)} = \frac{.311}{.311 + .546} = 0.363$$

$$P(\text{favorable play|two dry wells}) = \frac{(.685)(.363)}{(.685)(.363) + (1.0)(.637)} = \frac{.249}{.249 + .637} = 0.281$$

$$P(\text{favorable play|three dry wells}) = \frac{(.685)(.281)}{(.685)(.281) + (1.0)(.719)} = \frac{.192}{.192 + .719} = 0.211$$

P(favorable play|a discovery) = 1.0

NOTES

1.   The Office has benefited from numerous discussions with Professor Gordon Kaufman of M.I.T. over the last several years; for a more detailed discussion of the relative merits of a process-oriented approach, see Kaufman et al. (1975) and Eckbo et al. (1978).

2.   Our selection of the play as the appropriate geologic unit was in large part the result of the work of and discussions with the Energy Subdivision, Institute of Sedimentary and Petroleum Geology of the Geological Survey of Canada. In particular, the NPRA Study Team is much indebted to Drs. Robert McCrossan and Richard Procter (see Roy et al., 1975).

3.   The importance and implications for modeling of regional geologic correlation was brought to our attention by Gil Mull of the Alaska Branch, Geologic Division of the U.S. Geological Survey.

4.   For example, the U.S. Geological Survey is responsible for the probability judgments for the National Petroleum Reserve in Alaska.

REFERENCES

Drew, L. J., Attanasi, E. D. and Root, D. H. (1979). Importance of Physical Parameters in Petroleum Supply Models, The Economics of Exploration for Energy Resources Conference, May 17–18, 1979, New York University.

Eckbo, P., Jacoby, H. and Smith, J. (1978). Oil Supply Forecasting: a Disaggregated Approach, *Bell Journal of Economics and Management Science* **9**: 218–235.

Jones, R. W., (1975). A Quantitative Geologic Approach to Prediction of Petroleum Resources, *AAPG Studies in Geology* **1**: 186–195.

Kaufman, G. M., Balcer, Y. and Kruyt, D. (1975). A Probabilistic Model of Oil and Gas Discovery, *AAPG Studies in Geology* **1**: 113–142.

Kaufman, G. M., Runggaldier, W. and Livne, Z. (1979). Predicting the Time Rate of Supply From a Petroleum Play, The Economics of Exploration for Energy Resources Conference, May 17–18, 1979, New York University.

Newendorp, P. D. (1975). *Decision Analysis for Petroleum Exploration*, Petroleum Publishing Company, Tulsa.

Roy, K. J., Procter, R. M. and McCrossan, R. G. (1975). Hydrocarbon Assessment Using Subjective Probability, AAPG Research Symposium, *Probability Methods in Oil Exploration*, Stanford University, Aug 20–22, 1975, pp. 56–60.

Wansbrough, R. S., Price, E. R. and Eppler, J. L. (1976). Evaluation of Dry Hole Probability Associated with Exploration Projects, 51st Annual Fall Technical Conference and Exhibition of the Society of Petroleum Engineers of AIME, New Orleans, Oct 3–6, 1976, SPE Paper No. 6081.

PREDICTING THE TIME RATE OF SUPPLY FROM A PETROLEUM PLAY

G. M. Kaufman, W. Runggaldier, and Z. Livne

I. INTRODUCTION

The time rate of additions to petroleum supply generated by exploratory effort is the principal focus of this study. Forecasting supply from discovery of new deposits differs from that drawn from known deposits both in the type of data available for generating predictions and in the substantially greater uncertainties characteristic of petroleum exploration as opposed to petroleum production from known deposits.

Our objective is to build an intertemporal model of exploration in a petroleum play that links together geostatistical data and probabilistic models of exploration, discovery, and economics—a model that can be used to generate probabilistic predictions of the time rate of additions to supply from new discoveries as a function of policy choice, i.e., of future prices, costs, and fiscal and regulatory regimes.

A schematic representation of such a model is shown in Figure 1.[1] The model is composed of two distinct types of submodels: first, submodels describing the generation of physical observables (drilling successes and failures and sizes of discovered deposits) as a response to

69

Figure 1. Intertemporal Model of Exploration in a Petroleum Play

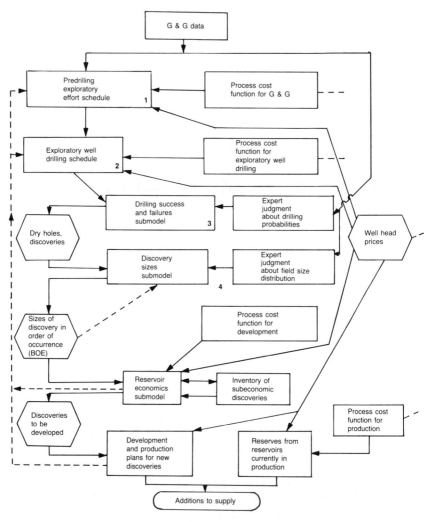

inputs of exploration effort (predrilling exploratory effort and exploratory wells drilled) and second, submodels of the economic processes that influence decisions as to how many wells to drill and when and as to what known deposits are to be developed and produced at what rate. The output of the drilling and of the discovery sizes submodels is the desired probabilistic forecast of future returns to exploratory effort in the form of drilling successes and failures and sizes of discoveries in order of occurrence.

The reservoir economics submodel brings the output of the drilling and discovery sizes submodels together with the economics of production. Once a normative economic criterion for choice is specified, a minimum economic reservoir size (MERS) can be computed, i.e., the smallest deposit that is economical to produce at a given point in time. The MERS is an economic gate, monitoring the flow of new discoveries into development and production. Discoveries that are currently uneconomical enter an inventory of subeconomic discoveries; a "favorable" change in prices, costs, and/or fiscal regime may induce members of this inventory to be developed and produced.

Essential attributes of exploration and discovery are captured by use of a probabilistic model of discovery studied by Barouch and Kaufman (1976, 1977). The setting is the North Sea, and we use cost functions constructed by Eckbo (1977) for this province. Exploratory drilling data and field size data are drawn from Beall (1976). We examine the behavior of drilling strategies and the consequent time rate of supply from an individual petroleum play in the North Sea under specific assumptions about future price and cost patterns and fiscal regimes, which are assumed to be known with certainty. The North Sea is considered here as a "price-taker" province, so exploration outcomes do not influence present or future prices, i.e., there is no feedback from the results of exploration to price. Uncertainty enters via the submodels describing exploration. The two key uncertain quantities are the outcomes of drilling exploratory wells (successes and dry holes) and the sizes of discoveries (measured in barrels of hydrocarbons in place).

In our formulation, the number of exploratory wells drilled at each time period t *is* exploratory effort, and this variable drives all succeeding submodels. *A priori* the rate of exploratory effort at each time period is an uncertain quantity, and we specify the joint probability law for rates of effort by forward-looking dynamic optimization, i.e., probabilistic dynamic programming. Once computed, this joint probability law for numbers of wells drilled at each time period is used together with that for drilling successes and failures to compute the probability law for the times at which the first, second, third, . . . , nth discoveries occur. The submodel for discovery sizes is the probability law for discovery sizes in order of discovery, so upon combining it with that for "waiting times" to the first, second, third, . . . , nth discoveries, we have a probabilistic description of both sizes of discoveries and the time periods at which they are made. Each field or reservoir of a given size possesses a prespecified production profile, and a superpositioning of these profiles according to times of discoveries of each possible size as dictated by the joint probability law for time and size of the nth discovery

($n = 1, 2, \ldots$) generates a probabilistic description of the future rate of production at each time period.

This *is* the supply function. Its properties depend jointly on the physical attributes of the play

- the size distribution of fields as deposed by Nature
- the number of prospects and the number of fields among these prospects

on how

- drilling successes and failures occur
- sizes of discoveries unfold
- production profiles for discoveries are determined

and on economic attributes, among which are

- a projection of (future) prices per barrel
- exploratory drilling, development, and production costs
- the fiscal regime in force (taxes, amortization, debt service, royalties, etc.)
- a normative criterion for making exploratory well drilling decisions and development and production decisions.

Whereas our approach to discovery and supply is superficially similar to that adopted by Eckbo, Jacoby, and Smith (1978), it differs in essential ways; perhaps the most important difference is that ours is an intertemporally dynamic analysis whereas theirs is static. In particular they assume that the rate of exploratory drilling is fixed for each future time period and known with certainty and that drilling successes and failures are Bernoulli-like, with known probability of success. In our approach, drilling rates are uncertain quantities with a probability law determined by dynamic optimization, and drilling successes and failures are adaptive as described in Section II.

Hnyilicza and Wang (1978)[2] study a model for intertemporal supply formally almost identical to that presented here. Their analysis is based on a computation scheme developed by the present authors and described in subsequent sections. However, their treatment of supply in the North Sea Jurassic Central play differs: it incorporates uncertainty about drilling successes and failures alone. Uncertainty about sizes of fields discovered and consequent effects on probabilities for future discoveries are ignored, and marginal expectations of discovery sizes in order of occurrence [cf. Eq. (7)] are adopted as certainty equivalents, i.e., sizes of all discoveries in order of occurrence are assumed to be known with certainty at the outset of the planning horizon. The only uncertainty remaining is at what well and in what time period they will be discovered. By contrast, a discretized version of the probability law for discovery sizes presented in Barouch and Kaufman (1977) is employed here, so predictive probabilities for future discoveries are explicitly dependent on past observations. Replacing the joint probability law for discoveries with certainty equivalents greatly reduces computation time at the expense of ignoring an essential feature of the discovery process. This approach may, however, be useful as an approximation. How robust an approximation it is is a topic for future research.

The economics of discovery and production enters the analysis through a projection of price per barrel for each time period in the planning horizon of time periods 1, 2, . . . , T and corresponding projections of exploratory drilling cost functions, reservoir development, and production cost functions, and a specification of the tax regime and production profiles for fields of sizes S_1, S_2, and S_3.

The time horizon T is defined to be the last time period at which a wildcat drilling decision can be made. That is, a decision to drill or not can be made at $t = 1, 2, . . . , T$, but no wildcat drilling may occur at time periods $t > T$. Production decisions are allowed at any time period $t = 1, 2, . . . , T$, but not beyond. Hence, the decision to produce a field of size S_i discovered at $t \leq T$ must be made at time period T or earlier. Because there is a time lag between time of discovery and the time when production begins, even when a decision to produce is made at the time of discovery, production may continue past time period T. Production ceases at a time period $T + \tau^*$ or earlier, where τ^* is the time period length of the longest production profile among all possible profiles (plus built-in lag). A finite time horizon introduces unwanted end effects. However, numerical analysis shows that T may be selected large enough to render these end effects negligible.

Eckbo (1977) used Wood–MacKenzie North Sea data to construct typical investment and production profiles for North Sea fields as shown in Table 1. We use these profiles in our calculations and assume that they remain fixed, i.e., do not change with the time period of discovery of a field. Then the fraction $\delta_{i,t+\tau}$ of a discovery at time period t of size S_i that is produced at time period $t + \tau$ is independent of the time t of discovery and $\delta_{i,t+\tau} = \delta_{i\tau}$ for all t.[3] If τ_i denotes the number of time periods to termination of production from a field of size S_i, the production profile for it is $S_i\delta_{i0}$, $S_i\delta_{i1}$, . . . , $S_i\delta_{\tau_i}$ for any t.

The process cost formula $C(S_i, t)$ for development and production from a field of size S_i discovered at time period t is expressed in net present value dollars at time period t and is a composite of fixed drilling

Table 1. Fraction of Total Exploration/Delineation Expenditures, Investment Expenditures, and Recoverable Reserves Occurring in Each Year Following Discovery.

Year	Exploration/delineation profile, all fields	FIELDS < 300ª Investment profile	FIELDS < 300ª Production profile	300ª ≤ FIELDS ≤ 1500ª Investment profile	300ª ≤ FIELDS ≤ 1500ª Production profile	1500ª < FIELDS Investment profile	1500ª < FIELDS Production profile
1	0.1	0	0	0	0	0	0
2	0.2	0	0	0	0	0	0
3	0.2	.04	0	.04	0	.04	0
4	0.2	.44	0	.12	0	.12	0
5	0.2	.27	.09	.20	.03	.20	.01
6	0.1	.11	.13	.24	.08	.24	.04
7		.08	.15	.16	.10	.16	.06
8		.06	.13	.07	.10	.07	.09
9			.13	.06	.10	.06	.10
10			.11	.06	.10	.06	.10
11			.08	.05	.10	.05	.10
12			.07		.10		.10
13			.06		.08		.10
14			.05		.06		.08
15					.05		.07
16					.04		.05
17					.03		.03
18					.03		.03
19							.02
20							.01
21							.01

Source: Eckbo, 1977.
ª Units: MM BBL.

costs C_0, variable drilling and production costs $a_i + b_i S_i$, production profile $\delta_{it}, \delta_{i,t+1}, \ldots, \delta_{i,t+\tau_i}$, and capital investment costs $A_i + B_i S_i$. In place of straightforward use of the investment schedule detailed in Table 1 Eckbo, 1977), we allocate capital investment costs to each time period $t, t + 1, \ldots, t + \tau_1$ for a production profile of length τ_i by averaging $(A_i + B_i S_i)/\tau_i$ per period. Costs are assumed to increase geometrically at a rate β per period. The cost factor β is distinguished from the net present value factor α, and in terms of α, β, and the aforementioned cost and production variables, total net present value of cost at time period t associated with a discovery of size S_i at t that begins development at $t + \tau$ is

$$C(S_i,t) = \beta^{t-1} C_0 + \left[(\alpha\beta)(a_i + b_i S_i) \sum_{j=0}^{\tau_i} \delta_{ij}(\alpha\beta)^j \right]$$

$$+ \frac{1}{\tau_i}(A_i + B_i S_i)\frac{1 - (\alpha\beta)^{\tau_j + 1}}{1 - (\alpha\beta)} \quad (1)$$

This function is a simplified version of that suggested in Eckbo (1977).

While any future price sequence is allowable within the framework of our analysis, we assume that an initial price per barrel p_1 is subject to geometric price inflation by a price growth factor γ, so that price p_1 at t is $p_t = p_1 \gamma^{t-1}$. Per-period tax payments are normally computed as a function of production rate and the per-period annual net reservoir operator profit. To simplify this computation, we introduce a tax and fiscal cost factor $0 < \theta < 1$ and represent the net present value of revenue flow at t from a field of size S_i commencing development at

$$R(S_i,t) = p_t S_i \sum_{\tau=t}^{t+\tau_i} \delta_{i,\tau-t}(\alpha\theta\gamma)^{\tau-t}$$

The total net present value of a discovery of size S_i made at time period t is thus

$$R(S_i,t) - C(S_i,t) \equiv v(S_i,t)$$

While this model for the net present value of cash flow from discovery of S_i at t is a reasonable approximation to reality, any nonanticipative model for $v(S_i,t)$, no matter how complicated in accounting detail, fits within the framework for dynamic optimization of drilling effort described subsequently.

We adopt maximization of expected net present value as a normative criterion and assume that once a field of size S_i is discovered, the decision as to when—if at all—to develop and produce it is separable from future drilling aimed at new discoveries and from the past history of exploration. If the interaction between the new discovery, fields already discovered, and possible future discoveries imposed by pipeline network considerations are ignored, this is reasonable. Given this assumption, commencing development at t of a discovery of size S_i made at t is desirable only if $v(S_i,t) > 0$. Optimal times for development to begin are at t^* such that $v(S_i,t^*) \geq \max\{v(S_i,t), v(S_i,t + 1), \ldots, v(S_i,T)\}$ provided that at least one $v(S_i,t)$ in this set is positive; otherwise never. Holding t fixed, a value $S^0(t)$ of field size such that $v[S^0(t),t] = 0$ is the minimum size for which development commencing at t is economically justifiable. In order for it to be optimal to begin development of a discovery of size S at t, it is necessary but *not* sufficient that $S > S^0(t)$.

An optimal sequential drilling strategy is computed by use of dynamic programming, and probabilities for number of wells drilled at time period t given the state history for drilling successes and failures and sizes of discoveries prior to time period t are a byproduct.

Figure 2 is an outline of major steps in the computation of probability laws for cumulative amount discovered by time period t, for cumulative

Figure 2. Major Steps in Computation of Probability Laws Associated with Intertemporal Model of Exploration

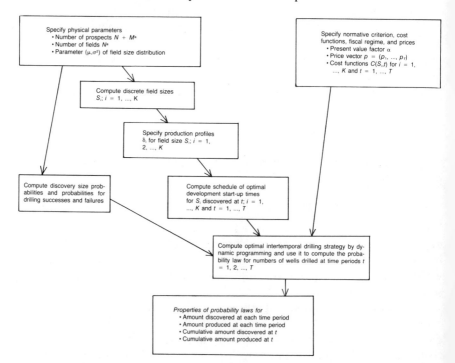

amount produced by time period t, and for the corresponding rates of discovery and of production when a sequentially optimal drilling strategy is employed.

A numerical example will introduce the discussion of the remaining sections. Consider a play with $N + M$ prospects, M of which are fields (prospects are in fact fields not known with certainty *a priori*). Drilling successes and failures are generated by hypergeometric sampling from the $N + M$ prospects.[4] The sizes of the N fields as deposed by Nature are generated by drawing independent sample values from a crude discrete approximation to a lognormal distribution with the mean μ of the log of size equal to 5.78 and the variance of σ^2 of the log of size equal to 6.38. These values of μ and σ^2 are maximum likelihood estimates computed using the discovery process model of Barouch and Kaufman (1976, 1977) applied to sizes of ten discoveries in the North Sea's Jurassic Central play as reported by Beall (1976). The discrete approximation is a partition of the range $(0, \infty)$ for size into three intervals of equal probability. The geometric mean for each of these three intervals is $S_1 = 100$ million barrels, $S_2 = 450$ million barrels, and $S_3 = 1500$ million barrels.

The planning horizon is $T = 20$ years (periods). (Exploratory drilling in fact drops to zero by the ninth period.) Expected discoveries and rates of production are computed for two initial prices per barrel: $5 and $12. Price is assumed to increase by $100(\gamma - 1)$ percent per year. Eckbo's cost formulation [Eq. (1)] is used and costs are assumed to increase by $100(\beta - 1)$ percent $= 6.6$ percent per year. Individual components of the cost function [Eq. (1)] are in 10^6 dollars ($)

exploratory drilling cost $= \$5$
total operating costs[5] $= \$18.87 + .04$ (size of field)
total investment costs (not including exploratory drilling)[5]
$\qquad\qquad = \$296.10 + 1.12$ (Size of field)

Investment costs are incurred according to the investment profiles shown in Table 1. For each discovery size, total operating costs are spread evenly over the time periods in which production takes place.

Numerical values of parameters for five runs of the model are given in Table 7. Output consists of:

- Mean of cumulative amount discovered before and including each time period (Table 3 and Figures 7, 8, and 9).
- Mean amount and mean of cumulative amount produced at each time period (Table 2 and Figures 5, 6, 7, 8, and 9).
- Mean and standard deviation of number of wells drilled at each time period (Table 4 and Figures 3 and 4).

Table 2. Mean Amount and Cumulative Amount Produced in Each Period (in 10^6 BBLS)

	1		2		3		4		4a	
	mean	cum.	mean	cum.	mean	cum.	mean	cum.	mean	cum.
1	—	—	—	—	—	—	—	—	—	—
2	—	—	—	—	—	—	—	—	—	—
3	—	—	—	—	—	—	—	—	—	—
4	—	—	—	—	—	—	—	—	—	—
5	15.64	15.64	15.64	15.64	10.33	10.33	1.11	1.11	.69	.69
6	30.37	46.13	30.38	46.02	21.42	31.74	4.84	5.95	3.29	3.98
7	41.53	87.54	41.66	87.68	29.32	61.06	9.81	15.76	6.70	10.68
8	42.63	130.17	42.74	130.42	32.29	93.35	10.07	31.83	11.28	21.96
9	42.51	172.28	42.55	172.97	33.37	126.73	21.51	52.92	15.18	37.14
10	38.71	210.99	38.68	211.64	31.59	158.32	25.12	78.03	17.71	54.85
11	32.46	243.45	32.45	244.09	26.81	185.12	27.05	105.08	19.22	74.07
12	28.27	271.72	28.24	272.33	23.58	208.71	27.68	132.75	19.87	93.95
13	24.50	296.22	24.46	296.79	20.51	224.22	27.56	160.32	20.20	114.14
14	20.76	316.98	20.74	317.53	17.24	246.46	25.56	185.88	18.91	133.05
15	10.30	326.27	10.25	327.78	10.05	256.50	22.89	208.77	17.13	150.18
16	5.62	332.90	5.58	333.36	5.87	262.37	19.21	227.97	14.42	164.60
17	3.32	336.22	3.26	336.62	3.87	266.24	14.92	242.89	11.09	175.69
18	2.75	338.97	2.73	339.35	2.37	268.61	11.77	254.66	8.80	184.49
19	1.60	340.57	1.50	340.93	1.49	270.10	8.62	263.29	6.61	191.10
20	0.79	341.36	0.79	341.72	0.76	270.86	5.94	269.23	4.66	195.76
21	0.48	341.84	0.00	341.72	0.45	271.32	4.15	273.38	3.39	199.15
22	—	—	—	—	0.27	271.59	2.28	275.66	1.91	201.06
23	—	—	—	—	—	—	1.20	276.85	1.04	202.10
24	—	—	—	—	—	—	0.48	277.35	0.05	202.50
25	—	—	—	—	—	—	0.16	277.49	0.02	202.60
26	—	—	—	—	—	—	0.08	277.57	0.01	202.61
27	—	—	—	—	—	—	0.00	277.57	0.00	202.61

Table 3. Mean Amount Discovered (Cumulative in 10^6 BBLS)

	Run			
Period	*1*	*2*	*3*	*4*
1	196.04	196.04	129.64	81.05
2	292.77	292.86	210.05	149.79
3	341.72	341.67	242.26	205.12
4	341.72	341.67	273.45	243.82
5	—	—	273.45	259.15
6	—	—	—	273.32
7	—	—	—	273.36
8	—	—	—	273.36

- Marginal probability distribution for number of wells drilled at $t = 1, 2, \ldots, T$ (Table 5).
- Joint probability distribution for number of wells drilled at t and cumulative number of wells drilled prior to t (not displayed here).
- Probability distribution for cumulative number of discoveries up to and including t (Table 6).

Table 5 is generated and displayed because expectations of rate of discovery at each time period and of the amounts produced at each

Figure 3. Mean and Standard Deviation of the Number of Wells Drilled in Runs 1 and 2

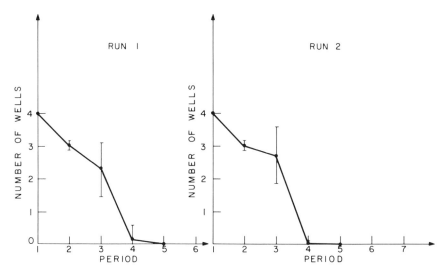

Table 4. Mean and Standard Deviation of Number of Wells Drilled

Period	Run							
	1		2		3		4	
	Mean	St. Dev.	Mean	St. Dev.	Mean	St. Dev.	Mean	St. Dev.
1	4.000	0.0	4.0000	0.0	4.0000	0.0	4.0000	0.0
2	3.0126	0.1540	3.0229	0.1541	3.5697	0.5208	3.9988	0.0639
3	2.3009	0.8503	2.7096	0.8539	1.8694	1.0341	3.9385	0.4845
4	0.1669	0.3779	0.0061	0.0779	1.4198	1.2331	3.4822	1.2175
5	0.0	0.0	0.0	0.0	0.0833	0.2771	1.3842	1.2171
6	—	—	—	—	0.0	0.0	0.7412	1.0789
7	—	—	—	—	—	—	0.0328	0.1867
8	—	—	—	—	—	—	0.0007	0.0366

Figure 4. Mean and Standard Deviation of the Number of Wells
Drilled in Runs 3 and 4

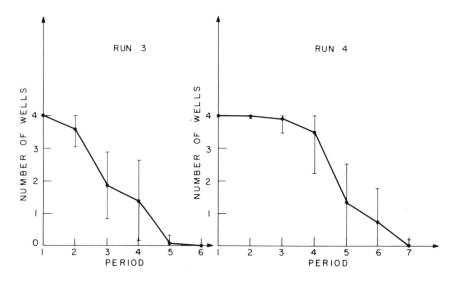

Figure 5. Mean Amount Produced in Each Period of Runs 1–3
(in 10^6 BBLs)

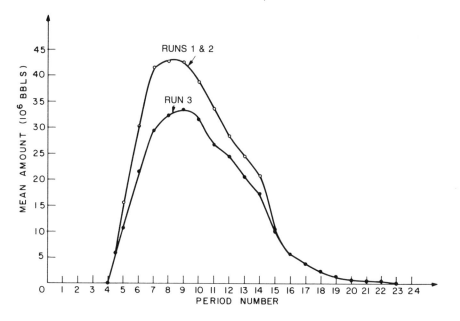

Table 5. Probabilities for n Wells Drilled in Period t

Run 1: t \ n	0	1	2	3	4
1	0.0	0.0	0.0	0.0	1.0000
2	0.0	0.0	0.0056	0.9762	0.0182
3	0.0854	0.0	0.4428	0.4717	0.0
4	0.8350	0.1632	0.0019	0.0	0.0
5	1.0000	0.0	0.0	0.0	0.0

Run 2: t \ n	0	1	2	3	4
1	0.0	0.0	0.0	0.0	1.0000
2	0.0001	0.0	0.0	0.9766	0.0233
3	0.0872	0.0	0.0289	0.8839	0.0
4	0.9939	0.0061	0.0	0.0	0.0
5	1.0000	0.0	0.0	0.0	0.0

Run 3: t \ n	0	1	2	3	4
1	0.0	0.0	0.0	0.0	1.0000
2	0.0020	0.0	0.0009	0.4204	0.5767
3	0.1242	0.1595	0.5169	0.1225	0.0769
4	0.3909	0.0460	0.3155	0.2476	0.0
5	0.9169	0.0829	0.0002	0.0	0.0

Run 4: t \ n	0	1	2	3	4
1	0.0	0.0	0.0	0.0	1.0000
2	0.0002	0.0	0.0002	0.0	0.9996
3	0.0144	0.0	0.0019	0.0	0.9837
4	0.1018	0.0	0.0052	0.1000	0.7930
5	0.3693	0.1083	0.3133	0.1872	0.0220
6	0.6508	0.0512	0.2039	0.0940	0.0
7	0.9687	0.0297	0.0016	0.0	0.0
8	0.9997	0.0	0.0003	0.0	0.0
9	1.0000	0.0	0.0	0.0	0.0

time period are functions of the joint probability law for cumulative number, $\bar{w}(t-1)$, of wells drilled at and prior to time period $t-1$ and number $\bar{d}(t)$ of wells drilled at time period t.[6]

The maximum number allowed for wells drilled per period is four. (Relaxing this constraint will alter the drilling rate, but will not, except with extreme values of model parameters, lead to a "bang-bang" drilling

Table 6. The Probability of n Discoveries Prior to or at Period t

Run 1: t \ n	1	2	3	4	5
1	.9762	.7381	.2619	.0238	0.0
2	1.0	1.0	.9167	.5000	.0854
3	1.0	1.0	1.0	1.0	.8350
4	1.0	1.0	1.0	1.0	1.0

Run 2: t \ n	1	2	3	4	5
1	.9762	.7381	.2619	.0238	0.0
2	1.0	1.0	.9170	.5018	.0871
3	1.0	1.0	1.0	1.0	.9938
4	1.0	1.0	1.0	1.0	1.0

Run 3: t \ n	1	2	3	4
1	.8586	.4061	.0667	.0020
2	.9899	.8671	.5099	.1242
3	1.0	.9818	.7636	.3909
4	1.0	1.0	1.0	.9169
5	1.0	1.0	1.0	1.0

Run 4: t \ n	1	2	3	4
1	.6244	.1620	.0134	.0002
2	.8978	.5346	.1531	.0144
3	.9855	.8468	.4654	.1018
4	.9990	.7737	.8172	.3693
5	1.0	.9965	.9123	.6508
6	1.0	1.0	1.0	.9687
7	1.0	1.0	1.0	.9997
8	1.0	1.0	1.0	1.0

policy.) In all cases drilling ceases by $t = 7$. The variability of drilling rates is greatest in the "middle" of the interval $t = 1$ to $t = 7$, at $t = 3$ for runs 1 and 2 and at $t = 4$ and $t = 5$ for runs 3 and 4, respectively.

Figures 5 and 6 display for runs 1 through 5 mean amounts produced each period by optimal drilling policies. The lumpiness in the graphs for runs 1, 2, and 3 is due in part to discretization of field sizes coupled with the behavior of the drilling rate: an uneven slowdown in the rate of drilling induces inflections in the time rate of production.

Figure 6. Mean Amount Produced in Each Period of Runs 4 and 5 (in 10^6 BBLs)

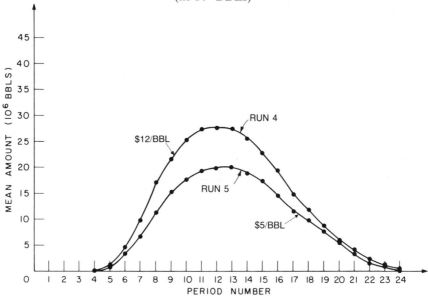

Figure 7. Mean Amount Discovered (Cumulative) and Mean Amount Produced (Cumulative): Runs 1 and 2

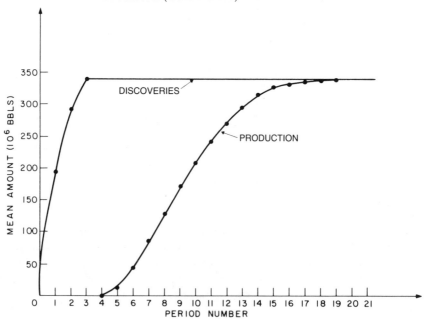

Table 7. Parameter Values for the Intertemporal Model

Run	Number of prospects M	Number of fields N	Initial price ($/BBL)	γ	θ
1	10	5	12	1.066	1.000
2	10	5	12	1.015	1.000
3	12	4	12	1.066	1.000
4	20	4	12	1.066	1.000
5	20	4	5	1.066	1.000

Finally, Figures 7, 8, and 9 show cumulative mean amounts discovered and produced for each of the five runs.

Having given a numerical preview of how our model works, we next examine the model's mathematical structure and discuss methods for computing the quantities presented as numerical output. Of particular interest is the use of dynamic programming to compute the probability law for drilling rates over time. A formal statement of the functional equation employed is given in V following specification of the mathematical structure of our models for deposition, drilling, discovery, development, and production in II, III, and IV.

Figure 8. Mean Amount Discovered (Cumulative) and Mean Amount Produced (Cumulative): Run 3

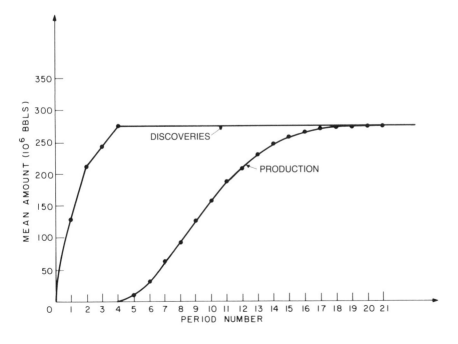

Figure 9. Mean Amount Discovered (Cumulative) and Mean Amount Produced (Cumulative): Runs 4 and 5

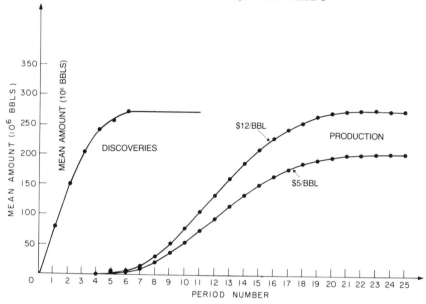

II. MODELING DISCOVERY

A petroleum *prospect* is a geologic anomaly conceived of as containing hydrocarbons and that forms a target for drilling. A petroleum *play* is a collection of prospects within a geographic region, all of which share certain common geologic attributes, i.e., there is lateral persistence of these attributes across the area in which the play is located. The petroleum play is a "natural" unit for analysis of the evolution of discovery effort over time and of petroleum supply because it is a conceptual template used by oil and gas explorationists to plan exploration programs.

Predrilling exploratory effort applied to a play generates a collection of prospects, each of which is appraised for its economic viability. Because it is never *a priori* certain (1) whether or not a prospect contains hydrocarbons, (2) if it does, how much petroleum is in place in it, and (3) how much petroleum can be recovered from it, uncertainty plays an important role in the explorationist's perception of the economic viability of exploratory drilling. Consequently, a model of exploratory drilling should reflect its essential geologic and technological uncertainties. We call a probabilistic model that does this a *discovery process model*. The particular structure of such a model depends on the level of informational detail about geologic and depositional attributes of prospects in the play assumed to be observable.

At one extreme are models for a small set of observable attributes, e.g., the number of dry exploratory wells drilled, the number that made discoveries, and the sizes (BOE in place) of discoveries. At the other extreme are models for descriptively rich sets of attributes, some of which bear on the presence or absence of hydrocarbons in a generic geologic anomaly and others that determine the amount of hydrocarbons in it. Presence or absence of source beds, favorable timing, favorable migration beds, adequacy of seal are typical of the latter; area of closure, porosity, connate water saturation are examples of the latter. These may be supplemented by maps that describe the spatial disposition of various combinations of attributes. This type of information can be used to construct a spatial probability law incorporating "lateral persistence" or probabilistic dependencies among attribute values across the area of the play. Probabilities for drilling successes and failures and for sizes of discoveries then become "spatial" in character.

Implementation of a play model incorporating this level of detail requires data generally available only to exploration companies or government agencies actively involved in the planning and execution of exploration of the play being modeled. The essential features of the evolution of exploration in a play can be captured by models more modest in their demand for input data. Prediction of the temporal flow of supply from the play can be done using a discovery model built from two key empirical features of petroleum plays: first, the size distribution of deposits is generally positively skewed with a very few large deposits and many small ones; second, on the average, the large deposits are found in the early stages of exploration of the play.

Our model for discovery is composed of three assumptions. The first two together compose a probability law for the sizes of discoveries in the order in which they occur. The third describes a probability law for drilling successes and failures. This latter assumption is somewhat simplistic and may be elaborated in several ways without severe analytical computation. However, in order to divide difficulties, we keep it simple; later on we discuss possible extensions of it.

Assumption I. Lognormal size distribution. Let A_i be the size of the ith pool among N pools deposed by nature in the geologic zone within which the play takes place. The A_i's are values of mutually independent, identically distributed lognormal random variables.

Assumption II. Sampling without replacement and proportional to random size. Given $A_1, \ldots, A_N$, the probability of observing $A_1, \ldots, A_n$ in that order is

$$\prod_{j=1}^{n} A_j/(A_j + \ldots + A_N).$$

Assumption III.   There are M prospects in the play of which N are known to be deposits. Drilling successes and failures take place via hypergeometric sampling of these M prospects.

The model for discovery sizes composed of I and II is imbedded in III in the sense that it describes a sequence of $n \leq N$ discovery sizes in order of occurrence conditional on n discoveries having been made. A discrete version of it will be used here. Assumptions I, II, and III together constitute a model for outcomes of a decision to drill a given number of wells independently of when these wells are made. That is, the model describes the *physical* consequences of a drilling program consisting of drilling a prespecified number of exploratory wells in the play.

The *economic* consequences of drilling will be attached to physical outcomes once models of exploration and production costs, prices, and fiscal regimes over time are specified.

The process generating sizes of discovered deposits in order of occurrence is embedded in the drilling process, i.e., deposit discovery occurs only when a well making a discovery occurs. Letting Z_i be barrels of oil in place discovered by the ith exploratory well, and defining

$$x_i = \begin{cases} 1 & \text{discovers a deposit} \\ & \text{if the } i\text{th well} \\ 0 & \text{is dry} \end{cases}$$

the ordered pair (x_i, Z_i) describes the outcome of the ith well drilled. If $x_i = 0$ then $Z_i = 0$ and if $x_i = 1$ then $Z_i > 0$. Consequently, if $x_i = 1$ and $\Sigma_{\ell=1}^i x_\ell = j$, then the jth discovery of size $Y_j \equiv Z_i > 0$ occurs at the ith well. The sequence $\tilde{Y}_j(j = 1, 2, \ldots, N)$ is assumed to be uninfluenced by the number of dry holes between discovery wells:

Assumption IV.   The sequence $\tilde{Y}_1, \ldots, \tilde{Y}_N$ of sizes of deposits discovered in order of occurrence is independent of the sequence $\tilde{x}_1, \ldots, \tilde{x}_i, \ldots,$ of drilling successes and failures.

Values $Y_1, \ldots, Y_n$ of the first $n \leq N$ discovery sizes may be interpreted as observations produced by sampling without replacement and proportional to size from a finite population $\{Y_1, \ldots, Y_N\}$ of deposit sizes whose elements were generated by independent sampling from a (lognormal) superpopulation. An exact computation of the probability of observing $\tilde{Y}_1 \, \varepsilon \, dY_1, \ldots, \tilde{Y}_n \, \varepsilon \, dY_n$ requires numerical evaluation of a rather complicated integral (cf. Barouch and Kaufman (1977) for discussion). In order to keep computational costs within reasonable bounds, we discretize the submodel for discovery sizes in the following way: Let $A(k)$, $0 \leq k \leq 1$, denote the kth fractile for $\tilde{A}_\ell$, $\ell = 1, 2, \ldots, N$, the sizes of deposits as deposed by Nature (Assumption I). Divide $(0,1)$ into K intervals of equal length and define S_m as the geometric mean of a generic $\tilde{A}_\ell$ conditional on $A_\ell \in \{A[(m - 1)/K], A[m/K]\}$, $m = 1, 2, \ldots, K$. These intervals are intervals for $\tilde{A}_\ell$ of equal probability $1/K$, and we shall interpret any $\tilde{A}_\ell \in \{A[(m - 1)/K], A[m/K]\}$ as having "size" S_m. This form of discretization enormously simplifies computation of probabilities for discovery sizes, replacing a density for $\tilde{A}_\ell$ concentrated on $(0,\infty)$ with a multinomial probability function attributing probability $1/K$ to each size $S_1, S_2, \ldots, S_K$

$$P\{\tilde{A}_\ell = S_m\} \stackrel{\text{def}}{=} P\left\{\tilde{A}_\ell \in \left[A\left(\frac{m - 1}{K}\right), A\left(\frac{m}{K}\right)\right]\right\} = \frac{1}{K}$$

Letting N denote the number of deposits in the play, defining N_m as the number of deposits of size S_m, and $\underline{N} = (N_1, \ldots, N_K)$, the probability that nature deposes N_1 deposits of size S_1, N_2 of size S_2, etc. is

$$P\{\underline{\tilde{N}} = \underline{N}\} = \binom{N}{N_1, \ldots, N_K} K^{-N} \equiv \binom{N}{\underline{N}} K^{-N}$$

Given that nature has generated $\underline{\tilde{N}} = \underline{N}$, the probability $P\{S_{j_1}, \ldots, S_{j_N}|\underline{N}\}$ of observing $S_{j_1}, S_{j_2}, \ldots, S_{j_N}$ in that order follows from Assumption II, sampling without replacement and proportional to size: letting $k(n,m)$ denote the number of discoveries of size S_m among the first n discoveries

$$P\{S_{j_1}, S_{j_2}, \ldots, S_{j_N}|\underline{N}\} = \frac{N_{j_1}S_{j_1}}{\displaystyle\sum_{m=1}^{K} N_m S_m} \cdot \frac{[N_{j_2} - k(1,j_2)]S_{j_2}}{\displaystyle\sum_{m=1}^{K} [N_m - k(1,m)]S_m}$$

$$\cdot \ldots \cdot \frac{[N_{j_N} - k(N - 1,j_N)]S_{j_N}}{\displaystyle\sum_{m=1}^{K} [N_m - k(N - 1,m)]S_m}$$

Putting these discretized versions of I and II together, we have the probability of observing $S_{j_1}, \ldots, S_{j_N}$ in that order as

$$P\{S_{j_1}, \ldots, S_{j_N}\} = K^{-N} \sum_{\underline{N}} \binom{N}{\underline{N}} P\{S_{j_1}, \ldots, S_{j_N}|\underline{N}\}$$

where summation is over $\{\underline{N}|N_m \geq 0, m = 1, 2, \ldots, K$ and $\Sigma_{m=1}^{N} N_m = N\}$.

Marginal and conditional probabilities for any ordered sequence of sizes $(S_{j_m}, \ldots, S_{j_n})$, $1 \leq m \leq n \leq N$ are calculable using the above probability function. Fortunately, the multinomial coefficients $\begin{pmatrix} N \\ \underline{N} \end{pmatrix}$ need not be computed in the course of computing these probabilities, for after some algebra we find that

$$P\{S_{j_1}, \ldots, S_{j_N} | \underline{N}\} = \frac{N!}{K^N}$$

$$\times \frac{S_1^{N_1} S_2^{N_2} \ldots S_K^{N_K}}{S[S - S_{j_1}][S - S_{j_1} - S_{j_2}] \ldots [S - S_{j_1} - S_{j_2} - \cdots - S_{j_{N-1}}]} \quad (2)$$

where $S = \sum_{m=1}^{K} N_m S_m$.

The above probabilities are probabilities for events that may obtain when *all* N fields in the play are discovered. The probability of observing discovery sizes $\tilde{Y}_1 = S_{j_1}$, $\tilde{Y}_2 = S_{j_2}$, $\ldots$, $\tilde{Y}_n = S_{j_n}$ in that order when $n < N$ may in principle be directly computed from Eq. (2). An alternative is to compute these "forward" probabilities as follows: Suppose that among $S_{j_1}, \ldots, S_{j_n}$, n_i are of size S_i and define $r_i = N_i - n_i$. Then letting

$$b_k = \left(\sum_{i=1}^{K} n_i S_i \right) - S_{j_1} - S_{j_2} - \ldots - S_{j_k}$$

$$P\{S_{j_1}, \ldots, S_{j_n}\} = \frac{N!}{K^N (N - n)!} S_1^{n_1} S_2^{n_2} \ldots S_K^{n_K}$$

$$\times \Sigma' \begin{pmatrix} N - n \\ r_1, \ldots, r_K \end{pmatrix} \prod_{k=1}^{n} \left[\sum_{i=1}^{K} r_i S_i + b_k \right]^{-1}$$

where Σ' is summation over $\{r_1, \ldots, r_K | \Sigma_{i=1}^{K} r_i = N - n, r_i \geq 0\}$.

Upon decomposing the products in the above sum by partial fractions and using the relation

$$\frac{1}{r_i S_i + b_k} = \int_0^{\infty} \exp[-\lambda(r_i S_i + b_k)] d\lambda$$

the above expression for $P\{S_{j_1}, \ldots, S_{j_n}\}$ becomes

$$K^{-n} \frac{N!}{N - n!} S_1^{n_1} \ldots S_K^{n_K} \int_0^{\infty} \left[\sum_{j=1}^{n} c_j \exp(-\lambda b_j) \right]$$

$$\times \left[\frac{1}{K} \sum_{i=1}^{K} \exp(-\lambda S_i) \right]^{N-n} d\lambda \quad (3)$$

where

$$c_j = \prod_{\substack{\ell=1 \\ \ell \neq j}}^{n} [b_\ell - b_j]^{-1}$$

Notice that $(1/K) \sum_{i=1}^{K} \exp(-\lambda S_i)$ is the Laplace transform of a probability function assigning probability $1/K$ to each of K values $S_1, \ldots, S_K$ of S. Each S_i is a function $S_i(K)$ of K and is chosen in such a way that

$$\lim_{K \to \infty} \frac{1}{K} \sum_{i=1}^{K} \exp[-\lambda S_i(K)] = \int_0^\infty \exp(-\lambda x) f(x) dx;$$

f is the density for a generic $\bar{A}_\ell$. In place of the expression in Eq. (3) $P\{S_{j_1}, \ldots, S_{j_n}\}$ may be represented as

$$K^{-n} \frac{N!}{N-n!} S_1^{n_1} \ldots S_K^{n_K} \int_0^1 \left[\sum_{j=1}^{n} c_j y^{b_j - 1} \right] \left[\frac{1}{K} \sum_{i=1}^{K} y^{S_i} \right]^{N-n} dy$$

When exploratory drilling is modeled as taking place at discrete points in time and more than one well may be drilled at each time point, there is no natural temporal ordering of discoveries made at a given point in time. Hence we are led to consider sampling as taking place without replacement and proportional to size, but for which the natural ordering of observations is partially lost. In the ensuing analysis of intertemporal rates of drilling, we need explicit formulae for probabilities of two types of events generated by such a sampling process: the probability that the first k discoveries are of sizes $Y_{1}, \ldots, Y_k$ and the probability that the next $n - k$ discoveries are of sizes $Y_{k+1}, \ldots, Y_n$ given that the first k discoveries are of sizes $Y_1, \ldots, Y_k$. To distinguish probabilities for events composed of ordered discovery sizes from events composed of discovery sizes without regard for order, we define $\sigma(Y_1, \ldots, Y_k)$ as the compound event composed of the union of all $k!$ orderings of Y_1, $\ldots, Y_k$, and present integral representations for $P\{\sigma(Y_1, \ldots, Y_n)\}$ and $P\{\sigma(Y_{k+1}, \ldots, Y_n) | \sigma(Y_1, \ldots, Y_n)\}$.

If observed sizes are generated by sampling proportional to size and without replacement, but the *order of observations is lost*, the probability of observing $S_{i_1}, \ldots, S_{i_n}$ possesses a simple integral representation that follows from the law of total probabilities and the following nice combinatorial identity. Given $Y_1 = S_{j_1}, Y_2 = S_{j_2}, \ldots, Y_n = S_{j_n}$ and a number S, it can be shown that

$$\left[\prod_{\ell=1}^{n} Y_\ell \right] \left\{ \sum_{\sigma} \prod_{i=1}^{n} [S + b_{j_i}]^{-1} \right\} = S \int_0^\infty \exp(-\lambda S) \prod_{\ell=1}^{n} [1 - \exp(-\lambda Y_\ell)] d\lambda$$

where for a fixed ordering $(Y_{j_1}, \ldots, Y_{j_n})$ of $Y_1, \ldots, Y_n$, $b_{j_i} = Y_{j_i} + $

$Y_{j_{i+1}} + \ldots + Y_{j_n}$ for $i = 1, 2, \ldots, n$ and Σ_σ denotes summation over the $n!$ permutations of $(1, 2, \ldots, n)$.

Using this combinatorial identity, the probability of discovering sizes $S_{i_1}, \ldots, S_{i_n}$ in the first n discoveries without regard to order is

$$\binom{N}{n} K^{-N} \Sigma' \binom{N-n}{r_1, \ldots, r_K} \left[\prod_{\ell=1}^{n} S_{i_\ell} \right] \left[\sum_\sigma \prod_{i=1}^{n} (r_i S_i + b_{j_i})^{-1} \right]$$

$$= (N - n) \binom{N}{n} K^{-n} \int_0^\infty \left[\frac{1}{K} \sum_{i=1}^{K} S_i \exp(-\lambda S_i) \right] \left[\frac{1}{K} \sum_{j=1}^{K} \exp(-\lambda S_i) \right]^{N-n-1}$$

$$\times \prod_{k=1}^{K} [1 - \exp(-\lambda S_k)]^{n_k} d\lambda \quad (4)$$

Letting $L(\lambda)$ denote the Laplace transform of f and L' the derivative of L, as $K \to \infty$ with N and the parameters of f fixed, Eq. (4) approaches

$$(N - n) \left[\prod_{j=1}^{n} f(Y_j) \right] \int_0^\infty [-L'(\lambda)][L(\lambda)]^{N-n-1} \prod_{k=1}^{n} [1 - \exp(-\lambda Y_k)] d\lambda \quad (5)$$

or in terms of the inverse function $U(L) = \lambda$ of L

$$(N - n) \binom{N}{n} \left[\prod_{j=1}^{n} f(Y_j) \right] \int_0^1 x^{N-n-1} \prod_{k=1}^{n} (1 - \exp[-u(x)Y_k]) dx$$

The marginal density for the size of the jth $(1 \leq j \leq n)$ discovery when n discoveries have been made is

$$(N - n) \binom{N}{n} f(Y_j) \int_0^\infty [-L'(\lambda)][L(\lambda)]^{N-n-1}$$

$$[1 - L(\lambda)]^{n-1} (1 - \exp(-\lambda Y_j) d\lambda \quad (6)$$

if the order in which the first n sizes discovered is "lost." If f has mean M_1, the marginal mean of $\tilde{Y}_n$ in this case is

$$(N - n) \binom{N}{n} \int_0^\infty [-L'(\lambda)][M_1 + L'(\lambda)] [1 - L(\lambda)]^{n-1} [L(\lambda)]^{N-n-1} d\lambda \quad (7)$$

when the order of $\tilde{Y}_1, \ldots, \tilde{Y}_n$ is "lost," while if the order of the $\tilde{Y}_j$'s is not "lost," it is

$$n \binom{N}{n} \int_0^\infty L''(\lambda)[L(\lambda)]^{N-n} [1 - L(\lambda)]^{n-1} d\lambda \quad (8)$$

Letting $E(\tilde{Y}_j)$ denote the expectation of the jth discovery when order is kept, it can be shown that Eq. (7) is equal to $(1/n) \Sigma_{j=1}^{n} E(\tilde{Y}_j)$.

Using the combinatorial identity presented twice earlier, the joint probability of $\sigma(Y_1, \ldots, Y_k)$ and $\sigma(Y_{k+1}, \ldots, Y_n)$ is

$$P\{\sigma(Y_{k+1}, \ldots, Y_n), \sigma(Y_1, \ldots, Y_k)\}$$

$$= \prod_{j=1}^{n} f(Y_j) \binom{N}{n} \binom{n}{k} \int_0^\infty \int_0^\infty d\lambda d\theta \left\{ \frac{d^2}{d^2\lambda} [L(\lambda + \theta)]^{N-n} \right.$$

$$+ (Y_{k+1} + \ldots + Y_n) \frac{d}{d\lambda} [L(\lambda + \theta)]^{N-n} \right\}$$

$$\times \exp[-\lambda(Y_{k+1} + \ldots + Y_n)] \prod_{j=1}^{k} [1 - \exp(-\lambda Y_j)]$$

$$\times \prod_{\ell=k+1}^{n} [1 - \exp(-\theta Y_\ell)] \qquad (9)$$

and $P\{\sigma(Y_{k+1}, \ldots, Y_n)|\sigma(Y_1, \ldots, Y_k)\}$ can be computed as

$$P\{\sigma(Y_1, \ldots, Y_k), \sigma(Y_{k+1}, \ldots, Y_n)\}/P\{\sigma(Y_1, \ldots, Y_k)\}$$

Because numerical computations are done by discretizing the size distribution, the above theoretical results are not directly employed. However, they provide a connection between the discrete version and the continuous version of the discovery process that can be exploited when adaptive updating of the parameters of the discovery process is considered, cf. Barouch (1978).

III. MODELING DEVELOPMENT AND PRODUCTION FOR INDIVIDUAL FIELDS

Once a discovery has been made, the field operator does an economic and engineering analysis to determine whether or not the field should be put into production, and if so, he specifies a development and production strategy for the field. At the individual field level, the problem of determining (relative to some prespecified normative criterion) the *optimal* development and production strategy for the field is in fact elaborately complicated and worthy of study in its own right. [Uhler's (1979) deterministic optimal control formulation of the individual field problem is a recent example of a long line of studies of the individual field problem.]

Our principal concern here is the temporal evolution of supply at the play rather than individual field level. Consequently we shall not consider dynamic optimization of production from individual fields. Rather, we propose a static model of individual field production over time, one that mirrors practical production experience: each field of size S has an associated production profile

$$\underline{\delta}(S) \equiv [\delta_0(S), \delta_1(S), \ldots, \delta_t(S), \ldots]$$

where $\delta_t(S)$ is the proportion of S produced at the tth period of time after the field's discovery; $\underline{\delta}(S)$ will be assumed to be independent of the time period at which the field is discovered. It will be convenient in subsequent analysis to define $\delta_t(S) = 0$ for $t < 0$.

Once the minimum economic reservoir sizes (MERS) for periods $t = 0, 1, 2, \ldots, T$ are computed, we can determine time periods at which a field of a particular size exceeds the MERS for that period.

In general, the MERS at t may depend on the past history of exploration prior to t. If, however, (1) prices and costs are known with certainty at $t = 0, 1, 2, \ldots, T$; (2) individual field production profiles are static over time; (3) maximization of expected net present value is the criterion for decision-making; (4) pipeline network decisions—requiring joint consideration at each time period of the sizes of all discovered fields, of potential future discoveries, and of past pipeline decisions—are ignored; and (5) the decision when, if at all, to put a discovered field into production is made in light of its economic desirability as a marginal decision-making unit independent of past history; then, the MERS at each time period is also independent of past history. We divide our difficulties by adopting these assumptions in subsequent analysis. If at t a field of size S_ℓ exceeds the MERS for at least one time period subsequent to t, a reasonable but not necessarily optimal rule is to put it into production at the first such time period.[8] More formally, let T_ℓ be the set of time periods among $0, 1, 2, \ldots, T$ at which size S_ℓ exceeds the MERS, and define

$$T_\ell(t) = \{\tau | \tau \; \varepsilon \; T_\ell \text{ and } t - 1 < \tau \le T\}$$

and

$$\tau_\ell(t) = \begin{cases} \text{smallest element of } T_\ell(t) \text{ if } T_\ell(t) \text{ is nonempty} \\ +\infty \text{ otherwise} \end{cases}$$

Then $\tau_\ell(t)$ is a time period at which a field of size S_ℓ discovered at period t and put into production at $T_\ell(t)$ has positive net present value. If $T_\ell(t)$ is empty, then fields of size S_ℓ discovered at time period t and subsequently will not be put into production at any time period within the planning horizon.

When future prices and costs are known with certainty and the decision-making criterion is maximization of expected present value, the optimal time to start production of a discovered field regarded as a production unit operating independently from other discovered fields and of its optimal production profile may be found by deterministic optimization. The optimal production profile for a field of given size will be a function of the time period subsequent to its discovery at which production begins, i.e., a discovery of size S_ℓ at period t will possess a physical production profile $\underline{\delta}_\ell[t + \Delta_\ell^*(t)]$ where $\Delta_\ell^*(t)$ is the number of time periods subsequent to period t at which physical production begins. The components of $\underline{\delta}_\ell[t + \Delta_\ell^*(t)]$ depend on *both* S_ℓ and $t + \Delta_\ell^*(t)$. With the above assumptions in force, a discovery of size S_ℓ at period t will physically begin production at period $t + \Delta_\ell^*(t)$.

IV. DRILLING, AMOUNTS DISCOVERED, AMOUNTS PRODUCED

We assume that drilling is done and outcomes are observed at discrete points 1, 2, ..., t in time and call the ith point in time "period t." As defined in Section II, the ordered pair (x_i, Z_i) describes the outcome of drilling the ith well: $x_i = 1$ if the ith well is a discovery and $x_i = 0$ if it is a dry hole. The size of deposit discovered by the ith well is $Z_i = 0$ if $x_i = 0$ and is $Z_i > 0$ if $x_i = 1$.

At the outset the numbers $\tilde{d}(t)$ of wells drilled at periods $t = 0$, ..., 2, ..., T are RVs whose joint probability law is determined by dynamic optimization given a normative criterion for decision making by the operator, a specification of the economic structure of the operator's optimization problem, and the joint probability law for the $\tilde{x}_i$'s and $\tilde{Z}_i$'s as described in Section II. Once the joint probability law for numbers $\tilde{d}(t)$, $t = 0, 1, 2, \ldots, T$ is computed, *all essential properties of amounts discovered and amounts produced are computable using it and the joint probability law for* $(\tilde{x}_i, \tilde{Z}_i)$, $i = 1, 2, \ldots, T$, i.e., the probability law for the total amount of hydrocarbons discovered at periods 0, 1, ..., t, ..., T and the probability law for amounts produced at periods 0, 1, ..., t, ..., T. The amounts produced at t depends on both the production profiles of deposits discovered at $\tau \le t$ and on whether or not a deposit of a given size discovered at $\tau_0 \le t$ is "profitably" put into production at some τ, $\tau_0 \le \tau \le t$.

The basic idea is simple: Let $\omega(t) = d(0) + d(1) + \ldots + d(t)$ denote the total number of wells drilled at 0, 1, ..., t and compute the probability distribution of the waiting time ω_n to the nth discovery, measured in number of wells drilled. Then compute the probability that $\omega(t - 1) < \omega_n \le \omega(t)$—that the nth discovery is made at period t. The probability distribution for sizes $\tilde{Y}_1, \ldots, \tilde{Y}_n, \ldots$ of discoveries is as described in Section II and is independent of times of discoveries. Consequently, if the nth discovery is made at period t, the amount discovered $\tilde{Y}_n$ has a probability distribution given $Y_1, \ldots, Y_{n-1}$ as shown in Eq. (3); the marginal probability distribution for $\tilde{Y}_n$ is as given in Eq. (6). Letting $h_{n,\ell}$ denote the marginal probability that the nth discovery is of size S_ℓ, the marginal probability that a discovery of size S_ℓ is made at period t is $P\{\tilde{\omega}(t-1) < \tilde{\omega}_n \leq \tilde{\omega}(t)\}h_{n,\ell}$, so the marginal expectation of amount discovered at period t is $E(\tilde{Z}_{\tilde{\omega}(t-1)+1} + \ldots + \tilde{Z}_{\tilde{\omega}(t)})$ and is equal to

$$\sum_{n=1}^{N} P\{\tilde{\omega}(t-1) < \tilde{\omega}_n \leq \tilde{\omega}(t)\}E(\tilde{Y}_n) \tag{10}$$

with $E(\tilde{Y}_n)$ as given in Eq. (7). The probability $P\{\tilde{\omega}(t-1) \leq \tilde{\omega}_n < \tilde{\omega}(t)\}$ can be computed in two stages. First compute $P\{\tilde{\omega}_n = \omega_n\}$; then compute $P\{\tilde{\omega}(t-1) < \tilde{\omega}_n \leq \tilde{\omega}(t)\}$ using the joint probability law for $\tilde{d}(0)$, $\tilde{d}(1)$, $\ldots$, $\tilde{d}(t)$.

Among simple possible characterizations of $\tilde{\omega}_n$ are

1. $\tilde{x}_1, \ldots, \tilde{x}_i, \ldots$ is a Bernoulli process with known parameter p. Then $P\{\tilde{\omega}_n = \omega_n\} = \begin{pmatrix} \omega_n \\ n-1 \end{pmatrix} p^n(1-p)^{\omega_n}$

2. $\tilde{x}_1, \ldots, \tilde{x}_i, \ldots, x_{\omega_n}$ is a subsequence of an infinite sequence of exchangeable RVs. Then the probability that $n-1$ 1's appear among the first $\omega_n - 1$ x_i's and $\tilde{x}_n = 1$ possesses a representation of the form

$$\begin{pmatrix} \omega_n - 1 \\ n - 1 \end{pmatrix} \int_0^1 \xi^n(1-\xi)^{\omega_n - n} \, dF(\xi)$$

where F is some *cdf* concentrated on $(0,1)$. If F is beta with parameter (α,β)

$$P\{\tilde{\omega}_n = \omega_n\} = \begin{pmatrix} \omega_n - 1 \\ n - 1 \end{pmatrix} \frac{B(\alpha + n, \omega_n + \beta - n)}{B(\alpha,\beta)}$$

3. $\tilde{x}_1, \ldots, \tilde{x}_{N+M}$ are hypergeometric as in Assumption III. Then

$$P\{\tilde{\omega}_n = \omega_n\} = \left[\begin{pmatrix} N \\ n-1 \end{pmatrix} \begin{pmatrix} M \\ \omega_n - n \end{pmatrix} \middle/ \begin{pmatrix} N+M \\ N \end{pmatrix} \right] \left[\frac{N - n + 1}{N + M - \omega_n + 1} \right]$$

Explicit calculation of the time period at which the nth discovery is made may be done by use of

$$P\{\tilde{\omega}_n \leq \tilde{\omega}(0)\} = \sum_{j=n}^{\infty} P\{\tilde{\omega}_n \leq j\}P\{\tilde{\omega}(0) = j\} \tag{11}$$

for $t = 0$, and by use of

$$P\{\tilde{\omega}(t-1) < \tilde{\omega}_n \leq \tilde{\omega}(t)\} = \sum_{k=0}^{\infty} \sum_{j=n}^{\infty} P\{\tilde{\omega}(t-1)$$

$$= j, \tilde{d}(t) = k\}[P\{\tilde{\omega}_n \leq j + k\} - P\{\tilde{\omega}_n \leq j\}] \tag{12}$$

for $t > 0$. Equation (11) is the probability that the nth discovery is made at period 0 and Eq. (12) is the probability that the nth discovery is made at period $t > 0$.

The marginal probability distribution for the starting time of production from the nth discovery follows directly from Eqs. (11) and (12). Letting $\tau_\ell(t) \equiv t + \Delta_\ell(t)$, the marginal probability that the nth discovery is of size S_ℓ and discovered at t is the marginal probability that a production profile $S_\ell \underline{\delta}_\ell$ commences at $t + \Delta_\ell(t)$. Hence the marginal probability that an amount $S_\ell \delta_{\ell,t-\tau-\Delta_\ell(\tau)}$ is produced at t from the nth discovery is the probability that the nth discovery is made at τ and is of size S_ℓ.[9]

Defining $h_{n,\ell}$ as the marginal probability that the nth discovery is of size S_ℓ, the marginal expectation $E[\hat{\rho}_n(t)]$ of the amount $\tilde{\rho}_n(t)$ produced at period t by the nth discovery is

$$\sum_{\ell=1}^{K} h_{n,\ell} \sum_{\tau \in \{j \mid j + \Delta_\ell(j) - t\}} S_\ell \delta_{\ell,t-\tau-\Delta_\ell(\tau)} \, P\{\tilde{\omega}(\tau - 1) < \tilde{\omega}_n \leq \tilde{\omega}(\tau)\} \qquad (13)$$

and so the marginal expectation of the amount produced at period t is

$$\sum_{n=1}^{N} E[\tilde{\rho}_n(t)]$$

To sum up, we have given explicit formulae for computation of the expectation of amount discovered at t and for the amount produced at t [Eq. (13)]. First moments of these quantities are relatively easy to compute, but higher moments of $\tilde{\rho}_1(t) + \ldots + \tilde{\rho}_n(t) + \ldots$ are quite complicated, so we defer presentation here.

V. COMPUTATION OF PROBABILITY LAW FOR $\tilde{d}(t)$, $t = 0, 1, 2, \ldots, T$ BY DYNAMIC OPTIMIZATION

The character of the operator's optimization problem is partially determined by the information available to him at each point in time when he must decide how many wells to drill. Within the context of the drilling and discovery size models presented in Sections II through IV, the most complete set of information about drilling successes and failures and discovery sizes possibly available at the beginning of period t is composed of three pieces (subsets):

1. Knowledge of the *structure* of the drilling model and discovery sizes model.

2. Knowledge of the *parameters* of these two models, e.g., if drilling is hypergeometric, the operator knows the values of the number M of prospects and the number N of fields; if drilling is an exchangeable sequence as defined in Section IV, the operator has assigned a mixing *cdf* F (prior distribution). He also knows the functional form and parameters of the field size distribution, e.g., if this distribution is lognormal, he knows its scale and location parameters with certainty.

3. Knowledge of the *history of drilling outcomes and of sizes discovered.* Recalling that the ordered pair (x_i, Z_i) describes the outcome of the ith well drilled

$$x_i = \begin{cases} 1 \text{ if the } i\text{th well is a discovery} \\ 0 \text{ otherwise} \end{cases}$$

and

$$Z_i = \begin{cases} \text{size of discovery by } i\text{th well if } x_i = 1 \\ 0 \text{ if } x_i = 0 \end{cases}$$

a *complete* state history of drilling successes and failures and of discovery sizes in order of occurrence at the end of period t is represented by the vector

$$H_t \equiv [(x_i, Z_1), \ldots, (x_{\omega(t)}, Z_{\omega(t)})]$$

or equivalently (since $Z_i = 0$ iff $x_i = 0$)

$$H_t \equiv (Z_1, \ldots, Z_{\omega(t)})$$

Because the time period at which the ith well is drilled conveys no information about future discovery sizes or about future drilling successes and failures, H_t is a complete or sufficient descriptor.

Assuming that the operator knows both model structure and model parameters with certainty is a strong assumption; in practice, neither model structure nor model parameters are known with certainty. This assumption is a tactical compromise, for if it is assumed that the operator knows model structures with certainty, but not the model's parameters, the operator's dynamic optimization problem—determine a sequentially optimal drilling strategy—becomes computationally unwieldy, i.e., at each period t, *parameters* of the predictive distributions for future drilling successes and failures and future discovery sizes are then dependent on past history H_t and the computational dimensionality of the optimization problem becomes very large. This can be true even when the dependence on H_t of parameters of the predictive distributions is through a sufficient statistic of low dimension and the random process generating drilling successes and failures is independent of the process generating discovery sizes.[10]

In what follows we shall assume that parameters of the process generating discovery sizes—the number N of fields deposed by nature, the functional form, and the parameters of the field size distribution—are known with certainty. Similarly, we assume that parameters of the drilling successes and failures process are known with certainty. We note however, that if $\tilde{x}_1, \ldots, \tilde{x}_i$ is assumed to be an exchangeable sequence, then for any positive integer i, (i,r), $r = x_1 + \ldots + x_i$ is a sufficient statistic;[11] predictive probabilities for drilling successes and failures $\tilde{x}_{i+1}, \ldots, x_{i+k}, \ldots$ are "adaptively updated" through interaction of (i,r) and the mixing (prior) *cdf F*, and the computational burden is roughly equivalent to assuming that $\tilde{x}_1, \ldots, \tilde{x}_{n+M}$ are hypergeometric RVs with parameter (N,M) *provided* that an *ad hoc* stopping rule for the total number of wells drilled over the planning horizon is introduced.

We determine the joint probability law describing the evolution of an optimal sequential drilling policy by use of dynamic programming. Let $\underline{\sigma}_t$ denote the history of exploration at period t: $\underline{\sigma}_t = (Z_{\omega(t-1)+1}, \ldots, Z_{\omega(t)})$. The number $d(t)$ of wells drilled at t is the number of components of $\underline{\sigma}_t$, and $Z_{\omega(t-1)+k}$ denotes the size of field discovered by the kth well drilled at period t ($Z_{\omega(t-1)+k} > 0$ is the size of a discovery and $Z_{\omega(t-1)+k} = 0$ denotes a dry hole). The history of exploration up to and including period t is $H_t \equiv (\underline{\sigma}_0, \underline{\sigma}_1, \ldots, \underline{\sigma}_t)$ and H_t in terms of H_{t-1} is $(H_{t-1}, \underline{\sigma}_t)$.

Adopting maximization of expected net present value as a normative criterion for decision making, let $v_t(\cdot)$ be the net present value at t over $t, t + 1, \ldots$ of discovery of sizes $Z_{\omega(t-1)+1}, \ldots, Z_{\omega(t)}$ made at t and let $E_{\underline{\sigma}_t|H_{t-1}}$ denote expectation with respect to the distribution of $(\tilde{Z}_{\omega(t-1)+1}, \ldots, \tilde{Z}_{\omega(t)})$ given H_{t-1} and $d(t)$. If $V_t(H_{t-1})$ is the expectation of an optimal policy over $t, t + 1, \ldots, T$ given H_{t-1}, then given a constant discount rate α, by the principle of optimality

$$V_t(H_{t-1}) = \max_{d(t)\varepsilon D(t)} \{E_{\underline{\sigma}_t|H_{t-1}} v_t(\underline{\tilde{\sigma}}_t) + \alpha E_{\underline{\sigma}_t|H_{t-1}} V_{t+1}[(H_{t-1}, \underline{\sigma}_t)]\}$$

where $D(t)$ is a set whose elements are numbers of wells that are allowable at t.[12] At $t = 0$, there is no history of drilling, H_{-1} is empty, and so we define

$$V_0(H_{-1}) = \max_{d(0)\varepsilon D(0)} \{E_{\underline{\sigma}_0} v_0(\underline{\tilde{\sigma}}_0) + \alpha E_{\underline{\sigma}_0} V_1(\underline{\tilde{\sigma}}_0)\}$$

No exploratory drilling takes place at $t > T$, so we define

$$V_{T+1}(H_T) = \max_{d(\tau)\varepsilon D(\tau)} E_{\underline{\sigma}_\tau|H_{T-1}} v_T(\underline{\tilde{\sigma}}_T)$$

Optimal times for development to begin at t^* such that $v(S_i, t^*) \geq \max \{v(S_i, t), v(S_i, t + 1), \ldots, v(S_i, T)\}$ provided that at least one $v(S_i, t)$ in this set is positive; otherwise never. Holding t fixed, a value $S^0(t)$ of field size such that $v(S^0(t), t) = 0$ is the minimum size for which development commencing at t is economically justifiable. In order for it to be optimal to begin development of a discovery of size S at t, it is necessary but *not* sufficient that $S > S^0(t)$.

Given $d(t)$ exploratory wells to be drilled at period t, the expectation operator $E_{\sigma_t | H_{t-1}}$ can be viewed as operating in two stages: one corresponding to expectation with respect to drilling successes and failures and a second corresponding to the sizes of discoveries given the number of discoveries made by these $d(t)$ wells.

If n discoveries are made by $\omega(t - 1)$ wells drilled at periods 0, 1, $\ldots, t - 1$ and we define, as earlier, $R(Z, t)$ as the net present value of revenue from a discovery of size Z at t, then *given* that m discoveries of sizes $Y_{n+1}, \ldots, Y_{n+m}$ are made at t by $d(t)$ wells, the net return at period t, $v_t(\underline{\sigma}_t)$ is

$$v_t(\underline{\sigma}_t) = R(Z_{\omega(t-1)+1}, t) + \ldots + R(Z_{\omega(t-1)+d(t)}, t) - c_t[d(t)]$$

$$= R(Y_{n+1}, t) + \ldots + R(Y_{n+m}, t) - c_t[d(t)]$$

where $c_t[d(t)]$ is the net present value cost of drilling $d(t)$ wildcats at period t. By Assumption III, the sequence $\tilde{Y}_1, \ldots, \tilde{Y}_N$ of RVs is independent of the sequence $\tilde{x}_1, \ldots, \tilde{x}_i, \ldots$. Hence given $\underline{Y} = (Y_1, \ldots, Y_n)$ discovered prior to period t, and defining $\xi = x_{\omega(t-1)+1} + \ldots + x_{\omega(t)}$

$$E_{\sigma_t | H_{t-1}} \, v_t(\tilde{\underline{\sigma}}_t) = E_{\xi | H_{t-1}} \, E_{Y_{n+1}, \ldots, Y_{n+\xi} | H_{t-1}} \, v_t(\tilde{\underline{\sigma}}_t)$$

$$= \sum_{m=1}^{d(t)} P\{\xi = m | x_1, \ldots, x_{\omega(t-1)}\} \sum_{\ell=1}^{m} E_{Y_{n+\ell} | \underline{Y}} \{R(\tilde{Y}_{n+\ell}, t) - c[d(t)]\}$$

When the well drilling history can be summarized by a sufficient statistic of low dimensionality [in cases (1), (2), and (3) of Section IV, the number $\omega(t - 1)$ of wells drilled prior to period t and the number r of discoveries made by these wells], the state history of the process at period t is fully summarized by this statistic and $\underline{Y}$.

ACKNOWLEDGMENTS

This manuscript is an account of work sponsored by the Electric Power Research Institute Inc. (EPRI). The responsibility for accuracy, completeness, and usefulness rests solely with the authors. However, we wish to thank EPRI's technical officer, Al Halter, for guidance. We also wish to thank Paul Eckbo for his assistance in formulating cost and price structure. WR was supported jointly by Electronic Systems Laboratory (ESL) and the Italian National Research Council.

NOTES

1. From "The Interface Between Geostatistical Modelling of Oil and Gas Discovery and Economics" (forthcoming in *Mathematical Geology*).
2. Revised and extended version by J. W. Wang.
3. This independence assumption is discussed in more detail in Section III.
4. Modeling drilling successes and failures as hypergeometric sampling is proposed by Jacoby, Eckbo, and Smith (1978: 232).
5. Operating costs consist of platform operating costs, administrative costs, transportation costs, and harbor and terminal operating costs. (See Table 5, in Eckbo.) Investment costs include platform costs, drilling costs, pipeline costs, terminal costs, and miscellaneous costs.
6. Henceforth we distinguish a random variable (RV) from a value assumed by it with a tilde; e.g., the RV $\tilde{d}(t)$ takes on a value of $d(t)$.
7. Integrating Eq. (9) with respect to $Y_{k+1}, \ldots, Y_n$ and then with respect to θ, Eq. (8) reduces to $P\{\sigma(Y_1, \ldots, Y_k)\}$ and is formally identical to Eq. (5).
8. Throughout, reference to the time period at which a field is "put into production" means that the decision to produce is made at that time period. Physical production may, because of time lags, occur subsequent to this time period.
9. Recall that $\delta_{t,\tau} \equiv 0$ for $\tau < 0$, so that if the nth discovery is made at $\tau' > t - \Delta_t(\tau')$ the amount produced from it at period t is zero.
10. See Barouch (1978) for what is required to update adaptively predictive distributions for discovery sizes alone.
11. In the Bayesian sense that the predictive distribution for $\tilde{x}_{i+1}, \ldots, \tilde{x}_{i+k}, \ldots$ given $x_1, \ldots, x_i$, depends on observations $x_1, \ldots, x_i$ only through (i,r).
12. $D(t)$ may depend on past history H_{t-1}.

REFERENCES

Arps, J. K. and Roberts, T. G. (1958). Economics of Drilling for Cretaceous Oil and Gas on the East Flank of the Denver-Julesberg Basin, *Am. Assoc. Petr. Geol. Bull.* **42:** 2549–2566.

Barouch, E. (1978). Blending Subjective Probability Assessments with a Petroleum Field Discovery Model (Task #2a).

Barouch, E. and Kaufman, G. M. (1976). Oil and Gas Discovery Modelled as Sampling Proportional to Random Size, Sloan School of Mgt. Working Paper, WP888-76, December 1976.

——— (1977). "Estimation of Undiscovered Oil and Gas," *Proc. Symposia in Appl. Math.*, American Mathematical Society, Vol. XXI, pp. 77–91.

——— (1978). "The Interface Between Geostatistical Modelling of Oil and Gas Discovery and Economics," *Math Geology*, Vol. 10, No. 5, Oct. 1978, pp. 611–628.

Beall, A. D. (1976). Dynamics of Petroleum Industry Investment in the North Sea, M.I.T. Energy Lab Working Paper, WP888-76.

102 / *The Economics of Exploration for Energy Resources*

Drew, L. I., Scheunemeyer, J. and Root, D. H. (1978). Resource Appraisal and Discovery Rate Forecasting in Partially Explored Regions: Part A: An Application to the Denver Basin, unpublished USGS manuscript in review.

Eckbo, P. (1977). Estimating Offshore Exploration Development and Production Costs, M.I.T. Energy Lab Working Paper, WP 77, September, 1977.

Eckbo, P. and Hnyilicza, E. (1978). Optimal Exploratory Drilling in the North Sea Petroleum Basin, M.I.T. Energy Lab Working Paper No. 78-012WP, August 1978.

Eckbo, P., Jacoby, H. and Smith, J. (1978). Oil Supply Forecasting: a Disaggregated Approach, *Bell Journal of Economics* **9**: 218–235.

Hnyilicza, E. and Wang, J. "Optimal Wildcat Drilling Programs Under Uncertainty" MIT Energy Laboratory Report MIT-EL 78-014WP (Revised and extended by J. Y. Wang) Nov. 1978.

Jacoby, H., Eckbo, P. and Smith, J. (1978). "Oil Supply Forecasting: A Disaggregated Process Approach." *The Bell Journal of Economics* Vol. 9 No. 1 Spring pp. 218–235.

Pindyck, R. S. (1977). Optimal Exploration and Production of a Non-renewable Resource, M.I.T. Energy Laboratory Working Paper No. 77-018WP, May 1977.

Uhler, R. S. (1979). The Rate of Petroleum Exploration and Extraction (forthcoming).

Witsenhausen, H. S. (1971). Separation of Estimation and Control: Discrete Time Systems, *Proc. IEEE*, **59**: 91–94.

AN ECONOMETRIC FRAMEWORK FOR MODELING EXHAUSTIBLE RESOURCE SUPPLY

Dennis Epple and Lars Hansen

I. INTRODUCTION

Econometric models of the supply of exhaustible resources have performed poorly. Markedly different supply paths are predicted by models subjected to uniform changes in the values of a set of exogenous variables common to the models.[1] The models have generally overestimated the actual response of supply to changes in price.

The poor performance of econometric models has been cited as evidence that econometric methodology is inapplicable to modeling exhaustible resource supply. This conclusion is incorrect. The specifications of econometric models of exhaustible resource supply have been based largely on intuitive judgments about the appropriateness of a particular set of explanatory variables. The specification errors that are likely to accompany such an *ad hoc* procedure can result in very large prediction errors, particularly when the values of explanatory variables used for model simulation differ substantially from those used for estimation.

Reliance on intuition in model specification cannot be attributed to a lack of theoretical analysis; much attention has been devoted to theoretical models of resource extraction.[2] The difficulty is that the theoretical models are mathematically complex and not easily translated into a form suitable for estimation. Our objective is to provide a formulation of the resource extraction problem that is applicable to a large class of exhaustible resources and that gives rise to supply equations that can be readily estimated with available techniques.

There are three important features that we believe the model should possess:

1. The econometric supply equations should be explicitly derived from maximization of the objective function of suppliers.
2. The derivation of the econometric equations should include an explicit treatment of the sources of uncertainty or unobservability of variables that give rise to the residuals in the supply equations.
3. If future values of exogenous variables are uncertain, the model should incorporate a specification of how producers expectation of those variables are determined.

There are several reasons for requiring that the model possess these features. Parameters appearing in the econometric equations will be either parameters in suppliers' objective functions or parameters in suppliers equations for forecasting exogenous variables. A clear interpretation of the parameters will thus be available. In addition, the theoretical model may place restrictions on the algebraic signs and, possibly, on the magnitudes of the coefficients.

Probability distributions determining exogenous variables and random components are part of the theoretical model. Explicit treatment of these distributions permits the selection of estimation procedures that are appropriate for the econometric equations derived from the model.

The parameters in equations determining producers' expectations of exogenous variables will generally appear in the equations determining supply.[3] Thus, a change in the producers' equations for forecasting future values of exogenous variables can change supply even if current values of exogenous variables appearing in the supply equation do not change. By estimating both the parameters in producers' objective functions and the parameters in their equations for forecasting exogenous variables, it is possible to state how a change in equations determining expectations will affect supply.

Our formulation of the resource extraction problem and our derivation of the econometric equations is developed rigorously and in detail in Epple and Hansen (1979).[4] The purpose of this article is to present the model in an intuitive and relatively nontechnical manner. Issues raised above will be illustrated with examples, and potential applications will be discussed. The theoretical formulation is presented in Section II; examples and potential applications are discussed in Sections III, IV, and V. In this article we will consider a model in which a single resource is being extracted. However, the framework in Epple and Hansen (1979) is general enough to apply to simultaneous extraction of several resources.

II. THEORETICAL FRAMEWORK

As the extraction of a resource proceeds, the easily accessible high quality deposits are exploited first. The unit cost of production rises as cumulative production rises because the quality and accessibility of unexploited deposits declines. This increase in unit production cost as cumulative production rises, is common to all exhaustible resources.

The unit cost of production also rises as the current rate of production rises. In mining, this results from the need to increase the area of the seam face being mined, which, in turn, requires the construction of additional points of access (e.g., tunnels) to the seam. It is typically not possible to increase the facial area of the seam being mined without a more than proportional increase in cost. In exploitation of petroleum reservoirs, increasing the rate of production requires drilling additional wells. The additional wells will permit more rapid depletion of the reservoir, but need not enhance—and may actually reduce—ultimate recovery. When exploring for undiscovered deposits, sequential search of potential sites is less costly per unit discovered than simultaneous searching of several potential sites. When search is conducted sequentially, the outcome of one trial provides information that improves the choice of location of subsequent trials. Therefore, increasing the rate of new discoveries requires a more than proportional increase in exploration costs.

These effects of current and cumulative extraction on extraction cost are incorporated in the following cost function:

$$K_t = \phi \Delta y_t + \theta \Delta y_t^2 + \pi \Delta y_t y_t + c_t \Delta y_t \qquad (1a)$$

In this expression K_t is the cost of production in period Δy_t is production in the current period, and y_t is cumulative production. Current and cumulative production are related by the accounting identity $\Delta y_t = y_t - y_{t-1}$. A random "technology shock" c_t is assumed to affect production in period t. Current and past values of c_t are assumed to be observed by the supplier but not by the econometrician. These technology shocks will give rise to the disturbance terms in the regression equations.

The role of the parameters in the cost function is more easily understood by rewriting Eq. (1a) using the definitional relationship $y_t = y_{t-1} + \Delta y_t$ to obtain:

$$K_t = \phi \Delta y_t + (\theta + \pi) \Delta y_t^2 + \pi \Delta y_t y_{t-1} + c_t \Delta y_t \qquad (1b)$$

Using Eq. (1b) the average and marginal cost of current extractions are

$$k_t = \frac{K_t}{\Delta y_t} = \phi + (\theta + \pi)\Delta y_t + \pi y_{t-1} + c_t \qquad (2)$$

and

$$
\begin{aligned}
m_t = \frac{\partial K_t}{\partial \Delta y_t} &= \phi + 2(\theta + \pi)\Delta y_t + \pi y_{t-1} + c_t \\
&= \phi + (2\theta + \pi)\Delta y_t + \pi y_t + c_t
\end{aligned}
\qquad (3)
$$

The average and marginal cost functions with the technology shock $c_t = 0$ are illustrated in Figure 1. The rate at which average and marginal extraction costs increase with current output is determined by the sum $\theta + \pi$. Therefore we require $\theta + \pi > 0$. In the derivation of the decision rule for current production, it proves to be necessary to impose the stronger restriction $2\theta + \pi > 0$. The last expression on the right hand side of Eq. (3) suggests why this restriction is needed. A portion of the increase in marginal cost πy_t is due to a rise in cumulative extraction. The remaining portion, $(2\theta + \pi)\Delta y_t$, is due to a rise in current output. The restriction $2\theta + \pi > 0$ implies that both components of this rise in marginal cost must be positive. Note that we do not rule out $\theta < 0$ as long as $2\theta + \pi > 0$. Because costs must be positive for nonnegative y_t and Δy_t, we require that $\phi > 0$.

The resource owner is assumed to have the objective of maximizing the expected present value of revenues less extraction costs. The maximization problem is

$$E_t \sum_{j=0}^{\infty} \beta^j \{q_{t+j}\Delta y_{t+j} - \phi\Delta y_{t+j} - \theta\Delta y_{t+1}^2 - \pi\Delta y_{t+j}\, y_{t+j} - c_{t+j}\Delta y_{t+j}\} \qquad (4)$$

The price of the resource at data $t+j$ is q_{t+j}. The discount factor is β. The expectation E_t is conditioned on the information available to the supplier at date t. Because this objective function is quadratic, the decision rule that maximizes Eq. (4) will be linear in a subset of the variables in the suppliers information set if the equations generating q_t and c_t are linear.

In order to derive the decision rule, it is necessary to specify how q_t and c_t are generated. We assume that the price q_t is an element of

Figure 1.   Average and Marginal Cost Curves at Date *t*

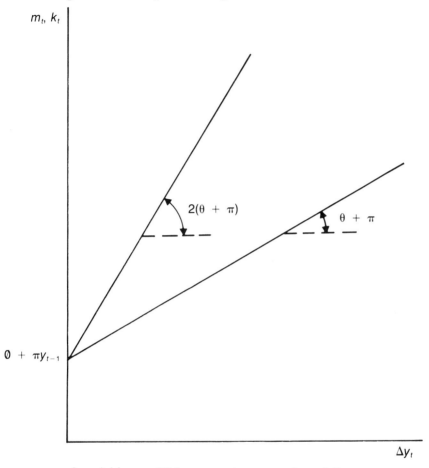

a vector of variables x_t. This vector is assumed to follow an autoregressive process

$$x_t = \zeta_1 x_{t-1} + \zeta_2 x_{t-2} + \ldots + \zeta_r x_{t-r} + s_t^x \qquad (5)$$

where $E_{t-1}(s_t^x) = 0$, and the ζ_i are parameters. As Eq. (5) indicates, variables included in x_t are variables that are useful in predicting the price of the resource. The stipulation $E_{t-1}(s_t^x) = 0$ implies that the mean of the disturbance term s_t^x conditioned on information available at $t-1$ is assumed to be zero.

Similarly, technology shock c_t is assumed to be an element of a vector e_t where e_t follows the autoregressive process

$$e_t = \gamma_1 e_{t-1} + \gamma_2 e_{t-2} + \ldots + \gamma_r e_{t-r} + s_t^e \qquad (6)$$

where $E_{t-1}(s_t^e) = 0$. The variables other than c_t that enter e_t are variables useful in predicting c_t. The mean of the disturbance term s_t^e conditioned on information available at $t-1$ is assumed to be zero. In addition, we assume $E_{t-1}(s_t^e s_t^x) = 0$.

Using the forecasting Eqs. (5) and (6), the solution to Eq. (4) derived in Epple and Hansen (1979) is

$$y_t = \frac{\psi_1}{(\beta)^{1/2}} y_{t-1} + \frac{1}{\psi_0} \sum_{j=0}^{\infty} [\psi_1 (\beta)^{1/2}]^j E_t(q_{t+j} - \beta q_{t+j+1}$$

$$- c_{t+j} + \beta c_{t+j+1)} - \frac{(1 - \beta)\phi}{\psi_0 [1 - \psi_1(\beta)^{1/2}]} \quad (7a)$$

where ψ_0 and ψ_1 depend on the parameters of objective function (4) in the following way

$$\psi_3 = \frac{2[(1 + \beta)\theta + \pi]}{(\beta)^{1/2}(2\theta + \pi)}$$

$$\psi_1 = \frac{\psi_3 - (\psi_3^2 - 4)^{1/2}}{2}$$

$$\psi_0 = \frac{(\beta)^{1/2}(2\theta + \pi)}{\psi_1}$$

The derivation of Eq. (7a) requires the restriction $\psi_1 < 1$. Equation (7a) can also be written in terms of the current rate of extraction by subtracting y_{t-1} from both sides of Eq. (7a) to yield

$$\Delta y_t = \left(\frac{\psi_1}{(\beta)^{1/2}} - 1 \right) y_{t-1} + \frac{1}{\psi_0} \sum_{j=0}^{\infty} [\psi_1(\beta)^{1/2}]^j E_t(q_{t+j}$$

$$- \beta q_{t+j+1} - c_{t+j} + \beta c_{t+j+1}] - \frac{(1 - \beta)\phi}{\psi_0[1 - \psi_1(\beta)^{1/2}]} \quad (7b)$$

Equations (5), (6), and (7a) [or (7b)] constitute our econometric model of exhaustible resource supply. Equation (7) specifies optimal cumulative extraction as a function of the parameters of the objective function (β, ϕ, θ, π), current and expected price, and current and expected technology shocks. For convenience of reference, let

$$v_t = \sum_{j=0}^{\infty} [\psi_1(\beta)^{1/2}]^j E_t(q_{t+j} - \beta q_{t+j+1}) \quad (8)$$

$$u_t = \sum_{j=0}^{\infty} [\psi_1(\beta)^{1/2}]^j E_t(c_{t+j} - \beta c_{t+j+1}) \quad (9)$$

By using Eqs. (4) and (5), u_t and v_t can be written in terms of current and past values of x_t, e_t, and the parameters in Eqs. (4) and (5). The expressions are presented in Epple and Hanson (1979). Illustrations using relatively simple forecasting schemes will be presented in Section III.

III. ILLUSTRATIVE EXAMPLES

In this section we consider special cases of the model to illustrate the points raised in Section I and to exhibit various properties of the model.

In discussing the cost function in Eq. (1), we noted that when $\pi = 0$ the resource is not an exhaustible resource. It is instructive to consider the decision rule that results in this special case. When $\pi = 0$, the parameter relationships following Eq. (7) imply $\psi_1 = (\beta)^{1/2}$ and $\psi_0 = 2\theta$. These values substituted into Eqs. (8) and (9) imply $v_t = q_t$ and $u_t = c_t$. The equation determining optimal current production (7b) reduces to

$$\Delta y_t = \frac{q_t - \phi}{2\theta} - \frac{c_t}{2\theta} \tag{10}$$

Equation (10) follows directly from Eq. (7b) regardless of the forecasting equations determining q_{t+j} and c_{t+j} for $j > 0$. This is precisely as one would expect. When $\pi = 0$, the maximization of Eq. (4) reduces to solution of a sequence of static maximization problems. Choices made in the current period have no impact on future costs and revenues, and future prices and technology shocks are irrelevant to the current decision. The producer observes q_t and c_t and obtains Eq. (10) as the optimal solution to the static maximization problem. The disturbance term in the regression equation (10) arises because the technology shock c_t, observed by the producer, is not observed by the econometrician.

Returning to the general model, we next consider the implications of alternative specifications of the equations determining q_{t+j} and c_{t+j}. The cases we consider concerning price are expected price equal to last period's price (A), expected price equal to a constant (B), and expected price converging to an asymptote (C). These three cases can be represented in the form given in Eq. (5) as

$$q_t = q_{t-1} + s_t^q, \ \zeta_1 = 1, \zeta_2 = \ldots = \zeta_r = 0 \tag{5A}$$

$$\begin{bmatrix} q_t \\ 1 \end{bmatrix} = \begin{bmatrix} 0 & \bar{q} \\ 0 & 1 \end{bmatrix} \begin{bmatrix} q_{t-1} \\ 1 \end{bmatrix} + \begin{bmatrix} s_t^q \\ 0 \end{bmatrix}, \ \zeta_1 = \begin{bmatrix} 0 & \bar{q} \\ 0 & 1 \end{bmatrix}, \ \zeta_2 = \ldots = \zeta_r = 0 \tag{5B}$$

$$\begin{bmatrix} q_t \\ 1 \end{bmatrix} = \begin{bmatrix} \gamma & \zeta \\ 0 & 1 \end{bmatrix} \begin{bmatrix} q_{t-1} \\ 1 \end{bmatrix} + \begin{bmatrix} s_t^q \\ 0 \end{bmatrix}, \ \zeta_1 = \begin{bmatrix} \gamma & \zeta \\ 0 & 1 \end{bmatrix}, \zeta_2 = \ldots = \zeta_r = 0 \tag{5C}$$

The corresponding expressions for v_t, defined in Eq. (8), are

$$v_t = \frac{q_t}{1 - \psi_1(\beta)^{1/2}} \tag{8A}$$

$$v_t = q_t - \bar{q} + \frac{\bar{q}(1 - \beta)}{1 - \psi_1(\beta)^{1/2}} \tag{8B}$$

$$v_t = \left(q_t - \frac{\zeta}{1 - \gamma}\right) \frac{(1 - \beta\gamma)}{[1 - \gamma\psi_1(\beta)^{1/2}]} + \frac{\zeta(1 - \beta)}{(1 - \gamma)[1 - \psi_1(\beta)^{1/2}]} \tag{8C}$$

As examples of alternative processes generating the technology shocks, we consider serially uncorrelated shocks (D) and first order serially correlated shocks (E). These are represented in the form given in Eq. (6) as

$$c_t = s_t^c, \qquad \gamma_1 = \cdots = \gamma_r = 0 \tag{6D}$$

$$c_t = \rho c_{t-1} + s_t^c, \qquad \gamma_1 = \rho, \gamma_2 = \cdots = \gamma_r = 0 \tag{6E}$$

These expressions combined with Eq. (9) defining u_t imply:

$$u_t = c_t = s_t^c \tag{9D}$$

$$u_t = \frac{c_t(1 - \beta\rho)}{1 - \rho\psi(\beta)^{1/2}} = \rho u_{t-1} + \frac{(1 - \beta\rho)s_t^c}{[1 - \rho\psi_1(\beta)^{1/2}]} \tag{9E}$$

The cases enumerated above all give rise to an equation of the following form when the expressions for u_t and y_t are substituted into Eq. (7):

$$y_t = \alpha_0 + \alpha_1 y_{t-1} + \alpha_2 q_t + \frac{u_t}{\psi_0} \tag{11}$$

The relationship of α_0 and α_2 to the parameters of the underlying structural model are quite different in the three price regimes under consideration, however. In addition, the appropriate estimation technique differs between the two regimes generating the technology shocks.

Consider first the choice of estimation technique. If the technology shocks are uncorrelated (D), consistent estimates of the parameters in Eq. (11) may be obtained by ordinary least squares. If the technology shocks are correlated (E), the presence of the lagged dependent variable in Eq. (11) will give rise to inconsistent estimates if Eq. (11) is estimated by ordinary least squares. These cases thus illustrate the general point that choice of estimation procedure will depend on the way that the technology shocks affect production costs.

Next, consider the alternative price regimes. Using Eqs. (8A)–(8C) and Eq. (11), it is easily established that the following relationships prevail for the three cases under consideration.

$$\phi = \frac{\alpha_0}{(1 - \beta)\alpha_2}, \quad \psi_0 = \frac{1}{\alpha_2[1 - \psi(\beta)^{1/2}]} \qquad (12A)$$

$$\phi = \bar{q} - \left(\frac{\alpha_0}{\alpha_2} + \bar{q}\right)\frac{[1 - \psi_1(\beta)^{1/2}]}{(1 - \beta)}, \quad \psi_0 = \frac{1}{\alpha_2} \qquad (12B)$$

$$\phi = \delta - \left(\delta + \frac{\alpha_0}{\alpha_2}\right)\frac{(1 - \beta\gamma)[1 - \psi_1(\beta)^{1/2}]}{(1 - \beta)[1 - \gamma\psi_1(\beta)^{1/2}]},$$

$$\qquad (12C)$$

$$\psi_0 = \frac{1 - \beta\gamma}{\alpha_2[1 - \gamma\psi_1(\beta)^{1/2}]}$$

In all cases $\psi_1 = \alpha_1(\beta)^{1/2}$.

The following numerical example illustrates the importance of correctly specifying the price regime. Suppose that the parameter values obtained by estimating Eq. (11) are $\alpha_0 = -10$, $\alpha_1 = .889$, and $\alpha_2 = 2.0$. Suppose further that the discount factor is $\beta = .9$, the mean price under regime B is $\bar{q} = 6$, and the parameters under regime C are $\gamma = .9$ and $\delta = 2$. Use of Eq. (12) and the parameter relationships following Eq. (7) gives the following estimates of the parameters of the cost function:

$$\phi = 20, \theta = .833, \pi = .536 \qquad (13A)$$

$$\phi = 4, \theta = .167, \pi = .111 \qquad (13B)$$

$$\phi = 6.076, \theta = .113, \pi = .0753 \qquad (13C)$$

If the price regime does not change during the period of estimation, and is not expected to—and does not—change subsequently, then an equation of the form of Eq. (11) will determine extraction. The above examples illustrate that a given set of values for α_0, α_1, and α_2 will generate very different values for the parameters of the cost function depending on which price regime prevails. From the standpoint of predicting extraction rates, this will be of no consequence if the price regime that prevailed during the period of estimation continues to prevail subsequently.

However, should the price regime subsequently change, the predictions from Eq. (11) could prove to be very inaccurate. For example, suppose that price regime B prevailed during the period of estimation. Then the correct cost function parameters are given in (13B). Suppose that after the period of estimation an unanticipated change in the price regime occurs; regime C replaces regime B.[5] The parameters in (13B) are not affected by this change because they characterize the underlying technology. The parameters in Eq. (11) do change, however, because they depend on the cost function parameters *and* the parameters of the equation determining prices. The parameters of price regime C combined with the cost function parameters (13B) yield new values for the parameters in Eq. (11) of $\alpha_0 = -1.22$, $\alpha_1 = .889$, and $\alpha_2 = .1158$. Thus Eq. (11) changes from

$$y_t = -10 + .889y_{t-1} + 2.0q_t + 2u_t$$

to

$$y_t = -1.22 + .889y_{t-1} + .1158q_t + 2u_t$$

when the price regime changes from B to C.

These examples illustrate why the regime determining prices (5), the process generating the technology shocks (6), and the decision equation of producers (7) are all important components of the model determining resource extraction.

IV. CUMULATIVE COST CURVES AND ULTIMATE RECOVERY

The concept of "reserves" plays an important role in many discussions of exhaustible resources. It may be possible, in principle, to determine the quantity of a resource that remains unexploited. However, it is widely recognized that such data would have limited usefulness in the absence of information about the conditions under which the resource will be produced.

This has led to efforts to determine "economically recoverable reserves." A great deal of ambiguity accompanies the use of this term. For example, the widely cited estimates of proved reserves of the American Petroleum Institute are defined as the amount of oil "which geological and engineering data demonstrate with reasonable certainty to be recoverable in future years from known reservoirs under existing economic and operating condition."[6] The meaning of "existing economic conditions" is far from obvious. Existing conditions generate expectations of future prices. Are they reflected in estimates of proved reserves? Users of the data must judge for themselves.[7]

One approach to making the concept of reserves more precise is to construct a cumulative cost curve. The curve specifies cumulative production as a function of unit production cost.[8] We argue in Section II that the total unit cost of extraction will depend on both the current extraction rate and the cumulative quantity extracted. Our Eq. (2) is one such unit cost function. Unit cost as a function of cumulative production is not defined unless the extraction rate is also specified. As we will show later, our approach allows us to provide a precise characterization of the relationship of price and cumulative output.

Our framework also permits an unambiguous definition of economically recoverable reserves. The cost function and the equation determining prices permit a precise statement of economic conditions. Once those economic conditions are specified, our framework determines both the rate of extraction and the amount that will ultimately be extracted. The extraction rate is given by Eq. (7b). The amount ultimately extracted is obtained by solving the difference equation [Eq. (7a)]. Ultimate recovery given conditions at date t is

$$
y_{\infty,t} = \lim_{k \to \infty} \frac{1}{\psi_0} \sum_{i=0}^{k} \left[\frac{\psi_1}{(\beta)^{1/2}} \right]^i \sum_{j=0}^{\infty} \{ [\psi_1(\beta)^{1/2})^j
$$
$$
\times E_t[q_{t+k+j-i} - \beta q_{t+k+j+1-i} - c_{t+k+j-i} + \beta c_{t+k+j+1-i}] \} \quad (14)
$$
$$
- \frac{(1 - \beta)\phi}{\left[1 - \frac{\psi_1}{(\beta)^{1/2}} \right] \psi_0 [1 - \psi_1(\beta)^{1/2}]}
$$

We will illustrate Eq. (14) using the examples from Section III. The appropriate expressions for the various cases are easily shown to be

$$
E_t(y_\infty) = \frac{(1 - \beta)(q_t - \phi)}{\left[1 - \frac{\psi_1}{(\beta)^{1/2}} \right] \psi_0 [1 - \psi_1(\beta)^{1/2}]} \quad (15A)
$$

$$
E_t(y_\infty) = \frac{(1 - \beta)(\bar{q} - \phi)}{\left[1 - \frac{\psi_1}{(\beta)^{1/2}} \right] \psi_0 [1 - \psi_1(\beta)^{1/2}]} \quad (15B)
$$

$$
E_t(y_\infty) = \frac{(1 - \beta)\left[\left(\frac{\delta}{1 - \gamma} \right) - \phi \right]}{\left[1 - \frac{\psi_1}{(\beta)^{1/2}} \right] \psi_0 [1 - \psi_1(\beta)^{1/2}]} \quad (15C)
$$

These expressions can be given a straightforward interpretation. First, note that the parameter relationships following Eq. (7) imply

$$
\left[1 - \frac{\psi_i}{(\beta)^{1/2}} \right] \psi_0 [1 - \psi_1(\beta)^{1/2}] = (1 - \beta)\pi
$$

Second, note that the price terms appearing on the right-hand side of Eq. (15) are the limits to which price is expected to converge as t approaches infinity. Let $E_t(q_\infty) = \lim_{j \to \infty} E_t(q_{t+j})$. Then $E_t(q_\infty)$ equals q_t,

$\bar{q}$, and $\delta/(1 - \gamma)$ for the three regimes under consideration. A general expression for expected ultimate recovery is then

$$E_t(y_\infty) = \frac{E_t(q_\infty) - \phi}{\pi} \qquad (16)$$

This is the result that would be obtained by equating expected marginal extraction cost in Eq. (3) to the expected ultimate price with current extraction equal to zero. That is, $E_t(y_\infty)$ is the value of ultimate recovery such that further extraction would cause marginal cost to rise above the expected limiting price, $E_t(q_\infty)$. Equation (16) may be interpreted as a cumulative cost curve for the resource.

This and the preceding section have illustrated how "existing economic conditions" determine the path of resource extraction and ultimate recovery in our framework.

V. APPLICATIONS

It is our belief that the framework discussed in this article will be applicable to modeling supply of a variety of exhaustible resources. In this section we will show that this framework provides an economic interpretation of patterns of reserve development first noted by geologist M. K. Hubbert (1974) for crude oil and natural gas in the United States. We then briefly discuss work we are currently pursuing in modeling oil and natural gas discoveries and development of oil and gas reserves in the United States.

In his investigation of the development of oil and natural gas reserves in the United States, Hubbert fit the following relationship to the data:

$$Y_\tau = Y_\infty \{1 - \exp[-\gamma_0(\tau + \gamma_1)]\} \qquad (17)$$

where y_τ is the estimate of production plus proved reserves in a field τ years after discovery. Y_∞, γ_0, and γ_1 are parameters. Hubbert estimated $\gamma_0 = 0.076$ and $\gamma_1 = 1.503$ for oil and $\gamma_0 = 0.063$ and $\gamma_1 = 4.343$ for natural gas. Parameter Y_∞ is field specific. This relationship can be written equivalently as the difference equation:

$$Y_\tau = \eta_0 Y_{\tau-1} + \eta_1 \qquad (18)$$

where $\eta_0 = e^{-\gamma_0}$, $\eta_1 = Y_\infty(1 - e^{-\gamma_0})$, and the initial condition requires that $Y_0 = Y_\infty(1 - e^{-\gamma_0\gamma_1})$.

Consider our model of Section II with price regime (B) of Section III. In Section III we assumed that producers observed the price at time t before making their production decisions. Suppose instead that producers must make production decisions before observing the price at time t. Then the decision rule for production at date t is

$$y_t = \frac{\psi_1}{(\beta)^{1/2}} y_{t-1} + \frac{(1 - \beta)(\bar{q} - \phi)}{\psi_0[1 - \psi_1(\beta)^{1/2}]} + \frac{c_t}{\psi_0} \tag{19}$$

This relationship is of exactly the same form as Eq. (18). Thus the empirical regularities observed by Hubbert can be interpreted as resulting from optimal reserve development subject to the cost function we have chosen if the producer expects the future real price to remain constant.

Hubbert's results are not sufficient to identify all of the parameters of our cost function. However, Hubbert's estimates imply values for $\frac{\psi_1}{(\beta)^{1/2}}$ of .927 and .939 for oil and gas, respectively. These values satisfy the restrictions implied by our theoretical formulation.

It is natural to ask whether the price expectations assumption implicit in the above interpretation of Hubbert's observations is appropriate. Our formulation provides a procedure for simultaneous estimation of optimal reserve development equations and price expectations equations. This work is currently underway and preliminary results are reported in Epple and Hansen (1979).

This formulation of reserve development can also be used to determine a parameter that may be interpreted as the size of field discovered in a particular year. Consider the following specification of the cost of development of reserves in fields discovered in year i.

$$K_{t,i} = \phi \Delta y_{t,i} + \frac{\theta}{S_i} \Delta y_{t,i}^2 + \frac{\pi}{S_i} \Delta y_{t,i} y_{t,i} + c_t \Delta y_{t,i} \tag{20}$$

This function differs from Eq. (1) in that we have introduced an additional parameter S_i that may be interpreted as the size of fields discovered in year i. This function has the property that doubling of S_i, Δy_{t+i}, and y_{t+i} will double costs. That is, a given proportional increase in the amount discovered would permit the same proportional increase in amount produced per year with the same proportional increase in costs.

The decision rule that results from this specification is

$$y_{t,i} = \frac{\psi_1}{(\beta)^{1/2}} y_{t-1,i} + \frac{S_i}{\psi_0} (v_t + u_t) - \frac{S_i(1 - \beta)\phi}{\psi_0[1 - \psi_1(\beta)^{1/2}]} \tag{21}$$

where v_t and u_t are as defined in Eqs. (8) and (9), and q_t is now interpreted as the "price" of a unit of reserves. Note that Eq. (21) differs from Eq. (7) in that S_i now appears as a parameter. By pooling data for different discovery years, i, and different points in time, it is possible to estimate the S_i up to a constant of proportionality. This gives estimates of the relative amounts discovered across years.

The resulting S_i estimates may be used to model the oil exploration process. That is, the S_i can be viewed as the output of the exploration process. Discoveries can then be modeled as the result of an optimal resource exhaustion problem that is also of the form discussed in Section II. Preliminary results from this analysis can be found in Epple and Hansen (1979).

These examples illustrate how the model can be applied to oil and natural gas exploration and reserve development. The approach should also be applicable to modeling other exhaustible resources.

NOTES

1. See, for example, the comparisons of models in Neri (1977) and Pindyck (1974), and the review by Epple (1978).
2. See, for example, the review by Peterson and Fisher (1977).
3. The significance of this fact for econometric policy evaluation is developed by Lucas (1976).
4. This formulation is an application of the approach proposed by Hansen and Sargent (1979a,b).
5. The shift from regime B to regime C may be a simplified version of the change in world oil price regimes that occurred in 1973.
6. Another example is the U.S. Geological Survey (1975) definition of "Economic Resources" as "Those resources, both identified and undiscovered, which are estimated to be economically recoverable" (p. 8).
7. Attempts to come to grips with this problem often add to the ambiguity. The Geological Survey (1975) states "In this study, price–cost relationships and technological trends generally prevailing in the recent years prior to 1974 are assumed" (p. 8). And, later, "If fundamental changes in cost–price relationships are imposed or if radical improvements in technology occur, estimates of recoverable resources will be affected accordingly" (p. 9).
8. Zimmerman (1977) presents a careful development of a cumulative cost curve for coal in the United States.

REFERENCES

American Petroleum Institute, Reserves of Crude Oil, Natural Gas Liquids and Natural Gas in the United States and Canada, Washington, D.C., annual.

Epple, D. (1978). Studies of U.S. Primary Energy Supply: A Review, *Energy Systems and Policy* **2**: 245–265.

Epple, D. and Hansen, L. P. (1979). An Econometric Model of U.S. Petroleum Supply with Optimal Endogenous Depletion, Carnegie-Mellon University, Working Paper.

Hansen, L. P., and Sargent, T. J. (1979a). Formulating and Estimating Dynamic Linear Rational Expectations Models: I, Working Paper.

――――――(1979b). Formulating and Estimating Dynamic Linear Rational Expectations Models: II, Working Paper.

Hubbert, M. K. (1974). U.S. Energy Resources, A Review as of 1972, Part I, in *A National Fuels and Energy Policy Study*, U.S. 93rd Congress, 2nd session, Senate Committee on Interior and Insular Affairs, Committee Print, Serial No. 93–40 (92–75).

Lucas, R. E. (1976). "Econometric Policy Evaluation: A Critique," *in* K. Brunner and A. Meltzer (ed.), *The Phillips Curve and Labor Markets*, North Holland, Amsterdam, pp. 19–46.

Neri, J. A. (1977). An Evaluation of Two Alternative Supply Models of Natural Gas, *Bell Journal of Economics and Management Science* **8**, 289–302.

Peterson, F. M. and Fisher, R. C. (1977). The Exploitation of Extractive Resources: A Survey, *Economic Journal* Vol. 87: 681–721.

Pindyck, R. S. (1974). The Regulatory Implications of Three Alternative Econometric Supply Models of Natural Gas, *Bell Journal of Economics and Management Science* **5**: 633–645.

U.S. Geological Survey (1975). *Geological Estimates of Undiscovered Recoverable Oil and Gas Resources in the United States*, Circular 725.

Zimmerman, M. (1977). Modeling Depletion in a Mineral Industry: The Case of Coal, *Bell Journal of Economics* **8**: 41–65.

U.S. OIL AND GAS SUPPLY

Ben C. Ball, Jr., John C. Houghton,
James L. Sweeney, and John P. Weyant

BACKGROUND

Many government and industry decisions hinge on assessments of the extent of U.S. oil and gas resources and the rate at which they can be produced. The present study makes alternative assumptions about key uncertainties—world oil price, the extent of the resource base, and the oil and gas industry's tax environment—and focuses on the problem of projecting the rate at which the domestic resources will be discovered, developed, and produced. Public and private R&D and investment decisions, as well as government decisions on price regulations, depend on this type of information. The task of making oil and gas resource base and production estimates is controversial and clouded by uncertainty, but perhaps formal modeling can help frame the debate.

Many approaches to oil and gas production forecasting have been taken. Some have been judgmental, whereas others have relied heavily on the structure a formal modeling approach can provide. Traditional approaches to oil and gas resource and supply modeling have disaggregated the problem by region, geologic structure, technology, and/or behavioral response. Methodologies have included those based primarily on extrapolation of historical trends using statistical methods, and those based primarily on the normative assumption of optimizing behavior on the part of oil and gas producers. But, even the latter methods depend heavily on extrapolations of historical data for crucial relationships such as that between the amount of exploratory effort and the amount of oil and/or gas discovered. Thus, virtually all the approaches rely on some characterization of historical oil and gas supply response.

OVERVIEW OF OIL AND GAS SUPPLY ISSUES

Among the most prominent oil and gas policy issues are the extent to which the prices of the domestic supply of these two crucial resources should be controlled below the equivalent world oil price. The post-1973 run-up in the world oil price provided the motivation for the creation of price controls on crude oil to avoid the adverse economic impacts that could result from a sudden jump in the price of all oil. On the other hand, natural gas prices have been controlled since the Natural Gas Act of 1936, but the Natural Gas Policy Act of 1978 put into effect a complicated scheme that will deregulate the price of all natural gas by 1986.

Besides the oil and gas pricing issues, other important U.S. oil and gas supply issues are (1) the rate at which federal lands are leased for the purpose of exploring, developing, and ultimately producing oil and natural gas; (2) the nature of the tax laws applicable to oil and gas producers, including the level of the depletion allowance, the investment tax credit, and the expensing of intangibles; (3) the impact of import quotas on domestic oil and gas production; and (4) the impact of a windfall profits tax on oil production.

Many factors that are uncertain today could have a large effect on the impacts of the various policy options. The most important of these seem to be the extent of the domestic oil and gas resource base and the world price of oil.

The study provides information about many of the impacts of the several policies under alternative assumptions about the resolution of the key uncertainties. It does not, however, provide all the information that is likely to be of interest to the policy maker. For example, the response of oil supply to higher prices with and without domestic price controls is projected under several alternative world oil price and domestic resource base assumptions. This is probably the most important information required to assess the efficacy of the controls, but information on the demand response to the higher prices, resulting U.S.

import posture, and distributional effects would also be of great interest during an administration/Congressional debate on oil pricing policy. These latter subjects are *not* addressed in the present study.

ENERGY MODELING FORUM MODEL STUDIES

The concern for oil and gas policy issues and the central importance of oil and gas in our energy future are evident from the attention that has been devoted to modeling the oil and gas supply process. Many sophisticated models have been developed incorporating extensive detail of the oil and gas discovery, development, and production process. The complexity of this process provides fertile ground for the application of these models. Each of these models emphasizes different aspects of the array of oil and gas policy problems.

Not all oil and gas models have been used to their full potential. The realization of this full potential requires a thorough understanding by users of their capabilities and limitations. Better communication between decision makers and modelers is needed to accomplish this end. One objective of the Energy Modeling Forum (EMF) is to stimulate such communication and thereby improve the use and usefulness of energy models. The EMF operates through a series of *ad hoc* working groups. Focusing on important issues, such as U.S. oil and gas supply, the working group applies a set of models and contrasts the results. The investigation of similarities and the explanation of differences in the key results help clarify the specific energy issue while isolating the most important characteristics of the models. This improves the user's understanding of the models and illustrates the requirements for the application of these models to other questions. At the same time, new areas for modeling research are indicated.

The first EMF study effort concentrated on the investigation of the use of models of "Energy and the Economy." "Coal in Transition: 1980–2000" was the second attempt of an EMF working group to study and compare an important class of models in the context of a pressing set of energy policy questions. The third EMF study focused on "Electric Load Forecasting: Probing the Issues with Models," and the fourth on "Aggregate Energy Demand Elasticities." The present study, "U.S. Oil and Gas Supply," is the fifth study that the Energy Modeling Forum has initiated.

The goals of the working group are threefold: (1) to compare and contrast the results obtained from the several participating models in order to understand the general behavior, strengths, and limitations of the models both as a class and as individual models; (2) to provide information that might be useful in national and international energy decision and policy making; and (3) to provide a guide to the models for potential users. The insights obtained from the models and their use may be in the context of a particular policy option or may focus on the implications of alternative model structures.

INTRODUCTION TO THE PARTICIPATING MODELS

Ten models were employed in the study. The American Gas Associations's (AGA) Total Energy Resource Analysis (TERA) model was developed in conjunction with Decision Science Corporation and Mathematica, Inc. over the period 1971–1973 and has been expanded, refined, and documented over the past few years. It has three main components: the Offshore Gas and Oil Supply Model, the Demand Marketplace Model, and the Onshore Gas and Oil Supply Model. Only the onshore and offshore supply models are used in the present study.

Developed by ICF, Inc. for the Federal Energy Administration in 1974 and patterned after the National Petroleum Council's (NPC) 1972 *U.S. Energy Outlook* analysis, the EIA/ICF model has been substantially enhanced and is updated annually for the Energy Information Administration (EIA). The model presently consists of three separate components: a lower-48 onshore and offshore oil and gas supply forecasting model (MOGSMS); an Alaskan hydrocarbon forecasting model (AHM), and an enhanced oil recovery model (EORM) developed for EIA by Lewin Associates.

In 1976 and 1977, Young Kim and Russell Thompson of the University of Houston constructed the Kim–Thompson model of new onshore lower-48 crude oil and natural gas discoveries. Their work was sponsored by the Texas Energy Advisory Council (TEAC).

The Long-Range Energy Development and Supplies (LORENDAS) model was developed over the period 1974–1977 by Leo A. Rapoport and others at Virginia Polytechnic Institute and State University. Originally conceived under a National Science Foundation grant to help assess national and international energy policy issues, the LORENDAS model has been refined and updated since that time. It currently models worldwide energy production, transportation, and consumption of oil, gas, coal, and uranium.

The LEAP model was developed during 1977–1979 by Decision Focus, Incorporated. It builds on the methodology of the Gulf–SRI model, which was designed by SRI during the early 1970s to help Gulf Oil Corporation make its corporate decision on a synthetic fuels investment strategy. LEAP is designed for comprehensive U.S. energy system forecasting and planning.

The Aggregate Supply Model of the MIT World Oil Project is a much simplified model based on "collapsed" versions of development expenditures and the associated production profiles. This simple structure was designed to be applicable to all countries in the world, particularly those for which data problems exist, yet still capture the essence of the petroleum development and production process. Only the U.S. model is used in the present study.

Developed in 1975 by Patricia L. Rice of Oak Ridge National Laboratory, the Rice model is an econometric representation of the domestic supply of crude and refinery petroleum products. It has recently been used to evaluate the impact of the petroleum-related provisions in the National Energy Plan (NEP).

The Erickson–Milsaps–Spann model was designed by Edward W. Erickson of North Carolina State University, Robert Spann of Virginia Polytechnic Institute, and Stephen W. Milsaps of Appalachian State University. This model builds on a previous model developed by Erickson and Spann. The development of the final version of the model was funded by the Brookings Institution; it is designed to project long-run crude oil reserves held by the oil producing industry.

The Epple–Hansen model has been under development and revision by Dennis Epple of Carnegie-Mellon University since 1975. It is a model of oil and gas production in the lower-48 states, with an explicit representation of the discovery process.

The FOSSIL2 model—the only systems dynamics model included in the study—was recently implemented by the Office of Policy and Evaluation of the Department of Energy by Roger F. Naill and associates and builds on the FOSSIL1 model developed by Naill and others at Dartmouth College in 1976–1977. FOSSIL2 was designed for comprehensive U.S. energy system forecasting and policy analysis.

CHARACTERISTICS OF THE PARTICIPATING MODELS

Most of the models explicitly model explorations, discoveries, extensions and revisions, and reserves and production, explicitly examining the role of depletion on new discoveries and on existing reserve levels. Most models examine both oil and gas supply within this framework.

The ten models in this study span a wide range of approaches to modeling oil and gas supply. Whereas the methodologies employed are widely divergent, each model is trying to explain the same process of petroleum supply. In order to understand and evaluate the models, one must first understand the actual process of finding pools of oil and gas, installing production facilities, and then using these facilities to supply crude oil to refineries and natural gas to pipelines.

The major uncertainty about future oil and gas production concerns the amount of oil and gas that has yet to be discovered. As with any depletable resource, it is expected that the larger, shallower, and less costly resources will be found and developed first. While some information about future oil and gas discoveries has been obtained through past exploration, the success of future ventures is still very uncertain. This makes gas and oil supply uncertain, because future drilling activity will be the primary determinant of the level of oil and gas production 20 years from now. A description of the oil and gas supply process begins, then, with a characterization of the amount of recoverable resources that has yet to be found, i.e., the stock of undiscovered resources.

Given the amount of oil and gas still to be found, an exploration decision is made to locate the remaining undiscovered pools of oil and gas. Elements of this decision include where to drill and how deep to go. These decisions are affected by considerations of drilling costs, the expected price of oil, and the size of the pool being drilled, among others. Exploration, the result of a conscious decision, moves pools of oil and gas from the stock of undiscovered resources to a state where they are known to exist but are as yet undeveloped.

The link between exploration and discovered resources is a difficult one to make. If the exploration process can be described as a random event, a new discovery will reduce the probability of success in future exploratory efforts simply because there is a reduced amount of oil yet to be found. As a result, one would expect the success rate for exploratory drilling to decline over time.

On the other hand, exploration involves a substantial amount of learning. All other things equal, exploratory efforts are believed to become more efficient over time as more expertise is gained, thus offsetting the normal decline of new discoveries by an uncertain amount. In any event, as exploration proceeds, new resources are discovered and are added to the stock of discovered resources and subtracted from the amount of oil and gas yet to be found.

Once a stock of resources has been discovered, a second decision is made about how much production capacity should be installed, or equivalently, how intensively a given field should be developed. For oil fields, this decision usually involves drilling additional wells, treating the well bore to increase flow rates, or opening additional zones of oil-bearing rock within the same well. Gas field development usually has the same options as for oil fields, but also includes rock fracturing techniques. In addition, the size of the pipeline and processing plant connected to the well must be considered. Sometimes the gas distribution network must be enlarged to allow for increased flow rates from the field. The extent of development determines the maximum rate at which gas and oil can be produced.

After development is completed, there is still some latitude for deciding on the utilization of existing production capacity. Prior to the 1973 embargo, oil and gas were usually produced near capacity unless it could not be sold or because a regulatory body restricted production. Since the embargo, the divergence between regulated and market prices for oil and gas has raised the possibility of voluntary production cutbacks.

The entire supply process, beginning with undiscovered resources and ending with cumulative production, is addressed in each of the ten models. There are, however, important similarities and differences in the way the several models represent the various stages of the supply process.

A TAXONOMY OF OIL AND GAS SUPPLY MODELS

Table 1 contains a catalog of the ten oil and gas supply models that participated in this study. Although the meaning of most of the columns is clear, some further explanation may be necessary. The third column gives the dates over which the model was developed. A date of 1978 indicates that current work may be in progress. The fourth column identifies the models that formed a basis for the development of the model in question. Column 8 classifies model methodology into two types: econometric or engineering-process.

An econometric model of production is a model that relies extensively on statistical analysis of historical data pertaining to the oil and gas industry. Models of this type are usually formulated in two stages. First, an economic theory is developed as to what variables are thought to have primary impact on the various aspects of oil and gas supply. Second, historical data is collected and statistical methods are employed to estimate the linkages between the dependent and independent variables in the model.

Engineering process models differ in a fundamental way from the econometric models in terms of their methodology. Whereas econometric models concentrate on the important economic relationships in a process, engineering process models concentrate on the process itself. Engineering process models spend relatively more effort modeling the

Table 1. A Catalog of Oil and Gas Supply Models

Name	Builders	Users (Funders)	Dates	Ancestors	Resources	Geography	Methodology	Mode of operation	Integrated
Epple–Hansen	Epple, D. (Carnegie-Mellon)	—	1975–1979	—	Oil & gas	Lower 48 on & offshore	Econometric	Simulation	No
E-M-S	Erickson, E. (NCSU) Spann, R. (UPI) Millsaps, S. (ASU)	Brookings Institution	1974	—	Oil	Lower 48 on & offshore	Econometric	Simulation	No
FOSSIL2	Naill, R. (Dartmouth-DOE)	DOE	1976–1979	—	Oil, gas, & others	All U.S.	Engineering process	Simulation	Yes
GEMS	Marshalla, R. (DFI) Nesbitt, D. (DFI)	EIA/DFI	1977–1978	SRI/Gulf	Oil, gas, & others	All U.S.	Engineering process	Intertemporal optimization	Yes
K–T	Kim, Y. (U of Houston) Thompson, R. (U of Houston)	TEAC	1977–1978	NPC	Oil & gas	Lower 48 onshore	Engineering process	Optimization	No
Lorendas	Rapoport, L. (VPI)	VPI/NSF	1975–1979	—	Oil, gas, & others	All U.S.	Engineering process	Intertemporal optimization	Yes
MIT–WOP	Adelman, M. A. (MIT) Paddock, J. (MIT) Jacoby, H. D. (MIT)	MIT/NSF	1976–1979	—	Oil	World	Engineering process	Simulation	No
EIA/ICF MOGSMS AHM EOR	Stitt, W. (ICF) Everett, C. (EIA)			NPC/FEA	Oil & gas Oil & gas Oil only	Lower 48 on & offshore Alaska Lower 48 on & offshore	Engineering process	Simulation Intertemporal optimization Simulation	Yes
Rice	Rice, P. (ORNL)		1975–1979	—	Oil & gas	Lower 48 on & offshore	Econometric	Simulation	Yes
TERA Onshore	Tucker, L. (AGA)	AGA	1971–1979	—		Lower 48 onshore	Econometric	Simulation	No
TERA Offshore				—	Oil & gas	Lower 48 offshore	Engineering process	Optimization	No

126

process of exploring, developing, and producing oil and gas. This does not mean that engineering process models do not use any econometric techniques; they often do. It is just that econometric models concentrate on the important economics relationships that govern a process, while engineering process models concentrate on simulating the process itself.

The ninth column in Table 1 indicates the calculational procedure used to generate the forecasts with the model. Three of these procedures or "modes of operation" are distinguished:

1. Simulation: In this case, the model solves the set of equations that form the model, for the endogenous variables, given a set of values for the exogenous variables. When this system of equations is recursive (i.e., the equations can be ordered in such a way that every equation only depends on exogenous variables and endogenous variables determined in previous equations), then the solution is trivial. If the model is not recursive, then iterative procedures are used to find the solution (e.g., for DFI–LEAP and FOSSIL2).
2. One-period optimization: For each time period of the model, at least one variable is determined in order to optimize an objective function.
3. Intertemporal optimization: The model solves simultaneously for an optimal set of values for all endogenous variables for all time periods in order to optimize one objective function. Therefore, the model determines the values of the endogenous variables for all periods all at once, so that exogenous variables (e.g., prices) of future periods directly affect endogenous variables in the current period.

ASSUMPTIONS AND SCENARIOS

The study is built around an examination of a set of alternative scenarios, each designed to explore some important facet of the U.S. oil and gas supply system and models. The processing of the scenarios by the models provides a set of conditional projections for analysis and interpretation.

The scenarios do not represent forecasts. No attempt was made to develop a consensus in the working group about the likely outcomes in the future. Instead, the scenarios are designed to provide a common basis for comparing the results from the alternative scenarios, with an emphasis on the response of U.S. oil and gas supply to higher prices. The details of these scenarios are explained elsewhere, but the broad thrust of each case is outlined here to establish the context for the comparison of the results.

There are 15 scenarios in all. The Reference Scenario provides a basis for comparison. It assumes undiscovered oil and gas in place at mean values from USGS Circular 725, and a 2.5 percent real rate of increase in the price of world oil (from $14.50/BBL on 7/1/78) through the end of the century. Wellhead pricing for natural gas is assumed to be as per the Natural Gas Policy Act, with decontrol in 1986, whereas wellhead pricing for crude oil is assumed to be as per the Energy Policy and Conservation Act, with price controls phased out between now and October of 1981. In the absence of price controls, the price of natural gas is assumed to equal the BTU equivalent price of crude oil. Thus, in the high price scenario, the price of new natural gas increases about $1.00 per MCF in 1986. Leasing rates, tax structures, and the Alaskan export ban mimic the existing federal policies.

Some of the most important information that the models can provide as inputs to policy analysis are projections of the response of U.S. oil and gas supply to price. The intermodel price responsiveness comparisons are driven by three alternative assumptions (reference, high, and low) about the world price of oil (with corresponding increases in the price of natural gas). Additionally, the price response was investigated under continued crude oil price controls (with a maximum composite price increase of 4.5 percent per year) and high geology (twice the reference level assumption about resources in place) assumptions. This defines 8 of the study's 15 scenarios.

Seven additional scenarios represent additional variations from the Reference scenario. In the No Tax Break scenario, the investment tax credit is decreased from 10 to 0 percent, the percentage depletion allowance is abolished, and expensing of intangibles is not allowed. In the Surprise scenario, prices are initially expected to follow the reference trajectory, but then jump to the high level in 1990. This scenario highlights the differences among the models with different degrees of foresight. In the Retarded Leasing scenario, the offshore average leased in each year drops to half the reference level. This should retard exploration, development, and production from the Outer Continental Shelf (OCS). In the Price Shear scenario, gas prices are calibrated to the high world oil price level, but the world oil price is, in fact, set at its reference level. This scenario isolates how the models differ in representing "directionality" in drilling for gas instead of oil. Another scenario (High Geology/Controls) combines the high geology assumption with continued price controls. This combination of assumptions should lead to a slow rate of domestic depletion (measured in terms of cumulative production as a fraction of ultimate recovery).

The final two scenarios balance the scenarios that include high geology assumptions by including more pessimistic geology assumptions than in the Reference scenario. The Low Geology scenario assumes undiscovered oil and gas in place at half their reference levels. The final scenario—Resource Shear—reflects the recent pessimism about oil relative to gas resource estimates by combining the low geology assumption for oil with the reference assumption for natural gas. Table 2 summarizes the study's 15 scenarios.

BROAD FINDINGS

The quantity of oil and natural gas that will be produced in the next 20 years depends significantly upon a number of factors that currently

Table 2. EMF Scenarios

			Reference leasing, taxes, expectations				Reduced leasing	No tax break	Unanticipated price increase
			Low oil geology	Medium oil geology		High oil geology	Medium oil geology		
			Low gas geology	Medium gas geology		High gas geology	Medium gas geology		
Continued controls	High oil price	High gas price			D				
	Medium oil price	Medium gas price			E	N			
Controls expire	High oil price	High gas price			B	G			K^a
	Medium oil price				M				
	Medium oil price	Medium gas price	P	Q	A	H	L	J	K^a
	Low oil price	Low gas price			C	I			

ᵃ In scenario K, prices unexpectedly change from medium to high.

are uncertain. Geologic uncertainty, price uncertainty, and policy uncertainty add to the uncertainty stemming from model data and structure. The range of projections from the models (Table 3) reflects the degree of our uncertainty about these factors. But, several key messages can be derived from analysis of the model results, given the scenario assumptions.

Domestically produced oil and natural gas will remain a significant source of energy in the U.S. for the rest of this century. Under almost every scenario, most of the models utilized project conventional oil and natural gas production of at least 25 quadrillion BTUs per year through the 1990s.

Despite the uncertainty in expected production levels, no dramatic changes in total U.S. production of conventional oil and gas are expected during this period; the changes tend to be gradual rather than sudden. For example, observe the slow rate of change of the projections of conventional oil and gas production shown for the High Price scenario in Figures 1 and 2, respectively. The dramatic market changes that occurred during 1979 have already resulted in a world oil price exceeding that implied for 1990 in the Reference scenario, making the High Price scenario a better benchmark. To construct Figures 1 and 2, Alaskan production projections from the MOGSMS/AHS system are added to the projections of the several models that project lower-48 production only (Epple–Hansen, Erickson, AGA–TERA, Kim–Thompson, Rice–Smith); these composite projections are represented with dashed lines in the figures. This seems reversible because the pipeline capacity on Alaskan production leads to similar results from the models that project Alaskan production (MOGSMS, DFI–GEMS, LORENDAS, and FOSSILS). Data used to construct Figures 1 and 2 are summarized in Tables 4 and 5.

The 1990 projections of oil production (which was 9 MMB/D in 1978) from the alternative models in the high price case range from 5 to 11 MMB/D, as illustrated in Figure 1, which also shows the corresponding oil price assumptions. However, enhanced oil recovery is excluded from the results presented here and not represented in most of the models. It might be sufficient to reverse any downward trend in production. In fact, the models that project enforced oil recovery production project 1–2 MMB/D from that shown by 1990 (Figure 3 and Table 6). Under conditions of more favorable geology, the estimates increase by about 2 MMB/D. At the lower extreme, in a case with lower prices and less favorable geologic assumptions, the 1990 conventional production estimates range from 3 to 9 MMB/D.

The 1990 projections of conventional natural gas production (which was 19 TCF in 1979) from the alternative models range from 15 to 25

Table 3. Ranges of Conventional Oil and Gas Production Projections for 1990

Model	OIL (MMBD)					NATURAL GAS (TCF)				
	Onshore	Offshore	Lower 48	Alaska	Total	Onshore	Offshore	Lower 48	Alaska	Total
AGA–TERA						6.10–10.00	4.67–6.38	11.24–16.38		
Epple–Hansen			2.98–3.49					12.57–15.75		
E–M–S			4.10–6.29							
FOSSIL2			5.90–7.10	2.00–2.60	8.00–9.70			14.10–15.70	1.70	15.80–17.40
Kim–Thompson[a]	0.88–1.45									
DFI–GEMS			3.71–11.03	1.20–2.40	5.10–12.2	9.59–30.34		18.93–25.06	0.91–1.34	19.91–25.97
LORENDAS	4.40–8.99	0.40–0.75	4.81–9.38	0.60–1.66	5.98–9.99		0.98–2.62	10.57–31.03	0.52–2.08	11.08–33.45
MIT–WOP			5.22–5.98	0.95	6.17–6.93					
MOGSMS–AHM	5.84–9.79	1.21–2.00	7.55–11.80	1.69–2.70	8.74–14.50	10.71–16.15	2.20–3.97	13.88–20.13	1.17–1.46	15.08–21.57
Rice–Smith			7.65–10.70					14.53–33.82		
1977	6.74	1.04	7.78	0.46	8.24	14.70	4.27	18.97	0.19	19.16

[a] New–new oil only.

Figure 1A. U.S. Total Crude Oil Production,[a] High Price Scenario

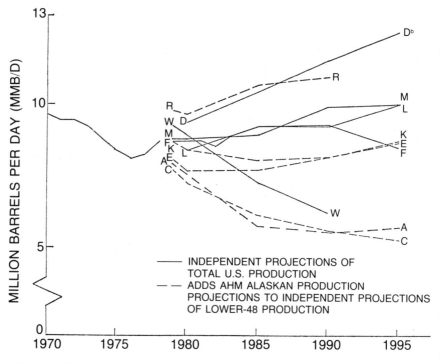

[a] Excludes NGL.
[b] See Table 4 for key to models.

TCF in 1990 under the high price case, which also shows the corresponding gas price assumptions (see Figure 2). However, unconventional gas supplies that are excluded from the results presented here and not represented in most of the models might be sufficient to reverse any downward trend. In fact, the one model that considers unconventional sources of natural gas (FOSSIL 2) projects a material increase in total natural gas supply despite significant decrease in supplies from conventional sources (Figure 4 and Table 6). Even under the most favorable cases, depending on the models and the resource assumptions, production for natural gas is still unlikely to ever reach its historic peaks of 22.6 TCF—except in the LORENDAS model projections. Furthermore, even in the most unfavorable cases, annual production levels of conventional gas are projected to be at least 13–14 TCF during this period.

Policy actions taken today can have a significant impact on future production levels. In particular, key policy levels include the extent and

Figure 1B. Price of World Oil, High Price Scenario

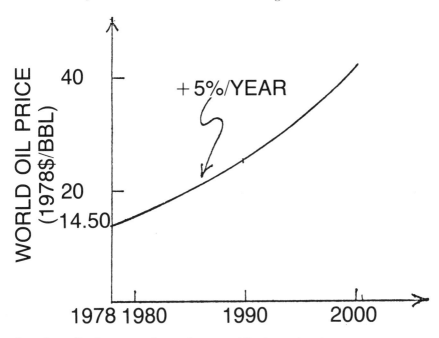

duration of price controls, tax laws, and limits on leasing rates. However, lead times tend to be long: 5 to 10 years must typically pass before a significant share of the impact of a policy action taken today is felt.

A critical element affecting the model projections is the nature and extent of the undiscovered resource base. Cumulative production projected during the next 10-15 years will exhaust current proved reserves. Therefore, the availability of currently undiscovered resources is fundamental to longer term production. The reference estimates of undiscovered resources employed here are tied to the USGS Circular 725 estimates, which are severely out of date. This makes the sensitivity analysis on resource base assumptions included in the study of critical importance.

Various assumptions about world oil prices, discount rates, and undiscovered resources have impacts on production that, like those of the policy actions, grow progressively over time, with relatively little variation prior to 1990 and greater impacts after that time.

Although the models included in the study are the best available tools at our disposal for projecting oil and gas supply over the next 10–20 years, their results crucially depend on many assumptions about key uncertainties that influence oil and gas production, as well as implicit assumptions embodying alternative, and generally untested, theories.

Figure 2A. U.S. Total Natural Gas Production, High Price Scenario

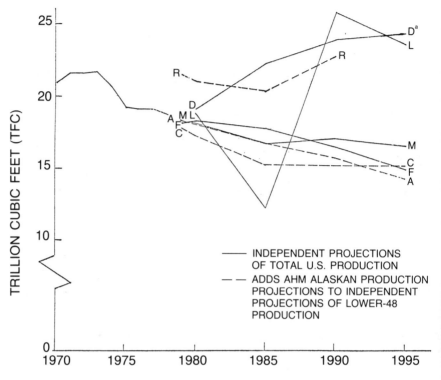

^a See Table 4 for key to models.

Figure 1A exhibits a large dispersion in conventional crude projections for 1990. This variation stems from a combination of factors: slightly differing definitions of crude oil, differences in the historical data series underlying the models, alternative assumptions about short-run adjustments of the reserve/production ratio, and different degrees of model calibration. These differences, so readily apparent in a model comparison study, are generally not taken into account in policy debates based upon results from a single model.

The normal concept of price elasticity of supply seems difficult, if not impossible, to apply correctly to depletable resources, such as oil and gas. Thus, the EMF chose not to display such a summary measure.

These broad findings indicate the direction and magnitude of the results, but several key factors must be examined in greater detail to understand the variations in projections between model scenarios.

Figure 2B. Price of Natural Gas, High Price Scenario

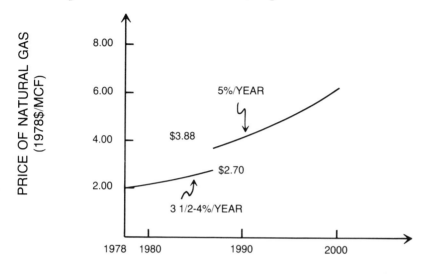

Figure 3. FOSSIL2 and MOGSMS–AHM Enhanced Oil Recovery

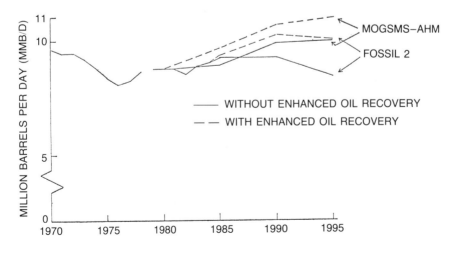

Table 4. U.S. Total Production Projections, High Price Scenario

Model[a]	CRUDE OIL PRODUCTION (MMB/D; EXCLUDING NGL)					NATURAL GAS PRODUCTION (TCF)				
	1979	1980	1985	1990	1995	1979	1980	1985	1990	1995
A – AGA–TERA[b]	7.91	7.21	5.52	5.36	5.50	18.38	18.16	16.89	15.81	14.26
C – EPPLE–HANSEN[b]	7.69	7.23	6.08	5.47	5.15	17.90	17.31	15.32	15.34	15.25
E – EMS[b,c]	8.03	7.64	7.63	8.09	8.54					
F – FOSSIL2[d]	8.70	8.70	9.10	9.20	8.40	18.30	18.40	17.90	16.60	15.00
K – KIM–THOMPSON[b]	8.68	8.38	8.00	8.08	8.62					
D – DFI–GEMS	—	9.34	10.38	11.43	12.36	—	19.12	22.37	24.02	24.38
L – LORENDAS	—	8.40	9.13	9.16	9.91	—	18.90	12.27	25.88	23.64
W – MIT–WOP	9.28	8.96	7.23	6.17						
M – MOGSMS–AHM	8.73	8.73	8.91	9.81	9.87	18.37	18.06	16.88	17.16	16.68
R – RICE[b]	9.74	9.61	10.54	10.87		21.59	21.08	20.46	22.87	

[a] Listing of models is to be used as master listing throughout EMF 5, except use spellout of EMS (per John Weyant, 12/05/79).
[b] No data for Alaska.
[c] Erickson–Milsaps–Spann.
[d] 1981, 8.7; 1982, 8.5; 1983, 8.8; 1984, 9.0.

Table 5. U.S. Total Production, Historical Data

Resource	1970	1971	1972	1973	1974	1975	1976	1977	1978
Crude oil (MMB/D)	9.64	9.46	9.44	9.21	8.77	8.38	8.13	8.25	8.70
Natural gas (TCF)	21.02	21.61	21.62	21.73	20.71	19.24	19.10	19.16	18.83

Table 6. U.S. Total Production Projections, High Price Scenario

Model	ENHANCED OIL PRODUCTION					UNCONVENTIONAL GAS PRODUCTION				
	1979	1980	1985	1990	1995	1979	1980	1985	1990	1995
FOSSIL2	0	0	0	0	1.20	0	0	0	1.50	4.00
MOGSMS–AHM	0	0	0.67	1.29	1.53					

Figure 4. FOSSIL2 U.S. Total Gas Production, High Price Scenario

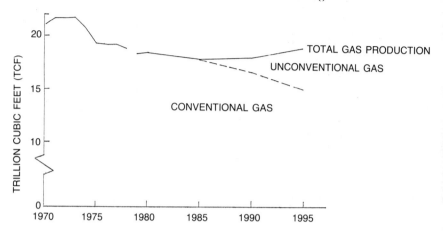

KEY FACTORS INFLUENCING SUPPLY

Many factors influence oil and gas supply; some, such as the size of undiscovered resource base, cannot be influenced by policy actions; others, however, are subject to direct policy control (price controls, taxes, lease offer rates) or are indirectly influenced by policy actions (world oil price, natural gas market prices, discount rates). In the present study, all three classes of factors are studied.

An easy but crucial result of the comparative model study was the observation that some of the scenarios could not be implemented by all of the models—their systems not having been designed to explore the issues reflected in those particular scenarios. Table 7 records the kinds of changes that can be accommodated by the models represented in the study. If a model cannot accommodate a particular change, it could not be used to analyze the study scenarios shown in the last row of Table 7. For some models, the parameter changes called for in the scenario design could not be implemented directly because the model does not represent that parameter explicitly. But, as noted in Table 7, in some cases the modeler is able to manipulate another associated variable to mimic the intent of the study scenario; however, in these cases the exact relationship between the scenario variable and the model variable used to represent it was not made explicit.

Central to the supply projections are estimates of the resource base. The impacts of doubling the assumed size of the undiscovered resource base crude oil projections vary from 2 to 20 percent in 1985 but grow to a 10 to 40 percent range in 1995 (Figure 5A). Similarly, the impact

Table 7. Capabilities of EMF 5 Models

Model	CAPABILITY TO EXAMINE CHARGES IN				
	Oil price	Gas price	Geologic resource base	Leasing schedules	Tax laws
Epple–Hanson	Yes	Yes	No	No	Yes
Erickson–Milsaps–Spann	Yes	No	Indirect	No	No
FOSSIL2	Yes	Yes	Yes	No	No
GEM	Yes	Yes	Yes	No	No
Kim–Thompson	Yes	Yes	Yes	Yes	Yes
LORENDAS	Yes	Yes	Yes	No	No
MIT–WOP	No	No	Yes	Yes	No
EIA–ICF MOGSMS AHM EOR	Yes	Yes	Yes	Yes	Yes
Rice	Yes	Yes	Indirect	Indirect	No
TERA Onshore Offshore	Yes	Yes	Yes	Yes	Yes
EMF 5 scenarios precluded by omission of this capability	B,C,D,G	B,C,D,M	G,H,I,N,P,Q	L	J

on natural gas projections range from 0 to 35 percent in 1985 but grow to 15 to 50 percent in 1995 (Figure 5B). The slow response is explained by the quantitative dominance of presently existing reserves in early years and of new reserves in later years.

Extreme uncertainty characterizes future world oil prices and the role of U.S. policies in moderating price increases is not well understood. While the models generally indicate that price increases will increase production, increases in the expected rate of future price increases leads to ambiguous results depending on the nature of the economic incentives incorporated in the model. Figure 6 shows the percentage change in the projections of oil and gas production attributable to a decrease in prices from high price level to the reference level. Some models project increases in mid-range supply, to take immediate advantage of the higher prices. In models that assume perfect foresight and assume that perfectly competitive firms can shift production over time to maximize profits (DFI–GEMS and LORENDAS), however, increases in the price growth rate may lead to mid-range production decreases, so that reserves can be held in anticipation of future price increases. For example, in the Reference scenario the price of natural gas increases only gradually to the BTU equivalent oil price in 1986,

Figure 5. Total Production for Oil (A) and Natural Gas (B), High Price–High Geology Scenario for Lower-48 Onshore and Offshore

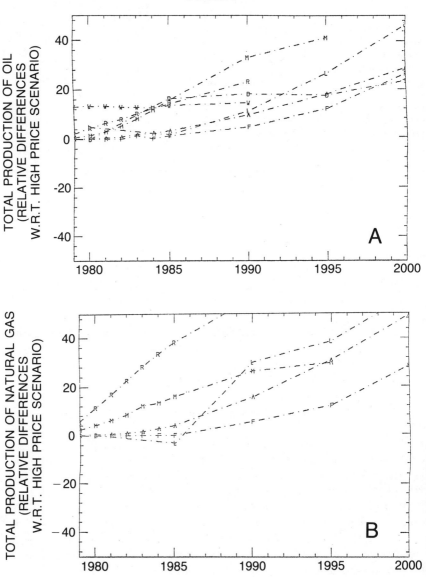

See Table 4 for key to models.

Figure 6.   Total Production of Oil (A) and Natural Gas (B), Reference
Scenario for Lower-48 Onshore and Offshore

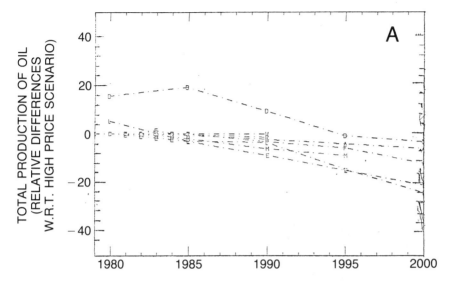

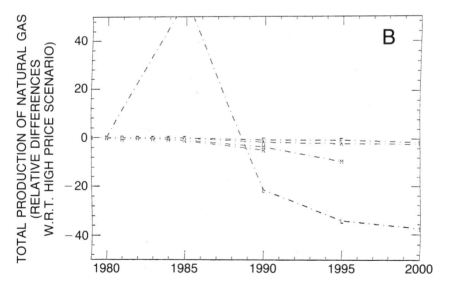

See Table 4 for key to models.

but in the High Price scenario, the jump is about $1.00/MCF. In the LORENDAS model this creates an incentive to produce less before 1986 in the High Price scenario than in the Reference scenario in anticipation of even higher prices after 1986. Other models project production decreases in oil or in gas in response to increasing prices of both due to greater profitability and, hence, production of the other resource (FOSSIL 2 and Epple–Hansen in Figure 6A).

High gas prices relative to oil prices invariably yield higher levels of exploration for gas relative to oil; and in models that treat total drilling as insensitive to price, the absolute level of oil drilling each year will decrease. However, in models for which total exploration is price sensitive, higher gas prices could either increase (Figure 7) or decrease (Figure 8) oil exploration.

Figure 7. Exploratory Effort for Gas and Oil, MOGSMS Model for Total United States

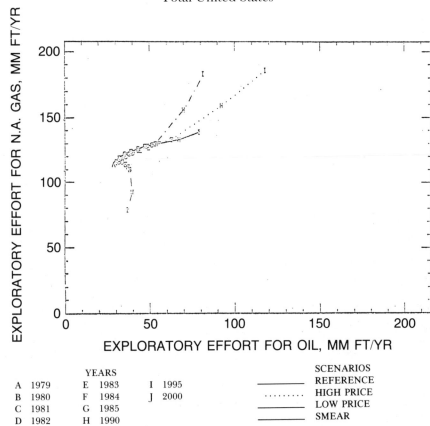

	YEARS				SCENARIOS	
A	1979	E	1983	I	1995	———— REFERENCE
B	1980	F	1984	J	2000	········· HIGH PRICE
C	1981	G	1985			———— LOW PRICE
D	1982	H	1990			———— SMEAR

Figure 8. Exploratory Efforts for Gas and Oil, Kim–Thompson Model for Lower-48 Onshore

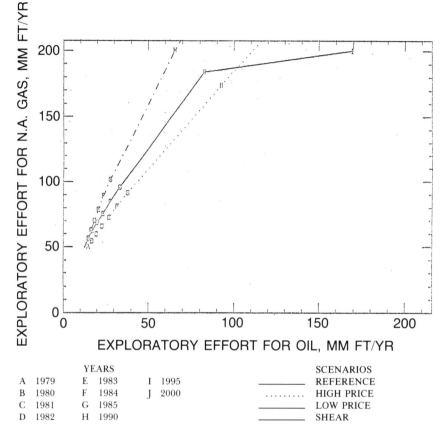

	YEARS			SCENARIOS
A	1979	E	1983	I 1995 · REFERENCE
B	1980	F	1984	J 2000 · HIGH PRICE
C	1981	G	1985	· LOW PRICE
D	1982	H	1990	· SHEAR

Discount rates can be influenced by governmental policy decisions but the appropriate value of this key parameter is uncertain. Results from LORENDAS, a full intertemporal optimization model, suggest that changing the assumed real interest rate from 8 to 16 percent reduces the year 1995 projected production from 9 ½ to 4 MMB/D. While this range probably overestimates the actual extent of interest rate uncertainty, the effect of moderately higher discount rates could be significant.

Several variables under direct federal control have been examined. Prominent in current debates are federal price controls on natural gas and on oil. A continuation of crude oil price controls is projected to reduce conventional lower-48 crude oil supply in the high price case from between 0 to 15 percent in 1985 for those r odels that include the effects of price, whereas in 1995 the impacts are even greater, ranging from 0 to 35 percent (Figure 9A). Similarly, the impacts on conventional lower-48 natural gas productions range from 0 to 6 percent in 1985 growing to 0 to 12 percent by 1995 (Figure 9B).

Price controls by reducing the production of oil imply that additional resources will be available to be produced at a later date (Figure 10A). To some extent, the issue to be examined is *when* oil and gas will be produced rather than *how much* in the aggregate will be produced. For example, price controls that create expectations of future discontinuous price jumps create incentives for even perfectly competitive firms or landowners to not explore for, develop, and produce reserves until after the price discontinuity. Whether these incentives lead to corresponding actions is open to debate.

Under direct control of the government is the rate at which federal lands are made available for lease. Current discussions on leasing rates significantly influence future production quantities through influencing reserve additions. For example, halving the federal offshore leasing rate reduces natural gas production by 1 to 7 percent in 1985 and 2 to 15 percent in 1995 (Figure 10B). Corresponding reductions for oil production are 1 to 3 percent in 1985 and 5 to 10 percent in 1995.

While it is impossible to use the aggregate models to examine fine issues in tax treatment of oil production, broader issues can be addressed. Elimination of (1) the percentage depletion allowance, (2) provisions for expressing of intangible drilling expenses, and (3) the investment tax credit leads to reductions in oil and gas supply by 0 to 15 percent and 5 to 30 percent in 1985 and 1995, respectively (Figure 11).

MAJOR ISSUES IN USING THE MODELS

The working group identified a number of important issues in the comparison of the models and the forecasts. Each model contains critical untested assumptions that the user must judge and evaluate.

- Expectations: The models differ significantly in the degree of foresight attributed to oil and gas producers. The forecasts of models with complete foresight, for instance, are very sensitive to the trend as well as the level of prices.
- Exploration and Discovery: The models employ finding rate functions to translate exploratory effort into discovery of oil and gas resources. Different functions, which fit the historical data equally

Figure 9. Total Production of Oil (A) and Natural Gas (B), High
Price–Controls Scenario for Lower-48 Onshore and Offshore

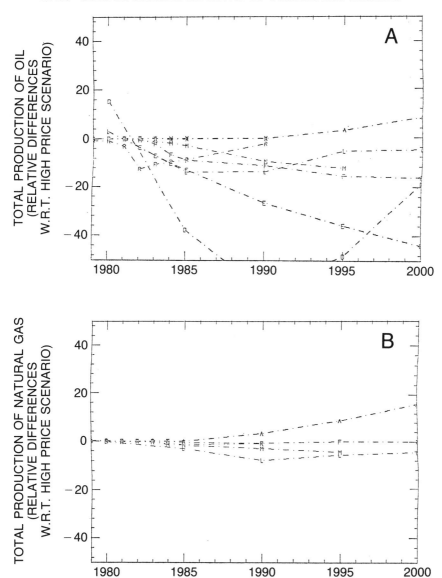

See Table 4 for key to models.

Figure 10. Total Production of Oil (A) and Natural Gas (B), Retarded Leasing Scenario for Lower-48 Onshore and Offshore

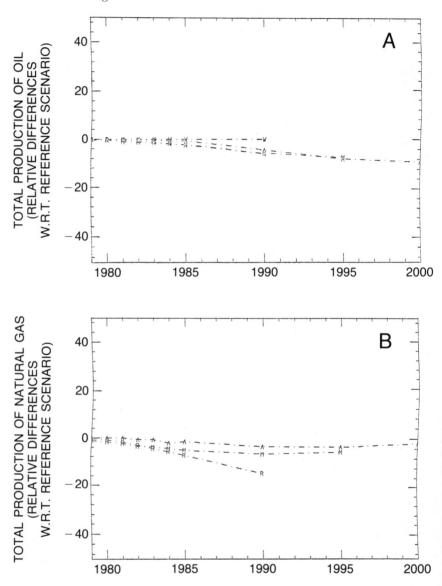

See Table 4 for key to models.

Figure 11. Total Production of Oil (A) and Natural Gas (B), No Tax Break Scenario for Lower-48 Onshore and Offshore

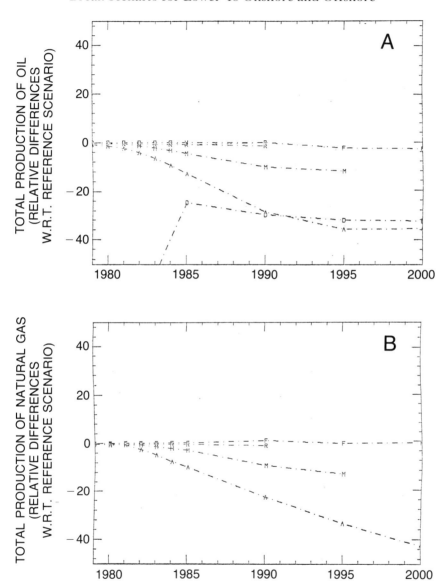

See Table 4 for key to models.

well, extrapolate to produce very different forecasts of the level and price responsiveness of future oil and gas production.

- External Constraints: Many of the modelers rely on drilling constraints to control the rate of exploration and discovery. This assumption often reduces the forecasts of production, when the unconstrained logic of the model would produce a more rapid pace of development. These constraints may cause the models to understate the rate of production because drilling capacity does seem to respond to price incentives.

- Development and Production: Many models treat the development and production patterns from a reserve, once found, as exogenous. Yet, firms do make decisions on the so-called intensive margin, and, therefore, can influence development and production patterns. The quantitative significance of this issue is not well understood. However, qualitatively, omission of this flexibility understates the role of prices or other incentives in influencing supply.

- Indirect Effects of Controls: The modelers assume that oil and gas price controls affect only the production that is directly regulated. But the complexity of controls may create unwanted incentives, e.g., to reduce output to qualify as a small well, or may create an environment wherein future regulations are anticipated, i.e., where today's uncontrolled new production will be controlled as tomorrow's new "old" production. Thus, the effects of controls may be to create unexpected incentives to either increase or decrease production in the near-term in anticipation of future prices.

- Interactions with the Economic System: Most of the models take as exogenous the state of financial markets, the health of the economy, and the world oil prices. The interactions of oil and gas supply decisions on these other aspects of the economic system have not been addressed within this study.

Modelers have not fully standardized the inputs, coverage, or outputs of these models.

- Enhanced Oil Recovery and Unconventional Resources: The models differ in the definition and description of opportunities for enhanced oil recovery (EOR) and unconventional oil and gas resources. Some modelers treat EOR and unconventional sources explicitly; others include them only implicitly in the total reserve data. These differences in definition of coverage can produce wide variations in the price responsiveness of the model.

- Geographic Coverage: The models differ in the geographical coverage and degree of regional disaggregation of oil and gas supply.

For example, not all of the models include Alaska, and the disaggregation of lower-48 production range from 1 region in the price model to 12 regions in the MOGSMS model.

* Historical Values: Comparability of model projections (even for the more straightforward statistics such as production as contrasted with reserves) is frustrated by multiple, inconsistent sources for current and historical information and by an inability to validate those statistics that do exist. For example, two prominent sources of data—the Energy Information Administration and the American Petroleum Institute—exhibit a 0.4 MMB/D difference in their reported 1977 data on crude oil production. However, the focus of the study was not to review current statistical series and their quality.

These difficulties in standardization are particularly disturbing when we consider their implications for past and present policy discussions. Public and private debates over conflicting production forecasts seldom, if ever, replicate the effort expended in the present study to put the forecasts on a common footing. But midway through the study, the oil production forecasts for 1979 differed by 2 MMB/D because of different accounting conventions, and the working group never achieved a complete standardization of the models. It is likely that similar problems account for much of the disagreements in different forecasts in less careful comparisons.

Finally, the working group recognized differences in the structure and assumptions of the models included in this study and the proprietary models used by oil and gas companies. The visibility of the USGS Circular 725 resource base estimates is very low in the oil and gas industry; none of the companies interviewed use it in their modeling efforts. The company models operate on a more disaggregated, but less comprehensive, level than the 10 models employed in this study. However, the federal "Interagency Task Force Project," which moves in the direction of data collection at the individual basin level, may lead to a greater convergence of the public and private sector models.

NOTES

Disclaimer: This paper represents the authors' preliminary assessment of the conclusions of an Energy Modeling Forum study. Many of the study's participants have contributed to the ideas presented here, but this paper has not been approved by the working group. The shape of many of the conclusions may change during the process of obtaining the group's approval of the final report over the next several months.

AN ACADEMICIAN'S THOUGHTS ON MODELING

Richard Engelbrecht-Wiggans

A variety of models have been presented during this conference. They vary in the amount of detail included and in the extent of their scope. Some are very quantitative whereas others are more qualitative.

The models provoked lively discussions. Shortcomings of each model in accurately representing the real world were identified. No model appeared to reflect the real world perfectly.

Although each of the models failed in some respect to represent the real world, this in itself does not make the models useless. Indeed, models inherently are only approximations of the real world. However, I feel that models have a very definite and useful role in basic research and in practical decision making. Some thoughts on what models are, what they should be, and how they may be used follows.

Webster defines a model as "a system of postulates, data, and inferences presented as a mathematical description of an entity or state of affairs." In short, a model is a mathematical abstraction. It isolates and incorporates the relevant aspects of the real world situation while pruning away irrelevant aspects.

All models are approximations of the real world. Indeed, no such thing as a perfectly representative model could exist—it would no longer be a model. A model is useful, however, if it accurately captures those aspects of a situation relevant to a particular application or set of questions. The determination of which aspects are relevant depends on what questions are being asked.

The temptation may be to include every possible detail into a model, and to make the model include all related and possibly external aspects explicitly. Such a thorough approach results in a model closely representing the real situation. However, such a model is not necessarily particularly good or useful.

Very thorough models have several shortcomings. Much time may be spent specifying the details. Outside expertise may be necessary to parameterize the model. In general, such a model may be difficult to build.

More important than the difficulties in specifying a very thorough model are the disadvantages of using such a model to study the real world situation. Of course thorough models may require more time to analyze. Of greater concern though, is their tendency to obscure the basic relationship between general characteristics of the real world and their influences and effects; in a thorough model, it is unclear which conclusions are a result of the specific details of the model and which are true for all models with similar general characteristics.

The usefulness of any model depends on the fidelity of the model to relevant aspects of the real world situation. Which aspects are relevant depends on what question is being asked. A model that captures all the relevant aspects for one question may be inappropriate for some other question; however, the inadequacy of the model with respect to the latter question does not necessarily make the model useless. In short, the model must be matched to the intended application or set of questions.

The applications intended for a model may differ in their detail and in their scope. Some questions are quantitative whereas others are qualitative. For example, a modeler may be interested in the probability of drilling a dry hole for one of several reasons. If the interest is to decide whether or not to drill, a sufficient answer may be whether or not the probability exceeds a fixed critical threshhold. Alternatively, if the question is asked while estimating the nation's future oil production, a numerical estimate may be desired. In some cases the question may be asked for a particular location, whereas in other cases the probability of a dry hole for a variety of locations is needed. For some applications, the question is qualitative rather than quantitative, e.g., "has the probability of drilling a dry hole increased or decreased over the last few years" rather than "how much has the probability of drilling a dry hole changed over the last few years?".

There are tradeoffs between models that are appropriate for a large variety of questions and those models appropriate for fewer or for less specific questions. A more thorough model requires more aspects to be accurately portrayed; a sloppy broad or detailed model may be useless with regard to all questions. The more thorough model also requires agreement among potential users of the details; the details may happen to be irrelevant to any of the questions being asked. A detailed model is more situation specific and less applicable to other, possibly related situations; the conclusions of the detailed model may depend critically on the details.

The best model may well be the most abstract model which includes at least some of the relevant aspects of the real situation. Certain general properties may be best discovered by looking at such abstract models. For instance, the well-known winner's curse is that if each bidder has roughly similar objectives, has access to similar estimating procedures, and on the average bids the true value for an object whose value is uncertain but the same for all bidders, then the winner will, on average, lose money. The model in the above statement, although not precisely stated, has three main aspects; to wit: symmetry of bidders and estimating techniques, uncertainty in the value of the object, and unbiased bidding. It is a very abstract model in that it includes descriptions of only these three aspects.

The model is clearly inadequate for many questions, e.g., any questions involving asymmetries in bidding philosophies or estimation techniques. It does not precisely represent any real situation in that there is always some asymmetry or some possible deviation from unbiased bidding. However, the model illustrates the very important phenomenon of the winner's curse, focuses on the aspects of a bidding situation that gave rise to the curse, and does not cloud the issue with details having no effect on the curse.

In many situations, such abstract models will not give specific or detailed enough information. The questions asked may be very detailed and specific. However, again, the best model may well be the simplest model that includes the relevant aspects. For example, in estimating the amount of resources to be allocated to exploration in the immediate future, it may be perfectly acceptable to assume that the price of oil decades from now will have no effect. In such cases, uncertainties in the long-term future price of oil need not be included in the model.

With any model, the basic assumptions of the model and its basic applications should be clearly stated. A good model will be appropriate for at least some questions in certain situations; the model user must decide for what questions and in what situations a particular model is adequate. However, I doubt if any model is appropriate universally.

Each model may have shortcomings with respect to representing certain aspects of the real world. This may render the model inappropriate or even useless for some questions and applications. Indeed, most models will have shortcomings with respect to some questions or possible applications. However, this does not imply that the model is inappropriate or useless for providing insight into the questions and applications for which the model was built.

The concern should be whether a model is appropriate for the question being asked. This determination is subjective; there may be disagreement whether or not a particular model does indeed represent all the relevant aspects sufficiently and accurately. There may even be questions for which no satisfactory model can be built. In particular, for certain detailed or specific questions, the model may require so many details to be specified that no two individuals will ever agree that the model is accurate in all its details.

Models have, however, proven useful. This is especially true of carefully constructed seemingly abstract models; models that are so abstract that they clearly fail to represent any real world situation. Such models provide insight into the relationship between basic, general characteristics of the real world and their effects. Taken together, the results of many such models provide an overall picture of how various factors affect each other. The previously mentioned model giving rise to the winner's curse is an example of one such model.

In some instances, models reflect the best available understanding of the real situation. If the current understanding of the real situation is imperfect, then the model will reflect the real situation imperfectly. Such models may still be useful if they are the best currently available and are sufficiently accurate for the question being asked. Many abstract models fall into this category.

There are purists who insist that abstract models that fail to represent any real situation can not give meaningful insight into real situations; they feel there is too much uncertainty about how the properties of such an abstract model should be interpreted in situations roughly, but not precisely, represented by the model. Such individuals should reflect on some of the abstract models currently being used, some of which are centuries old and are still being extensively used in spite of a consensus that they do not represent any real situation accurately. For example, the basic model of classical physics in which energy and momentum are conserved and in which length and time are independent of velocity has been used very successfully for many years even though inaccuracies of the model have been known for decades. It is still considered to be a sufficiently good approximation in many, many instances, and is thus still extensively used. Thus, the usefulness of a model does not depend on it being a perfect representation of the real situation being studied, but on its being a sufficiently good representation, or possibly the best available representation, of the real situation with respect to the particular questions being asked.

NOTE

This article is based on a presentation made at the Economics of Exploration for Energy Resources Conference, New York University, May 17–18, 1979.

PART II
NEW THEORIES OF
EXPLORATION IN RELATION TO
THE SUPPLY OF ENERGY

SOME OF THE POLICY
IMPLICATIONS OF THE
ECONOMICS OF EXPLORATION

James B. Ramsey

I.   SOME OF THE POLICY IMPLICATIONS OF THE
ECONOMICS OF EXPLORATION

The study of the economics of exploration is most important for the simplest, yet most profound, of reasons. Once people become convinced that there is little oil to be found from further exploration, especially in new and technologically challenging areas, the belief becomes permanently self-fulfilling. This is true no matter how much oil there might be nor how low in cost its recovery might be. To cease looking is to ensure nondiscovery. Current policies seem to be beginning to have this effect, however unintentional this result might be.

The importance of oil has recently been rediscovered by both academicians and the members of the various media, not to mention politicians of all political persuasions. Unfortunately, the immediate and naive assumption that provided the motive force for almost all discussion and analysis to date was that current inventory stocks, no matter how defined, provided a rough guide to ultimate resources that were obviously imminently to be depleted. Thus began the great economics of exhaustion debate.

Forgotten in all this argumentation was the elemental idea that what the "experts" currently estimate as our available resource stock of recoverable oil is a function of the process of discovery itself. The next step is to realize that economists, as well as everyone else, know very little about how the process of exploration functions, which circumstances aid it, which impede it, and even how we recognize successful exploration.

The analysis presented in this paper discusses in nontechnical language the formal mathetmatically based theory developed by the author (Ramsey, 1980). The reader interested in further details and a fuller understanding of the theory should consult that article.

While the theory presented in this paper was being developed, two other interesting, but similar, approaches to the analysis of exploration were being developed. Gilbert (1976a) and Attansi (1978) used theoretical work of Burt and Cummings (1970) to provide two early and highly laudable attempts to model the exploration process as an alternative to increased rate of production from existing wells. In contrast, the approach taken in this article concentrates on exploration in its own right and builds up a market supply function for discovered reservoirs from the analysis of individual firm behavior of a very specialized and to some extent abstract concept of an "exploration" firm.

The policy implications, even from this initial analysis and provided the theory stands up to empirical testing, are profound and of far-reaching significance. The main shift in emphasis arising out of this work is the recognition of the importance of concentrating attention on the distribution of exploration firm sizes and on the *distribution* of exploration areas by type. Policy changes that alter the distribution of firm sizes or the distribution of firm specialization in exploratory areas may have more serious long-run consequences for discovery success than policies that do not alter distributions, but lower the overall rate of search.

II.   A NONMATHEMATICAL STATEMENT OF THE ECONOMIC THEORY OF EXPLORATION

The theory developed in Ramsey (1980) is based on the idea that there is a market in exploration, or rather in discovered pools and reservoirs, which are the output of exploration. For some, this may be a novel abstraction about this particular portion of the oil industry, particularly if one recognizes that, especially for the majors, exploration is carried out by the designated division of the firm and that the division's financial support is a function of the economic status of the firm and of the market for delivered oil products.

Nevertheless, it is clear that there is a well-defined market in reservoirs as shown by the fact that the market prices for rights to drill, the exchange of tracts, or even the sale price of a discovered pool are easily ascertained. The economic theorist recognizes that the individual firm is restricted in its optimizing behavior by market conditions and that this is true even for the integrated firm that may not directly enter the exploration market but whose decisions will be guided by the prices determined within the market. After all, with open entry any firm can easily move into or out of the oil exploration business; therefore, by this fact one can see that market forces impinge even on the fully integrated firm.

It is with this realization that, in contrast to the excellent work by Attanasi (1978), Epple (1975), and by Gilbert (1976a), I have isolated the exploration market for separate study. The objective is to understand more clearly the economic forces bearing on decision making in this area. Hence, exploration divisions will be regarded as decision-making entities or "firms" in their own right. Because the emphasis in this paper is on the effect of risk on decision making and the specialization in risk taking rather than on the technical problems involved in geographically locating the next well, this assumption in fact does little violence to reality. As the funding of an exploration group grows or decreases, one has the market equivalent of "firm" entry and exit of various sizes; an increase in funding is equivalent to the "exit" of a small decision-making unit and entry of a larger, whose size is measured in terms of net worth.

Because the main interest of the analysis is on the behavior of "exploration firms" that are assumed with good reason to be in a competitive market, the economic conditions underlying the supply of tracts and the demand for reservoirs will be ignored; it is assumed that tracts are bid competitively by exploration firms. Tracts are assumed to be supplied at a rate to maintain a steady state in the market; it is also assumed that there exists a steady-state known "price" for reservoirs.

By concentrating on the role of risk in exploration and the specialization in types of risk taking, the analysis in this paper defines exploratory areas in a novel, but enlightening, manner. Exploratory areas are not defined by play, basin, or geographic region, but in terms of certain statistical characteristics regarding the distribution of oil. All regions with similar statistical characteristics will be treated as one "area"; in general an "area" so defined is simply the sum of a wide variety of geographic regions, each of which has the same (or more accurately, is thought to have the same) statistical characteristics.

The two major statistical characteristics on which the analysis concentrates are the probability of a "hit" (λ) and the expected value of a hit (η), once one has a hit; a hit is the discovery of oil to some measurable extent. While the concentration on just these two parameters does some violence to the complexity of the situation, the simplification involved will enable us to gain some useful insights as a first step.

Further, the initial assumption that the values of λ and η are known with certainty is far too strong. All that is required is that different areas are recognizable in terms of their statistical characteristics, that the parameter values are estimable, and that firm decisions are made on the basis of the firm's knowledge about the probable range of values of the selected parameters.

The strong initial assumption of knowing λ and η with certainty simplifies the theoretical development with little cost in essential realism.

The analysis is built up in stages. The first step is to clarify the nature of individual firm decision making in this area under the simplest of circumstances; the complexity of decision making is increased in stages in order to allow for a more realistic and insightful formulation of the problem. The next major step is to examine how the market as a whole functions and begin the analysis of the dynamics of interaction and adjustment at the very end.

A. Step I. Exploration by Firms Facing a Single Type of Exploratory Area

The "firm's" objective function is quite simply the maximization of its expected net discounted present value of its future income stream: in short, maximization of net worth. The effects of risk are brought into the analysis by recognizing that the concept of the probability of ruin is important in these situations. This approach to the firm decision-making problem is unusual, but has a number of key advantages.

It has long been recognized that risk affects the decisions of even very large firms (large in the sense of size of net worth). Yet, and especially for large firms, one cannot utilize neoclassical risk theory because it is based on the assumption that the "decision maker" has a well-behaved preference function over alternative outcomes. However, insofar as decisions are not made by one individual but are the outcome of committee deliberations, then no well-behaved preference function can be assumed to hold.

It will be shown in the following pages how the "probability of ruin" approach enables one to generate risk averse type behavior without assuming that committee's have well-behaved preference functions.

The phrase "probability of ruin" is overly dramatic but is used for its historical precedence and recognition. One need not assume that firms must actually and frequently go bankrupt in order for the concept to be useful. As will be seen, the notion is more one of recognizing that a long stream of dry holes is an event with nonnegligible probability of occurrence and that because bankrupt firms cannot borrow and continue operations, the simple examination of expected returns from drilling overstate the "bankrupt limited" actual expected return. While prudent management seldom leads to bankruptcy for large firms, no firm is too large to avoid it with incautious policies.

We begin by assuming that the firm has an initial net worth of W. The firm contemplates the problem of maximizing additions to net worth by exploratory activity and "selling" the output, i.e., discovered reserves. The first problem is to find the net worth maximizing level of exploration E given that the firm faces a given fixed probability of getting a hit (λ) and a given expected value of a hit (η). Thus, in each time period, E units of exploratory effort are expended with certainty and the return of y_t, the value of a hit in period t, is a random variable whose distribution depends on the probability distribution of hits given the value of E and the distribution of pool sizes (the mean of which is evaluated in terms of the net value of the pool given existing prices of oil and costs of extraction). The higher the value of E for given costs of exploration, the greater the expected number of hits, since one is essentially taking a larger "sample" with higher values of E. Each hit can be regarded as a random drawing from a distribution of net reservoir values with mean η.

This simplification in assumptions does some violence to the complexity of exploration as actually carried out but does provide a useful first step in understanding firm reaction to a risky environment.

Define E to be the level of exploration effort, let V_t denote the discount factor so that the product EV_t is the present value of a sum of a stream of expenditures at level E from now until time period t, and let Y_t denote the present value of the sum of the stream of discounted random net incomes from discoveries in each period from now until time period t. With these definitions, ruin occurs in period t if

$$W + Y_t - EV_t \leq 0$$

Simply, ruin occurs at time period t when a firm's sum of expenditures on exploration exceeds the sum of accumulated income and initial wealth. The greater the wealth, the larger the value of E that can be financed. Y_t is a function of E as well in so far as an increase in exploration increases the expected number of hits per unit time period.

The firm's objective function in this first simple version of the problem is to maximize with respect to E, the expression

$$PV = r^{-1}(E\lambda\eta - E)[1 - \sum_{t=1}^{\infty} Q(t,W)v^{t-1}]$$

where r denotes the relevant interest rate to the firm, $v^{t-1} = (1 + r)^{-(t-1)}$, and $Q(t,W)$ is the probability of ruin in period t given wealth W and exploration effort E. PV stands for the present value of net returns to exploration.

The first part of the expression, $r^{-1}E(\lambda\eta - 1)$ is the present value of exploring at rate E *without* consideration for the effect of ruin. Ruin enters the analysis through the expression $(1 - \sum_{1}^{\infty} Q(t,W)v^{t-1})$.

The condition for maximizing the present value PV with respect to level of exploration is that the value of the optimum level of exploration is equal to the reciprocal of the relative rate of change in the probability of failure; in short, since E measures the incremental gain in net worth due to exploration, the optimum value of E is equal to the incremental cost in the increased probability of ruin due to higher values of E.

One interesting and perhaps counterintuitive implication of this analysis is that an increase in the interest rate leads to an increase in the optimum level of exploration. Some insight is gained by noting that under the conditions of the problem a higher interest rate with given firm net worth implies that the firm can finance a larger value of exploration for a longer period of time.

Another interesting aspect is that an increase in initial net worth will only lead to an increase in the optimal level of exploration if the rate of increase in probability of ruin to increases in E changes sufficiently slowly; in short, conditions can prevail under which a larger firm in terms of value of W would find it optimal to explore at a slower rate.

In preparation for the next section, a lengthy algebraic analysis demonstrates the intuitively plausible result that an increase in either λ or η will lead to a higher value for E and for the optimum value of PV; firms would always choose larger values of λ and η if given the opportunity. In fact, firms face a variety of opportunities in terms of alternative pairs of values for λ and η, which is an issue to be discussed in the next section.

B.   *Step 2. The Firm's Optimal Choice of λ and η*

This section introduces one of the most important assumptions in the analysis—that an efficiency frontier in terms of pairs of (λ,η) values can be found. The idea is simply that in choosing between areas, there are some areas for which a choice of an increase in λ can be obtained only with a sacrifice in the value of η. This primitive notion is refined and formalized in Ramsey (1980) in terms of a function η = g(λ), which defines the efficiency frontier and which satisfies the condition that an increase in λ implies a decrease in η. Firms are thus forced to trade off *along* the efficiency frontier large values of λ for smaller values of η or *vice versa*. It is easy to show that all firms will locate on the efficiency frontier. Indeed, the power of this concept of an efficiency frontier is enhanced when one recognizes that even a choice between only two areas will enable the firm to pick out a point on a continuum of exchange possibilities generated by the firm's chosen proportions for exploring in the two areas as shown in Figure 1. If all exploration is in area 1 or 2, then the firm operates at points (λ_1, η_1) or (λ_2, η_2), but the firm, by dividing its total exploration between areas 1 and 2 in various proportions, can achieve any point on the curved line joining (λ_1, η_1) and (λ_2, η_2) as shown in Figure 1. In short, the firm seeks its optimum portfolio of exploration areas. Some few firms may specialize solely in areas such as that characterized by (λ_1, η_1) or (λ_2, η_2), but most firms will explore in both areas simultaneously and thereby try to achieve a point such as (λ_a, η_a) shown in Figure 1.

The stage has now been set for the next major step, the analysis of the firm's joint determination of the optimal level of exploration E and the optimal distribution of exploration in order to achieve desired values for λ and η. Indeed, the chief item of interest here is the notion of the firm using a portfolio of areas in order to specialize in its optimal (λ, η) combination, which is some point on the efficiency frontier.

The general problem can be separated into stages. First, the firm can solve the optimal portfolio problem given a presumed level of E, λ, and

Figure 1. Illustrating the Efficiency Frontier

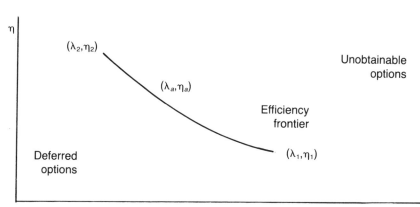

η. It is easily shown that the optimal portfolio is chosen so as to minimize the probability of ruin.

The second stage is to determine jointly the optimal triplet (E,λ,η) subject to the firm being on the efficiency frontier defined by the function $\eta = g(\lambda)$.

Since η can be eliminated from the problem by substitution and since the effect of variations in E has already been fully explored, one need only consider the effects of variation in λ. The first result is similar to that obtained for variations in E, namely that the optimum value for *PV* is obtained where the *relative* increase in expected revenue to change in λ is equal to the relative increased cost due to the increase in probability of failure.

Let $M(\lambda)$ denote the relative increase in revenue as a function of λ and let $S(\lambda|W)$ denote the relative increase in cost of probability of failure; the notation stresses that $S(\lambda)$ depends on the firm's initial net worth W (see Figure 2).

As W gets big, the curve $S(\lambda|W)$ flattens out as illustrated in Figure 2 and eventually goes to zero in the limit for all λ. Thus, if W is very large, the optimal solution will involve setting $M(\lambda)$ to zero; in short, the firm maximizes net worth and *ignores* risk and the effect of its actions on the probability of ruin.

Figure 2. Illustrating the Firm's Optimal Conditions with Respect to λ and the Effect of Wealth

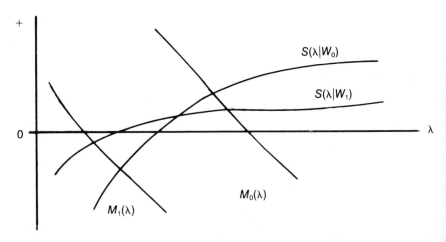

Note: $W_0 < W_1$; $M_i(\lambda)$, relative increase in revenue, $i = 0, 1$; $S(\lambda)$, relative increase in cost due to probability of failure. Points of intersection indicate optimal equilibrium solutions.

Figure 2 illustrates two alternative situations for the relationship between the functions $M(\lambda)$ and $S(\lambda|W)$. If $M_0(\lambda)$ is the relevant curve, then as W increases from W_0 to W_1, the optimal solution for λ increases. But if $M_1(\lambda)$ is the relevant function then an increase in W leads to a decrease in the optimal value for λ. Which function applies is an empirical issue.

However, a necessary and sufficient condition for an increase in W to produce a decrease in the optimal value of λ, say λ^*, for *any* initial wealth W_0, is that $S(\lambda^*|W_0) < 0$ and hence that $M(\lambda^*) < 0$.

As a practical matter, for small W it is most likely that the result will hold and less likely for very large W. Alternatively, the faster marginal revenue declines with increases in λ, the more likely is the result that increases in wealth give rise to smaller optimal values of λ and hence larger optimal values of η. The situation of increases in W leading to decreases in λ with corresponding increases in η seems to be the empirically relevant case.

C. Step 3. Equilibrium in a Competitive Oil Exploration Market

The analysis to date has concentrated on the behavior of the individual firm under increasingly more complex assumptions about the firm's extent of choice. We should now consider the implications of equilibrium in the market. The reason is not that equilibrium is observed as the common course of events but that it provides further understanding of the comparative statics of the model, indicates the situation toward which the market in disequilibrium would move, and hence provides the basis for a dynamic study of adjustment processes.

The theoretical development discussed in this paper leads to more complex notions of entry, exit, and equilibrium than in the standard comparative static analysis. Because actual outcomes are random and decisions are made on the basis of assumed and imperfect knowledge using estimates for parameters, actual performance by each firm is random. Second, the simple notion of entry by counting the number of firms will no longer suffice.

A firm will enter if its maximized solution to the problem posed in the previous section indicates a net expected gain in wealth and exit, or nonentry, otherwise. Hence, because firms specialize in terms of the optimal E,λ,η values chosen for each firm size as measured by initial net worth, a nontrivial distribution of net worth-sized firms implies that exit and entry can proceed simultaneously, for example, small firms exiting and large firms entering. Equilibrium is achieved when all firms estimate that they face zero expected competitively determined net increase in wealth. There is no reason for firms to leave and no reason to enter.

It can be shown that this equilibrium is stable in the Hicksian sense, that is, if the market is in disequilibrium, the adjustment forces thereby engendered are to reestablish equilibrium. In equilibrium the following condition holds for each firm

$$r = \frac{E^* (\lambda^*\eta^* - 1)(1 - \phi)}{W}$$

where r is the relevant *market* interest rate and the right-hand side is the firm's expected internal rate of return given W and its optimal choices for E^*, λ^*, and η^*. $(1 - \phi)$ is the probability of survival using the optimal values for E, λ, and η. From the equation we see that the effect of the probability of ruin is that the internal rate of return as conventionally measured will be somewhat greater.

Further, in equilibrium and if certain conditions mentioned in the previous section hold, then all firms will be distributed along the efficiency frontier and will be distributed such that higher values for W will be associated with higher values for η, but lower values for λ. In short, large firms will specialize in high η, low λ type areas and small firms will specialize in low η, high λ areas. One way in which this is done is for large firms relative to small firms to specialize in capital intensive exploration expenditures that will yield, for a given unit of E, a "small" λ.

Returning to the concept of entry and the complication of an equilibrium *distribution* of firms by size, one can see that entry or exit cannot be spoken of simply in terms of numbers of firms, since the size distribution by net worth can change. One can have entry in terms of the sum over $E^*_i, i = 1, 2, ..., n$ for n firms in or entering the market, or in terms of the sum over $\lambda^*_i \eta^*_i, i = 1, 2, ..., n$, that is, in terms of the expected output. What is important about this realization is that entry can occur, in one sense, but exit in the others. Further, one can have situations such as that in which firms enter but total expected discovered reserves fall, and so on.

The theoretical discussion can be completed by relating the above concepts to the behavior over time of the exploration of a fixed set of geographical regions. Figure 3 illustrates the idea. Suppose at some time period $\tau = 0$ we have just two regions characterized by (λ_1, η_1) and (λ_2, η_2) and with a corresponding efficiency frontier. Over time as region (λ_1, η_1) becomes better known and further explored, its (λ, η) characteristics change and move it in the general direction of (λ_2, η_2),

Figure 3. Illustration of the Variation in Exploration over Time for a Fixed Set of Georgraphic Regions

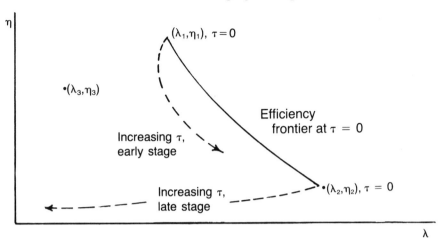

i.e., λ rises and η falls as exploration proceeds within a given fixed geographic region.

Contemporaneously, an area like (λ_2, η_2), on even further exploration, suffers from a decline in both λ and η values. The equilibrium process described above can only continue if new areas like (λ_1, η_1) are continuously supplied to the system so as to maintain the process. If no new areas are introduced, then the efficiency frontier moves toward the left so that previously inefficient, deferred options now constitute the new efficiency frontier, but at lower levels for both λ and η than before; for example, an area like (λ_3, η_3) might after time with no replacement for (λ_1, η_1) constitute part of a new efficiency frontier.

III. SOME POLICY IMPLICATIONS OF THE THEORETICAL ANALYSIS

There are a number of policy implications arising even out of this initial development of the theory of the economics of exploration, some more important than others. More specific conclusions and a wider variety of policy implications will be introduced by the extension of the analysis, especially to a dynamic analysis of adjustment processes.

At a general level, one of the most interesting developments is the shift in attention away from the idea of simple levels of exploration or the number of firms to concentrate on the *distribution* of exploration by area types and the *distribution* of firms by size. The previous section indicated that the theoretical deduction from an analysis of equilibrium was that there is an equilibrium distribution of firms by size and of areas of type to be explored. Consequently, policies that may not immediately and directly affect the overall level of exploration may well affect the distributions and therefore in the long run the overall levels of exploration and output. It appears that the distributional effects are of greater importance.

For example, if large firms as defined in this paper are forced to become smaller, or are impeded in their productive efforts, which lowers profitability net of taxes, or which increases risk, or reduces the firm's ability to diversify against risk, then the type of exploration in which large firms specialize will be shifted *down* the efficiency frontier.

However, the effects do not end here, because there appears to be a symbiotic relationship between large and small firms in that the type of exploration carried out by large firms provides the very area types used by small firms in their exploration. In short, by restricting the exploratory effectiveness of large firms, the effectiveness of all firms' exploration is eventually impeded. Worse, the inevitable decay of each geographic region's exploration potential over time would lead under such circumstances to the eventual elimination of effective exploration. Meanwhile, one could well observe increases in exploratory activity as conventionally measured, but with a corresponding *decrease* in the total expected amount of oil discovered.

Second, the fact that there exist areas known to have some oil potential but that are not currently being explored is not necessarily evidence of firm collusion in restricting supplies, nor of firm ignorance or irrationality, but is the natural result of firms seeking to locate on the efficiency frontier.

Next, the analysis indicates that competitive market conditions will lead to the expected internal rate of return being somewhat larger than the corresponding real market rate of return. Also, one should expect an increase in the rate of exploration with an increase in the real, as opposed to the nominal, rate of interest.

Clearly much further analytical work is required because only the very first steps have been taken in this analysis. However, what has been accomplished so far should be an indicator of the potential analytical payoff to be expected. While the testing and empirical application of these ideas will require detailed data far beyond what is currently available, this lag in operationalizing the theory should not seriously impede the theroetical insights that can be gained meanwhile. In any case, the policy implications are sufficiently startling and serious to engender considerable effort to begin testing and refining the ideas enunciated herein.

REFERENCES

Attanasi, Emil D. (1978). Firm Size and Petroleum Exploration Behavior, Council of Economics of AIME Proceedings, 107th Annual Meeting, 57–61.

Burt, O. R. and Cummings, R. G. (1970). Production and Investment in Natural Resource Industries, *American Economic Review* **60**: 576–590.

Epple, D. N. (1975). *Petroleum Discoveries and Government Policy*, Ballinger Press, Cambridge, Mass.

Gilbert, R. (1976a). Optimal Depletion of an Uncertain Stock, SEER Technical Report No. 10, Stanford University.

_____(1976b). Search Strategies for Nonrenewable Resource Deposits, SEER Technical Report No. 11, Stanford University.

Ramsey, J. B. (1980). The Economics of Oil Exploration: A Probability-of-Ruin Approach, *Energy Economics* Jan.: 14–30.

THE SOCIAL AND PRIVATE VALUE OF EXPLORATION INFORMATION

Richard J. Gilbert

I. INTRODUCTION

The search for deposits of nonrenewable resources serves two different economic functions. Exploration is a means to expand the capacity to extract a natural resource. Production capacity can be increased by more intensive development of known deposits or by identifying and developing new deposits. Exploration also serves to produce information about the resource stock.[1] Knowledge of the resource stock has a social value that differs from the value of the resource output, just as the value of information about sustaining a fusion reaction differs from the value of the energy produced.

The market offers financial reward for exploration that increases production capacity if the average cost of identifying and producing deposits is less than the market price. Exploration may also be profitable as a means to produce information about the value of resource assets, in particular, the value of mineral leases. In this way the market indirectly rewards those who produce information about the resource stock.

The indirect compensation provided by the market need not generate the socially desirable level of investment in exploration. Section II gives a detailed account of the social value of information about the amount of the resource, the cost, and the location of different deposits. The socially optimal timing and pattern of exploration are characterized assuming that the probability distribution describing the resource stock is known. The market (i.e., profit-maximizing) investment in exploration is described in Section III. The market allocation may differ from the social optimum because exploration may benefit people who are not required to pay for the information and because the private speculative value of exploration information may exceed its social value. Section IV is a very brief discussion of the effects of selected government policies on the market allocation of exploration.

The emphasis in this chapter is a qualitative analysis of the efficiency of the market in providing incentives for resource exploration. The primary concern is the analysis of exploration as the production of information. In this respect we draw a close analogy between exploration and research and development, drawing heavily on recent advances in the economic theory of information. Studies of extractive resource industries [such as those by Fisher (1964) and Adelman (1972) for the crude petroleum industry and MacAvoy and Pindyck (1973) and Erickson and Spann (1971) for the natural gas industry] have treated exploration solely as the process for expansion of supply capacity. There has been some discussion of the value of exploration as information (notably Allais, 1957 and Massé, 1962), but the authors do not compare the private value of exploration information to its social benefits. Kaufman (1974) and Uhler (1972) treat the uncertain returns from exploration as a statistical decision problem, but do not discuss questions of market efficiency. A partial investigation of externalities in resource exploration can be found in Gaffney (1967), Peterson (1975), and Stiglitz (1975a), but no explicit characterization of the social value of exploration is given.

It is difficult to estimate the direction, let alone the magnitude, of market distortions in the production of exploration information. There are some incentives for excessive investment in exploration, and simultaneously there are factors that imply too little incentive for exploration. However, the analysis presented in this chapter strongly suggests that the market does not provide adequate incentives for a particular kind of exploration. This is exploration of deposits that at the time of exploration are not commercially exploitable. Yet information about the distribution of such deposits can be of value in determining the appropriate rate of extraction from deposits of higher quality, and therefore there may be a case for subsidizing this kind of exploration.

II. THE SOCIAL VALUE OF EXPLORATION INFORMATION

A. Introduction

Information is a "signal," the observation of which leads to a revision in the subjective probability of some event. The data from seismic surveys and samples from core drillings may revise a prospector's probability that a particular location contains a commercially exploitable pool of oil. Information has value only to the extent that it may modify the planned actions of individuals. Seismic surveys and core drillings would be of no value to a prospector already committed to drill at a particular location, but the information may have considerable value to someone with more flexible plans. The demand for information is a derived demand that depends on individuals' beliefs about environmental uncertainties and the expected consequences of different actions.

Exploration produces at least three different kinds of information, often as joint products along with the output of a resource. These are information about (1) the amount of the total exploitable stock of a resource, (2) the cost of extraction of different deposits (including such characteristics as the level of impurities in different ores), and (3) the location of different deposits.

Information about the location of deposits avoids or reduces the error of drilling "dry" holes. The value of information about total resource stocks is more subtle. Improved knowledge of the total stocks of resources permits choice of current consumption rates that in an expected value sense allows a better balance between the welfare of present and future generations. Without this information, there may be a greater risk of an unexpected shortfall, or surplus, in future resource supply.

For some fossil fuels, such as coal and bituminous shales, and for several minerals, the total crustal abundance may be considered virtually inexhaustible. However, crustal abundance is a very poor measure of resource supply because it aggregates important economic characteristics. For convenience we lump these characteristics that affect the market value of a resource under a general heading of extraction cost, but they include diverse factors such as level of impurities (e.g., the sulfur content of coal and oil), proximity to markets, and environmental impacts associated with extraction, processing, and transportation. In most cases where the total stock of a resource is very large, the total amount of high quality ore may be small enough to be a constraint on the rate of economic growth. For this reason it may be necessary to estimate the joint distribution of the amount of a resource with a particular extraction cost.

In actual circumstances it is difficult to separate the three components of exploration information mentioned earlier. We have argued that it may be necessary to view size and cost as jointly distributed random variables, because the size of the total resource stock means little unless the stock can be profitably exploited. Similarly, the value of information about the location of resource deposits depends on the extraction costs of those deposits.[2]

Considerable simplicity is achieved by examining separately the value of size, cost, and location information. In the following pages of this section we show how information about each of these parameters of the resource endowment affects extraction decisions under uncertainty. We take the view of a central planner whose objective is the maximization of a utility function defined on the consumption flow of a (hypothetical) exhaustible resource. This approach ignores issues associated with diversity of preferences and beliefs, but otherwise provides a well-defined norm for the measurement of distortions in the market allocation of exploration investment.

The choice of the appropriate utility function to represent social preferences is a traditionally vexing problem (see Arrow, 1963, for a discussion of the impossibility of defining democratic social utility functions). However, we can sacrifice some generality and accept the approach of conventional cost–benefit analysis (and accept its criticisms as well). The objective in cost–benefit analysis is to maximize consumer plus producer surplus. For extraction of a resource at rate $q(t)$, the net surplus at time t can be written as

$$u[q(t),t] - c[q(t),S(t),t] \qquad (1)$$

In Eq. (1), $c[q(t),S(t),t]$ is the cost of extraction at time t when the remaining stock is $S(t)$. Whenever possible we will simplify (and sometimes ignore completely) this cost function. The first term in Eq. (1) is the total consumer benefit at time t. This is the total dollar amount a consumer would be willing to spend for $q(t)$ and is by definition

$$u[q(t),t] = \int_0^{q(t)} P(x,t)\, dx \qquad (2)$$

where $P(x,t)$ is the inverse demand function for x.

As a further simplification (and a standard one in cost–benefit analysis), we will assume that Eq. (1) can be written in present-value dollars as

$$e^{-rt}\{u[q(t)] - c[q(t),S(t),t]\} \qquad (3)$$

where r is the rate of interest including adjustment for inflation. Moreover, when we deal with the impacts of uncertainty, we shall assume that consumers obey the Von Neumann–Morgenstern axioms for the logical consistency of expected utility or expected net consumer surplus maximization (see Savage, 1954, for an axiomatic discussion of decision making under uncertainty and the implications of different objective functions).

Before we begin analysis of the planning problem, it is worth emphasizing that the value of information about size and extraction cost depends not only on geologic uncertainty, but also on the structure of demand for the resource. Thus, in general terms, demand elasticity and rates of time preference enter into the value of size information. As a specific example, air quality standards have increased the demand for low sulfur fuels and have also increased the value of information about coal and petroleum deposits with a low sulfur content.

B. The Value of Information about the Size of a Resource Stock

1. Uncertainty and Efficient Rates of Resource Depletion. One function of exploration is to provide information about the total resource stock in order to improve the allocation of the resource over time. Without knowledge of the actual total stock, extraction may be too rapid, leaving future generations with too little of the resource, or it may be too conservation minded. In this section, we show that the value derived from extracting a stock whose size is uncertain is strictly less than the value of the stock when information about its size is made available. This provides a sound basis for placing a positive social value on exploration information relating to the size distribution of total reserves.

Because little is gained in the way of policy conclusions by mathematical generality, in this section we consider a simple parameterization of uncertainty (a more detailed analysis of the value of exploration information is in Gilbert, 1979a). Suppose the total resource endowment is unknown, but it is agreed that the size of the endowment can take on only two possible values, which we denote by S_1 and S_2, where $S_2 > S_1$. Furthermore, assume all agree that the probability the endowment is S_2 is π, and the probability of S_1 is $(1 - \pi)$.

The expected value of the stock is $\bar{S} = (1 - \pi)S_1 + \pi S_2$. Consider the maximum social value from extraction of $\bar{S}$. If we neglect extraction costs, this is

$$V(\bar{S}) = \max_{q_t} \int_0^\infty u(q_t)\, e^{-rt}\, dt \qquad (4)$$

subject to $\int_0^\infty q_t\, dt \le \bar{S}$.

Since any extraction program must use up an amount S_1 in finite time, $V(\bar{S})$ can be written as

$$V(\bar{S}) = \max_{q_t,T} \left[\int_0^T u(q_t)e^{-rt}\,dt \right] + \max_{q_t} \left[\int_T^\infty u(q_t)e^{-rt}\,dt \right] \qquad (5)$$

where $\int_0^T q_t\,dt = S_1$ and $\int_T^\infty q_t\,dt \leq \pi(S_2 - S_1)$.

A change in the variable of integration in the second term of Eq. (5) gives $e^{-rT}\,V[\pi(S_2 - S_1)]$, while the first term can be written in abbreviated notation as $V(S_1,T)$, which is the maximum value from depleting S_1 over a time horizon of T. Thus Eq. (5) is equivalent to

$$V(\bar{S}) = \max_T \{V(S_1,T) + e^{-rT}\,V[\pi(S_2 - S_1)]\} \qquad (6)$$

Now consider the problem of depleting the uncertain stock. The size of the stock is *at least* S_1, and may be S_2 with probability π. We can plan on depleting a stock of size S_1 with certainty over some time period, and then we will find out that [with probability $(1 - \pi)$] none remains, or with probability π the remaining stock is $S_2 - S_1$. If $V(\tilde{S})$ denotes the maximum benefit from the uncertain stock, this can be written in a manner paralleling the development of Eq. (6) as

$$V(\tilde{S}) = \max_T \{V(S_1,T) + e^{-rT}[(1 - \pi)V(0) + \pi V(S_2 - S_1)]\} \qquad (7)$$

If we assume $V(0) = 0$, then[3]

$$V(\tilde{S}) = \max_T [V(S_1,T) + e^{-rT}\pi V(S_2 - S_1)] \qquad (8)$$

If $u(q)$ is a concave function, then $V(S)$ is concave in S. In that case, $V[\pi(S_2 - S_1)] > \pi V(S_2 - S_1)$. Thus the right-hand side of Eq. (6) must exceed the right-hand side of Eq. (8), or $V(\bar{S}) > V(\tilde{S})$. This implies that there is a cost to society imposed by the stock uncertainty. The uncertain stock is of expected size $\tilde{S}$, however there is a cost in "not knowing" whether the size of the stock is high or low before extraction begins. It is shown in Gilbert (1979a) and Loury (1976) that uncertainty lowers the initial extraction rate relative to the rate that is optimal for the mean value $\bar{S}$.

What this slower initial rate does, in effect, is leave future generations with more of the resource if $\tilde{S} = S_2$ in order to compensate them for the risk that they will be left with little or nothing if $\tilde{S} = S_1$, relative to, say, an optimal program for the mean endowment $\bar{S}$.

2. The Optimal Timing of Exploration when the Size of the Stock is Unknown. The discounted cost of exploration information is minimized by investing in exploration at a time as close as possible to the anticipated date of extraction, but the cost brought about by extraction under uncertainty implies that information about the size of the resource has positive social value. This is important, because if uncertainty did not impose a cost, there would be no gain from advancing the date of exploration or from holding reserves to hedge against the risk of unanticipated exhaustion of the resource stock.

Consider again the case where the resource endowment can only take on two possible values, S_1 or S_2, and assume that we already know of the existence of a stock of size S_1. These are known or proven reserves.[4] There may or may not exist another reserve of the resource; however, if it exists, we know it would be of size $S_2 - S_1$. For example, seismic data might give a good idea of the size of a structural trap, but the trap need not contain oil. Of course in practice there are many more sources of uncertainty, but this example allows considerable simplicity without losing the essence of the timing decision.

Now suppose that once a reserve has been proven, its extraction cost is negligible and assume it is possible to prove the existence of a deposit by sinking a well at cost A. Thus an investment of amount A is sufficient to determine whether the actual resource endowment is S_1 or S_2. This is an extreme instance where exploration provides perfect information about the size of the resource stock. Of course this is an abstraction, and more generally, exploration provides information that changes the prior subjective probability distribution on the resource endowment. Usually better information costs more and perfect information may be unattainable. Still, the problem posed here is a useful beginning for analysis of the optimal timing of exploration investment. More sophisticated analysis, particularly analysis based on estimated exploration costs and estimated stock probability distributions, would be worthwhile.

Although delaying exploration until proved reserves (S_1) are exhausted minimizes exploration costs, we show below that this strategy does not in general maximize the social benefits from the resource stock. In particular, let $u(q)$ be the surplus from consumption of the resource at rate q. If

$$\lim_{q \to 0} u'(q) = \infty,^5 \tag{9}$$

and if exploration at any time is desirable, then exploration should occur before known reserves are exhausted.

To prove this proposition, assume known reserves are exhausted at time T. Exploration would be desirable if expected benefits exceed the cost or if

$$\pi V(S_2 - S_1) > A \tag{10}$$

Assume Eq. (10) holds and exploration is advanced slightly to time $T' = T - \delta$. The cost of this change is $r\delta A$, the loss of interest from accelerating the exploration investment.

Suppose the extraction policy up to time T' is unchanged by the advance in the exploration date. Then at time T', there would be approximately $\delta\bar{q}_T$ remaining in the proved reserves, where $\bar{q}_t$ is the rate of extraction from proved reserves at time t. If a new deposit is found, the total available stock would be $(S_2 - S_1 + \delta\bar{q}_T)$. If no new deposit is found, the remaining stock is just $\delta\bar{q}_T$, the amount left in proved reserves. The expected value of the stock conditional on early exploration is

$$\pi V(S_2 - S_1 + \delta\bar{q}_T) + (1 - \pi)V(\delta\bar{q}_T) \tag{11}$$

The timing of events from the change in the exploration date is illustrated in Figures 1A and B. The small amount $\delta\bar{q}_T$ becomes a new stock of proved reserves that can be used in case exploration is not successful. The net benefit from the change in the exploration date is

$$W(\delta) = [\pi V(S_2 - S_1 + \delta\bar{q}_T) + (1 - \pi)V(\delta\bar{q}_T)]e^{r\delta} \tag{12}$$
$$- \delta u(\bar{q}_T) - \pi V(S_2 - S_1) - r\delta A$$

The first term is the value of the new information produced, the second represents the value of the stock that would have been extracted under uncertainty, the third is the value of exploration at the original date, and the last is the increase in cost from the change. To first order in δ, Eq. (12) is

$$W(\delta) = [\pi V'(S_2 - S_1)\bar{q}_T + (1 - \pi)V'(\delta\bar{q}_T)\bar{q}_T \tag{13}$$
$$+ r\pi V(S_2 - S_1) - u(\bar{q}_T) - rA]\delta$$

If $\lim_{q\to 0} u'(q) = \infty$, then $\lim_{\delta\to 0} V'(\delta\bar{q}_r) = \infty$. Since $\bar{q}_T$ is finite, for sufficiently small δ the value of advancing exploration must be positive.

Note that the condition $A < \pi V(S_2 - S_1)$ is necessary for exploration to be profitable at the date when known reserves are exhausted. However, this condition is not necessary for exploration to be socially profitable, since advancing the date of exploration increases its value. This has important policy implications, which we discuss in Section III.

In general, any change in the date of exploration should be anticipated and would lead to a revision in the rate of extraction prior to exploration. It is not difficult to show that this is a second-order effect that can be ignored when looking at marginal changes in the date of exploration.[6]

The assumption that exploration provides perfect information about the existence of additional reserves is not crucial to the result. The proposition can be generalized easily to show that if the resource is sufficiently valuable on the margin, it is socially profitable to maintain a stock of known reserves at all times.[7] Exploration need not provide

Figure 1. Timing of Exploration Date. (A) Exploration at T.
(B) Exploration at T'

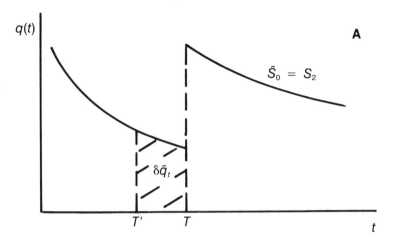

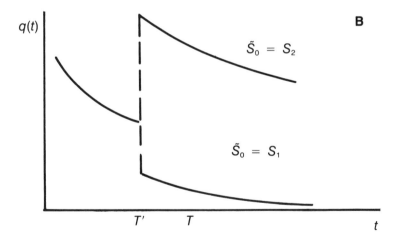

perfect information about the resource base; it need only identify a stock of known reserves. Exactly how much exploration is enough and when it should take place depend on the cost of exploration and extraction, the uncertainty in remaining resource stock, and the demand for the resource.

While we have shown that exploration should take place before proved reserves are exhausted, we have not determined the optimal timing of exploration. To do this, suppose exploration is planned at time T. The social value of the stock when exploration occurs at T is

$$W(T) = \max_{S} \{V(S,T) + e^{-rT}[\pi V(S_2 - S)$$

$$+ (1 - \pi)V(S_1 - S) - A]\} \quad (14)$$

If $V'(0)$ is sufficiently large, the optimal S in Eq. (14) will not exceed S_1 when T is chosen optimally. Let $S(T)$ be the solution to Eq. (14). At $S(T)$

$$\frac{d}{dS}V[S(T),T] = e^{-rT}\left\{\pi\frac{d}{dS}V[S_2 - S(T)]\right.$$

$$\left. + (1 - \pi)\frac{d}{dS}V[S_1 - S(T)]\right\} = 0 \quad (15)$$

This implies

$$P(T) = \pi P_2(T) + (1 - \pi)P_1(T)$$

where $P(T)$ is the spot price of the resource at time T, $P_2(T)$ is the spot price at T conditional on the discovery that $\tilde{S}_0 = S_2$ and $P_1(T)$ is the spot price conditional on $\tilde{S}_0 = S_1$. In other words, the current resource price immediately before exploration occurs must equal the expected price conditional on exploration.

An increase in T increases the left-hand side of Eq. (15) and decreases the right-hand side. Since the converse is true for an increase in S, it follows that $S(T)$ is an increasing function of T. At the optimal exploration date $d/dt\ W(T) = 0$, or

$$\frac{d}{dt}V[S(T),T] = re^{-rT}\{\pi V[S_2 - S(T)] + (1 - \pi)V[S_1 - S(T)] - A\} \quad (16)$$

The optimal exploration date maximizes a certainty equivalent stock

$$\tilde{S}(T) = S(T) + V^{-1}\{\pi V[S_2 - S(T)] + (1 - \pi)V[S_1 - S(T)] - A\} \quad (17)$$

This follows from the definition of $\max_T W(T)$, since

$$V[\tilde{S}(T)] = \max_{T} (V[S(T)] + e^{-rT}\{\pi V[S_2 - S(T)]$$

$$+ (1 + \pi)V[S_1 - S(T)] - A\}) = \max_{T} W(T)$$

It is not difficult to see that an increase in the cost of exploration delays the optimal exploration date. An increase in A increases $S(T)$ for any T. Since $S(T)$ is an increasing function of T, the optimal exploration date also increases.

C. Exploration and the Search for Low Cost Deposits

If the location and extraction costs of deposits of a natural resource were known with certainty, an efficient depletion policy would call for extraction in order of increasing costs. Herfindahl (1967) and Nordhaus (1973) discuss efficient extraction programs when marginal costs are constant, and Weitzman (1976) analyzes depletion with arbitrary (deterministic) cost functions. This section summarizes results in Gilbert (1979b), which extends the theory to the case of constant, but uncertain, costs of extraction.

Let $\{CE_j\}$, $j = 1, \ldots, n$, denote marginal extraction costs, assumed constant, with $CE_1 < CE_2 < \ldots < CE_n$. Each location, or "tract," is characterized by a joint probability distribution on the size and extraction cost of the deposit at that location. Within a "basin," the probability distribution is assumed identical for all tracts. There are m basins, indexed $i = 1, \ldots, m$.

In this section we impose the following conditions

1. Each deposit with extraction cost CE_j is a negligible proportion of the total amount of the resource with extraction cost CE_j in basin i.
2. There is no intermediate technology for the production of information about the characteristics of tracts. Exploration is simply the decision to drill in an area where the return at each location is uncertain.

If $\bar{S}_k^i$ is the expected size of deposits in basin i with extraction cost CE_k, then

$$w_k^i = \frac{\bar{S}_k^i}{\sum_{j=1}^{n} \bar{S}_j^i} \tag{18}$$

is the expected proportion of discoveries with extraction cost CE_k in basin i. Of course, the expected deposit sizes and hence the proportions w_k^i may change as deposits are discovered.[8] It is shown in Gilbert (1979b) that this complication does not change the efficient strategy if depletion only increases extraction costs.

Let $d(t)$ be the total rate of discovery of the resource, aggregated over all extraction costs. Suppose for now that the marginal discovery cost in basin i, CD^i, is constant. Not all deposits that are discovered need be extracted. It is easy to see that in general there may be a cutoff grade, CE_k, such that extraction from deposits with $CE_j > CE_k$ should be postponed (perhaps indefinitely). The efficient cutoff grade minimizes the total marginal cost of exploration and extraction in a basin. If

$$W^i(k) = \sum_{j=1}^{k} w_j^i$$

the total cost is

$$C^i(CE_k) = \frac{1}{W^i(k)}\left[CD^i + \sum_{j=1}^{k} CE_j w_j^i \right] \tag{19}$$

Differentiating Eq. (19) with respect to k gives the result that the efficient cutoff grade in basin i is the largest CE_k^i for which

$$CD^i \geq \sum_{j=1}^{k} (CE_k^i - CE_j)w_j^i \tag{20}$$

Equation (20) implies that the expected savings in extraction cost from the search for deposits better than CE_k^i are less than or equal to the cost of search. If a deposit with $CE_j < CE_k^i$ is discovered, the expected saving from continued search is less than the cost of search and the deposit should be extracted. Conversely, for $CE_j > CE_k^i$, there is a positive net benefit from continued search and extraction from the deposit should be postponed.

Equation (20) parallels the result obtained in the theory of consumer search with random price offers (see Rothschild, 1974). The cutoff grade, CE_k^i, may be interpreted as a reservation or acceptance cost. Substitution of Eq. (20) in Eq. (19), with equality assumed in Eq. (20), shows that

$$C^i(CE_k^i) = CE_k^i \tag{21}$$

One should be indifferent between search in basin i and extraction from a deposit with known extraction cost CE_k^i, where CE_k^i is the solution to Eq. (20).

Of course, it is possible that

$$CD^i > \sum_{j=1}^{n} (CE_n - CE_j)w_j^i$$

in which case the cost of search in the ith basin exceeds the expected cost savings from exploration. All deposits would be extracted upon discovery and there would be no accumulation of deposits for possible extraction at future times. The effective production cost in the ith basin would then be

$$CD^i + \sum_{j=1}^{n} CE_j w_j^i = CD^i + \langle CE \rangle^i \tag{22}$$

The analysis indicates that exploration should continue as long as the cost of discovering and extracting new deposits is less than the cost of extracting known deposits. The notion of maintaining an inventory to keep costs down does not necessarily arise.

In the process of exploration, extraction from some deposits that are discovered may be postponed. These deposits add to the stock of identified reserves.

When stocks of a particular quality are exhausted, effective production costs increase. At this point, the efficient production choice may call for exploration and extraction in a different basin or extraction from the stock of identified reserves. It is clear, then, that the efficient depletion policy may entail the recurrence of intervals of search and extraction from identified reserves, without any regular pattern. The sequence depends on the distribution of exploration and extraction costs in different basins.

It should be noted that the search strategy described in this section relates only to the efficient *sequence* of extraction from different deposits. The appropriate *rate* of resource extraction depends on factors including estimates of the total resource stock.

The preceding results depend on the assumption that exploration is only a means of search and does not change subjective estimates of the size or cost distribution of reserves in a particular basin. The value of exploration in producing information about the size of the stock (or the size of reserves with different extraction costs) has already been discussed. The following example illustrates that information about the cost of extraction from reserves may be of value in determining the efficient current rate of resource utilization in much the same way as information about the total size of the resource stock.

Assume that the earth's petroleum resources are located in two basins. Deposits in the first basin have zero extraction cost, and we shall assume that the location of these deposits and the total amount of oil they contain are known. The second basin contains a known amount of oil but the extraction cost of this oil is uncertain. If the elasticity of demand for the resource is nonzero, the efficient rate of extraction from basin 1 would depend on the cost of extracting oil from basin 2. In other words, the rate of depletion of low cost oil should depend on the cost of producing oil from bituminous shales. Because deposits of oil shale are plentiful, information that these resources could (or could not) be extracted at, say $30 per barrel would influence the efficient rate of extraction from oil fields and in general, the value of this information would be positive.

D. The Socially Optimal Pattern of Exploration

In the preceding section we showed that those tracts with the lowest total of expected discovery plus extraction costs should be explored first. When all tracts in the same basin have the same expected costs, the pattern of drilling within a basin is of no consequence. However, success or failure at any one tract often gives information about the probability of success at neighboring tracts, and the efficient pattern of drilling should exploit their interdependence.

Suppose a basin is subdivided into tracts as in Figure 2. With no information, all tracts are equally favorable for drilling, however those along the edges are of less value in planning future drilling decisions than those toward the center. The center tract (25) yields external information benefits that are at least as great as those derived from drilling at any other location. An efficient pattern of drilling would start at the center. If this were a failure, drilling should proceed to another tract that yields significant information benefits, such as number 9.

If exploration at tract 25 is successful, selection of the next site for drilling should consider both the likelihood of discovery and the information benefits from success or failure.[9] The decision is how far to "step out" the next well or mine shaft. Consider the choice of drilling

Figure 2. Subdivision of Basin into Tracts.

1	2	3	4	5	6	7
8	9	10	11	12	13	14
15	16	17	18	19	20	21
22	23	24	25	26	27	28
29	30	31	32	33	34	35
36	37	38	39	40	41	42
43	44	45	46	47	48	49

at 26 or 27. If exploration at 27 is successful, this might almost guarantee success at 26. The reduced probability of success at tract 27, relative to 26, could be offset by the information gained about tract 26. While the design of exploration strategies is best left to geologists and engineers, we show in Section III that decentralized exploration may offer opportunities to exploit information produced by others, and this may lead to an inefficient pattern of exploration.

E. A Digression on the Meaning and Measurement of Reserves

A number of terms are used in reference to the distribution of exhaustible natural resources. The U.S. Geological Survey (USGS) defines *reserves* as "economically recoverable material in identified deposits," and applies the term *resources* to include "deposits not yet discovered as well as identified deposits that cannot be recovered now."[10] The categories of reserves and resources are further divided to indicate extraction cost and the degree of uncertainty in the estimates. The end result of the classification scheme, as presented in the National Academy of Sciences report on *Mineral Resources and the Environment* is shown in Figure 3.

Figure 3.   Classification Scheme for Natural Reserves and Resources

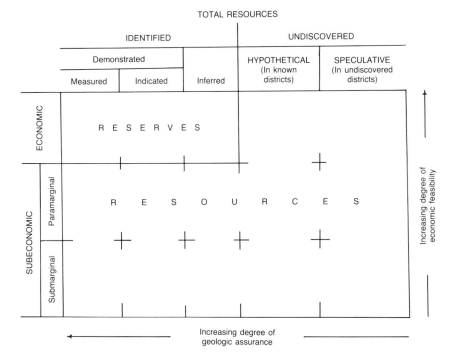

The classification scheme shown in Figure 3 represents a major and only recent advance in the characterization of resource endowments, but it is not without objection. The system partitions resource estimates according to "economic" and "subeconomic," "identified" and "undiscovered." However, the appropriate description of the resource endowment is the joint probability distribution of the total amount of the resource that can be extracted at a given cost. There are obvious difficulties in estimating and agreeing on a joint probability distribution function. However, this is not an impossible task, and the distribution function could be represented as in Figure 4. The vertical axis is total amount of the resource S, and the horizontal axis is extraction cost C. The figure graphs the total amount recoverable at a cost less than or equal to C. Each curve corresponds to a confidence level, with 1.0 representing absolute certainty. The level .95 is suggested for highly probable and .50 for speculative.

Figure 4. Distribution Function of Total Amount of Resource That Can Be Extracted at a Given Cost

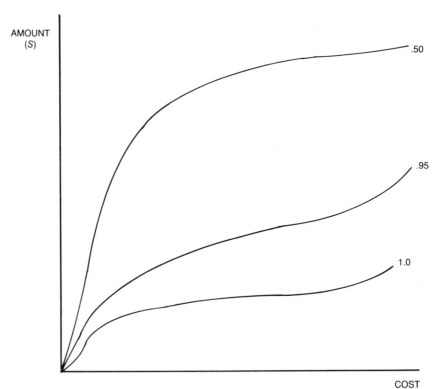

The advantage of Figure 4 over Figure 3 is that it avoids partitioning continuous parameters into discrete classes. There is and should be a fuzzy distinction between economic and subeconomic resources, but it is important to know estimates of the costs of deposits that are currently not exploited. This should be clear from the discussion of the efficient utilization of deposits that differ in cost. Some deposits that are discovered are postponed for later use, but the appropriate utilization of "economic" deposits depends on the distribution of "subeconomic" deposits.

A widely used resource statistic is the amount of "proved" or "measured" reserves, although this is probably more the result of the press than the USGS. The number is often given in years of supply at current consumption rates, which may suggest to some that proved reserves indicate the remaining stock of an exhaustible resource. There is no basis for this inference. We have argued that a stock of proved reserves often should be maintained, but the amount depends on factors such as the degree of uncertainty in the total resource stock, exploration costs, and demand. We argue in Section III that the amount of proved reserves actually maintained by a market economy is not generally equal to the socially optimal amount. Proved reserves generated by industry are usually the result of finding large deposits that take years to produce. They relate no more to the total recoverable stock than the number of automobiles at a manufacturer's plant relates to the total production capacity of the plant.

III. MARKET INCENTIVES FOR RESOURCE EXPLORATION

A. *Introduction*

An assessment of the net effect of market incentives on the level, timing, and pattern of exploration requires untangling a web of contrasting incentives, confounded by distortionary fiscal and regulatory policies. We postpone discussion of the direct effects of government intervention until the next section, and accept the criticism that some indirect effects of intervention may pass unnoticed.

There are several reasons why markets may fail to provide the signals necessary to achieve an efficient allocation of exploration investment. The returns from an exploration program are uncertain, and resource prospecting may be a risky activity although the risk to society from a single dry hole is negligible. We argue in Section III,B that in fact the risk in exploration is not a major source of market failure because adequate opportunities for diversification are available.

While risk may not be an important source of market failure, there are important externalities associated with the production of exploration information. Exploration information is to some extent a public good, and the consequences of this on the timing and pattern of exploration are discussed in Section III,C.

The public good aspect of information can bias the market allocation of exploration and cause delays in exploration expenditures if firms wait for potentially valuable information produced by others. A contrasting bias may result if exploration information can be kept private for use in speculation on the value of land and other assets. In Section III,D we show that exploration may be the source of monopoly profits that exceed the social value of the information produced. This is a particularly important issue in the design of government leasing programs.

Section III,E addresses distortions introduced by differences in the private and social rate of time discount. Of course to the extent that there is an important difference, this affects all investment decisions and not only the market allocation of resource exploration.

Surprisingly, the contrasting sources of market failure nonetheless allow some conclusions to be made concerning the general extent of distortions in the level, timing, and pattern of exploration, which are summarized in Section III,F. The conclusions lack the specificity that can only be supplied by modeling the particular effects of market failure in actual extractive resource industries; however, some qualitative judgements are possible.

B. Risk

From a societal perspective, the risk in resource exploration is the uncertainty in total discoveries. Any one well may be a failure, but with many thousands of wells, the total risk should be small if the returns from each well are uncorrelated. An analogy with farming is useful. A seed may or may not sprout, but when thousands of seeds are planted, the total yield depends on the average probability of germination and on uncertainties such as the weather and insect damage. Just as the farmer's return does not depend on whether any one particular seed sprouts, the social return from exploration does not depend on any one well (but does depend on technical progress and other factors common to all wells).

However, the costs of drilling wells and sinking mineshafts can be very high and the probability that any one venture is successful may be low. The private risk of failure can be significant even if the social risk is negligible, and market-determined investment in exploration activity responds to the private risk. Ramsey (1979) employs the "probability of ruin" concept to analyze in detail the effects of risk on the amount of exploration activity and on the choice of exploration ventures by firms. His analysis shows how exploration investment and the structure of the exploration industry are simultaneously determined conditional on the nature of private exploration risk. In general, investors in risky enterprises demand a premium to compensate for the uncertainty in returns, which ultimately results in higher prices for those goods and services where risk is significant. In the past, proponents of government subsidies for private exploration, such as accelerated depreciation schedules, have argued that such subsidies are necessary to compensate for the risks involved in mineral exploration.

Arguments to subsidize resource exploration on account of its risk are questionable in two respects. First, to the extent that exploration is a risky activity, the risk is a real cost that must be borne by investors. While measures to reduce risk may be desirable, subsidization of the cost of risk is no more justified on efficiency grounds than subsidization of any other costly activity in the economy.[11]

The second objection to exploration subsidies is the more basic question of whether the private risk in resource exploration is in fact significant relative to the private risk in other sectors of the economy. Statistics of drilling for hydrocarbons in new fields indicate that over the past decade only approximately one well in ten drilled in the U.S. has been classified a commercial success. The average cost per well over this period has averaged $50,000 to $100,000, and in specific cases, costs have reached more than an order of magnitude higher. The thought of spending $100,000 with only a one-in-ten probability of success does seem to be a risky prospect. Indeed, there is a popular image of the independent oil prospector (the "wildcatter") as a person who enjoys taking risks.[12]

In spite of these spectacular figures, it is likely that the risk in resource exploration is not particularly great relative to the risk present in other sectors of the economy. The reason is that exploration is a diversifiable risk. It is not the return from any single venture that determines the financial risk but rather the total return from a portfolio of ventures. A typical firm will drill several wells in a given year. Provided the manager of that firm does not make systematic errors in assessing the costs and prospective returns from drilling, then the disappointments at some locations should be at least partially offset by success at other locations.

The opportunities for diversification are not limited to a company's own drilling activities. Oil prospectors typically issue shares in their drilling projects and buy shares in other projects, thereby spreading the risk per dollar over a larger number of projects. The joint arrangements of drilling ventures can take on many forms that effect a better allocation of risk bearing.[13]

Of course, the cost of drilling programs on the Outer Continental Shelf and the North Slope of Alaska may run into many millions of dollars, and even with a large number of shareholders the risk per investor may not be insignificant. However, the assets of the companies engaged in these drilling programs are quite large, and the risk of the very ambitious ventures can be balanced by returns from more modest programs.

The potential for diversifying against geologic risk need not extend to the uncertain market and regulatory determinants of the private returns to exploration. Capital markets afford some diversification possibilities, but it is difficult to hedge against shifts in world prices, aggregate demand, and changes in fiscal policies. For the exploration firm with a large portfolio of prospects, the uncertainties of the market and government likely present the greatest sources of risk.

C. Public Good Externalities in Exploration

1. Information as a Public Good. An important source of potential market failure is the allocation of public goods. A pure public good is not materially affected by use. Its value to any one consumer is not diminished by the consumption of others. Information, radio signals, national defense, and parks are examples of public goods. The congestion and abuse of many city parks sadly confirms that these are not pure public goods, but information is at least close to such an ideal.[14]

The social value of a public good is the sum of its values to each consumer. The social value of an exploratory well on a particular tract is not just its value to the owner of the mineral rights for that tract; the social value includes the benefits of that well to those who own neighboring tracts. Suppose the exploratory well provides information that the total resource stock is larger (smaller) than previously anticipated. This would result in a decrease (increase) in the resource price as producers and consumers change their production and consumption decisions to conform to the new information. The benefits of the well are diffuse, and whereas the value of the information produced by one well may be small for one individual, the aggregate value of the information from several wells is significant.

The possibilities for market compensation for the supply of a public good depend on whether persons can be excluded from the use of the good. Exploration information is "partially" excludable. It is impossible to conceal a major discovery for any reasonable period of time, and in this sense exploration information is not excludable. However, much of the information about the distribution of mineral deposits is the result of data analysis by skilled geologists and engineers. In many cases, the particular experiences, capabilities, and intuition of the technical staff of a prospecting firm lend an idiosyncratic element to the interpretation of a collection of data. With the same statistical information prospectors may arrive at different posterior estimates of the returns from exploration at different locations. There are many stories of successful exploration by firms that persisted in drilling in areas that others had long abandoned.[15] The fact that the statistical evidence is available to all does not preclude the generation of private information by individual firms. Disclosure of geologic data accumulated by a firm may be of little value to competitors who do not have access to the human capital of the firm.

When the returns from exploration of tracts owned by different firms are correlated and exploration information can be held secret, exploration activities may be redundant. This cost can be offset by the possible benefits derived from independent research, but there is no assurance that the gains from diversity are worth the added cost.

The inability to maintain secrecy in the results of an exploration program may lead to market failure of a different sort. The expectation that competitors may provide valuable information free of charge may encourage firms to postpone exploration in those areas where information from others may be forthcoming. Because firms do not receive compensation for the external information benefits they generate, there may be too little investment in exploration.

The remainder of this section on public good externalities of exploration is divided into two parts. The first deals with the local effects of informational externalities in the exploration of particular areas. The second part deals with information about the total resource stock and the transmission of the information via changes in market prices.

2. Local Information Externalities. If the returns from drilling at locations owned by different firms are not independent, exploration by any one firm confers external benefits on other firms. We call these external benefits "local" to differentiate them from the externality discussed in the next section. The term local should not be taken literally because the returns from drilling at contiguous tracts with very dissimilar geological characteristics may be perceived as independent, whereas the converse may be true for similar structures that are very far apart. In other words, tracts with a high correlation in the value of discoveries are considered "close."

This interdependence among tracts owned by different firms may distort both the timing and the pattern of exploration activity. The distortions depend on the correlation between locations and the extent to which exploration information can be kept secret. We give a general characterization of the inefficiency below, and then discuss specific cases.

Suppose for the sake of argument that there are only two tracts, owned by different firms. Let $V_i(E_i)$ be the expected value of the ith tract given an exploration investment of E_i. If the tracts were explored jointly, an efficient exploration strategy would maximize

$$R_{total} = \mathscr{E}\{V_1(E_1) + V_2(E_2)|I\} - (E_1 + E_2) \qquad (23)$$

The expectation is conditional on I, which summarizes the prior state of knowledge of both firms.

If the tracts were explored independently, each firm would maximize profits

$$R_i = \mathscr{E}\{V_i(E_i)|I_i\} - E_i \qquad (24)$$

Here I_i is the state of knowledge of the ith firm at the time of the exploration decision.

Case 1. Private Information. Suppose the results of exploration programs were not publicly available, perhaps due to the cost of processing the information, or because the firm intends to use its information for speculative purposes. Each firm knows nothing of the results of the other firm's activity. Both firms invest in exploration as if the tracts were independent, and choose

$$\max_{E_i} V_i(E_i) - E_i \qquad (25)$$

If the returns from drilling the two tracts are correlated, this could imply redundant investment in exploration because the firms are not aware of the interdependence between their discoveries. It is also possible that neither firm would find exploration profitable when joint exploration would be profitable. If the tracts are perfectly correlated, only one tract need be explored to determine the expected value of both.

For a more specific example, suppose that exploration is the decision to drill a well at cost E. If successful, the well discovers a pool of oil of value V, and nothing otherwise. With no information, the probability of discovery at either tract is π. If exploration at one tract is successful, the conditional probability of success at the other tract is $\pi_S > \pi$, and if exploration is a failure, the conditional probability is $\pi_F < \pi$. A joint exploration strategy would be sequential with expected value (ignoring time discounting) of

$$R_{\text{total}} = (\pi V - E) + \pi\{\pi_S V - E\} + (1 - \pi) \max\{\pi_F V - E, 0\} \quad (26)$$

The expected value of independent exploration at each tract is just

$$R_i = \pi V - E \quad (27)$$

Since $\pi_S > \pi$, it is clearly possible that $R_i < 0$, but

$$R_{\text{total}} = (1 + \pi)R_i + \pi(\pi_S - \pi)V > 0 \quad (28)$$

Case 2. Public Information. Now let us reverse our assumption and suppose that the results of all exploration activities fall in the public domain. In this case, the state of knowledge for both firms is the same as if exploration were performed jointly. However, the distribution of benefits from exploration are not necessarily shared equally.

Consider the example discussed earlier. The first firm to explore makes an expected profit of $\pi V - E$. The second firm explores conditional on the results at the first tract and makes an expected profit of

$$R_2 = \pi(\pi_S V - E) + (1 - \pi) \max(\pi_F V - E, 0) \quad (29)$$

If the two tracts have the same conditional probability distribution, then

$$\pi = \pi_S \pi + \pi_F(1 - \pi)^{16} \quad (30)$$

There is no value in the second firm waiting for the results at the first tract if $\pi_F - E > 0$, since in that case $R_2 = R_1 = \pi V - E$. However, if $\pi_F - E < 0$, substitution of (30) in (29) confirms that $R_2 > R_1$ and the second firm benefits from the information produced by the exploration activities of the first firm.

a. Distortions in the timing of exploration. The externality introduced by the correlation between tracts may result in market failure in both cases of information exclusion and free access to information. Consider the optimal time at which the two tracts should be explored. Assume that the size of the deposit, if it exists, is small and extraction costs are negligible, so that $V(t)$, the value of a deposit at time t conditional on successful exploration is just $P_t S$, where P_t is the market price at time t and S is the size of the deposit. If a sequential exploration strategy can be carried out in a single time period, the tracts should be explored at time t if

$$\pi(1 + \pi_S)V(t) - (1 + \pi)E$$
$$> \frac{1}{1 + r}\{\pi(1 + \pi_S)V(t + 1) - (1 + \pi)E\} \quad (31)$$

assuming

$$\pi_F V(t) - E < 0$$

This is equivalent to

$$\frac{P_{t+1} - P_t}{P_t - \dfrac{(1 + \pi)E}{\pi(1 + \pi_S)S}} < r \qquad (32)$$

If information is not made publicly available, the two tracts would be explored at time t if

$$\pi V(t) - E > \frac{1}{1 + r}\{\pi V(t + 1) - E\} \qquad (33)$$

or

$$\frac{P_{t+1} - P_t}{P_t - \dfrac{E}{\pi S}} < r \qquad (34)$$

Since $(1 + \pi)/(1 + \pi_S) < 1$, the market price may be increasing over time at a rate that satisfies the inequality in (32) but not in (34). In that case, exploration will be postponed relative to the socially optimal date. The effect of information exclusion is to raise the cost of exploration relative to the optimal strategy that utilizes the information about one tract in the exploration of the other. In a market economy, tracts with expected total marginal costs that are less than $E/\pi S$ will be explored and extracted first. Since the social cost of the two tracts is less than $E/\pi S$, the market allocation may be inefficient. However, these results depend critically on the *subsequent* uses of the information gained in the process of exploration. By exploring one tract, a firm may obtain information that can be used to speculate on other tracts. This opportunity, which is the subject of Section IV,D, can be a strong incentive to accelerate exploration. The conclusion that information exclusion delays exploration by raising costs is true if the information has no speculative value, but it is not true in general.

A similar result may occur when information is made public, only for a different reason. The possibility that useful information may become available without charge reduces the expected cost of waiting. Suppose a firm on one of the tracts expects that with probability α the other tract will be explored and the outcome will be public knowledge. With probability $1 - \alpha$ the other tract will not be explored, in which event the firm will explore its own tract with no additional information.[17,18] Exploration at time t is preferred to waiting for possible additional information if

$$\pi V(t) - E > \frac{1}{1 + r} \{\alpha\pi[\pi_s V(t + 1)$$

$$- E] + (1 - \alpha)[\pi V(t + 1) - E]\} \quad (35)$$

which is equivalent to

$$\frac{P_{t+1} - P_t}{P_t - \dfrac{E}{\pi S}} - \alpha\left[\frac{1 - \pi}{\pi}\right]\left[\frac{\pi_r P_{t+1} - (E/\pi S)}{P_t - E/\pi S}\right] < r \quad (36)$$

Since $\pi_r P_{t+1} - (E/\pi S) < 0$ (otherwise, the information from the neighboring tract is irrelevant), the left-hand side of Eq. (36) is strictly greater than

$$\frac{P_{t+1} - P_t}{P_t - (E/\pi S)}$$

The incentive to delay exploration when information is public exceeds the incentive to delay exploration when information is private, provided the information gained may change the decision to explore. In this sense, public information is worse than exclusive information. However, in the latter case there may be redundant exploration activities that would not occur when information is public.

    b. Distortions in the pattern of exploration. The external effects of exploration information will influence the choice of which locations would be explored in a market economy. This is related to the bias in the timing of exploration. The distortions in the timing and pattern of exploration occur because the market costs of exploration and extraction at different locations do not equal their social costs. Postponement of exploration may imply that exploration at some locations is relatively more expensive than at others, and hence the pattern of exploration may change.

    If information is public, there may be a tendency to postpone drilling in areas where other firms are conducting exploration activities. If information that points to success becomes available, there may be a rush of drilling in the neighborhood affected by the information. This is seriously aggrevated by the common-pool problem in the extraction of fugacious resources such as oil and natural gas. Neighboring landowners may help themselves to the bounty of the discovery. This was a serious problem until unitized or cooperative development of oil fields become a common practice. The common-pool problem resulted in excessive rates of extraction as evidenced in Figure 5, which shows the location of oil wells along the property lines of an Oklahoma oil field in the 1930s.

When information is not excludable, there may be a reluctance to explore where others may benefit. One solution is to own all land that may be affected by the exploration information. As Peterson (1975) argues, this may require very large capital outlays. Furthermore, there may be intransigent landlords who expect to capitalize on the exploration information produced. If there are significant economies of scale in exploration, and if holdouts do not have access to a common pool, it may be rational to cooperate; however, reason does not always prevail. Hence exploration may be undersupplied in areas where these effects are important.

Information exclusion raises production costs and may bias exploration away from these areas if the information produced has little

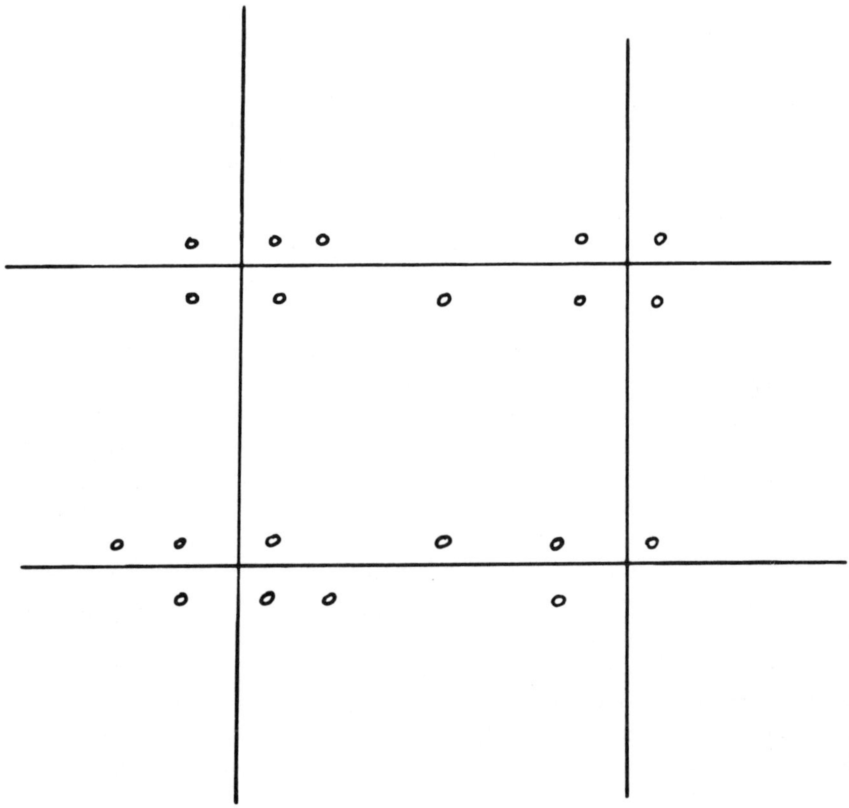

Figure 5. Location of Oil Wells along Property Lines of Oil Field

private value in other uses. However, when information can be kept secret, there are potential private gains from speculation. Since the value of speculative information depends on its scarcity, there may be a race to explore in areas where information may be kept private. Thus, areas where information exclusion is possible may be explored too early and perhaps too intensively. We consider the speculative value of exploration information in more detail in the next section.

3. Information about the Total Resource Stock. Exploration contributes to the fund of knowledge characterizing endowments of exhaustible resources. A major discovery or series of discoveries may lower the current price if the information leads producers to expect more supply in the future, and price may rise if a series of failures implies that there is less than originally anticipated.

It is important to ask whether there are private incentives to produce information about the resource endowment. We have already noted that exploration has private value in minimizing the costs of an extraction program. Furthermore, if the information can be kept private, exploration is a means to speculate on the value of mineral land.

Information about the total resource stock affects the market price and consequently the value of all resource lands, as well as the asset values of firms that use the resource in production. There are two reasons why the private return from speculating on the resource price may be less than the return from speculating on, say, the value of a particular tract available for lease. First, any particular discovery or failure may have a negligible impact on prices. Put another way, there may be significant scale economies in the rewards for information about the total stock. However, the second source of difficulty may obviate the private return to even very large exploration programs. In order to speculate profitably, the information produced by the exploration program must be kept secret until market trading is completed. It is very difficult to keep a major discovery or failure secret. Furthermore, an attempt to speculate may be revealed by the resulting movements of market prices. If traders may infer from the changes in these prices that someone has superior information, then they may be able to obtain that information free of charge simply by watching market prices. The extent to which this is possible depends on characteristics of financial markets (see Radner, 1970; Green, 1973; Grossman, 1975; and Grossman and Stiglitz, 1976).

These problems of scale and leakage of information are potentially more serious in reducing the private incentives to determine characteristics of the total stock relative to private incentives to search for particular deposits. Indeed, in the next section we show that the returns from speculation can lead to too much and too early exploration of particular tracts. It is useful to compare information about the resource stock with basic research. The primary output of basic research is information that may define the directions for future productive research and development. The search for resource deposits is analogous to applied research that has the immediate objective of developing new products or techniques. While it may be difficult to draw a fine line between basic and applied research, the social returns from research in areas such as fusion energy, cancer prevention, and mathematics are examples of basic research the benefits of which cannot be easily capitalized by competitive firms.

Is it possible that there can be too much exploration of specific areas and not enough exploration of the total stock? Clearly, if all areas are explored too much and too early, then there is too much exploration of the total stock. However, it is possible that private incentives to explore submarginal areas may be inadequate.

For example, Brobst (1977) suggests that for many minerals the distribution of resources according to extraction cost may be roughly bimodal, with a small concentration of high-quality deposits and a much larger stock of low-quality deposits. This is illustrated in Figure 6A, with the shaded area representing the total amount already extracted.

Typically, the distribution of resources is not known with certainty, and the uncertainty surrounding submarginal reserves may be particularly great. We emphasize this by approximating Figure 6A with Figure 6B. There is a known amount S_1 with (known) extraction cost C_1, and a much larger amount S_2 with uncertain cost $\tilde{C}_2$. If the elasticity of demand is finite, the efficient rate of extraction of low cost reserves depends on the uncertain cost $\tilde{C}_2$. The resource price should be higher if $C_2 \gg C_1$ than if $C_2 \cong C_1$.[19] However, suppose it is known that $\tilde{C}_2$ is at least as large as C_1. A price-taking firm would never explore the high cost deposits before the low cost deposits are depleted, because in no event will extraction from high cost reserves begin until the low cost reserves are exhausted. Yet this information has social value and should be produced if the cost of exploration is sufficiently low.

The problems of appropriating these benefits through market speculation have already been discussed, but there is another way a firm may benefit from exploration of the endowment. If the firm is large, it's own exploration activity may be a means to profitably speculate on it's own value. In this way, monopoly internalizes much of the external effects of information. (Of course, the presence of monopoly introduces distortions of its own.) A small firm may have to undertake the full cost of an exploration program but can only capture a small fraction

Figure 6. Distribution of Resources According to Extraction Cost

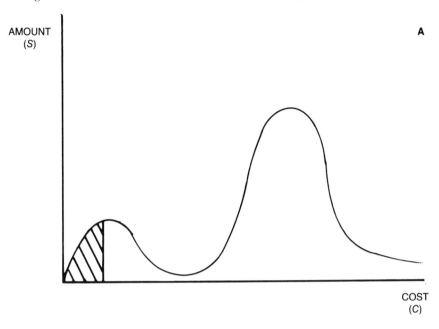

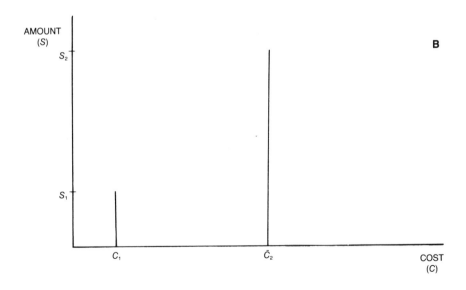

of the benefits of the program. Fragmented landowners could form cooperatives to undertake joint exploration programs, analogous to the informational activities of member-supported trade organizations. The difficulty of enforcing membership when the benefits are not excludable—the "free-rider" problem—is an important reason why such cooperatives are not more common.

D. The Speculative Value of Information

1. Distortionary Effects of Competitive Bidding. The owner of the mineral rights to a particular location has an incentive to explore the area in order to extract the resource at minimum total cost. If exploration information were not a public good, that is, if the information had no value in directing the use of the resource or the exploration decisions of other landowners, the incentive to minimize cost would assure an efficient investment in exploration.

However, the market offers another use for exploration. The information produced by exploration can be used in a competitive bidding market to speculate on the value of properties not owned by the prospecting firm. The incentives to speculate can lead to particular distortions in the market-determined allocation of exploration. To some extent, the incentives for speculation may offset the problems of "too little exploration too late" discussed in the previous section. However, they may only tip the scales in the direction of too much and too early exploration.

The problems that arise in competitive bidding relate specifically to presale exploration activities. Once a property is leased, in the absence of other distortions, a firm with the objective of producing the resource has the incentive to explore in order to minimize total private costs.

2. Locational Distortions of Exploration Prior to Leasing. The expected profits of participants in a sealed bid lease auction depend on each bidder's knowledge of the value of the lease and the strategies of other bidders.[20] There is much to be learned about the operation of complex auction markets, but there is a strong presumption that a participant with superior information may earn (monopoly) profits at the expense of less informed bidders. Gaskins and Teisberg (1976) cite a particular example (offered by Robert Wilson) where this is the case. Teisberg (1976) has simulated an auction in which participants bid a multiple of their estimates of the value of the lease. His results show that profits decrease as the number of bidders increase and that better information increases expected profit. Whereas the bidding strategy assumed by Teisberg is not necessarily individually optimal, it conforms to reports of actual bidding strategies in lease auctions (see Capen, Clapp, and Cambell, 1971, and Dougherty and Nozaki, 1975). In this section we assume that the simulation results of Teisberg (1976) are valid and show that the incentive to become informed prior to bidding for leases may result in wasteful exploration expenditures. In particular, exploration may be redundant and some leases may be explored even though the social value of the information may be less than its cost.

Gaskins and Teisberg (1976) note that exploration prior to a lease sale could be socially productive in assigning a lease to the firm that, as the result of its superior performance, places the highest value on the lease. However, the bidding process performs this matching function only if firms differ in abilities and not merely in their information. This information could be made public, and if firms have equal abilities and the same priors, they should calculate the same expected value for the lease.[21] Furthermore, firms can explore after the lease sale. If information has value only in locating minimum cost deposits (i.e., information about the total stock has no value), then firms have an incentive to optimally explore a lease after the sale. In this case, presale exploration can only be redundant if there are no other distortionary provisions in the lease (an example is the diligence requirement discussed in Section IV).

As a first step in modeling the incentives for exploration prior to a lease sale, let θ^- denote an uninformed state and θ^+ an informed state (not necessarily perfect information), which can be acquired at cost K. We shall assume that the lessor has a zero reservation price and firms are identical, so that the expected value of the lease depends only on whether or not it is explored. If there is only one bidder and a zero reservation price, the sole bidder captures the full expected value of the lease (by bidding an arbitrarily small amount), which we write as $V_1(\theta_1)$ where $\theta_1 = \theta_1^+$ or θ_1^-. The lease should be explored either before or after the sale if

$$V_1(\theta_1^+) - V_1(\theta_1^-) > K \tag{37}$$

When there are n bidders in the lease auction, the expected return to bidder j (i.e., the expected value of the tract less his bid times the probability of winning) depends on his state of information and the information of his competitors, which we write as $V_j(\theta_1, \ldots, \theta_n)$. By assumption, the expected profit from bidding decreases with the number of bidders. That is,

$$V_n(\theta_1, \ldots, \theta_{n-1}, \theta_n^+) > V_{n+1}(\theta_1, \ldots, \theta_{n-1}, \theta_n, \theta_{n+1}^+) \tag{38a}$$

and

$$V_n(\theta_1, \ldots, \theta_{n-1}, \theta_n^-) > V_{n+1}(\theta_1, \ldots, \theta_{n-1}, \theta_n, \theta_{n+1}^-) \tag{38b}$$

for all values of $\theta_1, \ldots, \theta_{n-1}$ and for $\theta_n = \theta_n^+$ or θ_n^- on the right-hand sides of Eqs. (38a) and (38b).

Each entract into the lease auction must decide whether it is profitable to become informed, knowing the number of firms already participating in the auction and their information states but without knowledge of the behavior of subsequent entrants. However, by Eqs. (38a) and (38b) each entrant may assume that if exploration is not profitable taking the existing number of firms as given, then exploration cannot be profitable for subsequent entrants into the auction. We may then assume without loss of generality that only the first $m < n$ firms explore prior to the lease sale.

In most circumstances, the total number of firms that will enter a lease auction is uncertain. We may resolve this uncertainty by assuming that there is a large pool of potential entrants and entry takes place as long as expected profits are positive. With this assumption, a tract would be explored by the first firm if the expected profit when one firm explores exceeds the expected profit if no firm explores prior to the lease sale, or if

$$V_1(\theta_1^+, \theta_{n-1}^-) - V_1(\theta_1^-, \theta_{n-1}^-) > K \qquad (39)$$

where θ_{n-1}^- denotes that all bidders other than the first are uninformed. The number of entrants, n and n' are determined by the zero profit (long run equilibrium) conditions

$$V_n(\theta_1^+, \theta_{n-1}^-) = C \qquad (40)$$

and

$$V_{n'}(\theta_1^-, \theta_{n-1}^-) = C \qquad (41)$$

where C is the cost of entry. Since $V(\theta_1, \ldots, \theta_n)$ is symmetrical, Eq. (41) can be substituted in Eq. (39) to give

$$V_1(\theta_1^+, \theta_{n-1}^-) > K + C \qquad (42)$$

as the necessary and sufficient condition for exploration prior to a lease sale. Condition (42) is very different from the necessary and sufficient condition for efficient exploration given by Eq. (37). Exploration is efficient if the *change* in the total value of the lease exceeds the cost of exploration. If entry costs are negligible, condition (42) says that presale exploration is profitable if the expected value of being informed when other bidders are uninformed exceeds the cost of the information.

It is possible that presale exploration will take place when the cost of exploration exceeds its social value. It is intuitive that the left-hand side of condition (42) should be an increasing function of the value of the explored tract, conditional on winning the lease. Gaskins and Teisberg (1976) quote results of Wilson showing that when the value of the lease is uniformly distributed between $0 and $B and entry costs are zero, a sole informed bidder makes an expected profit of $B/6 whereas uninformed bidders make zero profits. The left-hand side of Eq. (37) however depends only on the marginal value of exploration. Some lucrative tracts may require little or no exploration, but the lure of monopoly profits would motivate exploration in a lease auction.

For any particular lease, more than one firm may conduct a presale exploration program. The equilibrium number of informed bidders is the largest number m such that

$$V_m(\theta_1^+, \ldots, \theta_m^+, \theta_{n-m}^-) > K + C \qquad (43)$$

which is a straightforward extension of Eqs. (39) and (42). Since the expected profit of each informed bidder decreases with the number of informed bidders, a relatively large exploration cost implies a relatively small number of informed bidders in equilibrium. The quality of the information produced by exploration should also affect the equilibrium number of informed bidders. With perfect information, a second firm may not explore because two informed bidders with perfect information would bid away profits in a competitive auction (see Vickrey, 1961).

The speed with which the number of bidders reaches the equilibrium value may be an important factor in determining the market allocation of exploration. Suppose a firm obtains information about the presence of oil in an area where the time required for other firms to enter is significant (the North Slope of Alaska or the far reaches of the Outer Continental Shelf may be good examples). If the lessor accepts bids before the market reaches equilibrium, the existing firms may make large profits.[22] Furthermore, even if equilibrium is attained, the equilibrium number of informed firms may be small if the costs of exploration or entry are large or if the information obtained by exploration is particularly accurate. In equilibrium, an additional firm will make negative profits and therefore will not enter; but competing firms can make sizeable profits if their number is small.[23]

3. Competitive Bidding and the Timing of Exploration. Let $V(\theta,t)$ be the current expected value of a lease at time t conditional on the information state θ. If r is the rate of time discount, it is efficient to explore at some date if

$$\max_t \{[V(\theta^+,t) - K]e^{-rt}\} > \max_t [V(\theta^-,t)e^{-rt}] \qquad (44)$$

We shall assume that exploration is efficient and let T^* denote the optimal exploration date. This is illustrated in Figure 7A. Now suppose the lease is for sale in a competitive auction and assume entry costs are negligible. If the auction takes place at time t, the lease would be explored before the sale if

$$V_1(\theta_1^+,\theta_{n-1}^-,t) > K \qquad (45)$$

(We have amended the notation of the previous section to include the date of the sale.)

Suppose the lease auction takes place before date T^*. Now

$$V_1(\theta_1^+,\theta_{n-1}^-,t) < V(\theta^+,t)$$

but the actual value of $V_1(\theta_1^+,\theta_{n-1}^-,t)$ is difficult to determine, depending on factors such as the degree of uncertainty and bidding strategies. We have drawn two candidates in Figure 7B, labeled V_1^a and V_1^b. At date $T^a < T^*$ the return to the informed bidder just equals the cost of exploration when the expected value of the lease is V_1^a. The property would be explored before the sale if the lease auction takes place at date $t \geq T^a$. If $T^a \leq t < T^*$, exploration occurs at too early a date. For an informed expected lease value of V_1^b, no pre-sale exploration would take place if the auction occurs before $T^b > T^*$. After taking possession of the lease, the firm has an incentive to wait until T^* to explore the property, or to explore immediately if $t > T^*$.

The incentives of a competitive bidding market may lead to exploration at too early a date. We may also note that advancing the date of a sale could have desirable welfare effects. If the property for lease is not a very low cost deposit of the resource, it is possible to reduce its current present value by advancing the date of sale. If advanced sufficiently, there would be little incentive to explore the lease prior to the sale. If the exploration information is not a public good, this is desirable because after the sale the lease would be explored at the efficient date. However, such a policy could reduce the expected winning bid in the lease sale because with no presale exploration the uncertainty in the value of the lease would be greater. While loss of revenue in a sale of public lands may be criticized, this is a transfer of wealth and the loss of revenue could be recovered through a tax on profits. The loss due to the wrong timing of exploration is a real cost that cannot be recovered.

E. The Rate of Time Discount

Both extraction and exploration are affected by changes in the rate of time discount. If the market interest rate exceeds the social rate of

Figure 7. Timing of Exploration

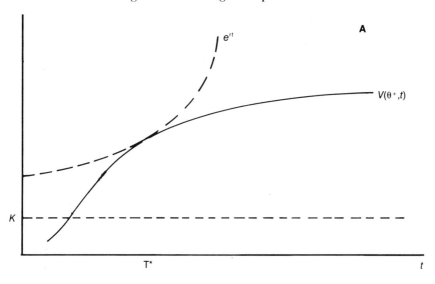

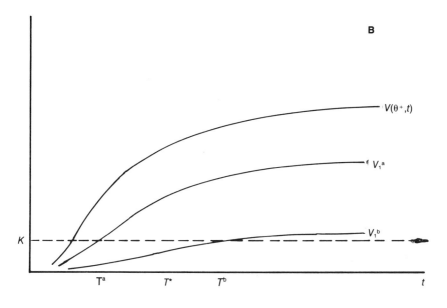

time discount, resource extraction would be too profligate. Because exploration calls for expenditures with the expectation of future returns, the incentives for exploration would be reduced. These conclusions must be tempered by the understanding that the social rate of time discount is crucial to all capital decisions, and general equilibrium effects must be taken into account.

An interesting consequence of possible distortion in the rate of discount is that the government, if it wishes to maximize social benefits, should not seek to maximize the royalties generated by lease sales because the rate at which firms extract resources would be excessive.

F. Summary

There are several reasons why markets fail to provide the correct signals for resource exploration. Leaving aside the broad implications of differences in the private and social rates of discount, the main reasons are the public good and speculative value of information. These tend to create opposing incentives; the speculative value of information encourages a rush for leases whereas the spillover effects lead to a wait-and-see approach. However, some unambiguous conclusions emerge from the analysis.

1. Locational Distortions. Both the speculative and public good nature of information bias the market toward exploration of economically remote areas. There is a greater probability of capitalizing on being first in these areas and also less to gain from waiting for the results of exploration by others, simply because the density of exploration activity is low. We have also shown that some areas where the net social value of exploration is negative may be explored if the expected value of the lease is sufficiently high.

If information about the total distribution of the resource endowment has social value in determining the appropriate rate of utilization of resources, exploration may be desirable even though its net private value is negative. Because potentially lucrative deposits may be explored even if the net social value of the information is negative, it is likely that only exploration of currently submarginal deposits would be inadequate if information about the endowment is socially valuable. Thus there may be too little exploration of shale oil deposits, whose costs are high but uncertain.

2. The Total Amount of Exploration. It is difficult to determine whether the total expenditure on exploration is too little or too much because the public good and speculative value of information work in opposite directions. Competition for leases probably results in redundant exploration, just as competition for patent rights generates redundant re-search. The extent to which this redundancy is socially excessive de-pends, however, on the extent to which firms with the same information may place different values on the same lease.

3. Distortions in the Timing of Exploration. If exploration information is of value only in locating the most valuable deposits and deposits are statistically independent, then there is no point in exploring an area until production from that area is intended to begin.[24] In a competitive economy, exploration may occur too early as a result of the incentives to participate in lease markets as an informed bidder. If deposits are not statistically independent and if information cannot be kept private, exploration may be delayed in areas where there is the possibility of learning from the activities of others.

The failure of the market to provide incentives to explore areas where extraction is not currently profitable is potentially important. Infor-mation about low grade ores, tar sands, bituminous shales, and other submarginal resources may be valuable in determining the appropriate rate of resource use if there is some probability that these deposits will be future sources of supply. It is difficult to assess the importance of this information in quantitative terms, just as it is difficult to place a a dollar value on basic research.

IV. ALTERNATIVE GOVERNMENT POLICIES: EFFECTS AND RECOMMENDATIONS

In this section we give a very brief overview of the implications of some existing policies that relate to natural resource exploration and discuss the desirability of alternative measures. Although these policies may be motivated by concerns other than those of the efficient intertemporal allocation of resources (i.e., efficient exploration and extraction), the consequences of these policies for the efficient use of our scarce re-sources is of sufficient importance that these effects need to be kept in mind.

A. Leasing Provisions and Procedures

The government faces a wide range of alternatives in the design of leasing programs for the exploitation of public lands. Some of the salient characteristics of existing and planned leasing programs are discussed in this section. The provisions of leases for privately owned lands are the result of market-mediated arbitration between the lessor and lessee. However, it is likely that lease conditions for private lands are also the result of legal precedent and sanctions.[25] The remarks here apply also to market leases to the extent that government intervention is desirable in changing these standardized provisions.

1. Diligence Requirements. Mineral leases often contain provisions to discourage the postponement of extraction after the sale. A diligence requirement simply states that production from the property must commence within a specified time period, otherwise the lease is void. Indirect measures such as rental fees may also serve this purpose.

If a tract is leased before the optimal date of exploration and extraction (T^* in Section III,D,3), it is efficient for the firm to postpone production until some time after the sale. The diligence requirement clearly discourages this postponement. The net result need not be an excessive rate of extraction from all deposits, but rather too early exploitation of some deposits accompanied by a curtailment or postponement of extraction from other deposits.

The use of diligence requirements is a confession of the belief that markets are providing incorrect signals for the extraction of exhaustible natural resources from identified reserves. Even if this claim could be substantiated, it would be desirable to institute corrective measures with less distortionary impacts on the pattern of extraction from reserves.

2. Royalty Bidding. Whereas a bonus bid is a lump-sum payment for mineral rights, a royalty bid is a share of either revenues or profits. The incentive for presale exploration under royalty bidding are much less than in a bonus bid auction because there is no risk involved in entering high bids. Unfortunately, a firm with superior capabilities has no advantage over less qualified firms in a pure royalty bid auction. Furthermore, if the royalty is a share of revenues rather than profits, there is less incentive to continue extraction as costs increase and leases may be terminated prematurely.

3. Unit Sales. This refers to the sale of mineral rights to an entire field so that exploration and extraction decisions can be coordinated. Coordinated exploration avoids the distortions in the timing and pattern of exploration caused by the statistical interdependence of discoveries at different tracts. These distortions lower the total profits from exploiting a field and provide incentives for voluntary unitization, which is frequently observed in petroleum exploration and extraction. Unfortunately, at times a unitization agreement can be blocked by a small landowner who refuses to accept the sharing agreement and capitalizes on the fugacious nature of oil. Stated differently, when either oil or the information about the location of oil is a common property resource, the core of the bargaining game may be empty.

Unitization can be made compulsory in a government leasing program. The government essentially establishes an exploratory–development corporation and sells shares to interested firms (who eventually manage the corporation as stockholders). This internalizes many of the informational externalities associated with exploiting deposits in a field.

B. Policies toward Exploration Information

1. Disclosure Regulations. Exploration information has speculative value only to the extent that it can be excluded from others. In a bidding market, two perfectly informed bidders with access to credit markets may compete against each other and bid away all rents. The requirement of disclosure of exploration information could have two desirable consequences. First, if there is a belief that there is too much investment in exploration for the purpose of speculating on the value of leases, forced disclosure can reduce the private incentives for exploration. Second, disclosure rules *may* increase the share of the lease's value captured by the seller, which is presumably a good thing if the seller is the government. Disclosure would equalize information among bidders, and Wilson (1975) shows that the seller should receive close to the expected value of the lease if there are many bidders.

However, there are three potentially important drawbacks to disclosure regulations.

1. Firms may easily circumvent disclosure rules, simply by randomizing the exploration data they make available to the regulatory authority.
2. If the disclosure rule were effective, firms may not invest at all in the production of speculative information. This information could be of value in determining the characteristics of neighboring deposits and in improving estimates of the total resource stock. Thus effective disclosure rules could result in too little exploration.
3. If disclosure reduces exploration and there are only a few bidders, the sellers share of the value of the lease could be reduced. Simulation results of Teisberg (1976) show that when there are few bidders and two or more are relatively informed, the average winning bid is higher than when all are equally uninformed. Since the number of bidders for a particular tract is typically small (less than ten for Outer Continental Shelf leases), the positive effect of disclosure on the seller's share when there are many bidders may be irrelevant.

2. Government Exploration Prior to Bidding. An alternative to disclosure requirements as a means of reducing excessive presale exploration is government exploration of leases prior to sale. The pattern of exploration chosen by the government would be an important factor in altering private incentives. Government exploration of isolated deposits could encourage speculative activity at neighboring tracts, and to avoid this the government would have to explore entire fields.

There are at least two important objections to centralized exploration. First, although the market does not provide optimal signals for the allocation of investment in exploration, it is not clear that the allocation determined under the rules and incentives of bureaucracy would be an improvement. Given information about the location of deposits, the market provides the correct incentives for extraction of deposits with the lowest cost. A government agency might not follow such a rule and might, for example, choose to explore all deposits with expected costs less than the market price.

The second difficulty is somewhat more subtle. There may be social gains from firms pursuing different exploration strategies. That is, there may be an optimal degree of redundancy in exploration (and research and development activities). Of course a single agency could carry on multiple exploration strategies, but the monolithic structure of a bureaucracy denies the opportunities for diversification that are fostered (perhaps excessively) by the market. These potential problems of centralized exploration warrant careful consideration of unitized private exploration of fields as an alternative.

ACKNOWLEDGMENTS

I am grateful to Partha Dusgupta, Geoffrey Heal, Joseph Stiglitz, James Sweeney, and Thomas Teisberg for valuable observations and suggestions.

NOTES

1. The generic term "stock" is used in this paper to represent the total endowment of a resource, which includes characteristics such as total amount, location, and cost. For a discussion of resource terminology, see Section II,B and Brobst and Pratt (1973).

2. As an extreme case, a "dry hole" can be viewed as a deposit with an extraction cost so large that it can never be profitably exploited.

3. The level for $V(0)$ is arbitrary unless $V(0)$ is unbounded below. If that is the case, it is not difficult to see that total extraction should never exceed the minimum level of reserves, S_1 (see Gilbert, 1976a).

4. This is implicit in the assumed probability distribution on the stock, since the endowment must be at least S_1, and possibly S_2.

5. The prime denotes the total derivative: $u'(q) = [du(q)]/dq$.

6. For changes in the date of exploration that are not marginal, taking account of the revision in the rate of extraction can only increase the value of advancing the exploration date.

7. By sufficiently valuable on the margin we mean that $V'(S)$ becomes sufficiently large as S is reduced to zero. This is equivalent to saying the demand price of the resource, $P(S) = V'(S)$, becomes sufficiently large as S decreases, which would be the case if the resource is essential to production.

8. An interesting analysis of the effects of depletion on the conditional distribution of petroleum deposits in developed fields is in Kaufman (1974).

9. The pattern of drilling that most efficiently extracts the resource should also be considered. In the case of oil or natural gas, spacing wells too far apart may impede reservoir recovery (see Muskat, 1949).

10. See Brobst and Pratt, (1973).

11. An interesting discussion of the incentives for risk taking in exploration is in Stiglitz (1975a).

12. See Grayson (1960), for a discussion of risk taking among independent oil prospectors.

13. McKie (1962) describes a representative oil prospecting deal that illustrates the possibilities for diversification.

14. To the extent that the use of information necessarily introduces random elements that reduce its value to others, information deviates from a pure public good.

15. See McKie (1962) for particular examples. Of course we cannot be certain that the success of these firms was not due to luck rather than better information.

16. This follows from $\mathscr{E}(X) = \mathscr{E}(X/Y)$, where Y represents success or failure and $\mathscr{E}(X/Y)$ is the expected return conditional on success or failure.

17. Clearly more complicated "wait and see" strategies are possible, but this seems reasonable enough to demonstrate the problems that can arise.

18. Note that if firms are identical, neither will benefit from the other, since either both will explore at time t or both will wait. This is yet another example of the "Prisoner's Dilemma" problen (see, e.g., Shubik, 1959).

19. Figure 6 may be a reasonable approximation of the distribution of world petroleum reserves. The high-quality deposits are primarily those of the Persian Gulf. The low-quality deposits are bituminous shales, tar sands, and coal. The cost of producing a natural crude oil substitute from these sources is uncertain, but definitely higher than the cost of extraction from Persian Gulf deposits.

20. In this section we consider only a bonus bid auction for the mineral rights at a particular location.

21. They may have different priors that result from previous exclusion of information. For an interesting discussion of information and agreement, see Aumann (1976).

22. It is to the advantage of the lessor to postpone the lease sale until the number of participants reaches equilibrium, provided his rate of time discount is not very much larger than that of the potential bidders. However, there are many examples where lessors have been too hasty in accepting bonus bids. Gaffney (1967) cites the example of the Houma Indians' disadvantageous bargaining with the Humble Oil Company over tracts in Louisiana in 1937.

23. Kaldor (1935) observed this result in a model of monopolistic competition.

24. Exploration could be of value in maintaining an inventory to avoid fluctuations in output.

25. Akerlof and Soskice (1976) emphasize the importance of "accepted behavior" in determining the outcome of market processes.

REFERENCES

Adelman, M. (1972). *The World Petroleum Market.* Johns Hopkins University Press, Baltimore.

Akerlof, G. (1970). The Market for Lemons: Qualitative Uncertainty and the Market Mechanism, *Quarterly Journal of Economics* 488–500.

Akerlof, G. and Soskice, D. (1976). The Economics of Sanctions, University of California, Berkeley, mimeo.

Allais, M. (1957). Method of Appraising Economic Prospects of Mining Exploration Over Large Territories, *Management Science* **3**.

Arrow, K. (1963). *Social Choice and Individual Values.* John Wiley and Sons, New York.

Aumann, R. (1976). Agreeing to Disagree, Stanford University, mimeo.

Brobst, D. (1977). The Systems Approach to the Analysis of Resource Scarcity, presented at Resources for the Future Conference on Exhaustible Resources, Washington, D.C.

Brobst, D. and Pratt, W. (eds.) (1973). United States Mineral Resources, U.S. Geological Survey Prof. Paper 820.

Capen, E., Clapp, R. and Campbell, W. (1971). Competitive Bidding in High Risk Situations, *Journal of Petroleum Technology* 641–653.

Dougherty, E. and Nozaki, M. (1975). Determining Optimum Bid Fractions, *Journal of Petroleum Technology* 349–356.

Erickson, W. and Spann, R. (1971). Price Regulation and the Supply of Natural Gas in the United States, *in* K. Brown (ed.), *Regulation of the Natural Gas Producing Industry,* Johns Hopkins University Press, Baltimore.

Feller, W. (1957). *An Introduction to Probability Theory and Its Applications* **1,** John Wiley and Sons, New York.

Fisher, F. (1964). *Supply and Costs in the U.S. Petroleum Industry,* John Hopkins University Press, Baltimore.

Gaskins, D. and Teisberg, T. (1976). An Economic Analysis of Presale Exploration in Oil and Gas Lease Sales, *in* R. Masson and P. Qualls (eds.), *Essays on Industrial Organization in Honor of Joe S. Bain,* Ballinger, Cambridge.

Gaffney, M. (ed.) (1967), *Extractive Resources and Taxation,* University of Wisconsin Press, Madison.

Gilbert, R. (1979a). Optimal Depletion of an Uncertain Stock, *Review of Economic Studies* **46:** 47–58.

—— (1979b), Search Strategies and Private Incentives for Resource Exploration, *in* R. Pindyck (ed.), *Advances in the Economics of Energy and Resources,* Vol. 2, 149–169, JAI Press, Greenwich, Conn.

Grayson, C. (1960). *Decision Under Uncertainty: Drilling Decisions by Oil and Gas Operators,* Harvard University Press, Boston.

Green, J. (1973). Information, Efficiency and Equilibrium, Harvard Institute of Economic Research, No. 284.

Grossman, S. (1975). The Existence of Futures Markets, Noisy Rational Expectations and Informational Externalities, Institute for Mathematical Studies in the Social Sciences, No. 182.

Grossman, S. and Stiglitz, J. (1976). Information and Competitive Price Systems, *American Economic Review* 246–253.

Herfindahl, O. (1967). Depletion and Economic Theory, *in* M. Geoffrey (ed.), *Extractive Resources and Taxation,* University of Wisconsin Press, Madison.

Hirshleifer, J. (1971). The Private and Social Value of Information and the Reward to Inventive Activity, *American Economic Review* 561–574.

Hotelling, H. (1931). The Economics of Exhaustible Resources, *Journal of Political Economy* **39:** 137–175.

Kaldor, N. (1935). Market Imperfection and Excess Capacity, *Economica* **2**.

Kaufman, G. (1974), Statistical Methods for Predicting the Number and Size Distribution of Undiscovered Hydrocarbon Deposits, presented at the American Association of Petroleum Geologists Research Conference, Palo Alto, California.

Loury, G. (1976). Optimal Exploitation of an Unknown Reserve, Massachusetts Institute of Technology, mimeo.

MacAvoy, P. and Pindyck, R. (1973). Alternative Regulatory Policies for Dealing with the Natural Gas Shortage, *Bell Journal of Economics and Management Science,* **4:** 454–498.

McKie, J. (1962). Market Structure and Uncertainty in Oil and Gas Exploration, *Quarterly Journal of Economics.*

Muskat, M. (1949). *Physical Principles of Oil Production,* McGraw–Hill, New York.

Massé, P. (1962). *Optimal Investment Decisions,* Prentice-Hall, New York.

Nordhaus, W. (1973). The Allocation of Energy Resources, *Brookings Papers* **3:** 529–570.

Peterson, F. (1975), "Two Externalities in Petroleum Exploration," in G. Brannon (ed.), *Studies in Energy Tax Policy,* Ballinger, Cambridge.

Preliminary Federal Trade Commission Staff Report on its Investigation of the Petroleum Industry, (1973), U.S. Senate, Committee on Interior and Insular Affairs.

Radner, R. (1970). Problems in the Theory of Markets Under Uncertainty, *American Economic Review* **60:** 454–460.

Ramsey, J. B. (1979). The Economics of Oil Exploration: A Theoretical Analysis Based on Probability of Ruin Concepts, presented at Conference on the Economics of Exploration for Energy Resources, New York University, May.

Rothschild, M. (1974). Searching for the Lowest Price When the Distribution of Prices is Unknown, *Journal of Political Economy* **82:** 689–711.

Savage, L. (1954). *The Foundation of Statistics,* John Wiley and Sons, New York.

Shubik, M. (1959). *Strategy and Market Structure,* John Wiley and Sons, New York.

Spence, M. (1973). Job Market Signaling, *Quarterly Journal of Economics* 355–379.

Stiglitz, J. (1975a). The Efficiency of Market Prices in the Long-Run Allocation of Oil, *in* G. Brannon (ed.), *Studies in Energy Tax Policy,* Ballinger, Cambridge.

——— (1975b). The Theory of Screening, Education and the Distribution of Income, *American Economic Review* 283–300.

Teisberg, T. (1976). A Model of Competitive Bidding with Application to Federal Oil and Gas Leasing, University of California, Berkeley, mimeo.

Uhler, R. (1972). Production, Revenue, and Economic Return in a Petroleum Exploration and Reservoir Development Program, unpublished.

Vickrey, W. (1961). Counter-Speculation, Auctions, and Competitive Sealed Tenders, *Journal of Finance* 8–37.

Weitzman, M. (1976). The Optimal Development of Resource Pools, *Journal of Economic Theory* **12:** 351–364.

Wilson, R. (1975). A Bidding Model of Perfect Competition, *IMSSS,* Stanford University, No. 184.

UNCERTAINTY AND THE PRICING OF EXHAUSTIBLE RESOURCES

Robert S. Pindyck

In this article the effects of both demand and reserve uncertainty on the behavior of exhaustible resource markets are examined. Demand and reserve uncertainty are introduced in a simple model of resource use by allowing the demand function and the reserve level to fluctuate via continuous-time stochastic processes with independent increments (Ito processes). Thus the demand function is given by

$$p(q,t) = f(q)y(t)$$

where $y(t)$ is a continuous-time stochastic process of the form

$$dy/y = \alpha dt + \sigma_1 dz_1 = \alpha dt + \alpha_1 \varepsilon_1(t)(dt)^{1/2}$$

Here $\varepsilon_1(t)$ is a serially uncorrelated normal random variable, so that $z_1(t)$ is a Wiener process (i.e., Brownian motion process), which implies that future values of $y(t)$ will be lognormally distributed. Note that in this representation of demand uncertainty, current demand is always known exactly but *future* demand is unknown, with the variance of the future demand increasing linearly with the time horizon.

Similarly, the reserve level R is characterized by a stochastic differential equation as follows:

$$dR = -qdt + \alpha_2 dz_2 = -qdt + \sigma_2 \varepsilon_2(t)(dt)^{1/2}$$

where q is the rate of production, and $z_2(t)$ is again a Wiener process, so that the current reserve level is known with certainty, but the effective reserve level ultimately available for production in the future is unknown. The Wiener processes dz_1 and dz_2 are assumed to be uncorrelated, i.e., $E[\varepsilon_1(t)\varepsilon_2(t)] = 0$ *for all* t.

The firm's optimal production problem is solved for both competitive and monopolistic markets using stochastic dynamic programming and it is shown that demand uncertainty has no effect on the expected dynamics of market price. Reserve uncertainty, on the other hand, will shift the expected rate of change of price if extraction costs are nonlinear in reserves. Also, if the demand function is nonlinear, both demand and reserve uncertainty will affect the dynamics of production, whatever the character of extraction costs.

We also extend the model to include exploration, first as a means of accumulating information and thereby reducing uncertainty, and second as a means of accumulating reserves, with uncertainty about the future response of discoveries to exploratory effort. It is shown that information regarding the future evolution of reserves has value only if extraction costs depend on the reserve level. Further, the result is derived that uncertainty over the future response of discoveries to exploratory effort affects the optimal rate of exploratory effort only if the stochastic parameter enters the discovery response function nonlinearly.

NOTE

Copies of this article are available from the author on request. A revised and expanded version of the article is to appear in the December 1980 issue of *The Journal of Political Economy* under the title "Uncertainty and Exhaustible Resource Markets."

COMMENT:
NEW THEORIES OF
EXPLORATION FOR ENERGY
RESOURCES

James L. Smith

It is appropriate that the models and arguments advanced in the papers by Gilbert, Pindyck, and Ramsey focus primarily on the influence of uncertainty in natural resource markets. In many ways, it is the presence of significant uncertainty regarding available resource stocks that distinguishes extractive resource industries from the more conventional manufacturing and service sectors of the economy. Unfortunately, whereas we do appreciate the significance of uncertainty in our natural resource markets, we still lack a comprehensive understanding of its effects. The articles included here are commendable both for their objective of enhancing our understanding of this topic and in their achievements to this end.

The differences in analytical method and technical approach among the articles are significant and fairly elaborate. Rather than focusing on the technical details, however, I believe it to be more instructive to confine my discussion to some of the broader conceptual issues raised by the authors' treatments of their subject.

The basic premise of Gilbert's analysis is that exploratory activity simultaneously serves two goals: the formation of productive capacity and the creation of information regarding ultimate reserve levels. The spirit of the theoretical argument is that the incentives for such activity, particularly for the creation of information, may be perverse, thereby affecting adversely the rate of exploration. Gilbert's position, I believe, is that the public nature of information flows is dominant and suppresses the rate of exploration below that rate that is deemed socially optimal. While I would agree with this proposition in general, instances do come to mind that could reverse this conclusion in particular circumstances. For example, we have the episode related by Gordon Kaufman in which an offshore petroleum leaseholder deliberately sunk a dry hole prior to a subsequent lease auction to convey misleading information to the group of competitors watching closely by the side.

Although Gilbert focuses on the incentive structure for investments in information, a similar treatment could be applied to investments in productive capacity. A variety of forces have conspired historically to influence the incentives for capacity formation in the oil industry, including the rule-of-capture, arbitrary rules of diligence, and the "maximum efficient rate of recovery," market prorationing, and multitier pricing schedules. The impact of these factors has probably been to stimulate the rate of capacity formation beyond the level that is socially optimal. Consequently, it is difficult to conclude what the net impact of capacity and information factors on the rate of exploratory activity has been. An unqualified policy recommendation in favor of exploration subsidies may at present be premature.

A possible avenue for further research on this question might be an empirical, cross-sectional study of the performance of distinct resource markets. The extent to which capacity formation is separable from information gathering varies widely across mineral markets, possibly providing an opportunity to isolate the magnitude of the separate effects. A further implication of this point is that appropriate policy recommendations may also vary across the affected markets.

Pindyck's article characterizes the temporal evolution of a resource market that is subject to both reserve uncertainty and demand uncertainty. It is a useful complement to Gilbert's analysis in that a particular valuation is induced on information and the incentive for exploration is illuminated from this point of view. In particular, investments in information are effective in reducing uncertainty regarding future reserve levels and corresponding production costs; thus informed producers are able to schedule a cost-saving production plan. I believe that a useful generalization of the model would also relate the stock of exploratory information to the future productivity and cost of the exploration process itself, rather than confining the impact to production (i.e., extraction) costs. Unlike Gilbert, Pindyck assumes that the value of information generated in this way is completely appropriable so the possibility of underinvestment does not arise. In fact, the question of appropriability is an empirical one, that again may vary across respective mineral markets. In the particular case treated by Pindyck (oil and gas), it seems reasonable to assume that some portion of exploratory information is not appropriable. Presumably, the model could be easily extended to account for this externality, and the under-provision of exploratory activity would then appear.

Pindyck attributes his results, which diverge from those of several discrete-time dynamic models, to his characterization of the exploration and production process as a smooth, continuous-time phenomenon. He does not emphasize the significance of another key assumption that is equally influential, that being the dependence of current production costs on the ultimate level of available reserves. This issue arises in determining the sensitivity of the price path to the presence of reserve uncertainty. If the average costs are nonlinear in the level of ultimate reserves, it is shown that the presence of uncertainty accelerates the rate of production and changes the rate of price change. The intuitive argument that supports this result is that prospective future fluctuations in the reserve level increase the expected average cost of production in those years. Consequently, there is a greater incentive to produce now. Unfortunately, it is not entirely clear from Pindyck's discussion why such random fluctuations in the reserve level (which may eventually be counteracted by further random fluctuations) should have any systematic impact on current production costs.

It is difficult to see why the real costs of production would be affected in any way by a random disturbance in our perception of ultimate reserves, especially if the disturbance is to be reversed at some point further in the future. One possible example supportive of Pindyck's formulation applies to the case of natural gas, where knowledge of an expanded resource base might facilitate long-term production contracting and more efficient resource recovery. However, even in this case, if it happens that the perceived expansion of reserves turns out to have been illusory, it would seem that the longer-term production plan could turn out to be suboptimal after all. I do not have a particular alternative cost function to propose at this time, but it seems important to explore this aspect of the model in more detail.

Ramsey's article is important both for the alternative characterization of producer behavior that it presents and its relevance to current policy debates that surround the method of leasing offshore oil and gas resources. A principle theoretical contribution of the article is the demonstration that oil and gas firms may exhibit risk averse behavioral tendencies even while operating in a manner that is traditionally described as being risk neutral. The key element responsible for this transition is the risk of bankruptcy—which is a significant factor in a market where firms engage in exploration for an unknown resource. The implication of the model is that, whereas firms may have equal access to venture capital and linear preferences for risk (as capital-asset-pricing theorists would have us believe), they may still have differential exposure to the risk of ruin. The extent of this exposure is determined by the level of their participation and diversification in the offshore oil market. Consequently, the model predicts specialization among firms regarding the type and quality of offshore tracts that are pursued.

The richness of testable hypotheses that devolve from the model is an attribute, especially in light of the extensive empirical record that records the pattern of company participation in this market. For example, it is known from previous research that, in the aggregate, companies have exhibited a preference for certainty over the size of potential returns in this market,[1] (i.e., small but less risky geologic structures are valued more highly than larger and actuarially equivalent, but more risky, structures). Ramsey's model provides a useful framework for interpreting such overall trends and any deviations that may be associated with certain types of firms.

The relevance of Ramsey's research to current policy discussions is obvious. Various proposals can be identified (e.g., royalty bidding, profit sharing, and government presale exploration) that would affect the risk-of-ruin and presumably influence the extent of the individual companies' participation in this market. Ramsey's model presents a framework within which the effects of such policies can be evaluated directly.

I suspect that Ramsey's model also contains implications regarding the degree of competition realized for tracts of varying quality—but the current treatment of this question seems incomplete. With different preferences over tracts, the extent of competition is an important equilibrating factor that, in principle, should adjust to leave firms indifferent among tracts at the margin. The mechanism by which this occurs is not specified. A related question concerns the stability of the allocation of tracts of differential quality through time, as the quality of offered tracts changes (deteriorates?). This supply side effect would have to be considered before meaningful empirical work could be performed. For example, if the quality of offered tracts were to deteriorate, should we expect the participation of small firms to decline, or the degree of specialization among firms to increase, or the degree of competition to change? These appear to be important policy questions that remain to be addressed within Ramsey's basic framework.

NOTE

1. James L. Smith, Bidding Behavior for Offshore Petroleum Leases, unpublished Ph.D. dissertation, Harvard University, July 1977, pp. 119–125.

PART III
SOME POLITICAL AND
ECONOMIC REALITIES

THE RELATIONSHIP BETWEEN BONUSES PAID AND REVENUE OBTAINED FOR INDIVIDUAL BIDDERS IN DIFFERENT FEDERAL OFFSHORE OIL AND GAS BONUS BID LEASE SALES

Elmer L. Dougherty, Myrle M. Johnson, Laurence A. Bruckner, and John Lohrenz

ABSTRACT

Some individual bidders in individual sales purchased more expensive acreage than others. What benefits did they obtain by buying dearer? We show that they obtained leases with revenue-yielding production more frequently. However, given any production, bidders obtained revenue proportional to bonus within uncertainty bounds unaffected by whether the bidder purchased cheaper or more expensive acreage.

I. INTRODUCTION

The acquisition of lands for drilling is one of the early major steps for the exploration of oil and gas. On Federal offshore lands, the principal policy for determining which operators can acquire lands for drilling has been bonus bidding. Specific leases are offered in sales. Leases may be issued to that operator offering the highest bonus for a lease.

The impact of these bonuses must loom large in the exploration process. Through 1977, bonuses paid for 3063 leases in sales from 1954 through 1977 have accumulated to $19.7 billion. Meanwhile, gross revenue from these leases has accumulated to $22.6 billion. The gross revenue was subject to a royalty of one sixth, leaving a revenue net of royalty of $18.8 billion. Obviously, bonuses have been more than revenues net of royalty through 1977. Certainly, there has been no "payout" on the aggregate of Federal offshore oil and gas leases where, in addition to the bonus, the operators have paid the exploration, development, and operating costs involved with any production obtained.

Dougherty et al. (1978) tracked the bonus and revenue profiles of individual Federal offshore oil and gas lease bidders through time. In particular, they examined the cumulative revenue to bonus ratios for individual bidders through time. Admittedly, a current revenue to bonus ratio is a flawed measure of an individual bidder's success. The ratio does not consider future revenue; costs other than bonus to obtain the revenue are not considered. On the other hand, such a ratio is a consistent measure of success as every bidder would prefer a higher ratio rather than a lower ratio.

There was a huge variation in individual bidders' cumulative revenue to bonus ratios through time. Likewise, there were large variations in the overall bonus per acre individual bidders paid. Obviously, comparisons using these revenue to bonus ratios through time may be clouded by differences in the entry and timing of the participation of individual bidders' participation in sales. A late entrant in bidding would have had less time to develop any revenue and would be more likely to have paid bonuses bloated by inflation. Dougherty et al. (1978) could not discern any pattern between the cumulative revenue to bonus ratio through time of individual bidders and the overall bonus per acre (i.e., how cheap or how expensive the acreage) the bidder purchased.

That led to the question addressed by this study. What are the benefits that a bidder derives from paying a higher bonus per acre? Presumably, among the benefits sought by a bidder paying a higher bonus per acre are (1) A higher probability that the lease, once acquired, will yield production. (2) A larger revenue per bonus paid, given that the lease is productive.

In this study we examined bonuses paid by bidders in particular sales and the corresponding revenues obtained to see if the record shows that either of these desiderata accrued for higher per acre bonuses. Does the frequency of obtaining production tend to increase as the per acre bonus increases? Likewise, how does the revenue obtained from productive leases increase as the bonus increases? (Note that by considering individual bidders in separate Federal offshore oil and gas lease sales, one need not be concerned with differences in the entry and timing of the participation of individual bidders through sales.)

Section II,A delineates the data used. The analysis performed is developed in Section II,B; the results are given in Section II,C. Section III interprets the results and shows that, of the two desiderata hypothesized, the first seems to be realized, but not the second.

II. STUDY OF BONUS BID LEASE SALES

A. *The Data Used*

For 23 of the Federal offshore oil and gas bonus lease sales from 1954 through 1977, 5 or more of the leases issued as a result of the sale had become productive through 1977 with a gross production revenue greater than $1 million. We restricted this study to these 23 sales, listed on Table 1, thereby eliminating sales that tended to be overall failures and also sales that might not have had time since issue of leases to develop some meaningful revenue.

B. *Analysis of the Data*

Table 1 shows an erratic, but perceptible trend of higher ratios of the sums of the bonuses paid to acres issued with later sales. The erratic nature of this trend would appear to be due to variations in the perceived overall quality of the leases offered in the sale. The trend to higher ratios would appear to be the response of the bidders to inflation. One would think a bidder in 1977 would usually offer a higher bid than he or she would have for the same lease in 1954.

Both ratios of the sums of the revenue to the acres and the revenue to the bonuses on Table 1 show the expected decreasing trend for the later sales. This trend also holds for the fraction of acres in productive leases. Leases issued in later sales have had less time to attain any production.

To look for interrelationships between bonuses paid by, acres issued to, and revenue obtained by individual bidders, their performance in each of the 23 sales must be measured on a common basis. To do this,

Table 1. Summary of Sales Used in This Study (Considering Any and All Production Through 1977)

Date	Location	Leases issued	Acres	Bonus (MM$)	Revenue (MM$)	Fraction of acres in productive leases	RATIO Bonus/ Acres	RATIO Revenue/ Acres	RATIO Revenue/ Bonus	Number of individual bidders	(BONUS/ACRE)$_N$ Highest	(BONUS/ACRE)$_N$ Lowest	Number of individual bidders with revenue (REVENUE$_N$ > 0)
10/13/54 & 11/09/54	Louisiana & Texas	109	461,811	139.73	1,611.66	.504	303	3490	11.53	19	4.03	.110	18
7/12/55	Louisiana & Texas	121	402,494	108.47	795.86	.218	270	1977	7.34	21	3.48	.062	13
8/11/59	Louisiana	19	38,820	88.04	52.29	.693	2268	135	.59	11	2.02	.034	9
2/24/60	Louisiana & Texas	147	704,133	282.47	3,099.48	.455	401	4402	10.97	23	3.02	.089	21
3/13/62	Louisiana	206	951,806	177.26	2,357.90	.417	186	2477	13.30	27	7.77	.164	22
3/16/62	Louisiana & Texas	205	953,996	268.27	2,227.68	.354	281	2335	8.30	28	10.96	.054	16
4/28/64	Louisiana	23	32,671	60.34	559.86	.650	1847	1836	9.94	9	4.21	.224	9
3/29/66	Louisiana	17	35,056	88.85	738.25	.850	2534	2106	8.31	11	2.41	.318	9
10/18/66	Louisiana	24	104,601	99.03	437.49	.590	947	4182	4.42	11	3.30	.058	9
6/13/67	Louisiana	158	743,809	509.62	1,731.21	.297	685	2327	3.40	34	4.80	.048	27
5/21/68	Texas	110	540,843	595.16	152.00	.138	1100	281	.26	28	2.95	.048	17
11/19/68	Louisiana	16	29,681	149.87	717.62	.405	5049	2418	4.79	11	5.43	.074	8
1/14/69	Louisiana	20	48,505	44.04	151.96	.515	908	313	3.45	12	2.38	.114	8
12/16/69	Louisiana	16	60,104	66.87	316.05	.654	1113	526	4.73	10	4.52	.049	7
7/21/70	Louisiana	19	44,632	97.74	393.49	.692	2190	882	4.03	12	3.75	.042	9
12/15/70	Louisiana	119	553,847	847.26	3,760.92	.367	1530	6791	4.44	37	3.86	.012	30
11/04/71	Louisiana	11	37,160	96.01	286.95	.295	2584	772	2.99	8	6.97	.089	4
9/12/72	Louisiana	62	290,279	585.77	165.78	.072	2018	571	.28	20	3.63	.038	5
12/19/72	Louisiana	116	535,873	1,665.52	665.08	.221	3108	1241	.40	36	6.96	.287	27
6/19/73	Louisiana & Texas	100	547,173	1,591.40	38.90	.050	2908	71	.02	37	2.52	.012	11
3/28/74	Louisiana	91	421,218	2,092.51	486.47	.214	4968	1155	.23	38	4.87	.288	20
10/16/74	Louisiana	136	634,832	1,427.24	314.87	.084	2248	496	.22	48	2.24	.067	23
5/28/75	Louisiana & Texas	86	406,942	232.92	12.48	.059	572	31	.05	44	5.29	.182	10
All 23 sales		1931	8,580,286	11,314.39	21,114.25	.287	1319	2461	1.87	535	10.96	.012	332

230

one can normalize each bidder's performance by the entire sale performance. Thus a bidder who paid zero bonus in a sale will most assuredly have generated no revenue in that sale. Likewise, any bidder who paid all of the bonuses in an entire sale would have been responsible for all the revenue that has been generated in the leases issued as a result of that sale. To this end, if we define

$$BONUS_N = \frac{\text{Sum of a bidder's bonuses paid in a sale}}{\text{Sum of all bonuses paid in a sale}}$$

and

$$REVENUE_N = \frac{\text{Sum of bidder's revenue obtained from the leases issued in a sale}}{\text{Sum of all revenue obtained from all leases issued in a sale}}$$

we know that

$$\text{when } BONUS_N = 0; REVENUE_N = 0$$

and

$$\text{when } BONUS_N = 1; REVENUE_N = 1$$

Further, *ceteris paribus*, we would expect that

$$BONUS_N = REVENUE_N$$

which simply means that a bidder who paid, say, half the bonuses in the sale would normally expect to get half of the revenue from the leases issued. That is merely an overall expectation, of course, from which bidders in individual sales can depart. In fact, characterization and quantification of any such departures with respect to higher and lower bonuses per acre paid would provide the answer to the question of this study.

An an index of whether bidders paid higher or lower bonuses per acre than for the aggregate of all bidders in the sale, we define

$$(BONUS/ACRE)_N = \frac{\dfrac{\text{Sum of a bidder's bonuses paid}}{\text{Sum of the acres issued to a bidder}}}{\dfrac{\text{Sum of bonuses paid}}{\text{Sum of acres issued}}}$$

Hence, for a bidder who purchased leases averaging the same bonus per acre as for the entire sale, $(BONUS/ACRE)_N = 1$. For a bidder who bought more expensive acreage than the overall for the sale, $(BONUS/ACRE)_N > 1$, the higher the more expensive; and for a bidder who obtained cheaper acreage, $(BONUS/ACRE)_N < 1$, the lower the cheaper.

Table 1 shows the range of $(BONUS/ACRE)_N$ for each of the 23 sales studied. The range of $(BONUS/ACRE)_N$ covers nearly three orders of magnitude. Clearly, bidders in individual sales obtained leases both very much more expensive per acre and cheaper per acre than the average for any sale. If we examine the relationship of REVENUE$_N$ versus BONUS$_N$ of individual bidders in individual sales with different (BONUS/ACRE)$_N$, we can see the departure from the expectation, BONUS$_N$ = REVENUE$_N$, with respect to bidders who paid higher and lower bonuses per acre than the average.

However, before we can apply this methodology, we must resolve the knotty problem of how exactly to define bidders in a sale. The problem arises because bidders (say, A, B, C, and D) bid jointly in a sale, but with varying ownerships in different bids for different leases in the sale. Sometimes A, B, C, and D may all hold ownership in a bid, but the amount may vary. Sometimes one or more of A, B, C, or D may not participate in a bid for some leases. Sometimes one of A, B, C, or D may bid "solo," i.e., A, for example, may desert the others or, for that matter, the others may desert A. In this situation, the question arises, "To what extent were A, B, C, and D 'one' individual bidder?" The answer one would like to give is that an individual bidder comprises any bidder or group of bidders that arrive at their bids together. Without being privy to the process by which a group of bidders collectively and individually decided to bid (and not to bid), that answer is, of course, not possible to implement.

We arrived at a very pragmatic answer to the question of how to define an individual bidder. We presumed that bidders who did did together and had substantially the same relative performance in a sale with respect to bonuses paid, acres issued, and revenues obtained computed on a basis of net ownership were actually bidding as one individual bidder. Those bidders who performed together were presumed to have bid together if they bid together at all. A precise algorithm was devised as follows:

1. For each bidder, the following were computed using the stated net ownership in any bid for a lease issued in a sale:

$$(B/A)_i = \frac{\text{Sum of bidder } i\text{'s bonuses paid}}{\text{Sum of the acres issued to bidder } i}$$

$$(R/B)_i = \frac{\text{Sum of bidder } i\text{'s revenue obtained}}{\text{Sum of bidder } i\text{'s bonuses paid}}$$

2. If bidder i and j bid together in a sale and

$$|(B/A)_i - (B/A)_j| < 0.05[\max(B/A)_i,(B/A)_j]$$

and

$$|(R/B)_i - (R/B)_j| < 0.05[\max(R/B)_i,(R/B)_j]$$

then i and j were considered to be one individual bidder.

3. Any bidder k who bid together with either i or j, and if the above two criteria applied to either i and k or j and k, was added to the individual bidder combine of i and j. And so on.

This algorithm does not guarantee an unambiguous definition of an individual bidder. For example, suppose A bids with B in one area and with C in another area of the same sale. Then, depending on outcomes, the algorithm may classify A, B, and C as 1, 2, or 3 individual bidders, with two possible groupings for 2 bidders, A–B and C or A–C and B. (One might, at first, opt for considering "A-with-B" and "A-with-C" as individual bidders. But, to what extent did A's impetus in bidding influence B and C? If it was overriding, the "best" individual bidder definition would be A, B, and C together.) The point is that no completely unarguable algorithm exists for defining individual bidders in Federal offshore oil and gas bonus lease sales precisely, given joint bidding as it occurs. As shown in Table 1, our algorithm defined 535 individual bidders in the 23 sales studied.

C. The Results

Figure 1 is a log-log plot of $REVENUE_N$ versus $BONUS_N$ for all bidders in the 23 sales. The individual points are divided into three approximately equal subpopulations according to $(BONUS/ACRE)_N$ as follows:

$(BONUS/ACRE)_N < 0.5$ — Representing bidders who tended to purchase the cheaper leases in a sale. These are plotted separately on Figure 2.

$.5 \leqslant (BONUS/ACRE)_N > 1.2$ — Representing bidders who tended to purchase the intermediate priced leases in the sale. These are plotted separately on Figure 3.

$(BONUS/ACRE)_N \geqslant 1.2$ — Representing bidders who tended to purchase the more expensive leases in a sale. These are plotted separately on Figure 4.

$REVENUE_N = 0$ for 203 of the 535 bidders; $REVENUE_N$ was greater than 0, but less than 10^{-4} for one bidder. These data points are shown on the lower border of Figures 1 through 4. Table 1 gives a breakdown of the number of bidders in the 23 sales with positive revenue ($REVENUE_N > 0$).

Figure 1. Plot of REVENUE$_N$ versus BONUS$_N$ for All Bidders

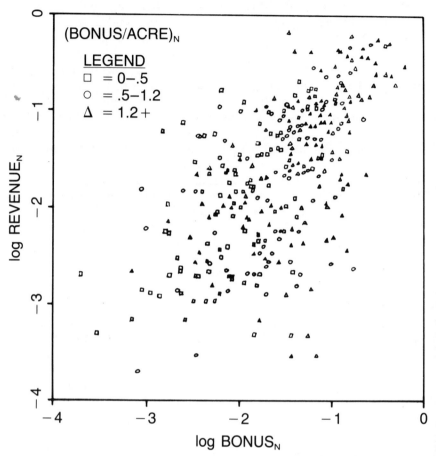

Table 2 shows the fraction of bidders in individual sales who obtained no revenue, i.e., lost their bonuses plus any exploration expenses, in the aggregation of the 23 sales by the (BONUS/ACRE)$_N$ subpopulations. It is unarguably apparent that those bidders who purchased the more expensive acreage were rewarded with leases having a higher frequency of yielding any production and revenue. [Lohrenz et al. (1979) showed a scattergram with no correlation between the fraction of acreage in productive leases and the bonus per acre paid by individual bidders aggregated through sales. However, here when we do not aggregate individual bidders across sales, a relationship is obvious.]

Figures 1–4 are scattergrams depicting the relationship between BONUS$_N$ and REVENUE$_N$ given REVENUE$_N$ > 0. The scattergrams

Figure 2. Plot of REVENUE$_N$ versus BONUS$_N$ for Bidders Who Tended to Purchase the Cheaper Leases, 0–.5 (BONUS/ACRE)$_N$

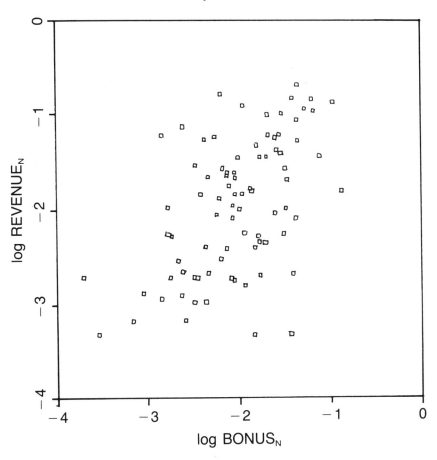

Table 2. Relation Between Price of Acreage and Frequency of Obtaining No Production

(BONUS/ACRE)$_N$	Number of data points	Data points with REVENUE$_N$ $\leq 10^{-4}$	Fraction of individual bidders paying bonuses in individual sale who obtained no revenue
$\leq$0.5	187	103	.551
>0.5 and $\leq$1.2	172	66	.384
>1.2	176	35	.199
All	535	204	.381

Figure 3. Plot of REVENUE$_N$ versus BONUS$_N$ for Bidders Who Tended to Purchase the Intermediate Priced Leases, .5–.12 (BONUS/ACRE)$_N$

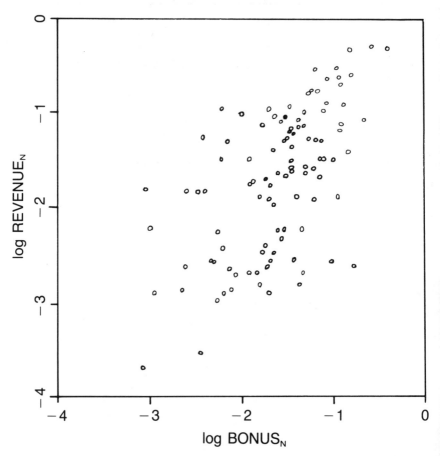

show the overall adherence of the data points to the expectation, BONUS$_N$ = REVENUE$_N$. What is interesting, however, is that the scatter around that expectation does not appear to be affected by whether one is considering the bidders buying cheaper, intermediate, or more expensive acreage. This is seen by comparing Figures 2, 3, and 4.

To measure that scatter, we defined a variance, $\hat{\sigma}^2$, which mimics a true variance, as follows:

$$\hat{\sigma}^2 = \frac{\sum_I (\ln \text{REVENUE}_N - \ln \text{BINUS}_N)^2}{I}$$

I is the number of individual bidders. The variance $\hat{\sigma}^2$ is a measure

Figure 4. Plot of REVENUE$_N$ versus BONUS$_N$ for Bidders Who Tended to Purchase the More Expensive Leases, 1.2$^+$ (BONUS/ACRE)$_N$

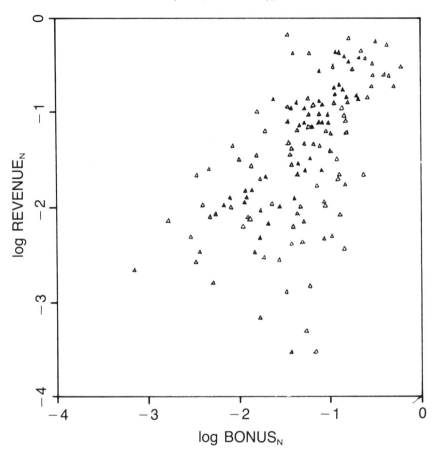

of the scatter of the data points with REVENUE$_N$ > 0 on Figures 1–4 about the overall expectation.

Table 3 shows the results for $\hat{\sigma}^2$ for all 23 sales and by subpopulations according to (BONUS/ACRE)$_N$. The variance $\hat{\sigma}^2$ for all 332 individual bidders in the 23 sales with REVENUE$_N$ > 0 was found to be 2.09; the variances for the subpopulations were near 2.09. A Bartlett chi-square test for homogeneity of the subpopulation variances (Snedecor and Cochran, 1967) gave a test statistic of a magnitude that would be obtained more than 50 percent of the time if variances were homogeneous and all other assumptions involved applied. Thus, this statistical test for

Table 3. Variance of the Departure from the Expectation, $BONUS_N = REVENUE_N$, by Ranges of $(BONUS/ACRE)_N$

$(BONUS/ACRE)_N$	Number of data points	$\hat{\sigma}^2$
≤0.5	85	2.11
>0.5 and ≤1.2	106	2.03
>1.2	141	2.13
All	332	2.09

homogeneity of variances is consistent with what we have visually concluded upon observing Figures 2, 3, and 4.

Wary, as they should be, correlators of real data such as those in this study might point out the possibility of spurious correlation between $REVENUE_N$ and $BONUS_N$. Both $REVENUE_N$ and $BONUS_N$ are ratios with a numerator that appears as part of a sum constituting the denominator. Both $REVENUE_N$ and $BONUS_N$ are constrained to values less than or equal to unity and as $REVENUE_N$ and $BONUS_N$ approach unity, their range of possible variability is perforce lessened.

Table 4 shows the results for $\hat{\sigma}^2$ by ranges of $BONUS_N$. Essentially, Table 4 examines the extent to which the $REVENUE_N$ versus $BONUS_N$ correlation may be spurious because the individual bidder's bonus and revenue are parts of the sums of all of the bonus and revenue in a sale. Table 4 shows values of $\hat{\sigma}^2$ that are quite constant except that the value is lower at the highest range of $BONUS_N$. On the other hand, the Bartlett chi-square test for homogeneity of variances (Snedecor and Cochran, 1967) gave the same result for the subpopulations by $BONUS_N$ of Table 4 as that for those of Table 3. It appears that the spurious correlation that one should be wary of is avoided because the bulk of the data for $REVENUE_N$ and $BONUS_N$ do not approach values near unity.

Table 4. Variance of the Departure from the Expectation, $BONUS_N = REVENUE_N$, by Ranges of $BONUS_N$

$BONUS_N$	Number of data points	$\hat{\sigma}^2$
>10^{-4} and ≤10^{-3}	7	2.43
>10^{-3} and ≤10^{-2}	75	2.06
>10^{-2} and ≤10^{-1}	187	2.24
>10^{-1} and <$10^0 = 1$	63	1.67
All	332	2.09

Thus, these results indicate that by purchasing more expensive acreage, individual bidders in individual sales have been able to obtain leases with a greater frequency of obtaining any production and revenue. On the other hand, given any production, the amount of revenue obtained was proportional to the bonuses paid with an uncertainty not correlated with whether the bidder purchased more expensive or cheaper acreage.

III. CONCLUDING REMARKS

When these 535 individual bidders purchased leases, some more expensive and some cheaper than the sale "average," we did not know their quantitative hope for what they wanted. We do know what they got. They did get a larger probability of acquiring a lease from which any production was obtained by purchasing the more expensive acreage.

However, given that production was obtained, individual bidders obtained production revenue according to the overall "average" revenue to bonus ratio for each sale with an uncertainty around the "average" that was unaffected by whether the acreage was more expensive or cheaper.

Naturally, a bidder would also seek acreage on which the cost of obtaining any production was less. For example, a lease in the Gulf of Mexico would presumably be more expensive than the same lease in the Beaufort Sea where climatic conditions amd location increase costs. All sales in this study were in the Gulf of Mexico. With the possible exception of costs affected by water depth, production costs should be roughly comparable.

Consider the size of that uncertainty, $\hat{\sigma}^2 = 2.09$. This means that, if a bidder was fortunate to have any production at all, the revenues he or she obtained will be between $4.26(e^{+\hat{\sigma}})$ times and $0.23(e^{-\hat{\sigma}})$ times the average obtained per dollar of bonus in that sale, at the "one sigma" level. The uncertainty by which an individual obtained revenue from bonus around the overall sale expectation (given production) was even higher than that of the bids of competing bidders for individual leases. The pooled variance of bonus bids for individual leases have been shown to be about 1.1 (Dougherty and Lohrenz, 1976, 1977).

In summary, this study shows individual bidders who purchased more expensive bonus acreage in a sale got a higher frequency of obtaining leases with any revenue-yielding production than those who purchased cheaper leases. But, given any revenue-yielding production, all bonus bidders and payers appear to be dealing with the same magnitude of uncertainty with respect to how much of the sale's revenue they will obtain for their bonus irrespective of whether they paid that bonus for more expensive or cheaper acreage.

ACKNOWLEDGMENTS

C. Kay King, Carolyn F. Mills, and Anthony F. Montoya of the Los Alamos Scientific Laboratory produced the computer-generated results and plots.

REFERENCES

Dougherty, E. L. and Lohrenz, J. (1976). Statistical Analyses of Bids for Federal Offshore Leases, *J. Petrol. Tech.*: 1377–1390.
Dougherty, E. L. and Lohrenz, J. (1977). Money Left on the Table in Sealed Competitive Bidding: Federal Offshore Oil and Gas Lease Bids, SPE 6501, *Proceedings of the SPE-AIME Symposium on Petroleum Economics and Evaluation*, pp. 291–300, Dallas, February 20–22, 1977.
Dougherty, E. L., Bruckner, L. A. and Lohrenz, J. (1978). Cumulative Bonus and Production Profiles with Time for Different Competitive Bidders: Federal Offshore Oil and Gas Leases, SPE 7134, presented at the 48th Annual California Regional Meeting of the SPE-AIME, San Francisco, April 12–14, 1978.
Lohrenz, J., Dunham, D. A. and Tomlinson, H. (1979). A Study of Factors Affecting Profit for Different Federal Offshore Oil and Gas Lease Bidders, SPE 7714, *Proceedings of the SPE-AIME Hydrocarbon Economics and Evaluation Symposium*, pp. 43–52. Dallas, February 11–13, 1979.
Snedecor, G. W. and Cochran, W. G. (1967). *Statistical Methods*, 6th edition, pp. 296–298. Iowa State University Press, Ames.

EFFECTS OF THE FEDERAL REGULATORY FRAMEWORK ON MINERAL EXPLORATION AND MINE DEVELOPMENT IN THE UNITED STATES

John W. Whitney

ABSTRACT

The Federal regulatory framework in the United States as it applies to the mining industry is composed of the Federal land management laws, Federal environmental laws, and Federal health and safety laws. The focus of this article is on the effects of the regulatory framework on mining industry functions, particularly at the exploration stage. The analysis required interviews with governmental and mining industry representatives and an extensive literature survey.

The Federal regulatory framework affects the nation's long term ability to develop the mineral supplies necessary to support its industrial base. The development of locatable, leasable, and salable mineral commodities is affected differently, and effects are most negative for locatable minerals. Effects are also different for the mineral exploration and mine development functions. Under current conditions, mineral exploration through mine development and construction takes more than 30 years. Social constraints created largely by the Federal regulatory framework are such that the time required for mineral supply development may lengthen more over the next 20 or 25 years.

I. INTRODUCTION

An important goal of this analysis is to determine the effect of the Federal laws on the nation's long-term ability to develop the mineral supplies necessary to support its industrial base. This article evaluates the relationship between the Federal regulatory environment (as expressed by Federal land management laws, Federal environmental laws, and Federal health and safety laws) and mineral exploration and mine development in the United States. Some of the effects of the Federal regulatory framework on locatable, leasable and salable commodities as they apply to exploration and development are identified. The data provided herein may help provide insights into why the "coming mineral shortage" that is often discussed in the trade press and other forums could develop.

Much of the material presented in this article was originally compiled for use by the Materials Program of the U.S. Congress Office of Technology Assessment (Whitney, 1977). Data presented in this report were derived from numerous sources, the most important being interviews with government and mining industry representatives. Extensive literature surveys and analytical research conducted by the author for mining companies and government agencies have also been used to build the data base presented here.

Mining companies serve as the nation's supply–development and production managers (Whitney and Dorr, 1977:143) and they develop the mineral raw material supplies necessary to satisfy its industrial needs. This article focuses heavily on the effects of the regulatory framework on mining company functions, especially at the mineral exploration stage. The author's perspective is based on experience gained from analysis of mineral supply problems resulting from government policies in many countries, including the United States. Although conditions in foreign countries are often quite different than in the United States, some of the effects, e.g., retardation of mineral supply development of their Federal laws, policies, and practices on mineral exploration and mine development are the same.

This article analyzes the regulatory framework in three ways: the first describes the problem in terms of mineral demand, supply, and the supply development process; the second describes the regulatory framework and its effects on mineral supply development by mineral commodity groups as well as effects on mineral exploration and mine development; the third summarizes the findings and presents the conclusions drawn from those findings.

II. THE PROBLEM: GROWING U.S. MINERALS DEMAND; DECLINING DOMESTIC UNITED STATES SUPPLIES

A. *Demand*

Mineral raw materials requirements in the United States are increasing at a prodigious rate. The current importance of mineral production to the United States and its increasing future importance is well illustrated in a speech given by V. E. McKelvey, formerly Director of the U.S. Geological Survey (McKelvey, 1976). McKelvey stated that

> Major urban areas are expanding at the rate of 1000 square miles annually, which is like adding a new Boston or Washington each year. The area coming under economic planning, development, and influence of metropolitan centers is expanding at ten times that rate: 10,000 square miles a year, an area larger than the state of New Hampshire. At these rates we will indeed duplicate our presently developed urban areas by the year 2000. All told, the land areas that are expected to undergo development just in urban centers and for highways and for surface mining will amount to more than 90,000 square miles during this period, an area nearly the size of Wyoming.
>
> This will amount to building a second America and will require prodigious amounts of resources, including energy, materials, water, and land. Just to maintain the present levels of consumption of oil and gas would require 150 billion barrels of oil and more than 500 trillion cubic feet of gas, substantially more than we have produced and used throughout our history, and the actual demand will be larger still due to the increased needs of a larger population. Some of this enormous bill of materials will have to be purchased from sources abroad, but most of it in the future, as in the past, will have to come from our own soil. Just the task of finding and producing the immense volume of materials that will be needed in the next twenty-three years will be a formidable assignment; doing so in ways that minimize damage to the environment and to other resources will be even more difficult . . .

Thus, as McKelvey points out, immense volumes of mineral raw materials will be required to satisfy anticipated domestic U.S. requirements over the next 21 years. A large proportion of these raw materials will have to be produced domestically.

B. *Supply*

Reduced, or in some cases, declining domestic mineral supplies contrast sharply with rapidly growing domestic mineral demand. Evidence for this reduced rate of domestic mineral supply development is provided by the United States mineral raw material import trends. Figure 1 shows that U.S. nonenergy mineral imports have been rapidly increasing since about 1971. If domestic energy and mineral production capacity is not expanded at a rate rapid enough to satisfy burgeoning demands, then mineral raw material imports will increase to satisfy those requirements.

New mineral supply development is often a slow process that requires long lead times. The length of time required for development is well illustrated by the fact that it often takes from 5 to 20 years to discover a mineral deposit and 3 to 6 years to conduct environmental studies and obtain construction permits; and it may take another 3 to 10 years to build a mine on the deposit and bring it into production. The lengthy time requirements result from the unpredictability of exploration results, from the complexity of the environmental permitting process, and from the detailed evaluation and design and special equipment fabrication that are often necessary due to unique physical and metallurgical characteristics of individual ore bodies.

Table 1 lists some of the more important time-related and technical factors that increase the cost and lengthen the time required for mineral exploration and mine development. Most of these factors result from the fact that mineral deposits are nonrenewable resources that occur in fixed amounts on or near the earth's surface. Over a long period of time it is natural to expect that mineral supplies will become more difficult, costly, and time consuming to develop. Consequently, planning horizons lengthen and a stable political–economic environment conducive to long-term planning becomes critically important to firms and individuals involved in new mineral supply development.

C. The Problem Setting

New mineral supplies are initially dependent on the exploration processes to define areas containing potential mineral deposits and then on the development process to define tonnage, grade, and economic feasibility of a deposit. Mineral exploration and mine development on both Federal and non-Federal land are constrained by combinations of technical and social factors, the most important of which are listed in Table 2. Some technical and many social constraints can be reduced or modified by changing the laws, policies, and practices governing the activities of supply–development managers, the mining companies.

This analysis is limited to nonfinancial social constraints that significantly affect mineral exploration, most of which have been imposed to minimize environmental damage resulting from exploration activities.

Figure 1. Value of United States Imports of Minerals, 1971–1976[a]

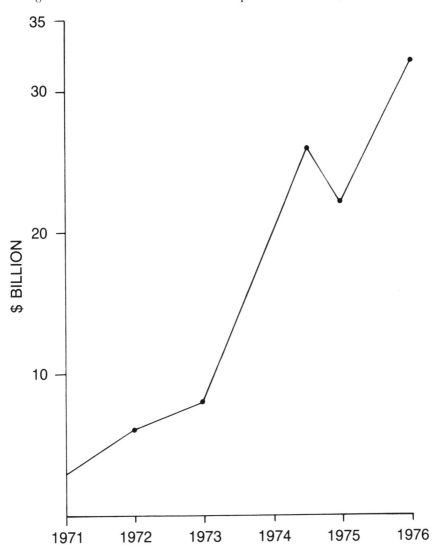

[a] Minerals includes raw materials, energy, and process materials.

Source: U.S. Bureau of Mines, U.S. Department of Interior, "Status of the Mineral Industries 1977,"
p. 4.

Table 1. Technical and Time-Related Factors Affecting the Mineral Exploration and Development Process

Exploration Factors

A. Number of deposits fixed: each discovery reduces by one the number remaining to be found.
B. Easiest to find mineral deposits found first.
C. Large areas of potentially *favorable* ground must be examined to find one mineral deposit: reduction of the amount of area available for mineral exploration reduces the chances of success.
D. Mineral deposits become more difficult to find over time: exploration requires increasing technical skill.
E. Mineral exploration process becomes increasingly costly.
F. Rate of mineral deposit discovery declines, even without reduction in area available for exploration.

Mine Development Factors

A. Richest deposits mined first: poorer deposits held until economic conditions warrant development.
B. Mine construction becomes more costly, construction times lengthen, ability to prepare reliable long term plans becomes critical.
C. Mineral supplies become more costly to produce because development of lower grade resources requires larger land surface areas, more water is used, and more energy is required for processing.
D. Larger number of deposits must be brought into production due both to lower grade of ore bodies and to increasing demand.

Source: John W. Whitney, derived from consultation with industry, state, and Federal government representatives, and literature review.

Mine development is also affected by socioeconomic constraints such as competing demands for the land, public perceptions of the need for mine development, and concern for the environment.

Statistics to support preservation of given areas with mineral potential often outweigh the generalities and conjecture that must be used to support and justify planning for mineral exploration and potential mine development. In addition, the mining industry constitutes a relatively small part of the total industrial economy and is becoming smaller in relative terms every year. For this and other reasons, there is sometimes little understanding on the part of the general public of how the development of new mineral supplies works and of how the social constraints imposed on the mineral exploration and mine development affect the United States' long-term ability to supply its raw material requirements.

The next section identifies and lists some of the most important social and environmental constraints imposed on mineral exploration and

Table 2. Technical and Social Constraints on Mineral Exploration and Mine Development[a]

CONSTRAINTS ON EXPLORATION

Technical	*Imposed by Society*
Availability of high risk capital	Access to Federal lands
Availability of land	Access to private lands
Highly trained manpower	Financial (taxes and subsidies)
Exploration technology	Environmental protection

CONSTRAINTS ON MINE DEVELOPMENT

Technical	*Imposed by Society*
Manpower (availability and training)	Socioeconomic pressures
Capital (cost and availability)	Legal pressures
Materials (lead times and cost of construction)	Environmental protection
Transportation (type and availability)	Land use restrictions (e.g., zoning)
Reserves (tonnage and grade)	Financial (taxes and subsidies)
Extraction (metallurgy)	
Consumption (markets)	
Water (availability)	
Energy (availability)	

[a] Not listed in order of priority, technical constraints represent physical limitations of manpower, materials, land, capital, and technology, whereas social constraints consist of legal restrictions imposed by government laws, policies, and practices at the Federal, state, and local levels.

Source: Independent analysis by John W. Whitney based on interviews with various levels of management within the mining industry and review of literature on mining industry financial investment.

mine development in the United States—constraints that largely result from the Federal regulatory framework.

III. THE REGULATORY FRAMEWORK

A. Categories of Federal Laws and Regulatory Agencies

A fundamental public issue that has arisen during the past 10 years is the question of how to make the required trade-offs between environmental protection on the one hand and mineral supply development on the other. During this 10-year period, numerous laws and regulations designed to protect the environment have been passed, often with little regard for their impact on U.S. ability to develop new mineral supplies. This promulgation of laws and regulations has dramatically changed the conditions for mineral exploration and mine development in the United States. Many mining industry and government representatives maintain that these changes severely reduce mining company ability to explore for new mineral deposits and develop new mines.

The Federal regulatory framework as defined for this report consists of the land management laws, the environmental laws, and the health and safety laws. Also included are the policies and regulations issued by administering agencies and their regulatory practices. The Federal administrative agencies that have the greatest effect on mineral exploration and mine development on Federal lands are the Bureau of Land Management and the Forest Service, whereas the Environmental Protection Agency and OSHA and MESA affect mineral exploration and development on both Federal and non-Federal lands. The Bureau of Land Management and the Forest Service have a direct effect through their administration of the public land management laws, whereas the EPA, OSHA, and MESA have an indirect effect through their issuance and enforcement of the environmental and health and safety laws.

The land management laws, the environmental laws, and the health and safety laws restrict mining companies by increasing administrative requirements and raising costs. Table 3 ranks the severity of these impacts on mineral exploration, mine development, and mine operation for each of the three categories of laws. Although the health and safety laws have the greatest effect on mine operation, they do have an indirect effect on exploration and development (B. Hillman, personal communication). The primary effect of the health and safety laws is to raise the cost of mine operation (Council on Wage and Price Stability, 1976:18), which, to the extent that it reduces mine profitability, reduces the incentives to explore for additional deposits.

One of the issues critical to national minerals supply is the need for low cost and relatively unhampered access to both public and private lands with reasonable environmental safeguards, especially during the early stages of exploration. The land management laws directly affect access to the public lands, and they indirectly affect access to private lands surrounded by public lands. The environmental laws and the

Table 3. Severity[a] of Impact of Federal Laws[b] by Activity

Activity	Exploration	Mine development	Mine operation
Land management laws	3	2	1
Environmental laws	1	3	2
Health and safety laws	1	2	3

[a] Ranked on a scale of 1 to 3, with 3 being most severe.

[b] State and local laws also affect exploration, mine development, and operation. The severity of impact varies from state to state; however, mine development and operation are generally more severely affected than exploration.

Source: John W. Whitney, derived in consultation with mining industry representatives.

health and safety laws indirectly affect access on both public and private lands. While the National Environmental Protection Act (NEPA) is a Federal law, states were required to either pass their own laws [for example, the Wisconsin Environmental Protection Act (WEPA)] or comply with the Federal statutes. This has resulted in a complex layering or overlapping of Federal, state, and local laws, practices, and policies, most of which have been developed since 1970.

Table 4 provides a perspective of the numerous government regulatory programs that affect mineral property acquisition, mineral exploration, and property evaluation; ore deposit development, pre-mine planning, mine construction, and mined land reclamation. The tabulation provided in Table 4 lists the Federal land management laws that consist of the laws governing disposition of minerals and acquisition of land for that purpose by mining companies. These laws apply to mineral commodities found on the public lands, which are classed by Federal land management laws as the locatable, leasable, and salable (disposable) minerals. Another group of surface management regulations governs the activities of mining companies as they explore for and evaluate mineral deposits on the public domain. Finally, mine development and mining operation on both public and private lands is governed by a large body of Federal, state, and local environmental and zoning laws and regulations.

One of the principal effects of land management and environmental laws is to increase the administrative requirements and costs of both the government agencies and the mining companies. These increased administrative requirements raise the cost of exploration to both the public and private sectors and slow the exploration process. Exploration and mine development on both public and private lands are affected, although the administrative requirements appear to be less complex for private lands.

Mineral exploration and mine development activities on private lands in which both the mineral and surface estates are in private hands are generally the subject of negotiated agreements between the owners and the mining companies and do not normally come under Federal or state land management laws. Mineral exploration and mine development on state lands are often more difficult to accomplish because of leasing and other requirements, which are often commodity specific. The Federal environmental laws do apply to mine development and operation on both private and state lands, although the degree of impact varies from state to state and often depends on both state and Federal agency enforcement practices.

Figures 2 and 3 illustrate the administrative steps that must be taken in order to prospect for and develop geothermal resources. Geothermal

Table 4. Overview of Government Regulatory Programs

PRIVATE LANDS	STATE LANDS
A. Mineral property acquisition	
Negotiations with property owners resulting in mutually acceptable terms; Wisconsin is the only state that has a law addressing this aspect of the mining business. The law provides special rights to the private property owner	State leasing laws and regulations. Each state has its own, and there are often significant differences between the relevant laws of the various states.

B. Exploration and property evaluation

State and county laws, regulations, and ordinances—some states provide little or no regulatory control whereas others are rather restrictive; Wisconsin is a prime example of a restrictive state

The recently enacted Federal Endangered Species Act may have a significant impact on future operations

The Federal Land Management Laws will affect those state and private lands surrounded by Federal Lands. Effects to date have not been obvious, but can be expected to be significant in the future due to rapid promulgation of new rules and regulations under recently enacted laws

PRIVATE LANDS	STATE LANDS
C. Ore deposit development, pre-mine planning, mine construction, mining, mined land reclamation	Mining and Mineral Policy Act of 1970
	National Environmental Protection Act (NEPA)
	Federal Water Pollution Control Act
	Clean Air Act—Regulations: 40 C.F.R. Subchapter C.—Air Programs; 40 C.F.R. Subchapter D.—Water Programs
	Occupational Health & Safety Act (OSHA)
	Mine Health & Safety Act (MESA)
	Endangered Species Act (New)
	Solid Waste Disposal Act (Proposed)
	State Surface Mining or Reclamation Laws and Regulations
	State Air and Water Quality Laws and Regulations
	State Stream Protection Laws and Regulations
	State Dam Safety Laws and Regulations
	State Mine Safety Laws and Regulations
	State Oil and Gas Conservation Laws and Regulations
	State Geothermal Resources Drilling Laws and Regulations
	State Mine Tax Laws
	State Zoning Regulations
	County Mining Ordinances
	County Zoning Ordinances

Table 4. Continued

	FEDERAL LANDS	
Locatable minerals	*Leasable minerals*	*Salable minerals*
A. *Mineral property acquisition*		
Act of May 10, 1872, as amended by the Act of July 23, 1955; Act of Sept. 2, 1958; etc.	Act of Feb. 25, 1920, as amended by the Act of April 17, 1926; Act of Feb. 7, 1927; Act of Aug. 8, 1946; Act of Aug. 6, 1947; Act of Aug. 7, 1953; Act of Sept. 2, 1960; Act of Dec. 24, 1970; Act of Aug. 4, 1976	Materials Act of 1947, as amended by the Act of July 23, 1955; Act of Sept. 28, 1962
Regulations: 43 C.F.R. Group 3800—Mining claims under the 1872 Mining Law	Regulations: 43 C.F.R. Group 3100, 3200, 3300 & 3500	Regulations: 36 C.F.R. Part 251 (Forest Service Only); 43 C.F.R. 3600 (BLM Only)
B. *Exploration and property evaluation*		
36 C.F.R. Part 252 (Forest Service) 36 C.F.R. Part 9 (Park Service), new 43 C.F.R. Part 3800 (BLM-Proposed), new	43 C.F.R. Part 23 30 C.F.R. Parts 211, 221, 231, 250 & 270	36 C.F.R. Part 251 (Forest Service only) 43 C.F.R. Parts 23 & 3600 (BLM only)

Source: John W. Whitney, modified from a table provided by T. S. Maley, Administrator of the Division of Earth Resources, Idaho Department of Lands, State of Idaho, April 1977, at the "Conference on Government Policy, Regulations, and Mineral Law," April 15–16, Coeur d'Alene, Idaho.

exploration and development is used as an example because the Geothermal Steam Act (84 stat. 1566; 30 U.S.C. 1001–1025) was passed in 1970 and the implementing regulations (43 C.F.R. 3200) were published in 1973 and made effective in 1974. These regulations are administered by the Bureau of Land Management. However, another set of regulations (30 C.F.R. 270) are administered by the Conservation Division of the U.S. Geological Survey and regulate exploration, development, and production operations under Federal leases, including those for geothermal steam. The application of two sets of regulations administered by two different agencies, in addition to all of the applicable environmental laws that have been passed during this same time period, further complicates the very complex administrative framework within which the geothermal explorationists must work. A similar framework would have been created for locatable minerals if the proposed Bureau of Land Management surface regulations (43 C.F.R. Part 3800) had

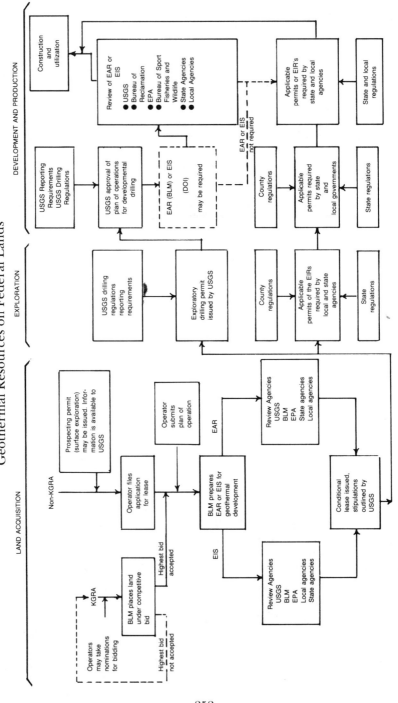

Figure 2. Administrative Requirements for Development of Geothermal Resources on Federal Lands

Source: A Study of Geothermal Prospects in the Western United States, TRW, Redondo Beach, Ca., 20 August 1975, Figure B-2, p. 66.

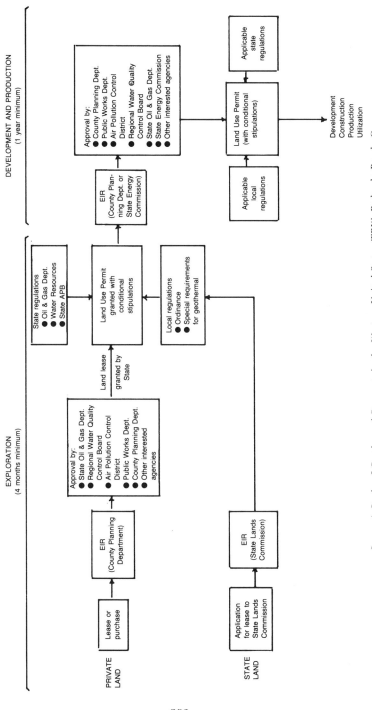

Figure 3. Administrative Requirements for Development of Geothermal Resources on State or Private Land in California

EXPLORATION
(4 months minimum)

DEVELOPMENT AND PRODUCTION
(1 year minimum)

PRIVATE LAND

Lease or purchase → EIR (County Planning Department) → Approval by:
● State Oil & Gas Dept.
● Regional Water Quality Control Board
● Air Pollution Control District
● Public Works Dept.
● County Planning Dept.
● Other interested agencies

State regulations
● Oil & Gas Dept.
● Water Resources
● State APB

Land Use Permit granted with conditional stipulations

Land lease granted by State

Local regulations
● Ordinance
● Special requirements for geothermal

STATE LAND

Application for lease to State Lands Commission → EIR (State Lands Commission)

EIR (County Planning Dept. or State Energy Commission)

Approval by:
● County Planning Dept.
● Public Works Dept.
● Air Pollution Control District
● Regional Water Quality Control Board
● State Oil & Gas Dept.
● State Energy Commission
● Other interested agencies

Applicable state regulations

Land Use Permit (with conditional stipulations)

Applicable local regulations

→ Development
Construction
Production
Utilization

Source: A Study of Geothermal Prospects in the Western United States, TRW, Redondo Beach, Ca., 20 August, 1975, Figure B-1, p. 61.

253

been passed. If a Federal leasing system for locatable (hard rock) minerals (as currently being proposed in Congress) is passed, then conditions will become even more complex.

Similar regulations have been passed and implemented by the U.S. Forest Service and the U.S. Park Service. Very little exploration and very little mining are done in the National Park System so that the new regulations will have little impact. The Forest Service regulations were implemented in 1974 and are deemed to be livable by the mining industry. However, there are now indications that late stages in exploration and mine development are encountering difficulties on forest lands. These difficulties (including both delays and administrative harassment) are attributed by mining industry representatives to practices of lower echelon field people who actually administer and enforce the regulations.

The constraints on mineral exploration and mine development resulting from the administrative requirements of regulations and policies depend on five factors:

1. Number of reviewing agencies in the approval process, e.g., in California as many as 40, in Arizona, 1.
2. Delays associated with the approval process; many procedures do not stipulate review time limits.
3. Administrative priorities of the reviewing agencies and attitude toward mining.
4. Attitude of private-interest groups such as the Sierra Club towards mining, e.g., prefers no development.
5. Complexity (Figure 2) and technical consequences of administrative and environmental requirements to be implemented, e.g., cost increases and complex environmental control technology.

Three case examples illustrate the complexity of administrative requirements. In the first case, El Paso Natural Gas Company applied for permission to build a coal gasification plant in northwestern New Mexico. By the time the proposal was dropped, El Paso Natural Gas was negotiating with more than 30 government agencies at all levels, and with more than 40 environmental interest groups (former company representative, personal communication). In a second case, Kennecott Copper Corporation proposed to build a copper mine near Ladysmith, Wisconsin in 1972. The company applied for 11 different water permits to gain access to process water (former company employee, personal communication). In the Kennecott case, 2 years were required just to get environmental approvals from the state of Wisconsin (Schilling and May, 1976:2). Environmental approval then meant that the company could proceed and apply for operating permits and operating plan approvals. In the third example, Noranda, a mining company that has found a promising lead–zinc–silver deposit on Admiralty Island, Alaska, has identified 25 Federal and state agencies that must review and/or approve the proposed mining project.

These examples illustrate the sociopolitical complexities resulting from the application of the Federal regulatory framework. The next section identifies some of the effects of the Federal regulatory framework as they apply to the locatable, leasable, and salable minerals and to mineral exploration and mine development.

B.   The Effects of the Regulatory Framework on Mineral Supply Development

1.   Effects by Mineral Commodity Group.   The land management disposal system for minerals on public lands in the United States has evolved over a period of more than 100 years (University of Arizona, 1969, Vol. IV:785). Three broad categories of minerals presently are administered under three different disposal systems. The locatable minerals, which include the metals and certain industrial nonmetallic minerals, are managed under the *location system*. The leasable minerals are essentially the fuel minerals (except uranium), phosphates, potash, sodium salts, and sulfur, and these are disposed of through the Federal *leasing system*. The salable minerals include certain common varieties of sand, gravel, and stone and are handled under the *commodities disposal system*. The locatable minerals, in contrast to the leasable and salable commodities, have been characterized as the "hard-to-find" minerals due to the fact that deposits of these minerals are often geologically obscured (Lee and Russell, 1976:33).

The Federal regulatory framework affects each commodity group differently, and each group has different general economic characteristics as displayed in Table 5. The locatable minerals are generally traded internationally and they are often most susceptible to cost and/ or price changes. For this reason, cost increases and delays in supply development, which are the product of the Federal regulatory framework, have a profound inhibiting effect on development of new supplies of locatable minerals.

The effects of the existing regulatory framework can be ranked by commodity group. Table 6 provides a ranking of effects on each commodity group by each group of Federal laws: land management laws, environmental laws, and health and safety laws. The severity of impact can be roughly translated as the effect of increased cost, reduced access, and/or time delays resulting from increased administrative requirements.

The effects of the land management laws apply directly to all commodity groups for the Federal lands, and they may apply indirectly to the commodity groups to the extent that they are found on nonfederal

Table 5. Important Economic Characteristics of Locatable, Leasable, and Disposable Minerals[a]

Economic characteristic	Locatable	Leasable	Disposable
A. Market and demand characteristics			
Type of commodities	Industrial materials, including metals	Energy and fertilizer materials	Construction materials
Market area	International	National and international	Local and national
Market demand for new material	Moderated by recycling for metals	Commodities consumed, not moderated by recycling	Commodities consumed, not moderated by recycling
Market stability	Large changes correspondent to changes in economic activity	Moderate changes correspondent to changes in economic activity	Moderate changes correspondent to changes in construction activity
B. Supply characteristics			
Production sensitivity to cost and/or price changes	High	Moderate to high	Low to moderate
Producer reaction to cost increases	Reduce production and/or exit from industry	Reduce production and/or raise prices	Raise prices
National impact of cost increases	Reduce domestic production and/or increase imports	Reduce growth in production and/or no effect	Reduce growth in production and/or no effect
Scope of exploration	International	International for some minerals; national for others	Local and national
Exploration risk	High to very high	Moderate to high	Low to moderate
Probable national impact of restrictions on supply development	Increased imports, exit of domestic producers from the industry	Increased imports of some commodities; price increases for others	Price increases
Need for access to public lands	High	Moderate	Low

[a] This table prepared by the author. The characteristics noted here are generally applicable to the three commodity groups, although they may not apply uniformly to all commodities in each group.

Table 6. Severity[a] of Impact of Federal Laws by Mineral
Commodity Group

Mineral group	Locatable	Leasable	Disposable
Land management laws	3	2	1
Environmental laws	3	2	1
Health and safety laws	3	2	1

[a] Ranked on a scale of 1 to 3, with 3 being most severe.
Source: John W. Whitney derived in consultation with mining industry and government representatives.

lands surrounded by or adjacent to public lands. The environmental
and health and safety laws apply to all commodity groups irrespective
of whether they are found on Federal or non-Federal lands.

2. Mineral Exploration Effects. This section focuses on the effect of
the closures of large areas of the public domain to mineral exploration
through "single use" land designations by Congress, the Bureau of
Land Management, and the U.S. Forest Service. Single use land management designations in the view of the minerals industry and representatives of the U.S. Bureau of Mines and the U.S. Geological Survey
restrict mineral exploration on Federal lands for development of future
mineral supplies needed for the benefit of the general public while
benefiting other special interest groups. Closure of large areas of the
public lands may have a more profound effect on mineral exploration
than any other aspect of the Federal regulatory framework.

As was noted in the previous section, the locatable mineral commodity
group is most severely affected by the Federal regulatory framework.
There are a number of reasons for this, the most important of which
is that deposits of the locatable minerals are difficult to find due to
their mode of occurrence. Much of the nonenergy mineral exploration
effort is focused on locatable minerals; successful nonenergy mineral
exploration is partially an art, although it is rapidly emerging as a
technically sophisticated science that incorporates the fields of economic
geology, geochemistry, and geophysics.

Successful exploration efforts for locatable minerals are of high national concern because exploration represents the beginning of the
mineral supply development process. Modern mineral exploration be-
came a reality during World War II as a result of the United States'
greatly expanded requirements necessary to maintain the war effort
(Bell, 1976:5). Table 7 lists the chief characteristics of full sequence
mineral exploration as currently practiced in the United States.

Two very important features of exploration deserve attention: (1) at
the early stages, exploration is a land extensive activity because large

Table 7. Chief Characteristics of Full Sequence Mineral Exploration Programs in the United States

Program factor	Reconnaissance	
Areal requirements	Several thousand square miles	
Time required	6 Months to 2 years	
Cost range	$20,000 to $1,000,000	
Number of exploration programs conducted per year nationally	Several dozen	
Annual aggregate national expenditure by exploration companies		
Scale of examination for:	*Regional appraisal*	*Detailed reconnaissance of favorable areas*
Typical number of prospects examined to produce one mine	10,000	1,000
Type of action required	Aerial reconnaissance and surface examination	Detailed geological, geochemical, and geophysical surveys
Type of access required	Road, trail, airplane	Road, trail, airplane
Continued access required for reexamination as exploration concepts and economic conditions change	Yes	Yes
Degree of environmental impact	Insignificant (use existing roads and trails)	Minor to insignificant (use existing roads and trails)
Permanency of environmental impact	Temporary	Temporary

areas of land must be surveyed to find a geologically favorable area, and (2) the early stages of exploration produce zero to minimal environmental damage. This latter point cannot be overemphasized because large areas of the public lands have been closed to mineral exploration, ostensibly to protect the environment. As a matter of fact, in the first two stages (Table 7), i.e., regional appraisal and detailed reconnaissance, a geologist on the ground does no more damage than a hunter, fisherman, or backpacker. Minimal surface disturbance is required for exploration drilling at the third stage, and today backpack drills are being used for shallow drilling so that very little surface disturbance results (W. Salisbury, personal communication). Thus, under current technological conditions, exploration causes little or no environmental disturbance until a mineral deposit has been positively identified.[1]

Table 7. Continued

Target Exploration

Fraction of a square mile for certain types of metal and nonmetal industrial minerals, deposits, several square miles for large tabular occurrences, such as coal and phosphate, and large disseminated occurrences, such as porphyry copper
1 to 5 years
$100,000 to $5,000,000
Several dozen
Greater than $100 million

Detailed surface appraisal	*Detailed three-dimensional sampling and preliminary deposit evaluation*
100	10
Exploration drilling and other testing	Detailed drilling, tunneling, shaft sinking; may be pilot plant tests
Road, trail, helicopter	Road
Yes	Yes
Minor to moderate (restricted to additional road construction necessary for temporary drill access)	Moderate (limited to road construction, but extensive road building may be required over a small area for drill access)
Temporary	Depends on timing of mine development; one in ten may be permanent

Source: Paul A. Baily, President of Occidental Minerals Corporation, "The Problems of Converting Resources to Reserves," in Mining Engineering, January 1976, Vol. 27, No. 1, pp. 29–31, other industry representatives, and John W. Whitney personal experience.

A third characteristic of mineral exploration is that of changing technology, economic conditions, and other factors that change the concept of what constitutes an ore deposit. For this reason known mineral areas that are not of current interest and areas that are believed to be nonmineral in character deserve to be kept open for reevaluation over time.

Numerous examples can be cited for development of mineral deposits in known mineral areas; now development of mineral deposits in areas formerly believed to be nonmineral in character are becoming much more common. A prime example that illustrates how changing technology and economic conditions can lead to recognition of the mineral importance of lands previously believed to be nonmineral in character is the land south of Tucson, Arizona (Haggard, 1977). In 1920 and 1922 the area south of Tucson was determined by the Department of Interior to be "nonmineral" in character. Today this land is the site of five major copper mines, which in 1974 accounted for 10 percent of the copper produced in the United States.

Another example of land previously classed as nonmineral in character that is now recognized as mineral bearing is a large area of the Colorado Plateau region of Utah, Colorado, New Mexico, and Arizona (University of Arizona, 1969, Vol. IV:811). Today this land is widely recognized as being mineral in character and it is the source of a large proportion of the United States' uranium production. More recently large areas in eastern Nevada have been recognized as having a very good potential for gold deposits of the Carlin type; large areas of the northcentral part of the state are experiencing rapid barite mine development; and uranium is now being found in the northcentral and northern areas of Nevada as well as in southeastern Oregon. These examples illustrate how changes in mineral exploration and mining technology often may lead to recognition of previously unidentified mineral belts that can make a significant contribution to domestic mineral supplies.

Prior to 1968 the public lands in the 11 western states served as the most important area for mineral exploration (University of Arizona, 1969, Vol. III:692–700). However, since 1968, increasingly large areas of the public lands have been withdrawn from mineral entry. Most of the land withdrawn from mineral entry has been designated as single-use land, primarily for recreational purposes and for wilderness areas. The classification of large areas of the public lands for single use began with the Wilderness Act of 1964 (Dare, 1974:5). By 1969 the rate of land withdrawn from mineral entry began to increase, and by 1974 approximately 67 percent of the Federal lands had been withdrawn from mineral entry (Bennethaum and Lee, 1975:4). A recent analysis (Walthier, 1977) suggests that in fact a much larger area of the public lands has been "clouded"[2] for mineral entry.

More than 90 percent of the public lands may now be "clouded" due to what Walthier describes as a "buffer zone" effect. The buffer zone effect results when various public groups and/or administrative agencies protest mineral developments within 5 to 10 miles of the boundary of a withdrawn area. This effect has been demonstrated for the Glacier Peak porphyry copper prospect in Washington state, and for a copper–nickel deposit in northern Minnesota. The prospect of denial of access for development of a mineral deposit found within buffer areas makes exploration managers reluctant to commit exploration funds, thus clouding an additional portion of nearby public and private lands. The effects of land withdrawals are over and above delays and increased costs resulting from the new administrative requirements of the land management laws noted in the previous section.

Restrictions on exploration activities on the public lands have led to a renewed interest in non-Federal (state and private) lands as a source of future mineral supply. The most important reasons for renewed interest in non-Federal lands are listed in Table 8. Despite this interest, mining company exploration geologists still feel that the public lands in the 11 western states and Alaska are the most important potential source of "future" domestic mineral supplies.

The most probable effect of the Federal regulatory framework on mineral exploration from delays due to increased administrative requirements and severely restricted access to public lands is a reduced rate of mineral deposit discovery. This in turn leads directly to a reduction in the rate of long-term development of domestic mineral supplies. As is illustrated in Table 9, the mineral exploration and mine development process is a very long one. Therefore, the effects of massive withdrawals and increasing administrative restrictions on access to the public lands may not be felt in terms of reduced mineral supplies for many years. Long-term reduction in mineral supply development on public lands may be partially offset by increased mineral exploration and mine development on private lands, although restrictions on mine development resulting from application of the environmental laws, as discussed in the next section, prevent or slow development of mineral supplies from private lands.

3. Mine Development Effects. Mine development and operation for locatable minerals, in contrast to mineral exploration, require only small areas of land, whereas vast amounts of capital are required. The primary cost to the mining industry of the environmental regulations and the

Table 8. Factors Contributing to Increasing Interest for Access to Non-Federal Lands for Mineral Exploration and Mine Development[a]

A.	Public land withdrawals that significantly reduce public land areas available for exploration.
B.	Federal practices, agency policies, and laws (in that order) that reduce the ability of exploration companies to conduct timely exploration programs by (a) increasing administrative requirements and (b) introducing uncertainty as to future access and tenure.
C.	Growing national minerals raw materials requirements that require increasingly intensive and costly exploration efforts.
D.	Growing domestic exploration needs by *both* domestic and foreign companies that result in increasing demands for land geologically favorable for exploration.
E.	Changing technology leading to new and/or renewed interest in different geologic environments that occur in different geographic regions.
F.	Changing exploration goals resulting from changes in local, national, and international mineral supply–demand conditions.

[a] Not ranked in order of importance.

land management regulations results from inflation that occurs during administrative delays and delays due to legal challenges under the environmental laws. The Federal regulations that affect mine development appear to be applied more restrictively by Federal and state agencies for locatable minerals in the eastern states than in the western public land states. The primary reason for the more restrictive practices by the administrating agencies in the eastern states is concern for the environment that stems partly from agency lack of experience with mining of locatable minerals.[3]

Capital requirements increase rapidly in an inflationary economic environment. Capital intensive projects such as mines, electrical power plants, and pipelines are especially vulnerable because of their large capital requirements. Capital requirements are high for mines being developed and built to extract locatable minerals, especially the metals.

Capital requirements for mine development are expected to continue to increase as lower grade ores are developed; continued inflation will exacerbate the rate of increase. For this reason, the cost effects of regulatory delays resulting from application of the environmental laws during development have become a major national issue for the domestic mining industry, and for others such as the electrical power industry, which requires large amounts of capital for new plant construction.

Delays due to increased administrative requirements and legal challenges by environmental groups dramatically raise the cost of mine development and construction due to the fact that the United States is experiencing a high rate of inflation. The greatest cost results from inflation in capital requirements that occurs during the period when Federal environmental reviews and applications for construction and operations permits that are required for the states and local communities are being carried out.

The most widely known example that illustrates the inflation that occurs during regulatory and environmental delays is the Alaska pipeline. In 1968 when the decision was made to build the pipeline, it was estimated to cost approximately one billion dollars. In 1977 when the pipeline was completed, it had cost in excess of eight billion dollars. This inflationary increase in capital required was due in part to delays arising from environmental challenges and in part due to design changes required to ensure greater environmental protection.

A recent example of how administrative delays increase mine development costs is illustrated by the Flambeau deposit in Wisconsin (Schilling and May, 1976). The environmental review process including the acquisition of data required to prepare an environmental impact statement (under WEPA passed by Wisconsin to conform to NEPA) took

4 years, i.e., from 1972 through 1976. In 1972 the cost of the project was estimated to be 18 million dollars; by 1976 costs had escalated to 27 million dollars. The project may now be postponed indefinitely because the company is uncertain that it can obtain the county permits required for mine development. Even if permits were obtained in a timely manner, it is not clear that the proposed mine would be profitable because of the greatly increased capital costs, in which case, development would still be postponed until prices had increased sufficiently to cover the increased costs.

Both Wisconsin and Minnesota have passed environmental acts (WEPA and MEPA) that conform to the requirements of NEPA, the Air Quality Act, and the Water Quality Act. Mining companies associated with the proposed mine developments are having great difficulty in obtaining required approvals (Gilliland, 1977:63–65, and Mining Engineering, Vol. 27:17). The commodities affected in Wisconsin are zinc and copper, whereas the commodities affected in Minnesota are copper and nickel.

Numerous examples can be cited for delays created by the Federal regulatory framework as it affects exploration in the western states; however, similar environmental and administrative problems affecting base-metal mine development have been rare. On the other hand, according to industry representatives, phosphate, coal, and uranium mine developments are now being delayed in Idaho, Wyoming, and Montana due to environmental concerns. It is probable that delays and even postponements of proposed mine developments will become more common in the future as more of the states pass and enforce legislation that is modeled after or conforms to the requirements of the various Federal environmental regulations.

Reference to Table 9 indicates that once a potentially profitable orebody is identified, it may take between 4.5 and 11 years to develop a mine. Now that environmentally founded administrative delays and

Table 9. Steps and Timing of Mine Development

Step	Time (years)
1. Detailed drilling, bulk sampling, engineering design, and feasibility analysis	2.0–5.0
2. Environmental permitting process	4.0–7.0
3. Plant construction	2.0–5.0
4. Plant start-up and shakedown	0.5–1.0
TOTAL TIME: Minimum and maximum	8.5–18.0

Source: OTA.

environmental challenges are increasingly common, mine development time may be extended by 4 to 7 years. Inflation during delays for environmental reviews may increase capital requirements to the point where the proposed project becomes unprofitable, leading to further postponements (William R. Tipton, Alument, Inc., personal communication). Table 9 lists the time requirements for creation of a mine. Using maximum times for each phase, including environmental review and approval, the maximum time required from initiation of exploration to new mine development now exceeds 30 years. Lead times of this magnitude make a rapid national response to materials shortages and intermediate term changes in supply conditions that require increased domestic supplies virtually impossible.

It is still too soon to fully assess the impact on domestic mineral supply development of delays in mine development resulting from the regulatory framework, increased administrative requirements, environmental challenges, and the effects of postponements due to inflationary increases in capital requirements and development delays by environmental reviews and challenges. Domestic mine development delays for minerals traded internationally could increase the opportunities for foreign producers so that imports may increase for those commodities.

IV. SUMMARY AND CONCLUSIONS

A review of important effects of the Federal regulatory framework on domestic mineral supplies has been completed. This review has suggested that the locatable, leasable, and salable mineral commodities are affected differently. It has also suggested that mineral exploration and mine development are affected differently, with both activities being more severely restricted now than ever before. The effects of these restrictions are important because the United States' mineral raw material requirements are growing at a prodigious rate. Domestic mineral supplies are increasing at a slower rate than demand and imports are filling the gap. Social constraints created to a large degree by the regulatory framework are such that the role of mineral supply development may slow even more over the next 20 or 25 years.

Mineral supply development is a lengthy process that begins with exploration, continues with mine development and construction, and ends with mine operation. Under current conditions, mineral exploration through mine development and construction takes more than 30 years. Part of the time required is attributed to technical factors, which include the unpredictability of exploration success and the size and complexity of the orebody found, as well as the technical and metallurgical requirements for extraction and processing of the ore. The balance of the time is attributable to the requirements of the Federal regulatory framework.

The social constraints that affect mineral exploration and mine development are founded upon the Federal regulatory framework, consisting of land management laws, environmental laws, and the health and safety laws. The consequences of Federal land management laws, land withdrawals, and increased costs attributable to administrative requirements and delays generally have the greatest effect on mineral exploration for locatable mineral commodities on Federal lands. The principal effects of these laws on exploration are to reduce the amount of area available and to raise the cost of entry for the remaining areas.

The environmental laws generally have the greatest impact on mine development. Mine developments for locatable minerals in eastern states are encountering the most severe problems, although mine developments for leasable minerals (notably phosphate and coal) are being encountered in some of the western states. Most of the effects of the environmental laws on mining stem from a combination of public concern for the environment, which results in legal challenges, and from restrictive enforcement of the environmental laws by state and local government agencies.

A large proportion of the current Federal regulatory framework as it applies to mineral exploration and mining has been put into place since 1970. Massive Federal land closures to mineral exploration and mine development have been mandated by Congress and by directives from both the Forest Service and the Bureau of Land Management since 1969. This combination of factors has changed the parameters of the whole mineral supply development process for the United States. Table 10 lists some of the most important mineral exploration and mine development effects.

Part of the reason for imposition of the Federal regulatory framework and for the massive closure of Federal lands to mineral entry is the belief that mineral exploration and mine development severely damage the environment. This belief has been shown by data presented in Table 7 to be false for the early stages of exploration, although some land disturbance must necessarily occur in the late stages of exploration and during mine development and mine operation.

Over the long term, the increased regulation of mining industry activities and closure of large areas of land to mineral exploration and mine development may result in reduced development of domestic supplies and increased imports of mineral commodities that are traded internationally. Inflation in capital requirements that occurs during delays arising from regulatory agency administrative requirements and

Table 10. Effects of the Federal Regulatory Framework on Mineral
Exploration and Mine Development

Exploration Effects

A. Reduced access to public lands due to land withdrawals.
B. Increased interest by minerals exploration companies in private lands.
C. Retardation in the exploration process due to administrative delays (regulatory agency practices).
D. Increased exploration cost, due to increase in bureaucratic requirements.

Mine Development Effects

A. Retarded development, which in an inflationary environment increases capital requirements.
B. Increased costs; expensive environmental impact statements and extensive public review results in higher costs due to increased litigation and expense of environmental impact statements.
C. Prevents mine development in certain cases, e.g., if inflation during delays makes the proposed mine unprofitable due to increased capital requirements and/or operating costs.
D. Reduced availability of domestic mineral supplies, resulting in greater import requirements and larger mineral trade deficit.

legal challenges by environmental groups may raise the cost of a proposed mine development to the point where it must be postponed until prices rise sufficiently to cover the increased costs and return a profit. Thus, the Federal regulatory framework may also result in higher prices for mineral raw materials.

Although a shift in mineral exploration to non-Federal lands may offset some reductions in mineral supply development resulting from restraints on exploration being imposed on Federal lands, the constraints on mine development on non-Federal lands are generally more severe than on Federal lands because of restrictive state and local enforcement of environmental laws. For this reason the non-Federal lands may not be able to supply sufficient quantities of the mineral raw materials that the growing United States economy requires.

NOTES

This article was presented at the Conference on the Economics of Exploration for Energy Resources, sponsored by the Department of Economics and the C. V. Starr Center for Applied Economics at New York University, May 17–18, 1979.

1. Most of the environmental damage resulting from exploration is due to *state* and *Federal* laws that require excavation and other surface disturbance to satisfy annual assessment work. With modern exploration techniques such excavations contribute little

to mineral deposit discovery, and mining industry efforts in two states (Arizona and Nevada) have led to a change in the law to recognize modern exploration requirements, as well as the need to protect the environment.

2. "Clouded" as used here means that an exploration manager would be reluctant to commit exploration funds in the affected lands.

3. The restrictiveness of various eastern states appears to be associated with and attributable to passage and enforcement of environmental laws that conform with requirements of Federal enabling legislation, e.g., NEPA, Air Quality Act, and Water Quality Act. Enforcement at the state and local level in some eastern states is more restrictive than enforcement at the Federal level.

REFERENCES

Articles and Books

Bailly, P. A. (1976). The Problems of Converting Resources to Reserves, *Mining Engineering* **27**:27–38.
Bell, E. B. (1976). The Future of Mineral Exploration in the U.S., *The Mackay Miner*, the publication of the John Mackay Club Chapter of AIME of the Mackay School of Mines, pp. 4–6.
Bennethum, G. and Lee, L. C. (1975). Is Our Account Overdrawn?, *Mining Congress Journal*, special print.
Council on Wage and Price Stability of the Executive Office of the President (1976). *A Study of Coal Prices*, a Staff Report.
Dare, W. L. (1974). *Pre-Emptive Land Use—Its Impact on the Mineral Base*, preprint of a paper presented Society of Mining Engineers of AIME Fall meeting, Acapulco, Mexico, Sept. 22–25, 1974.
Haggard, J. L. (1977). Indirect Regulation of Land Use, *Mining Congress Journal* :48–52.
Lee, L. C. and Russell, D., (1977). Federal Leasing: The Need for a Perspective, *Mining Engineering* **25**:23–24.
McKelvey, V. E. (1976). *Second America Must be Built in 25 Years*, U.S. Department of Interior, Geological Survey News Release, May 11, 1976.
Ohle, E. L. (1975). Economic Geologists, SEG, and the Future, *Economic Geology* **70**:612–623.
Schanz, J. J., Jr. (1977). United States Minerals—A Perspective, *Mining Congress Journal* :26–29.
Schilling, R. W. and May, E. R., (1976). *Case Study of the Environmental Impact, Flambeau, Wisconsin*, a paper presented at the 1976 Mining Convention of the American Mining Congress, Denver, Colorado, September, 26–29, 1976.
University of Arizona (1969). *Nonfuel Mineral Resources and the Public Lands*, Vol. I–VI, prepared for the United States Public Land Law Review Commission, Arizona Economic Information Center, Tucson, Arizona.
Walthier, T. N. (1976). The Shrinking World of Exploration, *Mining Engineering*, Part I, **28**:27–31 and Part II, **28**:46–49.
Whitney, J. W. and Dorr, A. L. (1977). *Policy Implications of Factors Affecting International Trade in the Copper and Aluminum Industries*, a paper presented in the Council of Economics Sessions at the National AIME Meeting in Atlanta, Georgia, March 6–11, 1977.
Whitney, John W. (1977). *The Federal Regulatory Framework: Effects on Minerals Exploration and Mine Development on Domestic Public and Private Lands*, working paper prepared for OTA in support of Assessment 404.1, Nonfederal Minerals Accessibility.

Interviews by Telephone

E. B. Bell, Vice President, Freeport Exploration Company.
John H. DeYoung, Jr., Mineral Economist in the Office of Resource Analysis, U.S. Geological Survey, Reston, Virginia.
Barry Hillman, Mineral Economist, New Jersey Zinc Company.
Bruce Imswiller, former Manager of Exploration in the Western U.S. for International Minerals and Chemical Corporation.
William G. Salisbury of Salisbury and Dietz, Inc.
William R. Tipton, General Manager, Alumet Company.

Talks Given at the "Conference on Government Policy, Regulations and Mineral Law," April 15–16, Coeur d'Alene, Idaho

Howard Banta, Acting Director, Division of Watershed and Minerals, U.S. Forest Service, Washington, D.C., Hard-Rock Mining Regulations on National Forest Lands.
Barney Brunelle, Mining Engineer, U.S. Bureau of Land Management, Boise, Idaho, The Federal Land Policy and Management Act of 1976 (BLM Organic Act): Mining Claim Recordation Requirements and the Proposed BLM Hard-Rock Mining Regulations.
Norman H. Day, Supervisor, Mineral Conservation Section, Idaho Department of Lands, Boise, Idaho, Hard-Rock Mining Regulations on the National Park System.
Norman H. Day, Supervisor, Mineral Conservation Section, Idaho Department of Lands, Boise, Idaho, State Laws and Regulations Governing Exploration, Mining and Reclamation.
David Hintzman, Western Zone Mining Engineer, U.S. Forest Service, Coeur d'Alene, Idaho, Minerals Input in the Land-Use Planning Process.
Professor Paul Matthews, J. D., Assistant Professor of Geography, College of Mines, University of Idaho, Moscow, Idaho, Federal Environmental Laws and Regulations.
Al Teske, Executive Secretary, Idaho Mining Association, Economic Impact of Environmental Controls.

PART IV
EXPLORATION FOR COAL AND
OTHER MINERALS

THE GEOSTATISTICAL ESTIMATION OF UNEXPLORED RESOURCES FOR NATIONAL COAL MODELING

Richard Newcomb

I. INTRODUCTION

The geology of United States bituminous coals differs from that of anthracites and other fuels in several respects important to exploration and development activities. The age and character of the deposition of these coals make the location and size of the major basins simpler to determine than for other solid or fossil fuel resources. Also, public information on resources is much greater. Nonetheless, the economics of exploration and development are of interest to their assessment to the extent these activities play a role (1) in the definition of the mineral endowment of a regional coal basin and (2) in the delineation of economic and subeconomic deposits for the derivation of long run potential supply functions. Broad mineral appraisal (Newcomb, forthcoming) is the inference of endowment in a relatively unexplored basin or seam from the experience or geology of developed parts of the basin and similar basins and seams. Because much is known about coal basin geology, there is less concern over the size of the fuel endowment.

However, there is reason to question the assumptions of relative regularity within or among coal seams in the matter of reserve delineation, the more so as variances in the characteristics of coal deposits significantly affect coal costs and qualities in use at various locations.

The current interest of economists in the definition of regional coal endowment is motivated by the desire of policy makers to conduct impact analyses that require the transformation of geologic data into parameters of coal supply functions capable of systematic integration into national energy models. The chief of these are allocation models in which the effect of alternative policies are measured on the efficient outputs and prices of coals in both producing and consuming regions. These assessments are termed geostatistical if geologic variables and their distribution functions enter explicitly into the analysis in an important way. At one extreme are the supply estimates of conventional econometric market models. These have the advantages afforded by the use of statistical theory. However, because they focus almost exclusively on nongeologic variables, they have not proved convincing for the direct estimation of long-run resource supply. Decomposing demand and supply sides has improved estimations. In general, despite the increased elaborateness of energy models in recent years, especially the Project Independence Energy Systems analysis (PIES), there has been little connection made between the geology of fuel resources, their characteristics or depletion rates, and the estimates made of long-term supply costs. In the case of coal, however, an attempt is being made to employ some geologic information along with cost engineering models to derive more meaningful supply schedules. The best-known of these attempts is the Federal Energy Agency's National Coal Model (NCM), which can be linked to PIES and to the Department of Energy (DOE) national scenarios. This model stands at the other extreme compared to the wholly empirical statistical estimation procedures of econometric supply models. In order to avoid the problems of identification, multicollinearity, and associated data deficiencies of conventional econometric approaches, the NCM incorporates key geologic and technical variables directly into cost engineering models of representative mines. There is no residual error admitted, and the analysis becomes wholly deterministic. This extreme has the merit of introducing full specification and the explicit consideration of geologic explanatory variables, but it does so by eliminating statistics and statistical inference. The NCM supply cost estimates assume that for every seam and place, one knows enough to site specific mines of optimum size, and on this basis it simulates all regional supply schedules.

This article defines exploration and development of coal resources for reserve estimations and potential supply functions (1) in theoretical terms as an aggregation (index) problem in which statistical inference can be useful and (2) in practical terms for national coal modeling efforts. Because the cost rather than the existence of sizeable reserves is the key issue for the resource appraisal of coals, many economists have accepted coal supply models with greater confidence than estimates for oil or gas. This paper examines the grounds for this confidence and finds them wanting. In view of data problems, an index approach is offered as a more efficient method than simulation for deriving supply schedules in major U.S. seams and basins.

In Section II I employ the framework of Harris (forthcoming) to give perspective for the definition of exploration and development activities in the NCM and the derivation of regional potential supply schedules. In Section III I describe an alternative index approach. For comparative purposes, I employ data on the supply functions simulated for West Virginia by the National Coal Model and for Electric Power Research Institute by my own geostatistical index. The robustness of these estimators is examined. Two criteria are used, one examining the adequacy of data assuming well-known distribution functions for the parameters of interest, the other examining simulation results directly through sensitivity analysis. In Section IV the implications of these analyses are discussed for information gathering and future supply modeling.

II. OPTIMAL EXPLORATION CONCEPTS AND THE DEVELOPMENT OF POTENTIAL SUPPLY IN THE NATIONAL COAL MODEL

The most highly calibrated program for the simulation of a potential supply system is that designed for the NCM effort developed within the Federal Energy Agency with the assistance of ICF, Inc. The model is based on U.S. Bureau of Mines data (ICF, Inc., 1976; Department of Energy, 1976) and cost evaluations of model mines (Katell and Hemmingway, 1974; Katell et al., 1972). The coal supply component both in the original NCM and in later versions of the model employed by ICF called the Coal Electric Utility Model (CEUM) are substantially the same. This component has been well reviewed elsewhere (Gordon, 1976a, 1977), so there is no need to comment at length on its detail. Here we only wish to establish the extent to which the NCM engages in the concepts of optimal exploration and development for unmined and undeveloped basins and seams.

Essentially the NCM is a data-driven regionally decomposable supply system in which 30 coal regions and 40 possible coal types are distinguished for 35 demand regions. In CEUM an intermediate and smaller number of inventories (piles) are distinguished for coals available to the six consuming sectors in consuming regions. The NCM is of interest chiefly as an example of the steps and assumptions that must be made in the simplest possible case: when the structure of endowment in all parameters and seams in a region are assumed fully specified. This is, indeed, assumed for coals. The coal case is useful because it addresses the question of the adequacy of data and information without the complicating problems of the metals in which the nature of the endowment is also frequently unknown. The heavy reliance on optimal exploration concepts in coal supply models is not widely recognized. However, this reliance is clearly demonstrated by placing the NCM supply component in the formal framework developed by Harris (forthcoming) for the geostatistical estimation of potential supply.

Harris characterizes the problem of developing the potential metals supply as the linking of three conceptually distinct models. Translated for coals, this means that three steps are also required: (1) fuel endowment must be defined, (2) an exploitation model must be explicitly developed to distinguish coal resources as economic or subeconomic within a range of economic and technical conditions. Finally, (3) optimal exploration must be defined as the means of transforming resources information into a useful economic concept of potential supply. The wide extent of both assumptions and techniques of simulation required for the NCM can be seen by showing its structure within the Harris framework.

In the Harris scheme, the mineral endowment of a region is described by the inventory of deposits D. Like the ores, coals are not homogeneous element concentrations, but heterogeneous rocks, with each deposit r_i characterized by a vector k describing both *in situ* seam conditions affecting mining ease and *within seam* deposit measures affecting yields and the quality of beneficiated coals. The fuel endowment m of the region can only be distinguished on the basis of some subset of these characteristics by aggregating over all such deposits forming D:

$$m = \sum_D Z(r_i) \qquad (1)$$

Without concern for mining economics or technology, the Bureau of Mines and U.S. Geological Survey estimates take as the relevant deposition coal resources by seam and basin (Averitt, 1973; U.S. Bureau of Mines, 1974). This is the inventory of all deposits known and discoverable by grade, tonnage, depth, and mode of occurrence. It is, more simply, just that subset of the coal resource base RB such that for every deposit r_i belonging to D, the characteristics vector k is above the USGS cutoff point k' for each of the k_i characteristics of the jth deposit. This partitions RB into discoverable and other deposits that constitute the physical coal inventory:

$$RB = D \cup \bar{D}$$

The coal inventory analysis begins by employing USBM data on coal resources (U.S. Bureau of Mines, 1971, 1975a,b) generally and by sulfur content (U.S. Bureau of Mines, 1972, 1974a, 1974b), and by partitioning this on the basis of three characteristics: depth, seam thickness, and sulfur to define Eq. (1). Data are designated for underground and surface mines.

Harris notes that for any specified economic and technical conditions E, a function can be defined (or a process evaluation or cost engineering exercise can be performed) to determine the present value for each r_i belonging to RB. This value set V^R can be used to partition RB into two subsets

$$RB = R \cup \bar{R}$$

R contains economically producible deposits over the range of feasible and near-feasible technologies. Coal resources cs are the quantity of carbon units in R obtainable by such an aggregation:

$$cs = \sum_R Z(r_i) \tag{2}$$

R is a subset of D if k' is selected at cutoff levels for each characteristic such that no coal deposit excluded would be economic to produce given the conditions for R:

$$cs \leqslant m$$

Thus, given an estimate of D and m, resources (cs) can be determined by using the value function and the economic conditions E to compute V^D where all individual values are nonnegative. In the National Coal Model, cs is the USBOM demonstrated reserve base, classified according to supply regions. Five categories of carbon content from 26 million British thermal units (MBTU) per ton or greater to under 15 MBTU per ton (Z,H,M,S,L) and eight categories of sulfur per MBTU raw (A to H) are defined (Tables 1 and 2). Table 3 gives the aggregation of coal resources cs. Examples throughout this article show only the West Virginia region's case. The exploitation model of Eq. (2) assigns reserves in demonstrated resources categories after elimination of negligible, inaccessible, illegal, and depleted reserves to both existing and potential deposits. For the former, an estimate of existing mine production and reserves committed to existing mines is necessary. For the latter, one must also, on the basis of existing information or inferences, allocate uncommitted surface resources to overburden ratio categories and uncommitted deep reserves to seam thickness and seam depth categories.

Table 1. BTU Content Categories and Codes, National Coal Model

Millions of BTU per ton	Code	Approximate rank of coal
≥ 26	Z	Bituminous
23–25.99	H	Bituminous
20–22.99	M	Bituminous
15–19.99	S	Subbituminous
< 15	L	Lignite

Source: "Coal Supply Analysis, Validation Workbook for West Virginia," unpublished manuscript by Federal Energy Agency, Dec., 1976.

These assignments in the NCM were made on the basis of a uniform distribution hypothesis for parameters, and weights were assigned on the basis of past production proportions. By specifying further *current* economic and technically *feasible* conditions, then the coal resources can be partitioned into economic (rs') and subeconomic (rs'') deposits:

$$R = R' \cup \bar{R}''$$

The exploitation model in the NCM does this by assuming no significant technical changes between now and 1990 and a range in prices within approximately one order of magnitude of present lower bounds (existing mines). The assignment of R' and R'' is made by allocating

Table 2. Sulfur Level Categories and Codes, National Coal Model

Pounds sulfur per million BTU	Code	Definition
0.00–0.40	A	Can be blended with higher sulfur coals to meet Federal new source performance standard
0.41–0.60	B	Meets Federal new source performance standard
0.61–0.67	C	Can be deep cleaned to meet new source performance standard (5 percent decline in sulfur content)
0.68–0.83	D	Roughly 1 percent sulfur
0.84–0.92	E	Can be deep cleaned to meet 1 percent SIP standard (10 percent decline in sulfur content
0.93–1.67	F	Roughly 2 percent sulfur
1.68–2.50	G	Roughly 3 percent sulfur
>2.50	H	Greater than 3 percent sulfur

Source: "Coal Supply Analysis, Validation Workbook for West Virginia," unpublished manuscript by Federal Energy Agency, Dec., 1976.

Table 3. Coal Resources of West Virginia by Coal Types, National
Coal Model

Coal Type	DEMONSTRATED RESERVES (millions of tons)	
	North	*South*
ZA	146	152
ZB	1752	8491
ZC	191	—
ZD	19	2820
ZE	—	365
ZF	2228	1359
ZG	4123	—
HB	107	914
HD	79	188
HE	654	—
HF	1536	—
HG	1888	118
Unknown	8846	3556
Total	21,569	17,963

Source: "Coal Supply Analysis, Validation Workbook for West Virginia," unpublished manuscript by
Federal Energy Agency, Dec., 1976.

uncommitted reserves to mine size categories and assigning production
estimates to mine types for the purposes of production cost estimation.
These estimates permit the aggregation of coal resources following Eq.
(2) of Harris' formulation. They are based on USBOM engineering cost
evaluation models by Katell (Katell and Hemmingway, 1974; Katell et
al., 1972) and modifications of his work by TRW systems. Mineral
processing costs are added by region as a constant. The NCM calls this
aggregation its "production flow estimation." The scale economies for
optimal size are taken from the engineering models.

Potential supply ps in the model is formed directly from R by defining
optimal exploration and development EX^*, which partitions R into R^d
$\cup \bar{R}^d$ such that R^d contains those deposits that would be discovered by
such an effort. Then

$$R^d \subset R \subset D \subset RB^d \text{ and } cs \leq m \leq \text{resource base}$$

Since ps is the sum of fuel in R^d, the relation between ps and the fuel
endowment is $ps \subset cs \subset$ resource base. The concept of coal supply as
a stock s_t at any time can be derived by a third aggregation, summing
over the known and exploited deposits $\bar{R}^{d_t}$ that would be delineated by
perfect markets, considering both technical change and depletion:

$$s_t = \sum_{\bar{R}^{d_t}} Z(r_i) \qquad (3)$$

This hypothetical Harris world applied to coal describes the potential supply system essentially as three aggregation problems, Eqs. (1)–(3). Sequentially, (1) the economic geologist, without considering economics or technical specifics, sets the characteristics defining the inventory of deposits or mineral endowment. (2) By employing a lower bound to such characteristics (k'), deposits can be classified resources, both known and conceptualized (inferred). Current economic conditions and feasible techniques, given the evaluation function, then order the deposits in terms of their present value for any given prices, i.e., the difference between potential supply price PS and cost C_i. Finally, (3) a concept of optimal exploration is employed to order in a third aggregation the known and discoverable deposits into potential supply.

Over time, $\lim(s_t) = ps$ as t approaches infinity. Thus,

$$s_t \leqslant ps \leqslant cs \leqslant \text{resource base} \rightarrow R^{d_t} \subset R^d \subset R \subset D$$

The exploration simulation in the NCM takes place in what FEA calls its "production cost estimation" for the range of prices and feasible technologies it assumes by accepting the Katell studies of representative mines. These are used to estimate the unit cost of production for each mine type and to arrange mine types and associated production levels in order of increasing unit production costs (minimum acceptable selling prices). Thus, exploration is simulated by "optimal" assignment of reserves by coal type and region among a variety of existing and hypothetical future mining operations. These project the potential annual production flow from each new or existing mine. The result is a set of economically producible and discoverable deposits within the coal seams. These, ranked in order of their mining cost, indicate the amounts of coal that will be supplied at any of the contemplated conditions of E. In the NCM, changes in the E conditions are simplified to changes in the single market clearing price PS employed as an index of change. Other elements of E have been fixed to simulate exploitation in Eq. (2) by assumptions of constant prices, constant technology, and homogeneous mines. Cost changes are limited to shifts in the point estimates (average costs) of given mine types or to changes in size by varying the number of tons reserves assigned to the mine type and the rate of annual production (depletion). Model mines are assumed to adjust output optimally but seam conditions and parameters remain homogeneous. Figure 1 graphs the FEA potential supply curve aggregated for West Virginia for a single coal quality averaging 23–25.99 MBTU per ton. Figure 2 graphs the potential supply curve for West Virginia for all coal types. The ordering is accomplished for new mines by the exploration simulation of the homogeneous mines. Table 4 gives the production estimates from existing mines in 1975 after depletion and in 1980, by mining techniques.

Figure 1. Potential Supply Curve for Bituminous Low Sulfur (.41–.60%) Coals in Northern West Virginia, National Coal Model

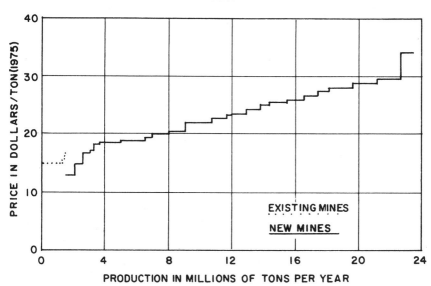

Coal Type HB: Supply Region West Virginia, South
Bituminous Coal
23.00 - 25.99 Million BTU per ton
0.41 - 0.60 pounds if sulfur per million BTU

Source: "Coal Supply Analysis, Validation Workbook for West Virginia," unpublished manuscript by Federal Energy Agency, Dec., 1976. Modified data subsequently published in *National Coal Model*; TM/ESA/78-02, September 1978.

The use of model mine point estimates without a clearly defined statistical relation being demonstrated between seam thickness, depth, and other parameters for the prediction of costs and assignment of reserves has been questioned by Zimmerman (1975) and Gordon (1976b), and by me (Newcomb, 1978). One can also question the adequacy of the data base and therefore the use of point estimates of seam conditions and other observed average parameter values from mined regions to assign costs and reserves. In the NCM, after existing mine capacity in 1980 is adjusted for depletion and removed from the reserves base along with "committed" and illegal reserves, all the uncommitted strippable and deep reserves must be assigned to mine sizes, seam thickness, and depth categories. Finally, the stock of reserves must be changed into potential production flows using assumed mine lives and recovery factors. The simplifying assumptions required for these steps are heroic, given the paucity of data. This is true even in major

Figure 2. Potential Supply Curve for All Coals in West Virginia, National Coal Model

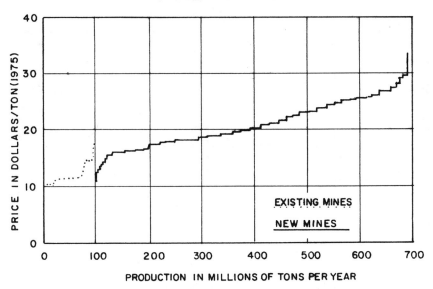

PRODUCTION IN MILLIONS OF TONS PER YEAR

Coal Type All Supply Region West Virginia
All Coal Types

Source: "Coal Supply Analysis, Validation Workbook for West Virginia," unpublished manuscript by Federal Energy Agency, Dec. 1976. Modified data subsequently published in *National Coal Model;* TM/ESA/78-02, September 1978.

(currently mined) seams. In minor seams, with no experience observable, the Eq. (3) elaboration stretches credibility further. Needless to say, the assumption of homogeneous mines ignores the intensive margin, even though the elaborateness of simulation is extreme in the NCM.

The alternative is the establishment of coal costing relations and reserve assignments statistically. Notable for ingenuity in this respect are studies by Charles Rivers Associates or CRA (1975) and Zimmerman (1975). The two approaches to the economic estimation of the coal supply are reviewed by Gordon, who notes the relatively low confidence levels regression analysis affords the statistical associations between costs per ton and seam thickness. In the CRA studies of shifts over time in cost, multiple regression explains only .23 of the variance in costs. Zimmerman's normalization for mine size greatly improves the fit using cross-section data in the regression of thickness and section numbers on productivities, but the major effects of influences other than seam thickness remain and show in the large standard deviation of the error term. Nonetheless, Zimmerman's analysis achieves an elegant and best

Table 4. 1975 and 1980 Production Estimate[a] for Existing Mines in West Virginia, National Coal Model.

Coal Type	ESTIMATED 1975 PRODUCTION			ESTIMATED 1980 PRODUCTION		
	Surface	Deep	Total	Surface	Deep	Total
North						
ZA	0.16	1.99	2.15	0.15	1.94	2.09
ZB	1.40	—	1.40	1.35	—	1.35
ZD	—	1.27	1.27	—	1.23	1.23
ZF	0.54	—	0.54	0.52	—	0.52
ZG	0.25	—	0.25	0.24	—	0.24
HB	0.21	—	0.21	0.21	—	0.21
HD	0.15	0.83	0.98	0.14	0.81	0.95
HF	1.32	0.29	1.62	1.26	0.30	1.56
HG	1.58	19.44	21.02	1.63	18.72	20.35
TOTAL	5.62	23.82	29.44	5.50	23.00	28.50
South						
ZA	0.14	23.20	23.44	0.22	21.33	21.55
ZB	10.77	4.06	14.82	9.95	3.68	13.63
ZD	1.85	7.12	8.97	1.73	6.52	8.25
ZF	0.64	7.91	8.55	0.55	7.31	7.86
HB	1.73	—	1.73	1.59	—	1.59
HD	—	8.67	8.67	—	7.98	7.98
HG	0.01	13.04	13.06	—	12.00	12.00
TOTAL	15.14	64.11	79.25	14.04	58.82	72.86

[a] In millions of tons.
Source: "Coal Supply Analysis, Validation Workbook for West Virginia," unpublished manuscript by Federal Energy Agency, Dec., 1976.

(maximum likelihood) estimate of reserve assignments statistically with an economy of assumptions. The major cost is the assumption of the lognormality of seam thickness. Given predetermined reserve sizes by sulfur content, his method can assign reserves to potential supply easily and show explicitly the variation of costs due to depletion. These fall as the median seam thickness of the exploitable reserves distribution "walks" toward the origin over time. In Appalachia, costs rose 22 percent over 14 years in low sulfur underground and in 38 years in other Appalachian coals. In the Illinois and western basins, the depletion effects are even less noticeable. However, the point is well made that changes in costs can be estimated statistically with far less trouble and time than by the replication of model mine sizes in preassigned reserves. Because both techniques must rely ultimately on the resource preassignments of USGS or USBOM, and these data are criticized by its sources as inadequate to this task, Occam's razor favors the use of inference over simulation. Statistical inference on D substitutes in the aggregation step of Eq. (3) for the elaborate simulations to define exploration. The merit of statistical inference is, then, the simplicity of defining optimal exploration and the economy of supply function estimation given the data base. Unfortunately, statistical functions often perform poorly in allocation modeling and the shortcutting of the Harris framework leaves a model difficult to validate. This leads to speculation whether a modified approach can be found to reduce the residual error term of the Zimmerman estimates and permit the adjustment of variances on the basis of observed trends over time, yet still make use of the "realism" of model mine simulations.

In the case of bituminous, subbituminous coals, and lignites, geologists agree on the earth processes that caused the depositions of carbon, while drill-core information and outcroppings have identified large areas of the resource base. This eliminates the need for complex simulations of optimal exploration efforts and related inferences to delineate the probable discoverable coal resources. Geologists are not so much in agreement with respect to other coal characteristics, especially the presence of sulfur, ash, and trace elements. These are associated with geologic features not so observable as those measuring carbon content or basin extent. In Section IV, I attempt to define the translation of such accessory element occurrence into cost.

Another important feature of the Harris endowment model is the characterization of the deposit as heterogeneous in grade. Because most coal models conceive of optimal exploration as a summing over individual homogeneous operations, they neglect the within-seam variances in parameters affecting cost, i.e., the internal margin. For example, the NCM exhibits only an extensive margin with new mine development occurring as economic conditions change. Says Harris (forthcoming),

> The description of both effects raises two issues: (1) the necessary structure of the potential supply model, and (2) the data which are available for the quantification of the model. Clearly the preferred endowment model would describe deposits, not ore, and it would contain those relationships necessary to convert the deposit to ore tonnage and grade ... Issue two (data availability) arises when thought is given to the quantification or calibration of such a model, for the data are customarily available on ore only ... Consider the data requirements for the transformation equations, equations which express simplistically the mining decision and associate with each deposit an *ore* tonnage and grade ... Statistical analysis of these data could provide the desired relations. In the event that this is not possible, an alternative approach could be employed: these transformation equations would be generated by simulating typical deposits for a variety of sizes, grades, grade variations, and depth and by determining that ore tonnage and grade that represents the optimum mining decision for a given set of economic

and technologic circumstances. Of course, such an approach would require appropriate costing relationships based upon engineering analysis and the modeling of the morphologies of deposits.

Addressing first the issue of structure, this section shows that the NCM does, in fact, produce precisely the sort of simulation described above in a deterministic way. Statistical approaches can do the same through inferences assuming something about the frequency distribution of seam thickness.

III. INDIRECT ESTIMATION OF POTENTIAL SUPPLY: AN INDEX APPROACH TO EXPLORATION

Potential supply *ps* can be formed directly from *R* through the simulation of exploration models or indirectly from *D*. Statistics on the coal deposits of North America include estimates of seam thickness, depth, and sulfur content. By assuming well-behaved frequency distributions of tonnage by seam thickness, one can derive *ps* statistically for high and low sulfur seams in a district if he assumes the relationship between thickness, mine size, and cost. Seam thickness, a proxy for productivity, becomes, in this analysis, a shift parameter in a total or average cost function for mining. Reference is made to the variables listed in Table 5. *B* represents the subset of characteristics *k'* that define the *in situ* mining

Table 5.   Variables Relating Engineering and Petrologic Factors to Coal Productivities and Yields

y	= output of coal, mouth of mine
y'	= output of clean coal
x	= vector of inputs in mining, beneficiation, or conversion
P	= y/x mine productivity
Y	= y'/y = yield
C	= total cost
C/y	= unit cost
B	= vector of coal characteristics *in situ*
B'	= vector of clean coal characteristics
T	= seam thickness
S	= sulfur content by weight
A	= ash content by weight
E	= percentage change in sulfur relative to percentage change in ash via cleaning
R	= washability, sulfur reduction potential
m	= mean seam thickness
s	= variance in seam thickness
K	= lower bound of cost for mining and cleaning
k	= own-price slope of long-run supply

conditions affecting the extraction costs of raw coal y. B' represents the characteristics affecting coal quality such as sulfur and ash, and washability, i.e., reduction of sulfur and trace elements through mineral preparation to obtain clean coal y'. The cost function is

$$C = g(y;B,B') \tag{4}$$

Zimmerman and others single out seam thickness as the single geologic variable of measurable importance that can be identified for seams of given depth and access to given mining techniques. However, the intraseam variance in thickness is very large. It can be argued (Newcomb, 1978) that this variance is as large within seams as among seams in a basin. But most importantly, there are many other variables affecting costs, so that the estimates of unexplained variance in the direct regression of seam thickness on productivities remain quite large. Because the definition of "deposit" in D is an individual seam in a basin, the mining industry is viewed in one period as able to mine selectively all tonnages from such seams of given thickness without losing for subsequent periods unmined tonnages. The realism of these assumptions can be questioned.

It seems more reasonable to "disaggregate" the unexplained variance in cost by attempting the further identification of other parameters relating to cost and coal quality. This extension leads naturally to the concept of a shift "index" for individual seams by county using all the information available in each area. The index is, therefore, an attempt to go further in the explanation of unexplained variance, and it permits one to simulate the industry more realistically. Here, I limit interest to major seams in counties with large remaining reserves.

This extension of the indirect exploration model to include a wider number of seam parameters is described by me fully (see Newcomb, 1977 and Newcomb and Fan, 1980). The index constructed is apt for the case of homothetic or "elasticity preserving" expansions of production in which output level changes or the order of their occurrence will not affect the index values. In such a case, it makes sense to define the weights (α) as elasticities of cost with respect to the key parameters B and the index (I) as of the form:

$$(I,\alpha) = f(P)g(Y)h(S)i(\#S) \tag{5}$$

where $B = \{P,Y\}$ and $B' = \{S,\#S\}$

The index runs on West Virginia are reproduced in Table 6. It yields an ordinal ranking that can be compared with an independently achieved rankings by researchers familiar with the analyses of typical West Virginia coals. The experts' ranking of the coals is not significantly different from the index's, i.e., the rank correlation between the index

Table 6. Index Results (I) for West Virginia and Rankings (R) Based on Variables for Seam Productivity (P), Yield (Y), Raw Sulfur (S) and Sulfur Reduction Potential (#S)[a]

County	Seam	P	Y	S_o	#S	I	R
Monongalia	Waynesburg	0.850	0.714	1.27	0.255	0.671	13
Monongalia	Sewickley	0.876	0.747	4.53	0.313	0.495	18
Brooke	Pittsburgh	0.926	0.500	4.04	0.267	0.431	23
Harrison	Pittsburgh	0.890	0.832	5.13	0.295	0.494	19
Marion	Pittsburgh	0.785	0.935	2.68	0.199	0.565	16
Marshall	Pittsburgh	0.669	0.772	3.84	0.213	0.450	22
Monongalia	Pittsburgh	1.092	0.913	2.46	0.331	0.687	11
Ohio	Pittsburgh	0.763	0.840	3.78	0.317	0.506	17
Grant	Bakerstown	0.728	0.436	3.01	0.764	0.464	20
Preston	Up. Freeport	0.457	0.639	2.16	0.581	0.459	21
Barbour	Md. Kittanning	1.455	0.621	2.07	0.634	0.768	10
Nicholas	Md. Kittanning	1.290	0.617	1.06	0.413	0.837	7
Boone	Lr. Kittanning	1.516	0.787	0.77	1.000	1.113	1
Logan	Lr. Kittanning	1.516	0.750	0.81	1.000	1.108	2
Logan	Stockton-Lwstn	0.578	1.000	0.71	1.000	0.804	9
Boone	Winifrede	0.838	0.657	0.72	1.000	0.829	8
Kanawha	Winifrede	0.759	1.000	0.66	1.000	0.955	5
Logan	Winifrede	0.866	1.000	0.58	1.000	1.008	4
Logan	Chilton	1.108	1.000	0.70	1.000	1.104	3
Logan	Cedar Grove	0.609	0.871	1.91	0.462	0.584	15
Mingo	No. 2 Gas	0.463	0.909	1.12	0.434	0.613	14
Logan	Powellton	0.832	1.000	0.74	1.000	0.938	6
McDowell	Lr. War Eagle	0.585	0.865	1.28	1.000	0.685	12

[a] Coals are from sample crushed to pass 1 to ½ inch screen and washed at specific gravity of 1.40.
Source: Cf. text.

and expert orderings is very high. In the application that follows, a simple log–linear functional form of the index is given to four shift parameters computed for each coal minable by underground methods using the data collected by seam and by county described previously. This version of the index is shown in the ranking of Table 6:

$$I = KP^{B_1}Y^{B_2}S^{B_3}\#S^{B_4}$$

where

P = Productivity underground in tons/man-day, normalized by the hypothetical (1969) "best" productivity of 25 tons per man-day. Except for this normalization, the index values would not exceed unity.

Y = Yield in terms of clean coal percent weight. Y is equal to unity if the sulfur content raw is less than that that would result in emissions of 1.20 lbs. per million BRU (MBTU) at the stack under the normalized heat rate and other conditions of combustion modeled.

S = Sulfur dioxide content of raw coal, SO2R, measured in lbs/ MBTU at the stack. In addition to this measure, the index requires lbs. SO2/MBTU from clean coal (SO2C) and the sulfur reduction rate.

$\#S$ = Adjusted Sulfur Reduction Rate = $\{[(\text{SO2R} - \text{SO2C})/ \text{SO2R}][(1.20/\text{SO2C})]\}^{1/2}$. R is equal to unity if SO2R or SO2C are less than 1.20 lbs/MBTU.

B_i = Weight accorded the ith index variable, the elasticity of I with respect to i.

K = A constant.

    A number of qualifications should be noted. Data on productivities are used directly rather than the proxy seam thickness. For estimations through 2000, only major seams, all of them currently undergoing mining, are included because little change in seams or techniques is assumed. The range of productivities currently achieved in seams 3 to 8 feet thick are therefore thought to be more reliable indicators of future costs than seam thickness over this period. Coal quality is defined by the BTU, ash, and sulfur content of raw coals and coal washabilities. The coal's washabilities are defined by the reduction potential of mineral preparation to desulfurize the coal, based on existing samples of ash and sulfur content raw and clean, mass yields, and thermal yields at conventional sizing levels. All the data on each coal in the sample are given in Table 6. If coals meet EPA standards without washing or scrubbing, yield is equal to unity.

The weights of the shift parameters in the index are not statistically estimated. Instead, they are determined from the "observed" elasticities of unit cost with respect to each variable distinguished in the simulations of models tracing the average cost functions of mining, beneficiation, and sulfur removal processes as a function of productivity, yield, and incremental scrubbing required. The elasticities for productivities in mining at the face and for yields in coal cleaning are taken from the simulation results of process evaluation models. Assuming these elasticities to be independent of scale effects, the unit cost functions for underground mines generally in the Appalachian basins can be obtained from these data. The index implies there is a trade-off or rate of substitution (ROS) discernible between P and Y and that proportional weights can be given S and $\#S$ to reflect the alternatives of scrubbing or beneficiation. The buyer, in effect, by offering premiums or discounts for sulfur content with or without beneficiation can also trade the costs of scrubbing for those of prior mineral preparation of mining. The weights selected sum to one and are derived from the cost models in

$$I = P^{.42}Y^{.22}S^{.28}\#S^{.08}$$

Thus, the index can be conceived of as a joint distribution function estimating the size of the shift in cost likely from changes in seam conditions B and coal characteristics B'):

$$I = f(B,B')$$

For the two-parameter mining cost case (P,Y), it is useful to show the derivation of ps from I that takes the place of exploration simulation.

The parameters influencing clean coal yield are ash content and the level to which mineral preparation is pressed, parameters on which we have some measures, but there are other factors that influence washabilities more difficult to measure. Variations in these influences may drive yields in given processing operations down below the standard for the average seam coal characteristics or mining method employed. The assumption is that the elasticity of output with respect to yield variation is proportionate to the elasticity of cost with respect to yield variation.

For the standard quality coal, defined by the buyer to have standard carbon, ash, and sulfur content, on a dry clean basis, there would be an upper bound to productivities and lower bound to cost K under ideal seam thickness and cover conditions. However, in practice, mining costs would vary depending on the variation experienced in productivities. The index assumptions imply that

$$C(P) = K - B_1(\ln P) \tag{6}$$

B_1 is simply the elasticity of unit cost with respect to variations in productivity. By defining a cost engineering model for ideal conditions and varying productivities, $C(P)$ and K can be determined and B_1 estimated:

$$C(P) = \$15 - 11.54(\ln P)$$

Under those conditions, those shift parameters (B) which change input productivities (P) by impacting neutrally on the relationship between coal output (y) and fixed inputs $(\bar{x})$ in mining

$$y = f(\bar{x};B) = f(P)$$

will change in the same way the unit costs (C) of that mine change by impacting neutrally on the relationship between costs and fixed input prices $(\bar{r})$:

$$c = f(\bar{r};B) = C(P)$$

The parameters influencing seam productivities are seam thickness and depth of overburden, on which we have some measures, but there are many others virtually impossible to measure. Variations in these influences will drive productivities in given mines down below the standard for the average seam thickness or depth of the mine. The assumption is that the elasticity of output with respect to productivity variation is proportionate to the elasticity of cost with respect to productivity variation.

Similarly, those shift parameters (B') that change yield (Y) by impacting neutrally on the relationship between clean coal output (y') and fixed inputs $(\bar{x})$ in processing

$$y' = g(x;B') = g(Y)$$

will change in the same way the unit cost of clean coal changes by impacting neutrally on the relationship between cleaning costs and fixed input prices:

$$c = g(\bar{r};B') = C(Y)$$

Similarly, the index assumptions imply for the standard sulfur and washability conditions:

$$C(Y) = -B_2(\ln Y) \tag{7}$$

B_2 is simply the elasticity of unit cost with respect to variations in yield.

By defining a cost engineering model for ideal conditions and varying yields, $C(Y)$ can be determined (see Newcomb and Peng, 1976; Peng and Newcomb, 1976) and B_2 estimated:

$$C(Y) = -15.66(\ln Y)$$

Clearly there is a trade-off between coals that are higher than average in the mining productivity achievable but lower in yield to effect standard and those that are lower than average in achievable mining productivity but higher in yield to effect standard. By stipulating the standard cost and holding it constant, while varying P and Y, the isocost function can be defined:

$$C(P) + C(Y) = C_i \tag{8}$$

Equations (6), (7), and (8) imply that

$$K - B_1\ln P - B_2\ln Y = C$$

and

$$P^{-B_1}Y^{-B_2} = \exp^{(C - K)} \tag{9}$$

where $\Sigma_i a_i = 1$ and $da_i = B_i$, $i = 1, 2$.
Equation (7) implies

$$(P^{a_1}Y^{a_2})^{-d} = \exp^{(C - K)} \tag{10}$$

where $I = P^{a_1}Y^{a_2}$. Whence

$$C = K - d\ln I \tag{11}$$

Because of this duality, knowing the elasticities of P and Y permits the estimation of the index weights (a). When $B_1 = 11.54$ and $B_2 = 15.66$ as above, $a_1 = 0.42$, $a_2 = 0.58$, and $d = 27.20$. Thus, $I = P^{0.42}Y^{0.58}$ and $C = 15 - 27.20(\ln I)$, and the derivation of the index values as a cardinal measure of associated unit costs is complete.

The index is a three-dimensional cost function [Eq. (11)] in its log form, i.e., a hyperplane with intercept K. It rises constantly as productivities and yields fall below their maximum values of unity. Productivity is defined as a ratio of actual to ideal (maximum) productivity attainable in a seam, while weight loss from mineral preparation cannot fall below zero. The tilt of the cost plane to that of any constant cost C_0 is a function of the relative weights, B_1/B_2.

The cost function in real terms is a concave function of Y and P, with constant rates of increase from the lower bound K. The origin is $O = (1,1)$. Because of the duality between costs and production, the index I is a mirror image of C, with origin $O = (0,0)$. As costs rise to infinity, the value of the index approaches unity asymptotically.

Table 7. Values of the Index (I) and Corresponding Costs (C) for Select Value of Productivity (P) and Yield (Y)

P	Y	I	C	$ Approximation
1	1	1	15.00	$15
1	0.6	0.744	23.06	$23
0.5	0.6	0.747	22.92	$23
0.5	0.6	0.556	30.98	$31

In Table 7, the four-parameter case results are given.

Coals are sold largely in intermediate goods markets and therefore their relative demand prices are not, for the most part, a matter of preferences but are the results of constrained profit maximization on the part of the users. Similarly, coals are supplied as the result of economic processes, and their supply prices are similarly constrained to maximize the profits of producers. In this derivation of demands, coals face substitution from rival fuels. Thus, there will be an upper bound in the price of coal relative to the cost of oil and gas (and to some extent equivalent nuclear energy) to which demand for boiler coals can accommodate price increases. Below this bound, coals will compete among themselves for demand as boiler fuels. The properties of each coal influence its value in use. The raw sulfur content (Katell and Hemmingway, 1974), given a coal's BTU, is the major component of concern in utilization. Low sulfur is worth a premium to the user because he avoids considerable variable cost in burning coals of admissible sulfur content even when the fixed costs of implementing sulfur control at the stack have been undergone. Low particle emission aids in the elimination of hazard from sulfur and other pollutants. The cheapest means to remove the major component of sulfur from coal, that related to ash, is by mineral preparation techniques prior to burning. Chemical means after combustion are the most costly. These two means describe the techniques respectively used to bring coals into compliance: mineral beneficiation and scrubbing. The properties of note for computing the costs of clean coal utilization, in addition to the raw sulfur content of the coal, are the percentage change in sulfur relative to changes in ash via cleaning and the washability or sulfur and ash reduction potential (#S).

On the supply side, also, coals produced from different seams and by various means will substitute for one another. An entry cost common to both surface and underground coals, where these are produced jointly, will establish a lower bound to the cost of production in a region. Between this point and the upper bound described by the ultimate value of any coal to the producer, a wide range of mouth-of-mine prices will be produced, depending on the variation of key factors of mining and processing. These factors can be reduced to two: those that pertain to productivity of production factors (P) and those that pertain to yield (Y) or the proportion of clean coal relative to raw coal output. Because all mineral preparation techniques cause some loss of weight, supply prices must be normalized to reflect a clean coal standard.

Clearly, the attempt of this research is to rank raw coals *in situ* to reflect their potential optimal order of mining and so derive meaningful long-run supply functions for modeling purposes. Such an attempt must account for the premiums assigned by users to low sulfur (S) and the washabilities ($\#S$) properties of clean coal as well as to the productivities and yields attainable by future producers. This definition leads, naturally, to the concept of an index number for reserves by seam and region ordering coals by their ultimate mouth-of-mine prices. To normalize for the cost of delivering comparable coal properties, it is desirable to develop the index number for a standard ton of coal after adjustment by premiums or discounts to the producer for quality differences as described earlier.

The transformation from index value to cost is through Eq. (11). One can show this cost function graphically. All costs are given in 1975 constant dollars. In terms of the Harris framework this represents the exploitation model. The yields, high sulfur and low reduction potential of the worst coals are well below the current Appalachian average. The result of indexing all coals for which data are available is shown in Table 8 for the states of West Virginia, Pennsylvania, Ohio, Maryland, Virginia, Tennessee, East Kentucky, and Alabama.

Clearly the highest ranking coals are found in Virginia, southern West Virginia, and eastern Kentucky; the lowest in Maryland and Ohio. Moderate ranking coals are found in all the states. Very similar costing coals are found in Ohio, Pennsylvania, and northern West Virginia. The index distinguishes county and seam. Note that coals in the same seam show a wide distribution of index values.

The index results transformed into incremental coal costs require a further refinement for the generation of a potential supply function. The tonnages of coal in each category of indexed reserves for that county or group of counties must be defined as a supply district for modeling. The assignment of tonnages makes primary use of the US-BOM and USGS references indicated in Section II. This represents the exploration model, assuming that in the next 30 years Appalachian coals will continue to come exclusively from the major seams and currently producing counties.

Table 8 thus displays the potential supply function for all Appalachia. The range of index values is .20 to 1.20. In terms of costs, the range is $10 to $60. The majority of reserves are obtainable within the West

Table 8. Index Detail, Coal Supply Function, Appalachia.

AL	EK	MD	OH	PA	TN	VA	WV	County	Seam	Index	Underground Reserves[a] (10^6 tons)
						x		Russell	Tiller	1.221	84.66
							x	Boone	Lr. Kittanning	1.113	0
							x	Logan	Lr. Kittanning	1.108	34.98
							x	Logan	Chilton	1.104	195.49
						x		Russell	Jawbone	1.078	185.31
							x	Logan	Winifrede	1.008	134.19
						x		Dickenson	Up. Banner	0.989	122.14
x								Jefferson	Black Creek	0.983	20.71
						x		Wise	Kelly	0.958	35.07
							x	Kanawha	Winifrede	0.955	0
							x	Logan	Powellton	0.938	0.82
					x			Scott	Poplar Lick	0.938	3.17
					x			Campbell	Walnut Mtn	0.933	17.92
						x		Wise	Taggart	0.900	40.61
					x			Claiborne	Jellico	0.897	2.74
				x				Centre	Brookville	0.866	83.88
				x				Jefferson	Lr. Kittanning	0.848	149.39
			x					Vinton	Md. Kittanning	0.843	85.35
							x	Nicholas	Md. Kittanning	0.837	68.25
							x	Boone	Winifrede	0.829	347.79
	x							Harlan	Low Splint	0.810	51.62
							x	Logan	Stockton–Lwstn	0.804	68.81
	x							Floyd	Up. Elkhorn #2	0.778	226.93
	x							Bell	Haddix	0.776	NA[b]
					x			Campbell	Jordan	0.776	6.62
							x	Barbour	Md. Kittanning	0.768	NA
				x				Clearfield	Lr. Freeport	0.760	170.21

						x		Wise	Dorchestor	0.755	62.10
				x				Clearfield	Up. Kittanning	0.753	118.45
				x				Clearfield	Up. Freeport	0.749	54.76
					x			Marion	Sewanee	0.742	25.23
			x					Perry	Md. Kittanning	0.740	515.41
						x		Dickenson	Splash Dam	0.715	50.25
				x				Indiana	Lr. Freeport	0.707	423.95
	x							Martin	Stockton	0.699	NA
						x		Wise	Imboden	0.688	33.55
							x	Monongalia	Pittsburgh	0.687	1342.14
							x	McDowell	Lr. War Eagle	0.685	14.54
x								Jefferson	Mary Lee	0.684	450.37
			x					Harrison	Lr. Freeport	0.683	391.05
	x							Floyd	Hazard #4	0.680	75.43
				x				Butler	Brookville	0.679	2.07
			x					Columbiana	Md. Kittanning	0.678	46.69
				x				Indiana	Up. Freeport	0.676	568.30
				x				Butler	Up. Freeport	0.674	NA
							x	Monongalia	Waynesburg	0.671	544.90
				x				Washington	Pittsburgh	0.652	2995.61
x								Marion	Black Creek	0.647	NA
				x				Armstrong	Lr. Freeport	0.644	172.58
				x				Lawrence	Brookville	0.636	0.09
				x				Centre	Clarion	0.636	75.39
		x						Garrett	Up. Freeport	0.630	312.99
							x	Mingo	Campbell	0.613	146.08
			x					Muskingum	Md. Kittanning	0.607	536.99
				x				Armstrong	Up. Freeport	0.606	359.10
				x				Allegheny	Up. Freeport	0.590	356.61
							x	Logan	Cedar Grove	0.584	503.27
	x							McCreary	Up. Elkhorn #3	0.583	0.40
		x						Garrett	Barton	0.579	0
		x						Garrett	Sewickley	0.576	NA

Table 8. Continued

AL	EK	MD	OH	PA	TN	VA	WV	County	Seam	Index	Underground Reserves[a] (10^6 tons)
x	x							Walker	America	0.575	155.35
x								Jefferson	Gwin	0.573	66.04
					x			Campbell	Jellico	0.569	10.99
							x	Marion	Pittsburgh	0.565	1022.93
				x				Clinton	Lr. Kittanning	0.565	7.98
				x				Centre	Lr. Kittanning	0.563	41.16
		x						Allegheny	Sewickley	0.555	4.16
			x					Belmont	Waynesburg	0.553	337.86
				x				Armstrong	Lr. Kittanning	0.552	463.69
				x				Clearfield	Md. Kittanning	0.552	74.46
				x				Butler	Lr. Freeport	0.551	117.07
			x					Coshocton	Md. Kittanning	0.551	80.55
					x			Anderson	Big Mary	0.551	12.16
				x				Indiana	Lr. Kittanning	0.549	694.12
				x				Greene	Sewickley	0.545	785.45
			x					Gallia	Pittsburgh	0.543	122.88
			x					Belmont	Pittsburgh	0.543	2431.25
			x					Belmont	Sewickley	0.542	1081.96
				x				Greene	Pittsburgh	0.535	3540.07
				x				Somerset	Up. Kittanning	0.521	444.87
				x				Somerset	Lr. Kittanning	0.520	294.43
			x					Harrison	Sewickley	0.518	63.28
			x					Harrison	Pittsburgh	0.517	258.90
			x					Jefferson	Pittsburgh	0.514	327.72
				x				Cambria	Lr. Kittanning	0.514	352.04
				x				Clearfield	Lr. Kittanning	0.514	372.74
				x				Bedford	Lr. Kittanning	0.514	27.36
	x							Bell	Hazard #4	0.510	4.64
							x	Ohio	Pittsburgh	0.506	273.29

								County	Seam		
				x				Monongalia	Sewickley	0.495	848.90
				x				Harrison	Pittsburgh	0.496	335.06
					x			Cambria	Lr. Freeport	0.478	426.43
			x					Allegany	Bakerstown	0.468	NA
				x				Grant	Bakerstown	0.464	72.31
			x					Preston	Up. Freeport	0.459	221.05
x								Walker	Clement	0.455	NA
				x				Marshall	Pittsburgh	0.450	1924.67
					x			Cambria	Up. Kittanning	0.444	359.01
					x			Wstmrland	Up. Freeport	0.437	528.58
			x					Brooke	Pittsburgh	0.431	131.15
		x						Jackson	Brookville	0.430	0.05
	x							Allegany	Franklin	0.419	0
	x							Garrett	Lr. Freeport	0.414	NA
					x			Somerset	Up. Freeport	0.406	209.34
		x						Monroe	Pittsburgh	0.400	413.33
	x							Allegany	Redstone	0.397	NA
	x							Allegany	Bakerstown	0.395	135.41
	x				x			Tuscarawas	Md. Kittanning	0.377	523.18
					x			Cambria	Up. Freeport	0.373	263.14
	x							Allegany	Waynesburg	0.373	2.34
	x							Garrett	Lr. Bakerstown	0.373	132.79
	x							Garrett	Pittsburgh	0.366	0
	x							Garrett	Lr. Kittanning	0.364	NA
	x							Garrett	Franklin	0.364	0
	x							Allegany	Lte Pittsburgh	0.356	NA
		x						Meigs	Clarion	0.303	0.20
	x							Garrett	Up. Kittanning	0.302	55.98
	x							Allegany	Up. Freeport	0.219	102.63
Totals											
6	7	17	17	33	7	8	23				32,469.87

a Include reserves base with thickness > 28 inches.
b NA, Not available.
Source: Newcomb, 1978.

Virginia index range between .35 and .89 or cost range from $15 to $45. This can be compared to the NCM supply function of Section II. The indexed underground supply function for Appalachia is graphed in Figure 3. This reflects the abundance of similar cost moderate sulfur coals in Ohio, Pennsylvania, and northern West Virginia, and the high quality of Virginia, southern West Virginia, and eastern Kentucky coals. In all, the potential supply covers some 30 billion tons of known and unexplored reserves out of the reported 100 billion coal resources of the region. This represents more than enough coal to provide the targeted eastern production through the year 2000 at even the highest projected rates.

The realism of the index simulation of exploration and development depends on (1) the completeness, stability, and reliability of the relationships specified and the goodness of fit over the entire sample and over time, (2) the assumptions about frequency distributions of index variables and their stochastic independence, and (3) the sample coverage and size. Some comment is due on each of these points.

A. Specification

Carbon content is assumed to be uniformly distributed over the seam and county. Productivities are assumed by the industry to be normally distributed within each seam with a large variance due to the wide variations within seam of thickness and other conditions affecting experienced productivities. These unspecified variables are assumed to have lognormal distributions. We assume that the most favorable seams are mined first. Present productivities are taken as good proxies of future conditions only because the industry has sufficient unexplored and undeveloped resources in these seams to continue to mine in the major counties through the year 2000. This subset of the demonstrated reserve base constitutes approximately 33 percent of coal resources. Yield, because it depends on ash content, is assumed lognormally distributed, as is its associated variable, sulfur. Washabilities also are assumed lognormally distributed. The model mine assumptions imply no major changes in techniques. The variance in values of each of the arguments of the index is known to be large. The choice of average experienced values is thus a Bayesian *a priori* assumption. As such, it is no better than the sample size for an individual seam and county permits. Consideration of both these interseam and intraseam variations are accommodated in the index by the process of computing the weights. Each argument was varied 40 percent on the basis of experienced ranges in these seams to simulate the change in cost associated with the argument's variability. However, once fixed, these weights determine cost

Figure 3. Indexed Long-Run Coal Supply, Appalachia

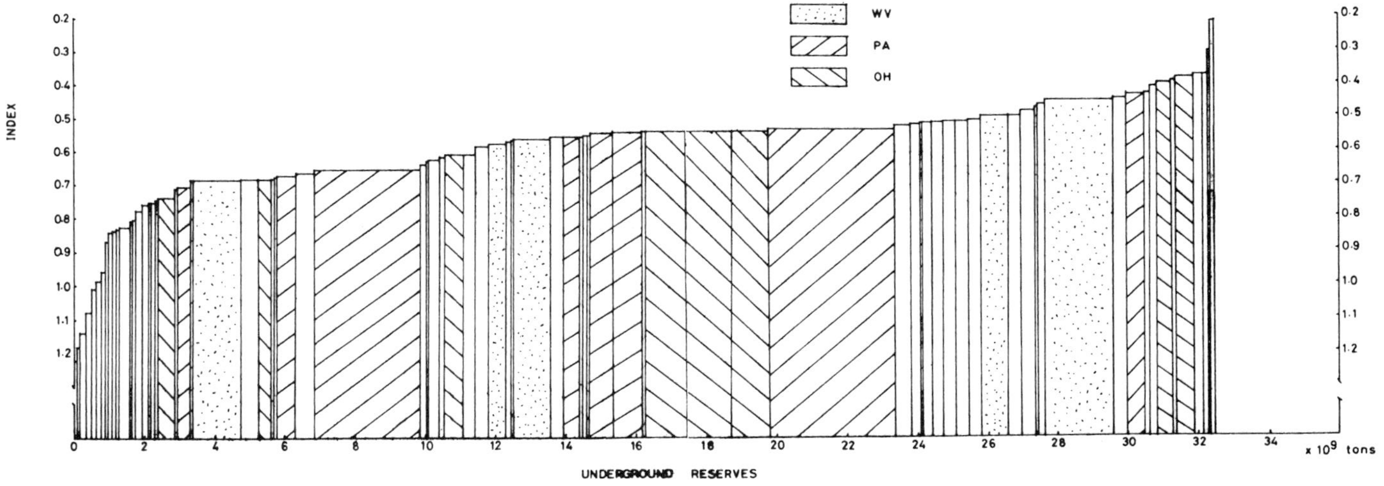

297

estimates and leave no way to estimate residual errors. As in all index applications, there will be an arbitrary number of index formulations that will fit sample data. The index approach has the advantage of a greater degree of specification, which it shares with the National Coal Model exploration simulation, and simplicity of estimation, which it shares with purely statistical exploration models. However, it lacks the maximum-likelihood properties of wholly empirical estimates of seam thickness and residual terms peculiar to the least squares approach. Moreover, the index implies that there will be as wide a range of costs from any group of new mines within a seam as there is within the district among seams at a given time.

B. Robustness and Independence

The index gives us a measured indication of what that range might be (e.g., $30 in West Virginia) and how large the tonnage of resource potential is that is associated with this cost range over the state or some number of counties. The confidence placed in the specification of the index can also be measured in two ways, by noting sample size and coverage.

When the number of data points permits, the index suggests the use of regression to estimate cost functions for other than major seams and for other definitions of k'. The stability of such regressions would then depend on the degree of collinearity of the index arguments. Some indication of the independence of these variables can be gained from the sample variances (s_{xi}), the covariances $[\text{cov}(s_i, x_j)]$, and pairwise correlations (r_{ij}) of the index variables. These are given in Table 9. These results from the sample of Table 8 do not indicate severe statistical problems of collinearity.

C. Coverage

The coverage spatially of coal supply data on reserves and productivities is excellent over the coal producing counties where remaining underground reserves are extensive. It is less adequate for counties in which little mining has, as yet, occurred (Table 10). The number of analyses on reserves of the principal mining states covering both productivities (P) and sulfur content (S) ranges from 20 to 402, adequate for mining district samples, but not for analysis by county and by seam. The coverage for seam washabilities based on sulfur reduction potential $(\#S)$ and yields (Y) is less than adequate for districts and quite inadequate for seam and county estimates if the level of confidence sought is above 20 percent. About 80 percent of the existing mineral preparation plants of any sophistication for cleaning bituminous coals are

Table 9. (Co)Variability of Index Arguments

Statistic	$x_1(\ln P)$	$x_2(\ln Y)$	$x_3[\ln(1.2/S)]$	$x_4(\ln R)$
		VARIABLE		
S_{xi}	.3399	.2292	.7469	.5962
r_{ij}	−.1478 (12)	.4912 (23)	.1657 (34)	
	.1243 (13)	.1657 (24)		
	.1164 (14)			
$\text{cov}(x_i,x_j)$	−.0128 (12)	.0841 (23)	.3389 (34)	
	.1315 (13)	.0226 (24)		
	.0236 (14)			

located in West Virginia. Table 11 shows the data available for the state, which has over 100 minable coal seams. Few seams have data on more than several counties. Even if variances could be known, the coverage of seams across counties with large reserves is quite poor. Clearly the base for exploration models is small.

The index calculations simulating exploration for the Appalachian states contain the major seams in which the numbers of observations warrant independent assessments of mine productivity and *at least one washability is available*. The variance is often extremely large for coal characteristics. Unless the sample is sufficiently large (15 to 25) there is a very low probability that several observations (3–4) will typify the mean or permit confidence in the estimates of seam statistics. Without a firm estimate of mean and variance, one cannot assign tonnages spatially by grade. In the case of seam or mine productivities, there are enough data from county inspectors' reports in West Virginia to test hypotheses concerning these variances. The same is true of raw coal characteristics in some counties from the county reports of the geologic surveys. However, these data have not been routinely published since 1940 by the survey and, in the case of washabilities, there are simply no comparable public data. Thus, small sample bias is a major problem even in the case of coal.

Table 12 shows the size of samples necessary were one to hope for 90 and 80 percent confidence intervals for hypothesis testing. Here the variances are of a known size, for the examples are of raw coal observations in seams with more than 35 observations, i.e., relatively large samples. However, seldom do the number of clean coal observations available approach this magnitude.

Thus the sample of characteristics from each major seam by county is too small to be a robust estimate of the unmined seam potential average productivity, and far too small to serve as a reliable estimate of seam washabilities. The method becomes credible, therefore, only

Table 10. Summary of Data Coverage by Seam and County

Region[a]	RESERVES ANALYSIS			WASHABILITIES ANALYSIS			INDEX			Total Underground Reserves[c] (10⁶ tons)	Index	Percent-age[d]
	Counties	Seams	Number of analyses[b]	Counties	Seams	Number of analyses[b]	Counties	Seams	Number of analyses[b]			
AL	12	21	37	5	5	8	3	5	6	1798.09	692.47	39
E.KY	30	42	219	5	6	7	5	6	7	9466.48	359.02	4
MD	2	13	20	6	14	17	2	14	17	901.91	747.30	83
OH	23	10	110	19	10	29	13	7	17	17423.26	7316.65	42
PA	28	25	183	18	10	43	15	9	33	22788.94	14532.33	64
TN	19	28	93	5	6	7	5	6	7	667.13	78.83	12
VA	7	48	92	3	8	8	3	8	8	2833.24	613.69	22
WV	43	66	402	16	15	25	14	14	23	34377.77	8230.62	24
Appalachia										90256.82	32469.87	36

[a] AL, Alabama; E.KY, eastern Kentucky; MD, Maryland; OH, Ohio; PA, Pennsylvania; TN, Tennessee; VA, Virginia; WV, West Virginia.
[b] Number of analyses on different seams in different counties.
[c] Include reserves base greater than 28 inches;
[d] Percentage calculated as index/total underground reserves × 100.

300

Table 11. Washability Data Coverage, West Virginia

Seam	County	Number of samples
Waynesburg	Monongalia (1)[a]	1
Sewickley	Monongalia (1)	1
Pittsburgh	Brook (1), Harrison (3), Marion (4), Marshall (2), Monongalia (4), Ohio (2)	16
Bakerstown	Grant (1)	1
Upper Freeport	Grant (1), Preston (5)	6
Md. Kittanning	Barbour (2), Nichols (1)	3
Lr. Kittanning	Boone (1), Logan (3)	4
Stockton–Lwstn	Logan (1)	1
Winifrede	Boone (1), Kanawha (2), Logan (1)	4
Chilton	Logan(1)	1
Cedar Grove	Logan (1)	1
Campbell Creek	Mingo	1
Powellton	Logan (1)	1
Lower War Eagle	McDowell (4)	4
Gilbert	Wyoming (1)	1

[a] Sample size in the county.

when observations are pooled over a number of counties and seams. It may, therefore, be a reliable *a priori* estimate only of the range one may expect in a district.

IV. SOME IMPLICATIONS

The utility of exploration and development constructs is clearest in the case of coal supply analysis for the impact analyses performed on allocation models of the industry that are spatial in the sense that these distinguish among competing supply regions and coal types. The results of potential supply estimations for coals are interesting because the construction is simplest in this case and data are far more available. This article implies that, even in this simplest case, the data problems are formidable and that if one attempts to reduce specification errors in the formulation of potential supply, small sample bias may reduce confidence in the estimates. One merit of the index formulation, however, may remain in its more efficient use of information in conjunction with quadratic programming (QP) than the more elaborate simulations of exploration and development model mines in linear programming.

Table 12. Sample Sizes Required for Interval Estimation of Raw Coal Sulfur Content.

Seam	County	α Levels (%)	Sample size required	Confidence interval	Assumption on the distribution of S[a]
Pittsburgh	Harrison	10	57	2.625 < Mean < 3.025	None
			49	2.392 < Median < 2.921	Lognormal
		20	58	2.671 < Mean < 2.971	None
			37	2.414 < Mean < 2.814	None
			36	2.212 < Median < 2.702	Lognormal
			46	2.387 < Median < 2.801	Lognormal
Campbell Creek	Fayette	10	22	0.865 < Mean < 1.065	None
			12	0.849 < Mean < 1.149	None
			15	0.829 < Median < 1.119	Lognormal
		20	15	0.908 < Mean < 1.108	None
			9	0.814 < Mean < 1.114	None
			11	0.807 < Median < 1.090	Lognormal

[a] Percentage weight sulfur content in raw coal.

Another merit, as a balanced Bayesian approach, may be its use of more information in a structured way than would be possible in a purely statistical approach. In either case, the degree to which such approaches to modeling exploration can reflect actual allocations, prices, and production shares with economy and realism is of interest.

In extensive research reported to The Electric Power Research Institute (Newcomb, 1977), I employ a version of a RAND corporation QP designed to test the dynamic properties of airfoils. The model was modified at West Virginia University (Yang, 1979; Liebenthal, 1979) to conform to the spatial equilibrium formulation given to quadratic programming by Takayama and Judge. This QP formulation, following the primal–dual described by Takayama, permits allocation simulations of coal markets in several forms, from the full incorporation of linear demand and supply functions to versions in which demands or supplies are fixed. The formulation is equivalent to the joint solution of two linear programs (LP) in which shipments are selected to minimize delivered costs while the dual constraints computing rents for underground and surface sectors are required. In its simplest versions, therefore, it is reminiscent of James Henderson's seminal LP model analyzing competitive equilibrium in the coal industry (Henderson, 1958).

The QP model operates like the NCM LP except that it is much more efficient. The individual linear supply functions effectively aggregate in two parameters of slope and intercept hundreds of model mine simulations required by the NCM. These simple functions thereby eliminate an enormous number of NCM constraints, reducing impressively the size and the cost of individual runs.

Simply stated, the model employs the indexed potential supply functions for each producing state and fixed demands in each consuming center to allocate coal flows on a least cost basis. Letting x_{ij} *represent the movement of coal from the i*th state to the *j*th center, the model maximizes the sum of producers' and consumers' surplus to assign the most efficient set of such flows. Thus it represents an exploration and development model for coal along the lines suggested by Harris that is empirically based without the need for elaborate simulation. The ability to reproduce existing and future market allocations and to predict prices can be tested. The results are good.

The optimal solutions for $L(x,d,s)$ and the joint dual $L'(\ell_i,\ell_j)$ are given in Table 13. These solutions are compared with the actual 1973 experience of the coal industry in Appalachia, shown in parentheses. Following Henderson (1958), the success of the model can be measured in a validation exercise. We compute the absolute values of deviations of simulated (*) from actual in all cases, i.e., for interregional flows,

Table 13. Current Demands (1973) Index QP without Regulations (in 10^{15} BTU)

Destination	ORIGIN[a]						Total Consumption	Delivered Price
	WV	PA&MD	OH	VA	TN&E.KY	AL		
New England	(0.03)[b] 0.03						(0.03) 0.03	(52.3) 51.4
Mid Atlantic	(0.23) 0.39	(1.03) 0.90		(0.03)			(1.29) 1.29	(48.0) 48.4
IN–MI[a]	(0.15)	(0.07)	(0.24) 0.66		(0.2)		(0.66) 0.66	(47.5) 44.7
No. Central	(0.01)	(0.01)	0.03		(0.01)		(0.03) 0.03	(43.9) 48.0
Ohio Valley	(0.38) 0.56	(0.09)	(0.69) 0.79		(0.56) 0.37		(1.72) 1.72	(38.8) 44.6
So. Central					(0.24) 0.39	(0.28) 0.13	(0.52) 0.52	(39.7) 50.0
So. Atlantic				(0.21) 0.29	(0.72) 0.68	(0.04)	(0.97) 0.97	(48.6) 50.1
Total output	(0.80) 0.98	(1.20) 0.90	(0.93) 1.48	(0.24) 0.29	(1.73) 1.44	(0.32) 0.13	(5.22) 5.22	
M.O.M. price	(31.7) 30.1	(38.8) 37.1	(30.6) 30.9	(41.1) 34.2	(34.4) 33.2	(39.8) 42.4		

[a] WV, West Virginia; PA, Pennsylvania; MD, Maryland; OH, Ohio; VA, Virginia; TN, Tennessee; E.KY, eastern Kentucky; AL, Alabama; IN, Indiana; MI, Michigan.

[b] Figures in parentheses are actual observations.

Source: Mineral Industry Survey, Bituminous Coal and Lignite Distribution, Calendar Year 1973, U.S. Bureau of Mines, Washington, DC: 1974, Steam Electric Plant Factors 1974, National Coal Association, Washington, DC, 1974; Minerals Year Book 1973, U.S. Bureau of Mines, Washington, DC, 1975.

supplies in producing districts, mouth-of-mine prices, and delivered prices. These are, respectively for the control case

(1) $\sum_i \sum_j (1/2)|x_{ij}^* - x_{ij}|/x_{ij} = 26.9/2 = 13.4$ percent

(2) $\sum_i (1/2)|s_i^* - s_i|/s_i \quad = 29.7/2 = 14.9$ percent

(3) $\sum_i (1/2)|p_i^* - p_i|/p_i \quad = \quad 6.6/2 = 3.3$ percent

(4) $\sum_j (1/2)|p_j^* - p_j|/p_j \quad = \quad 8.2/2 = \quad 4.1$ percent

These results "explain" 87 percent of the interregional trade flows observed for the coal industry in 1973, 85 percent of the observed production in the major mining districts, 97 percent of the mouth-of-mine average observed price in producing districts, and 96 percent of the observed price received for steam coals in the consuming centers. This performance is compared with the National Coal Model results in the Electric Power Research Institute publication of research (Newcomb and Fan, 1980).

Because of the economy of computation, model runs on the changes in solution for given changes in demand can be easily obtained. Table 14 shows the results, assuming demand requirements double by 1985 in all of the consuming centers. The total district output changes tell the competitive story with no changes in other conditions. West Virginia deliveries rise almost 300 percent, Ohio coals more than triple output, and Virginia coals increase 6-fold. This growth comes at the expense of Pennsylvania, Tennessee, and eastern Kentucky coals, which increase at much slower rates. Alabama coal production declines. This is in line with the much larger price increases required for the latter coals relative to the faster growing set. Changes in delivered prices reflect the rise in mouth-of-mine prices predicted. These results can be compared with the more elaborate National Coal Model in the various cases in which its NCM or CEUM versions have been published. Two such runs for a similar base case are shown in Tables 15 and 16 for the CEUM version used in a recent impact analysis.

While the focus of this article has been on the simulation of exploration and development and the formulation of exploitation components rather than the properties of the QP or LP allocation models, it is interesting to note that despite its substitution of almost continuous long-run potential supply functions for the step functions of LP models, the QP does not avoid some of the well-known problems of LP. These are, notably, irregularities and paradoxical results in district quantity adjustments and prices. In both examples prices fall as output increases

Table 14. Demand Requirements Double Index QP in 1985 without Regulations

Destination	ORIGIN[a]						Total consumption	Delivered price
	WV	PA&MD	OH	VA	TN&E.KY	AL		
New England	(0.03)[b] 0.06						(0.03) 0.06	(52.3) 55.4
Mid Atlantic	(0.23) 1.332	(1.03) 1.248		(0.03)			(1.29) 2.58	(48.0) 52.8
IN–MI[a]	(0.15)	(0.07)	(0.24) 1.32		(0.2)		(0.66) 1.32	(47.5) 48.7
No. Central	(0.01)	(0.01)	0.06		(0.01)		(0.03) 0.06	(43.9) 52.0
Ohio Valley	(0.38) 0.833	(0.09)	(0.69) 1.894		(0.56) 0.712		(1.72) 3.44	(38.8) 48.6
So. Central					(0.24) 0.856	(0.28) 0.183	(0.52) 1.04	(39.7) 54.0
So. Atlantic				(0.21) 1.371	(0.72) 0.569	(0.04)	(0.97) 1.94	(48.6) 54.1
Total output	(0.80) 2.225	(1.20) 1.248	(0.93) 3.274	(0.24) 1.371	(1.73) 2.137	(0.32) 0.183	(5.22) 10.44	
M.O.M. price	(31.7) 34.1	(38.8) 41.1	(30.6) 34.9	(41.1) 38.2	(34.4) 37.2	(39.8) 46.4		

[a] WV, West Virginia; PA, Pennsylvania; MD, Maryland; OH, Ohio; VA, Virginia; TN, Tennessee; E.KY, eastern Kentucky; AL, Alabama; IN, Indiana; MI, Michigan.
[b] Figures in parentheses are actual observations.
Source: *Mineral Industry Survey, Bituminous Coal and Lignite Distribution, Calendar Year 1973*, U.S. Bureau of Mines, Washington, DC, 1974; *Steam Electric Plant Factors 1974*, National Coal Association, Washington, DC, 1974; *Minerals Year Book 1973*, U.S. Bureau of Mines, Washington, DC, 1975.

Table 15. Estimated Coal Production[a] in 1985 by Scenario, Region, and Method of Mining

Region	Reference case (estimated production without regulations)	Implementation case (estimated production with regulations)
Central and Southern Appalachia		
Surface	214.5	188.5
Underground	129.1	142.8
Total	343.6	331.3
Northern Appalachia		
Surface	58.0	58.0
Underground	57.8	61.8
Total	115.8	119.8
Midwest		
Surface	57.9	57.9
Underground	136.9	143.1
Total	194.8	201.0
South Central		
Surface	64.1	64.1
Underground	0.6	1.1
Total	64.7	65.2
North Rocky Mountain		
Surface	284.0	286.7
Underground	0.0	0.0
Total	284.0	286.7
West		
Surface	72.1	72.6
Underground	30.5	30.5
Total	102.6	103.1
Total United States		
Surface	750.6	727.7
Underground	354.9	379.3
Grand Total	1105.5	1107.0

[a] Values in millions of tons.

Source: ICF, Inc., for the Office of Surface Mining, *Permanent Regulatory Program of the Surface Mining Control and Reclamation Act of 1977*, Draft Regulatory Analysis, Washington, DC, Sept., 1978. Production estimates are based on incremental cost estimates provided by Office of Surface Mining.

in one case and output can fall despite the increase in all demands (including own demands). While variously explicable, such paradoxes remain interesting. Equally interesting are the irregularities, i.e., in which the simulations produce fewer flows than actually observed, encouraging the user to employ higher levels of aggregation in reporting results and in validations of the model. Subsequent research will generalize the properties of allocation model stability and regularity through analytical and sensitivity analyses of the index QP.

Table 16. Estimated Interregional Production Shifts[a] by Method of Mining, 1975–1985, "with" and "without" Implementation of the Regulations Analyzed

Supply district	Actual[b] 1975	ESTIMATED[c]		CHANGE[d]	
		1985, Without regulation	1985, With regulations analyzed	Without regulation	With regulations analyzed
Appalachia					
Underground	224	224	243	0	+19
Surface	172	234	208	+62	+36
Total	396	458	451	+62	+55
Midwest					
Underground	57	79	85	+22	+28
Surface	84	116	116	+32	+32
Total	141	195	201	+54	+60
South Central					
Underground	0	1	1	+1	+1
Surface	21	64	64	+43	+43
Total	21	65	65	+44	+44
Rocky Mountain					
Underground	0	0	0	0	0
Surface	46	284	287	+238	+241
Total	46	284	287	+238	+241
West					
Underground	11	31	31	+20	+20
Surface	23	71	73	+48	+50
Total	34	102	104	+68	+70
Total					
Underground	293	418	434		
Surface	355	687	673		
Total	648	1105	1107		

a Values in millions of tons.
b Source: U.S. Minerals Yearbook.
c Total district tonnage only from NCM scenarios. The mix of underground and surface production is calculated based on existing trends as described in the text.
d Absolute change for surface tonnage only from NCM scenarios. Residual change assigned to underground.
Source: Office of Surface Mining, Permanent Regulatory Program of the Surface Mining Control and Reclamation Act of 1977, Draft Regulatory Analysis, Washington, DC, Sept., 1978.

Table 17. Rents and Outputs Index QP without Regulation

Supply region[a]	Types of mines	Rent (in 10^7 dollars)	Output (in 10^{15} BTU)
WV	Small mine	0.8502	0.541
WV	Low sulfur	0.0456	0.029
WV	Median sulfur	0.1025	0.065
WV	High sulfur	0.5481	0.349
PA&MD	Small mine	2.390	0.467
PA&MD	Low sulfur	0.0801	0.016
PA&MD	Median sulfur	0.0801	0.016
PA&MD	High sulfur	2.058	0.401
OH	Small mine	0.2866	0.176
OH	High sulfur	2.1063	1.298
VA	Small mine	0.2514	0.189
VA	Low sulfur	0.0552	0.0418
VA	High sulfur	0.0821	0.0619
TN&E.KY	Small mine	0.5015	0.1253
TN&E.KY	Low sulfur	0.4629	0.1149
TN&E.KY	Median sulfur	0.9894	0.2460
TN&E.KY	High sulfur	3.8074	0.9465
AL	Small mine	0.1419	0.0273
AL	Low sulfur	0.089	0.0152
AL	High sulfur	0.4853	0.0912
TOTAL		15.4055	5.22

[a] WV, West Virginia; PA, Pennsylvania; MD, Maryland; TN, Tennessee; E.KY, eastern Kentucky; AL, Alabama.
Source: This source is the QP with Index Base Case, 1975, from Liebenthal, 1979.

The QP's continuous functions permit the easy calculation of economic rents in producing regions that market clearing (marginal cost) prices would create under perfectly competitive conditions. Table 17 shows the producers' surplus for each region by type of mine in $10,000,000 units and its associated output in units of 100 trillion BTU. Rents average approximately $.80 per standard ton of 25 MBTU for the case shown. This may not be a bad approximation for the result, assuming the market was competitive for the period researched. Despite the plausibility of these and other results from the coal study, representing the simplest case of potential supply estimation conceivable, the inadequacy of sample size and coverage do not permit very high levels of confidence. Sensitivity studies will present further problems. If this is the situation for the simplest case of all, what is to be said of the exploration component of more complex discovery and production such as that for oil, gas, or uranium? This remains a central question for broad mineral appraisal techniques and their use in policy studies.

REFERENCES

Averitt, P. (1973). Coal *in* D. A. Brobst and W. P. Pratt (eds.), *United States Mineral Resources,* U.S. Geological Survey Paper 820.

Charles Rivers Associates, Inc. (1975). Analysis of the Supply Potential for Southern West Virginia Low Sulfur Coal, Cambridge, Massachusetts.

Department of Energy (1976). Coal Supply Analysis, Validation Workbook for West Virginia, unpublished manuscript by Federal Energy Agency.

Gordon, R. *Economic Analysis of Coal Supply,* Vols. 1 (1976a), 2 (1977), Electric Power Research Institute, Palo Alto, California.

——— (1976b). The Economics of Coal Supply—The State of the Art, *Energy* **1:** 283–289, Pergamon Press, Great Britain.

Harris, D. (forthcoming). Mineral Endowment, Geostatistical Theory and Methods for Appraisal, *in* Richard Newcomb (ed.), *Future Resources, Their Geostatistical Appraisal,* West Virginia University Press.

Henderson, J. M. (1958). *The Efficiency of the Coal Industry,* Harvard University Press, Cambridge, Massachusetts.

ICF, Inc. (1976). The National Coal Model, Description and Documentation, Final Report to the Federal Energy Agency, NTIS PB 236–334.

Katell, S. and E. L. Hemmingway, (1974). Basic Estimated Capital Investment and Operating Costs for Underground Bituminous Coal Mines, IC-8632, U.S. Bureau of Mines, Washington, D.C.

Katell, S. et al. (1972). Cost analysis of Model Mines for Strip Mining of Coal in the United States, IC-8535, U.S. Bureau of Mines, Washington, D.C.

Liebenthal, A. (1979). Interstate Supply Competition in Appalachian Steam Coal Markets, unpublished Ph.D. dissertation, Department of Mineral Economics, West Virginia University, Morgantown, West Virginia.

Newcomb, R. (1977). The Supply and Demand Potential of Eastern Coals, Report to Electric Power Research Institute on Contract No. 951-1 and National Science Foundation Contract No. AER 76-24680.

——— (1978). The Geologic and Statistical Characteristics of Coal Supply Models, *Materials and Science* **2:** 45–57, Pergamon Press, Great Britain.

——— (ed.) (forthcoming). *Future Resources, Their Geostatistical Appraisal,* West Virginia University Press.

Newcomb, R. and Julia Fan (1980). *Coal Market Analysis Issues,* Electric Power Research Institute, Palo Alto, California.

Newcomb, R. and Peng, F. (1976). Modeling the Role of Mineral Preparation in the Implementation of Clean Air Standards, *Application of Computers to the Mineral Industries XIV,* APCOM Symposium Proceedings, The Pennsylvania State University.

Office of Surface Mining (1978). *Permanent Regulatory Program of the Surface Mining Control and Reclamation Act of 1977,* Draft Regulatory Analysis, Washington, D.C.

Office of Surface Mining (1979). *Permanent Regulatory Program of the Surface Mining Control and Reclamation Act of 1977,* Final Regulatory Analysis, Washington, D.C.

Peng, F. and Newcomb, R. (1976). The Economics of Coal Preparation, *Proceedings of the Symposium on Coal Processing and Conversion,* West Virginia Geological and Economic Survey, University of West Virginia.

U.S. Bureau of Mines (1971). Strippable Reserves of Bituminous Coal and Lignite in the United States," IC 8531, Washington, D.C., 1971.

—— (1974). The Reserve Base of Bituminous Coal and Anthracite for Underground Mining in the Eastern United States, IC 8655, Washington, D.C.

—— (1975a). The Reserve Base of United States Coals by Sulfur Content, The Eastern States, Part I, IC 8680, Washington, D.C.

—— (1975b). The Reserve Base of United States Coals by Sulfur Content, The Western States, Part II, IC 8693, Washington, D.C.

—— (1972). Sulfur Reduction Potential of the Coals of the United States, Report of Investigation, 7633, Washington, D.C.

—— (1974a). Sulfur Reduction Potential of the Coals of the United States, FC 8281, Washington, D.C.

—— (1974b). Survey of Sulfur Reduction Potential in the Appalachian Regional Coals by Stage of Crushing, IC 8282, Washington D.C.

Yang, C. W. (1979). A Critical Analysis of Spatial Commodity Modeling: The Case of Coal, unpublished Ph.D. dissertation, Department of Mineral Economics, West Virginia University, Morgantown, WV.

Zimmerman, M. (1975). The Supply of Coal in the Long Run; the Case of Eastern Deep Coal, Report No. MIT-EL 75-021, Energy Laboratory, Massachusetts Institute of Technology, Cambridge, Massachusetts.

THE RELATION BETWEEN EXPLORATION ECONOMICS AND THE CHARACTERISTICS OF MINERAL DEPOSITS

D. A. Singer and D. L. Mosier

I. INTRODUCTION

A view held by many involved in exploration for metals is that the larger tonnage deposits tend to be discovered first. Empirical evidence to test this belief has not been forthcoming; however, validation of this assumption may seriously affect both exploration economics and resource estimates. If the larger deposits are discovered first, then diminishing returns of exploration expenditures can be expected under certain conditions. Reliance on grade–tonnage models in resource assessments of incompletely explored areas may provide biased estimates of the undiscovered deposits if larger deposits tend to be found first.

Because mineral deposit discovery dates are poorly documented and frequently conflicting, a different approach is taken here. Physical characteristics of one mineral deposit type are used with certain features of the exploration process to determine if larger deposits are discovered first. Results of this examination are then used to consider the effects of some physical properties of deposits on the economics of exploration.

II. SOME FEATURES OF EXPLORATION FOR METALS

Exploration can be characterized as a multistage search process in which only the last stage, drilling, is usually definitive. At each stage an attempt is made to reduce the area to which the next, typically more expensive, stage of search is applied. Each stage may be viewed as an attempt to discriminate between areas that contain valuable deposits and areas that do not. Because deposit detection is probabilistic at each stage, classification errors of both types (that is, rejecting valuable deposits and accepting nonvaluable occurrences) and their associated costs must be balanced against the possible gains of discovering a deposit.

Perhaps the nature of this process can best be understood through a few simplified examples of the search for porphyry copper deposits. Porphyry coppers are high-tonnage, disseminated copper sulfide deposits that are usually associated with rocks having granitic affinities. Frequently the copper-bearing zone is surrounded by a zone of disseminated pyrite; these two zones are commonly called the sulfide zone or system (Figure 1). A less obvious zone of alteration typically extends from the center of the deposit out to, and frequently beyond, the sulfide zone. Although there are other features of porphyry coppers that locally aid in exploration such as associated vein and skarn deposits, the basic properties discussed here will serve for the examples.

The first stage of exploration for exposed porphyry copper deposits entails reduction of the search area to geologic terrains containing certain favorable varieties of granitic rocks. The next stage relies on visual identification of sulfide zones. Frequently these zones are easily observed as "rusty" appearing areas. Alteration zones that extend beyond the sulfides are more difficult to recognize. Determining whether the sulfide system contains a copper mineralized zone during the next stage of exploration requires drilling. Many sulfide systems contain no copper zone; perhaps 50 percent of the sulfide systems in Arizona are barren.

Exploration for porphyry copper deposits that are covered by younger, unmineralized rocks involves more risk and more expense. The first stage reduction of search area has a greater chance of errors for the covered areas than it does for the exposed areas; geology and locally aeromagnetics are used for the extrapolation under the cover. In the next stage, geophysical techniques such as induced polarization are used to identify sulfide systems. Increasing depth of cover seriously reduces the ability of these tools to discriminate. The last stage is drilling.

An attempt is made through these examples to limit consideration of exploration to particular mineral deposit types, particular sets of exploration techniques, and particular geologic settings, such as covered

Figure 1. Schematic Plan of Zonations in Porphyry Copper Deposits

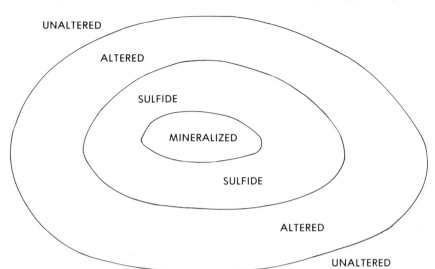

or exposed regions. This is necessary in order to properly address the question of whether size biasing occurs in the finding order of deposits. The history of exploration is full of examples of deposit types that were ignored because they were not economic to mine at a particular time, of deposit types that were not recognized, and of geologic settings that were not explored because exploration techniques were lacking that could find deposits in that setting. Thus, even if discovery dates were available, interpretation of the record could prove difficult or misleading.

III. SOME PHYSICAL CHARACTERISTICS OF MINERAL DEPOSITS

Like mineral deposit discovery dates, public information concerning the physical characteristics of mineral deposits is sparse and variable in quality. Probably the best documented deposit type is porphyry copper; most of the analysis in this paper will therefore concern these deposits. Estimates of tonnage, average copper grade, and contained metal along with alteration, sulfide, and copper mineralized areas were compiled from a large number of sources for porphyry coppers. Measurements could be made or estimates were available for either the sulfide, copper mineralized, or altered areas of all 89 deposits that had grade and tonnage estimates.

Table 1. Summary Statistics for Porphyry Copper Deposits

Variate	Number of deposits	Mean ($\log_{10}$)	Standard deviation ($\log_{10}$)	Median (arithmetic)	Asymmetry $(b_1)^{1/2}$	Peakedness (b_2)
Tonnage (metric)	89	8.450	0.605	2.78×10^8	0.05 NS[a]	3.49 NS
Copper grade (percent)	89	−0.238	0.191	0.578	0.21 NS	3.23 NS
Tonnage of metal (metric)	89	6.212	0.655	1.63×10^6	0.16 NS	3.00 NS
Area of sulfides (km²)	72	0.730	0.476	5.37	−0.39 NS	3.35 NS
Area of copper mineralization (km²)	61	−0.103	0.524	0.789	−0.65 NS[b]	2.81 NS
Area of alteration (km²)	29	0.717	0.550	5.22	−0.09 NS	2.80 NS

[a] NS. Not significant.
[b] Significant at 5 percent level.

316

Summary statistics for altered, sulfide, and mineralized zones, tonnage, average grade, and contained metal of the porphyries are presented in Table 1. Absence of estimates for all variates on each of the 89 deposits led to variable sample sizes for the statistics. The mean sulfide area that is larger than the mean altered area is due to sampling variability; for deposits that have estimates of both variates, the mean altered area is slightly larger. Tests of asymmetry and peakedness of logarithms of the samples demonstrate that the lognormal distribution is probably adequate as a model of each variate. The significant skewness of the copper mineralized area could be due to either errors of measurement or to the small sample size.

The adequacy of the lognormal distribution as a model of each variate suggests a strong skewness in the arithmetic data. This skewness is reflected by the ten largest deposits accounting for over 60 percent of the metal in the 89 porphyry copper deposits (Table 2). Sandstone uranium deposits apparently follow this pattern (Griffiths and Singer, 1973). The ten largest podiform chromite deposits in California also account for over 60 percent of the chromite found to date (Table 3). Over 85 percent of the mercury found in the California coast ranges is contained in the ten largest deposits (Table 4). Similar results for petroleum can be linked to the observation that larger deposits tend to be discovered early in the exploration of any region (Drew, Attanasi, and Root, 1978). Because the historical discovery record is not available for porphyry coppers, an indirect method of demonstrating this linkage must be used.

Table 2. Cumulative Proportion of Copper Contained in Porphyry Copper Deposits

Rank of deposits	Cumulative proportion of deposits	Cumulative proportion of metal
5	.056	.474
10	.112	.637
15	.169	.731
20	.225	.788
25	.281	.834
30	.337	.871
35	.393	.900
40	.449	.920
45	.506	.937
50	.562	.951
60	.674	.974
70	.787	.988
80	.899	.997
89	1.000	1.000

Table 3. Cumulative Proportion of Chromium Contained in the 43
Largest Podiform Chromite Deposits in California

Rank of deposits	Cumulative proportion of deposits	Cumulative proportion of metal
1	.004	.199
5	.019	.505
10	.037	.695
15	.056	.762
20	.075	.797
25	.093	.828
30	.112	.855
35	.131	.875
40	.149	.892
43	.160	.902

Source: Menzie and Singer, 1980.

In order to establish a linkage between the order of discovery and
size (tonnage) of deposits, the relationships among the physical characteristics of the deposits are analyzed. A plot of average copper grade
against tonnage displays no apparent relationship between the variates;
a test of the linear correlation of the logarithms of the variates confirms
this observation (Figure 2 and Table 5). However, contained metal is
so highly correlated with tonnage that the two variables could be in-
terchanged (Figure 3 and Table 5). The existence of a linkage between
rate of discovery and deposit size can be tested by examining the relations between tonnage or contained metal and the deposit characteristics that affect the chance of discovering the deposits. Tonnage and
contained metal are both significantly correlated with the areas of sulfides, copper mineralization, and alteration (Figure 4, 5, and 6 and

Table 4. Cumulative Proportion of Mercury Contained in the 12
Largest Mercury Deposits from the California Coast Ranges

Rank of deposits	Cumulative proportion of deposits	Cumulative proportion of metal
1	.007	.339
3	.021	.627
5	.036	.720
7	.050	.796
9	.064	.857
11	.079	.893
12	.086	.907

Source: Menzie and Singer, 1980.

Figure 2. Tonnages and Grades of Copper in Porphyry Copper Deposits

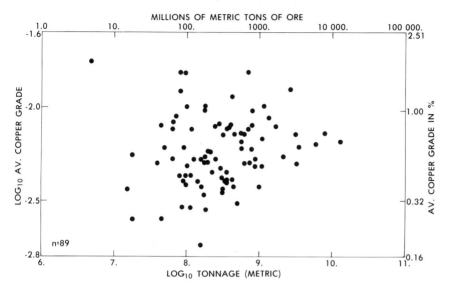

Table 5. Correlations among Porphyry Copper Variables

Variate	*Versus*	*Number of deposits*	*Correlation coefficient*
Tonnage	Copper grade	89	.110 NS[a]
	Contained metal	89	.957[b]
	Area of sulfide	72	.565[b]
	Area of copper mineralization	61	.654[b]
	Area of alteration	29	.657[b]
Contained metal	Copper grade	89	.398[b]
	Area of sulfides	72	.631[b]
	Area of copper mineralization	61	.660[b]
	Area of alteration	29	.660[b]
Copper grade	Area of sulfides	72	.385[b]
	Area of copper mineralization	61	.306[c]
	Area of alteration	29	.338 NS
Area of copper mineralization	Area of sulfides	45	.651[b]
	Area of alteration	25	.664[b]

[a] NS, Not significant.
[b] Significant at 1 percent level.
[c] Significant at 5 percent level.

Figure 3. Tonnages of Ore and Tonnages of Contained Copper in Porphyry Copper Deposits

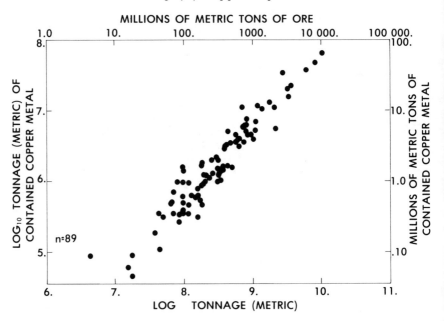

Table 5). Copper grade is also related to contained metal and the sulfide and copper mineralized areas, however the correlations are not particularly high (Figure 7).

For both covered and exposed porphyry copper deposits, the area of the sulfide zone is an important determinant of the chance of discovery. The high positive correlations between tonnage or contained metal and sulfide area suggest that the chances of discovering a large deposit are better than discovering a small deposit. Thus unless the exploration process is much more efficient finding small deposits than it is finding large deposits, the larger deposits should be discovered earlier on the average.

IV. EFFECTS OF PHYSICAL CHARACTERISTICS OF DEPOSITS ON RESOURCE ESTIMATES

Most resource estimation methods rely on some form of analogy where knowledge of what has been found is used to project what may remain to be found. For porphyry copper, podiform chromite, and mercury

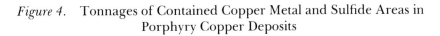

Figure 4. Tonnages of Contained Copper Metal and Sulfide Areas in Porphyry Copper Deposits

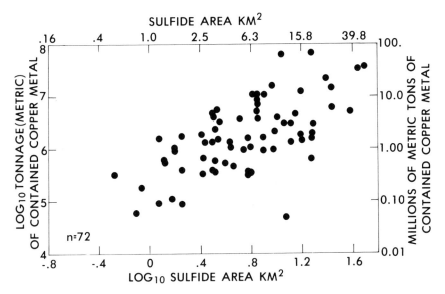

from California, for sandstone uranium, and for petroleum deposits, the observation has been made that the few largest deposits account for the majority of the discovered commodity from each deposit type or geologic setting. The adequacy of a lognormal model for tonnages of many types of mineral deposits (Menzie and Singer, 1980) suggests that the pattern of a few deposits containing most of the commodities may be appropriate for all mineral deposit types. If the deposits that have been found are not representative of the deposits yet to be found, then a biased estimate of the total resources and, in particular, the undiscovered resources may result.

The critical issue is whether larger deposits tend to be discovered early in the exploration process. Evidence presented here suggests that for porphyry copper deposits located in the same geologic setting, larger deposits should be discovered earlier than smaller deposits. Menzie (personal communication, 1979) has found that the large tonnage mercury deposits in the California coast ranges tended to be discovered early. Any deposit type for which deposit tonnage is positively correlated with the surface projection area of features that lead to discovery should tend to show a discovery sequence of large deposits being found early. It appears likely that most, if not all, mineral deposit types meet this

Figure 5. Tonnages and Mineralized Areas in Porphyry Copper
Deposits

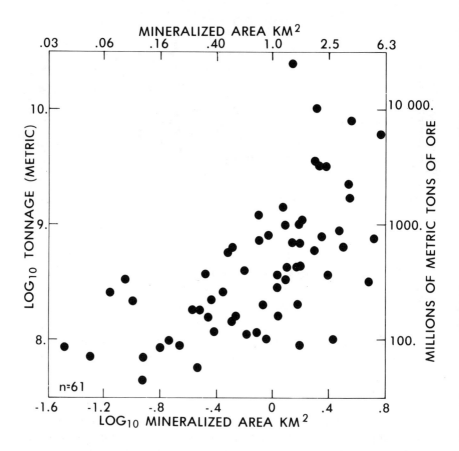

criterion. It should be noted that these conclusions only apply within
deposit types in common geologic settings. Even within deposit types
the actual record of discoveries may deviate from this pattern due to
chance, varying exploration starting times in different geologic settings,
and varying exploration starting times in different political units.

Given that the weight of evidence favors larger mineral deposits being
found earlier, care should be exercised in methods of resource estimation that use the size or tonnage of known deposits as estimators of
the size or tonnage of undiscovered deposits. If the historical record
of discoveries is available, then Barouch and Kaufman's (1977) method
of estimating the mean and variance of the parent population and the

Figure 6. Tonnages of Contained Copper Metal and Alteration Areas in Porphyry Copper Deposits

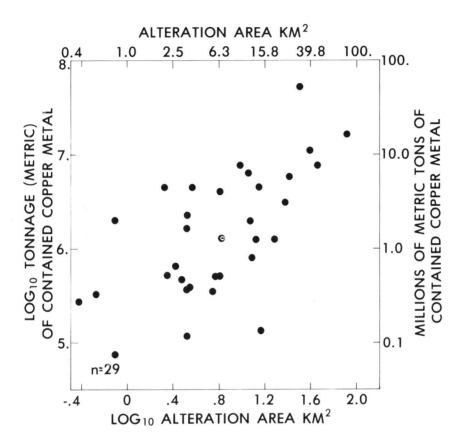

number of deposits might be appropriate. In many cases the historical record of discoveries is not available for metal-bearing mineral deposits and an alternative must be sought. One possible alternative is to construct models of the tonnages based on similar deposits from a well-explored region and to apply by analogy the models to all deposits in the incompletely explored region. Problems with this approach include the question of whether the analogy is reasonable and the possible loss of information from any discovered deposits in the incompletely explored region. A modification of the method whereby the tonnage model is adjusted to account for the tonnages of the discovered deposits in the incompletely explored region might be the most reasonable tack.

Figure 7. Tonnages of Contained Copper Metal and Average Copper Grades in Porphyry Copper Deposits

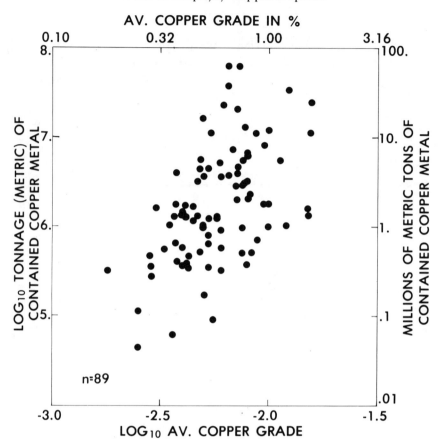

V. EFFECTS OF PHYSICAL CHARACTERISTICS OF DEPOSITS ON ECONOMICS

It is generally recognized that for two deposits of the same type, setting, and grade, the larger tonnage deposit will be more profitable to mine due to economics of scale. If the conclusion that larger deposits tend to be found earlier is correct, then it follows that earlier discovered deposits would tend to be less costly to mine than the later discoveries.

Typically, the exploration of a region is not systematic. There are multiple passes or attempts at exploring a region, and the only information common to the explorers is knowledge of successes. The first few passes over the region tend to discover the larger deposits first. The smaller, more difficult to find, and possibly less profitable deposits tend to remain for later passes over the region. The effectiveness of exploration may decrease because of redundancy of information obtained from adjacent samples (Singer, 1976). Many of the geologic features that might be confused with mineral deposits probably are small, and the possibility of errors of detection and associated exploration costs probably increase for smaller tonnage deposits.

VI. SUMMARY AND CONCLUSIONS

For deposit types that have been tested, the majority of total metal from known deposits is contained in the few largest deposits. Similar observations have been made for petroleum. The historical record of discoveries of mercury deposits in the coast ranges of California and petroleum deposits in many basins shows that the larger deposits tend to be discovered early. Analysis of the physical characteristics and exploration process of porphyry copper deposits indicates that, within each geologic setting, larger tonnage porphyries should also be found earlier than smaller deposits. It is likely that exploration for most mineral deposit types will display the same pattern.

The conclusion that large deposits of each type are probably discovered early affects both the economics of exploration and resource assessment procedures. Resource assessment methods that rely on analogy with what has been discovered must be used carefully in order to avoid biased estimates. Ideally the information available from the earlier discovered deposits can be used to adjust the estimates.

The economics of exploration and mining is also affected by larger deposits being discovered earlier. Exploration for metals is a multistage process in which each stage produces a smaller search area in which the next, typically more expensive, stage is applied. With the exception of the location of deposits found, explorationists for metals usually do not share information on the results of their efforts. Thus for a given deposit type in a region, there should be a tendency for exploration costs per ton of metal found to increase because the area to be searched is reduced slightly by the larger deposits discovered early, but the total target area remaining to be discovered is reduced significantly. Because of economics of scale, the earlier discovered deposits should also be more profitable to mine.

NOTE

This article was presented at the Conference on the Economics of Exploration for Energy Resources, New York University, May 17–18, 1979.

REFERENCES

Barouch, E., and Kaufman, G. M., (1977). Estimation of Undiscovered Oil and Gas. *in* Mathematical Aspects of Production and Distribution of Energy, Proceedings of Symposia in Applied Mathematics, American Mathematical Society. **21:** 77–91.

Drew, L. J., Attanasi, E. D., and Root, D. H., (1978). Importance of Physical Variables in Petroleum Supply Models, *in* J. H. DeYoung, Jr. (ed.), Proceedings of the 1977 Mineral Economics Symposium, AIME, Washington, D.C.

Griffiths, J. C. and Singer, D. A., (1973). Size, Shape, and Arrangement of Some Uranium Ore Bodies, 11th International Symposium on Computer Applications in the Mineral Industry, p. B82–B110.

Menzie, W. D., and Singer, D. A., (1980). Some Quantitative Properties of Mineral Deposits; *in* R. F. Meyer and J. S. Carman (eds.), The Future of Small Scale Mining, UNITAR, p. 27–34.

Singer, D. A. (1976). Area of Influence of Exploratory Drill Holes Under Conditions of Errors of Recognition, *in* A. Weiss (ed.), *World Mining and Metals Technology* (AIME) **2:** 1037–1048.

PART V
POSTSCRIPT

WHAT HAVE WE LEARNED;
WHAT DO WE EXPLORE NEXT?

James B. Ramsey

One matter that is abundantly clear from the conference is that the empirical modeling of exploration *per se* is virtually nonexistent, although there are some supply models that contain submodels of discovery. In addition, the difference between exploratory and discovery models is the difference between modeling purposive behavior and mechanistic outcomes. In short, models in which, for example, discovery is essentially a function of the proportion of the unsearched area that contains oil is a model of "discovery" and basically mechanistic. Models of exploration by contrast would concentrate on the factors affecting firm decision making about where, how, and when to explore, modified albeit by the firm's presumed knowledge of the geologic possibilities.

Insofar as either exploration or discovery has been considered, it has been in the context of general supply models. Extant supply models are of four major types: simple curve fitting, either of the Hubbert type or the early so-called "econometric" models; the operations research-oriented individual firm specifically using highly detailed data-type models; geologic–statistical models; and economic (or econometric) models. Let us compare and contrast these models very briefly.

One of the unfortunate ironies of statistical life is that with sufficient imagination any researcher can obtain "good fits" with some model to any data, but the mere fact of getting a good fit to historical data is irrelevant to the problem of using such a model in order to forecast future behavior. Consequently, the procedure of "curve fitting" on the basis of naive *ad hoc* rationalizations, no matter whether or not the variables involve economic terms, is doomed to failure both as an analytical tool and as a device for forecasting future supplies. These are models in which one can have no confidence.

This type of model was not considered directly in the conference, although Attanasi *et alia* did review the early econometric models and in the process indicated their major failings with respect to geologic constraints and the known facts with respect to discovery. What was not pointed out by these authors was that those models were not carefully considered economic structures either and the relationships estimated were not derived from basic economic theory.

The operations research-oriented models are in a far different category. In such models the attempt is made to simulate the firm's decision-making procedures. These models are usually characterized by being fairly simple in concept but highly complicated in form in that they involve a large number of variables, multiple decision-trees, arrays of feedback loops, and so on. Trying to understand the behavioral implications of these highly complicated models is frequently only possible by simulation techniques. Such models are data intensive. The object is to provide, through aggregation over the analysis of a series of specific prospects within plays, an "estimate" of future outcomes by "duplicating" the decision-making processes over known outcomes and previously exploited plays. In short, by simulating past behavior with respect to current opportunities, one hopes to estimate future supply. There is much to recommend this approach when handled by researchers having great familiarity with the decision process and when limited to forecasts in the near future and within the context of known experience. Simply stated, these models can, but not necessarily will, perform well under the maintained hypothesis that the way things were done in the past will be how they will be done in the future and that the economic system and the geologic constraints remain constant between fitting the model and using it as a forecasting tool. However, such models are not useful and can be most misleading if one wants to evelaute the outcome of new procedures, a new economic system of rewards and constraints, or a new geologic environment. Such models by their very design give very little insight into how the supply system or oil market functions.

In the conference, two researchers reported on work in this category: Kaufman, who has been successfully pursuing this approach for some time, and White. Because the MPRA model discussed by White owes so much to the work of Kaufman and Drew, the two articles can usefully be regarded as a pair of examples of this type of modeling.

Notwithstanding their potential, this type of model has pitfalls for the unwary; in particular, their heavy data requirements and intricate attention to detail is as much a deficiency as an advantage. Massive detail inhibits learning by the researcher and the rapid acquisition of insight into the fundamentals of the behavioral process under examination. The necessary reliance on large amounts of data means that one faces an enormous data-collecting task and, as is well known, analysis errors and mistakes rise exponentially with the size and complexity of the data set being used.

However, all of this attention to detail and massive quantities of data masks a more serious problem. The usefulness of these models depends upon the confidence one has in their ability to forecast reliably and our concept of reliability depends on the extent to which we believe that the circumstances underlying the generation of the model's particular structure continues to apply over the forecast period. Especially in those cases where sampling or Monte Carlo simulation procedures are used to generate results, the mistaken assumption is often made that such models are not subject to "inferential ills" as are "econometric" or "statistical" models. The truth, however, is quite the reverse, simulation models are even more prone to fitting errors because there are fewer checks on the model itself and the behavior of the residuals than is the case in regression analysis. Second, a crucial requirement with such models, but one not often pursued, is to investigate the sensitivity of the results to the structural form of the model and to the estimates, which are often mere guesses, about the values of the parameters used to generate the Monte Carlo simulations.

The model mentioned in the Attanasi *et alia* article is in an intermediate category. Basically, the model is mechanistic, being driven quite simply by the perceived proportions of reservoirs by size category. The addition added by the authors was to introduce the effects of search and development costs on the cutoff point for search effort and to estimate the parameters of a simple "find-the-biggest-first" type of model.

One very important factor raised by these authors stems from the obvious fact that the distribution of reservoirs or fields is highly skewed to the right, the lognormal distribution providing a rough approximation to the unknown distribution. With any such distribution, the *mean* is heavily affected by the low density of, but very large values contained in the tails of the distribution. Success rates on the other hand depend upon the density in the body of the function. So the observed mean is determined predominantly by the small number of gigantic fields, whereas the median or mode of the distribution is determined by the very large number of very small reservoirs or fields; consequently the median is a small fraction of the mean. Because sampling is nonrandom, one must recognize the trade-off over the life of a basin between large expected discovery sizes and low success rates in the early stages of exploration to very small expected discovery sizes and high success rates in the later stages.

Geologic–statistical models are a relatively new development and when restricted to the original use for which designed provide both useful forecasts and the requisite structural data analysis for the development of a rigorous theory of geologic relationships. For example, if one ignores the process of exploration itself and concentrates on being able to forecast volume of recoverable oil obtained from statistical analysis of the geologic characteristics of prospects within a given basin, then this limited objective is attainable with high probability by this type of model. A more important payoff from this type of research is that it provides the basic structure within which alternative geologic theories can be tested. Davis and Harbaugh, as illustrated by their article in this volume, are two of the major researchers in this area.

The last group of supply models discussed in the literature are "economic," or at least are intended to be. A good example is provided by Epple's model, which is presented in this volume. As the reader may recall, Epple began his article with a statement concerning three characteristics that useful econometric models in this area of application should exhibit: supply equations should be derived explicitly from the maximization of the objective functions of the suppliers; the specification of the model should include statements about the properties of the disturbance terms; and the formation of producer expectations must be carefully stated. These desirable traits, together with the usual requirements for good modeling, have in the past been more conspicuous by their absence than by their presence. The result, of course, has been to produce basically *ad hoc* regression functions for fitting historical data. Such methods do not produce useful and reliable forecasts, nor do they provide any insight into the functioning of energy supply markets.

The Epple model is straightforward and produces a very simple relationship between the observable variables. Basically, firms are assumed to seek to maximize their discounted present value of net returns from oil and gas production. The marginal (incremental) cost function is a linear function of output, but its intercept shifts upward with accumulated output. Both prices and "technological" shocks to production are assumed to be elements of an autoregressive series. While the model is very simple in structure, it allows for a rich variety of market conditions to be examined. Most importantly, it has the distinct scientific

advantage of spelling out very clearly the observable circumstances under which it can be rejected.

One important side benefit is to enumerate the conditions under
which the Hubbert model would be obtained as a special case of the
Epple system. In essence, a Hubbert model will be produced if one
assumes that firms make production decisions before observing price
in the productive period (plausible), that firms make decisions with
neither risk aversion nor concern about probability of ruin (most implausible), and finally that firms expect future real prices to remain
constant, which might have been moderately plausible in the past but
is clearly highly implausible for the future.

Given this theoretical analysis of the Hubbert model, it would appear
that his empirically determined model will have to be altered once firms
cease to believe future oil prices will remain constant, if this is not
already the case.

The second part of the book is quite short, but potentially of great
importance for policy. To date the attention of economists has not been
focused to any recognizable extent on a crucial aspect of supply modeling, namely the exploration phase. The two full articles in the theoretical part of this volume are the main exceptions in the theoretical
economic literature.

Gilbert addresses an issue of some controversy at this time, namely
to what extent will a "free" market in exploration produce the socially
desired level of exploration. The analysis in this article builds on some
of Gilbert's earlier work in which the firm's drive for exploration was
an alternative to increasing costs of extraction from existing fields.

Gilbert recognizes that exploration produces, or rather can produce,
two products: oil and information. It is the latter that may cause difficulties in the operation of an effective exploration market due to the
possible informational externalities generated by exploring firms; in
short, if exploration firms are unable to obtain from their revenues *all*
of the benefits generated by their efforts, too little exploration will be
undertaken.

The analysis of such markets is always in two parts: first, an analysis
of the structure of the situation together with an evaluation of the
specific implications of the presence of informational externalities. This
is the subject of Gilbert's article. The other step is to evaluate *empirically*
the probable extent and degree of externalities required. Currently,
there is some dispute about this matter; some claim that the informational externalities are significant and therefore have a substantial
impact on exploration rates and its geographic distribution, but others
claim that the externalities, even if present, are insignificant in size with
a corresponding negligible effect on exploration behavior.

The Ramsey article is considerably different, both in approach and with respect to those aspects of behavior on which greatest attention is placed.

With respect to the approach, the noteworthy aspect is that probability-of-ruin concepts are used with the assumption that the firm is a net-worth maximizer. The outcome, as the reader is now aware, is that what one might call "risk averse type" behavior is generated without the attendant difficulties of assuming that *firms,* as opposed to the managers, are risk averse.

The potential policy implications are, however, far more important than the resolution of mere technical difficulties. Thus, if the theory is empirically tested and not found wanting, then we will have gained considerable insight into the workings of the oil exploration market.

Perhaps the most important shift in attention that would occur as an outcome of this research is to recognize the importance of the *distribution* of oil exploration by type of area and the corresponding importance of the distribution of firm sizes that are engaged in exploration. Next, the symbiotic relationship between large and small firms is of vital importance to long-run success in exploration. Our improved understanding of the general process of exploration will enable us to disentangle the effects due to changes in geologic and technical constraints from those of political and economic forces. Finally, the pattern of historical time paths of exploitation of basins of various types will be understandable. This will lead in the end to useful and reliable forecast models of supply.

Part III of the volume contains two articles. The first by Lohrenz examines, to the extent currently possible, the relative returns from different bids for leases; the question quite simply is what did firms get by making bigger bids. The answer is equally straightforward: a greater probability of obtaining revenue.

In the companion piece in this part of the volume, Whitney examines the effect of Federal regulations by a number of agencies on the efficiency of mineral development. The analysis is qualitative rather than quantitative. However, a more precise conclusion is the increase in lead times between a firm initiating some phase of a project and being able to complete it. The lead time figures have already reached extraordinary limits. For example, Whitney estimates lead times range from 5 to 20 years for discovery, 3 to 6 years for drilling permits, and a further 3 to 10 years for building the mines. As Whitney views the matter, the major source of the difficulty is the lack of focus, diversity, and conflicting nature of a complex array of rules promulgated by a series of independent agencies. That is, the regulatory impact on efficiency would be considerably less if there were one agency with a simple set of relatively straightforward rules.

The last part in this volume discusses some ideas in exploration with respect to coal and other minerals. These discussions should help us understand the analysis of oil and gas exploration more fully by being able to compare and contrast with the exploration activities in other minerals and coal. The main distinguishing characteristic of coal discovery and the development of coal fields is that relative to oil and gas the risk is less, there is less uncertainty, and geologically useful information is greater. The concerns mentioned earlier by Gilbert about the greater social informational returns from exploration may be of greater moment in this situation than in oil and gas exploration.

However, Newcomb points out that the relatively lower degree of uncertainty has misled researchers concerning the reliability of existing coal supply models, which are neither as useful nor reliable as some would have us believe. One particular factor that Newcomb incorporates in his model is an allowance for heteroskedasticity of variance in seam thickness as an important element in exploring extraction costs, which is a variable formerly ignored.

The final article in this section (by Singer and Mosier) examines the issue as to whether fields of larger tonnage of mineral ores tend to be discovered first, as is the case in oil and gas exploration. The simple answer is that as with oil and gas the larger tonnages are found first, at least within common geologic settings. Further, as is well known with oil and gas deposits, mineral deposits are also distributed by size according to a heavily skewed distribution with a very long tail to the right.

What Do We Explore Next?

While it is true that the past few years have seen a rapid growth in interest in supply models and more recently, but as yet only hesitantly, in exploration models, there is still much work to be done. We cannot yet claim as economists or more generally as students of human decision making to understand the process of exploration. What is now recognized is that economic, political, and geologic factors are involved. At times one of these forces will dominate the others and thereby mask the importance of the other two. But the economist must recognize the geologic facts of life more explicitly in his models and the geologist must recognize that economic and political factors play an important role; exploration is not the mere mechanistic process of selecting from a basin of prospects ever smaller reservoirs. While if it were true geologically that if there is no oil to be found, no amount of economic pressure will create it, yet it is also true that no matter how abundant oil may ultimately be, the wrong economic signals will inhibit search for it. Oil not searched for is oil not discovered.

The deficiencies of existing supply models lie on two fronts. The development of the appropriate theoretical structure is one and the other is the empirical implementation. As the new theories become better focused and gain in acceptance as potentially useful analytical tools, this development will give rise to new demands for data, not just more observations on the existing variables of interest, but observations on new variables. In particular, one might reasonably predict that more and more attention will be focused in the future on distributional questions, rather than on aggregate levels. Thus, the new theories will generate an interest in the distribution of exploration by type of region, by type of firm, by type of exploration process, and so on.

Another potential lesson that should encourage much dramatic research is to devise models that are able to quantify the real cost of governmental regulations and procedures so that at last the costs can be weighed against the benefits, which themselves are as yet unquantified.

An important issue raised by Gilbert in this volume is the question of externalities in the exploration market in general and informational externalities in particular. Their presence or absence is an important empirical issue, which is as yet unresolved but hotly debated. Clearly the estimation of the degree of externalities should be a priority item. For, if found to be present to a significant extent with a measurable impact on exploration outcomes, efficiency considerations alone would lead us to consider whether the market can be improved and the externalities internalized or whether some form of centralized allocation is needed. If externalities are not found to be present, then the existing market can be left alone.

An unanticipated outcome from the conference is the warning that the geologic, economic, and political conditions in the exploration and mining of minerals is sufficiently similar to the exploration for hydrocarbons as to indicate a potentially more serious problem of rapidly escalating finding costs than for oil and gas. Indeed, because the media seem to relish a crisis, it would appear that the next crisis will be with respect to *nonenergy* deposits.

In conclusion, the economics (as opposed to the mere financial accounting) of exploration is the key to the future not just in energy (the contemporaneous "big issue") but also for nonenergy minerals, which is the "big issue" to come. We need to understand not just the geology of these issues, but also both the economic and political forces that impinge upon them. We certainly need to separate the effect of the first from the latter two factors.

Index